ENVIRONMENTAL LAW GUIDE

To my son, Ajan, and his father

With my love

ENVIRONMENTAL LAW GUIDE

Linda S Spedding, LLM, PhD, Solicitor (England and Wales),
Attorney at Law (USA) and Advocate (India)

OLD BAILEY PRESS

LAW IN PRACTICE SERIES

OLD BAILEY PRESS

200 Greyhound Road, London W14 9RY

ISBN 1 85836 079 X

British Library Cataloguing-in-Publication Data

A catalogue record for this book is available from the British
Library.

5   4   3   2   1

Printed and bound in Great Britain

Contents

Preface

Over the period during which this book has been written its intended message has been taken increasingly seriously as a result of the priorities set both by regulatory and voluntary measures. In addition to an explanation of the regulatory framework, therefore, the practitioner has to be aware of other aspects of environmental performance.

In recent years most businesses, whatever their size, have recognised the importance of compliance with environmental regulation and have at least heard of environmental auditing if not utilised this approach in one form or another, through interaction with colleagues, professional associations, membership of organisations, and the general public.

Significantly, the EU's Environmental Management and Auditing Scheme (EMAS) has been launched and there has been the broader discussion of environmental management and its significance in terms of business strategy. Accordingly, in addition to considering regulatory matters, a discussion of the meaning of environmental management both in a general sense and in the specific context of the International Standard ISO 14001 has been included in the book. Here again, a more practical discussion of the features of ISO 14001 is included in order to set out the position as it affects the business manager (as well as his or her adviser).

It is also true to say that the term 'environmental management' has become part of today's general business strategy, at least from the point of view of, for example, the Confederation of British Industry (CBI) and the International Chamber of Commerce (ICC). Nowadays it is quite common to hear the remark that good environmental management amounts to good business management. From a wider perspective, therefore, consideration is also given to the place of environmental management in corporate priorities, bearing in mind such issues as:

• environmental liability and exposure;

• environmental and business/investment planning;

• environmental and trade/competitiveness in the sense of 'benchmarking'; and

• the environmental opportunities both at home and abroad.

This has meant that the real focus of this book has moved to a broader debate on the role of standards as well as compliance.

Whereas certain issues have settled down in environmental legal developments there still remain various key matters that are open to change, at national, European and international levels. For example, the implementation and enforcement of the guidance of the UK

Environment Act 1995 in relation to the contaminated land provisions is a matter that remains to be seen. Meanwhile the whole question of environmental liability generally, within Europe, remains unanswered, although the former Environment Commissioner Britt Bjerregard indicated that this is a matter of urgent priority. As a result, a discussion of the Green Paper on Environmental Liability is included and the follow-up, including the debate on subsidiarity, has required some comment. This is particularly topical as we now await a White Paper on the subject, due to be published by the spring of 1999.

Of course, it is important to bear in mind the continuing expansion of the European Union which impacts on this debate. It is also useful to consider implementation and enforcement aspects through some comparison of the environment agencies established under the relevant regimes of the UK, the EU and the USA. This is especially true since the US looks to Europe, and vice versa, in terms of environmental developments.

The importance of the environmental technology business and the environmental industry in general has been recognised increasingly over the last three years. This has prompted the launch, in 1995, of the Environmental Industries Commission (EIC). It has been remarked that the environmental technology industry, for example, is larger than that of aerospace. Moreover, certain countries such as Japan and Germany have already taken the lead in grasping this opportunity. The Chief Executive of the Environment Agency, Ed Gallagher, has exhorted the industry to look to the positive business issues rather than to compliance and liability matters and the EIC has supported the view that the UK should try to catch up with the market leaders as soon as possible.

Finally, other practical matters include a discussion of the environmental 'bottom line' and the pros and cons of good environmental management as opposed to environmental mismanagement. Some practical examples and comparative case studies of other jurisdictions are included. The importance of the environment in business or investment planning, in terms of diligence in respect of transactions, mergers and acquisitions, project finance, joint ventures etc, are addressed.

It is hoped that this guide will assist those who advise on, or who are concerned with keeping abreast of, the ramifications of environmental developments.

Linda S Spedding

October 1998

Acknowledgements

In compiling this volume the author has been encouraged by, and has relied on contributions from, colleagues and friends. To all who have assisted with this publication the author wishes to express thanks. Particular contributions have been provided by Herbert Enmarch-Williams of Lawrence Jones Solicitors, John Voothees, Bob Woellner, Paul Onifade and Tobias Schumacher. As colleagues in Quest Environmental Management Consultancy, John and Bob were able to provide insight on the role of environmental management systems, particularly the ISO 14000 series. Lisa Fretton has provided invaluable assistance in handling secretarial matters. Thanks also to Professor Chris Arnold and Emma Richards at the Academy of Professional Training for their additional skills and suggestions.

Professor SRAG Purna, as an external consultant editor, has eased the production process greatly. Many thanks to my father for his encouragement of my writing potential, my mother for her unfailing support and tolerance during the long hours of proofreading. Thanks also to Paul Gregory for his 'last-minute' assistance.

Finally, I acknowledge the encouragement and support of my publishers.

Whilst author takes full responsibility for the final work readers should seek legal advice on specific issues and concerns.

Glossary

ACCA	Association of Chartered Certified Accountants
ACP	Advisory Committee on Packaging
AP	(EU) Action Programme
BAT	Best Available Technique/Technology
BATNEEC	Best Available Techniques/Technology Not Entailing Excessive Cost
BEO	Best Environmental Option
BPEO	Best Practicable Environmental Option
BPM	Best Practicable Means
BS	British Standard
BSI	British Standards Institution
BS7750	British Standard 7750 as a Specification for Environmental Management Systems
CBA	Cost-benefit Analysis
CBI	Confederation of British Industry
CEL	Contractors Environmental Liability
CERCLA (US)	Comprehensive Environmental Response Compensation and Liability Act
CFCs	Chloroflourocarbons
COPA (UK)	Control of Pollution Act 1974
COSHH	Control of Substances Hazardous to Health
CPL	Contractors Pollution Liability
Cradle to grave	Term used to express the life-cycle analysis of a product or process
DETR	Department of Environment, Transport and the Regions
Directive (EU)	Official European legislative instrument

DIS	Draft International Standards
DG	Director-General
DoE (UK)	Department of the Environment
DOJ (US)	Department of Justice
DSG	Draft Statutory Guidance
DTI (UK)	Department of Trade and Industry
DWI	Drinking Water Inspectorate
EA (UK)	Environment Agency
EA 1995	Environment Act 1995
EAP (EU)	Environmental Action Programme
EARA (UK)	Environmental Auditors Registration Association
ECE	European Commission for Europe
ECJ	European Court of Justice
Eco-label	Label identifying environmentally-friendly products
EEA (EU)	European Environment Agency
EEB (EU)	European Environment Bureau
EEC (EU)	European Economic Community
EFTA	European Free Trade Association
EIA	Environmental Impact Assessment
EIC	Environmental Industries Commission
EIL	Environment Impairment Liability
EIS	Environmental Impact Statement
EMAS	Environmental Eco-management and Auditing Scheme
EMS	Environment Management Systems
EPA (US)	Environmental Protection Agency
EPA 1990 (UK)	Environmental Protection Act 1990
EQSs	Environment Quality Standards
ERAS	Environmental Reporting Awards Scheme
ESA	Environmental Services Association
ETBPP	Environmental Technology Best Practice Programme

EU	European Union
FOE	Friends of the Earth
GAAP	Generally Accepted Accounting Principles
GATT	General Agreement on Tariffs and Trade
GEF	Global Environmental Fund
GEMI	Global Environmental Management Initiative
HCFCs	Hydrochlorofluorocarbons
HMIP (UK)	Her Majesty's Inspectorate of Pollution
HSE	Health and Safety Executive
ICC	International Chamber of Commerce
IEC	International Electro-technical Commission
IEM	Institute of Environmental Management
ILO	International Labour Organisation
IPC (UK)	Integrated Pollution Control
IPCC	Intergovernmental Panel on Climate Change
IPPC (EU)	Integrated Pollution Prevention Control
ISAR	International Standards of Accounting and Reporting
ISO	International Organisation of Standardisation
LA	Local authority
LAAPC	Local Authority Air Pollution Control
LCA	Life-cycle Analysis
Maastricht Treaty	Treaty on European Union 1992
MEP	Member of the European Parliament
NACCB	National Accreditation Council for Certification Bodies
NEEC	Not entailing excessive cost
NGO	Non-governmental Organisation
NIFES	National Industrial Fuel Efficiency Service
NRA (UK)	National Rivers Authority
OECD	Organisation for Economic Co-operation and Development
OFWAT	Office of Water Services

OJ	Official Journal of the European Communities
PCA	Planning and Compensation Act
PCB	Polychlorinated biphenyl
PGs	Process Guidance Notes
PIF	Property Information Form
PRP	Potentially Responsible Party
RCEP (UK)	Royal Commission on Environmental Pollution
RCRA (US)	Response Conservation and Recovery Act 1976
SAGE	Strategic Advisory Group for the Environment
SARA (US)	Superfund Amendments and Re-authorisation Act 1986
SEA	Single European Act 1987
SEPA	Scottish Environment Protection Agency
SHE	Safety, Health and Environment
SMEs	Small and Medium-sized Enterprises
SSSI	Site of Special Scientific Interest
Superfund (US)	A federal trustfund established by CERCLA to allow the US Government to act immediately to eliminate threats to human health and minimise future risks at seriously contaminated sites
Sustainable development	Development that meets the needs of the present without compromising the ability of future generations to meet their own needs (Source: 'Our Common Future' (1987) World Commission on Environment and Development)
TC	Technical Committee
TCPA	Town and Country Planning Act
UGs	Upgrading Guidance Notes
UKAS	United Kingdom Accreditation Service
UNCED	United Nations Conference on Environment and Development
UNECE	United Nations Economic Commission for Europe
UNEP	United Nations Environment Programme
VOCs	Volatile Organic Compounds

WA 1989	Water Act 1989
WHO	World Health Organisation
WIA 1991	Water Industry Act 1991
WRA	Waste Regulation Authority
WRA 1991	Water Resources Act 1991
WTO	World Trade Organisation

Chapter One

An Overview of the Developments in UK Environmental Law and Policy

Setting the Scene

The growing presence of government bureaucracy that regulates the state and its citizens' lives reflects the impact of the increase in peoples in the world. Not too long ago some believed that this regulation could be limited to the immediate human environment, namely the city and urban communities. However, the developing impact of modern technologies on nature, together with a mushrooming population that needed space to live in, thus encroaching upon nature, made it necessary for the state to intervene and start a process that led to an escalation in the regulation of the environment.

Until very recently, it may have been considered that nature had been providing human beings with a 'free lunch' of its goods and services. Resources have been widely available and little, if anything, was charged for them. Only now might the bill, according to a conservative estimate approaching £1.81 trillion a year,[1] be on the way, as humans realise that climate change and ever more limited resources are not a low price to pay.

Moreover, the 1990s have witnessed the environment coming into sharp and prominent focus as a political, commercial and social issue. Both legislative and economic incentives have placed the principle of sound environmental management high on many commercial agendas. By way of example, the chemicals industry has been conducting environmental audits for several years, while the Chemical Industries Association also has a well-established set of guidelines entitled *Responsible Care*.

The impetus for the 'greening of business' has developed through the national initiatives of different jurisdictions, including some in the UK that are mentioned below, and through specific regional initiatives such as the EU's Environmental Action Programmes, as well as through international imperatives. Therefore the 'Green Movement' is not some passing phase that will go away, thus enabling companies to revert to their previous practices. The principles and campaigns advocated by pressure groups in defence of the environment have done much to enhance public perception of the environment as an issue, but the Green Movement is now more sophisticated and multi-faceted.

Changes for Business

As referred to further below, business now has a responsibility for improving its environmental performance, just as other socially drawn changes to working practices and employment conditions have to be made over the years. The environment is a transnational issue and therefore has no geographical boundaries. Green change is accelerating and, in particular:

- manufacturing processes have to be greener, more efficient, less energy-intensive, using and producing fewer environmentally unfriendly chemicals and materials;

- products are being increasingly environmentally scrutinised to eliminate CFCs, raw materials from endangered species and wasteful use of resources;

- waste is growing as an issue – controls on what can be disposed of are becoming tighter and the actual cost of disposal is rising dramatically as landfills become scarcer and legislation places waste-disposal operators' practices further under the spotlight;

- recyclability is going to become an increasingly legislatively imposed requirement;

- greener utilisation of both renewable and non-renewable resources in general will be increasingly important, both to customers and employees.

Like it or not, businesses will have to change and practitioners will have to be aware of this when advising their clients.

A more recent development has added a new perspective to the older aspect of *regulation*: the *preservation* of the environment. This perspective, founded in the Green Movement, has many bases including:

- the attribution to the environment of a value of its own; and

- a mere manifestation of human survival instincts to protect future generations.

Whereas a detailed discussion of such issues goes beyond the scope of this text it should be understood that both aspects – the need to regulate and the need to preserve – are reflected in this century's development of UK environmental law and policy.

UK Environmental Law: Modern Developments

The modern development of UK environmental law has gone further than merely to increase the regulation and administration of environmental pollution. In fact, the UK government supports both deregulation and the use of economic instruments for environmental protection and has introduced a number of financial levies and taxes to promote more environmentally-friendly processes and techniques. The range of such mechanisms is set to increase in the near future.

UK Environmental Law: Key Statutes

*   From 1947 onwards a succession of Town and Country Planning Acts (TCPAs) established a regulatory regime of planning control. Environmental protection was not the objective of this legislation.

*   The same regulatory attitude could be observed in the Waste Regulation Act 1963 (WRA 1963), which was intended to manage the consequences of privatisation of the waste sector, that took until the 1980s to achieve.

*   Only in 1974 did the Control of Pollution Act (COPA 1974) introduce legislation to control pollution of the environment.

*   The protection afforded by COPA 1974 required enhancement and became the basis for the first milestone in environmental protection legislation: the Environmental Protection Act 1990 (EPA 1990).

*   The provisions of the EPA 1990 were further strengthened by the establishment of a unified environment agency and a proposed new regime on contaminated land under the Environment Act 1995 (EA 1995).

While Chapter 3 explains the relevant aspects of the EPA 1990 and the EA 1995, key points are summarised below.

The Environmental Protection Act 1990

The EPA 1990 brought about a regime of public accountability for environmental damage. Its more important aspects are that:

*   provisions, such as s73(6), allow individuals to take action for damages for certain offences under the Act;

*   provisions in Part I establish a system of integrated pollution control (IPC) which is concerned with the most seriously polluting processes, regulated initially by Her Majesty's Inspectorate of Pollution (HMIP) and subsequently by the Environment Agency (EA, or the Agency) as discussed below. IPC regulates the cross-media effect of pollution;

*   certain processes are prescribed under the Act, List A, or by subsequent regulations, and need authorisation from a relevant authority;

*   targets such as that of the Best Practicable Environmental Option (BPEO) are introduced;

*   HMIP is given certain enforcement powers: revocation and variation of authorisations, enforcement and prohibition notices, and powers of entry and seizure;

*   a Local Authority Air Pollution Control (LAAPC) system is established, mostly for processes less polluting than those that fall within the IPC regime;

- specific regulations of contaminated land are introduced: most importantly, a register of such land has to be maintained and citizens are given recourse through statutory nuisance provisions (ss79–83 inclusive);

- Part II contains provisions relating to waste on land, rectifying anomalies in the earlier Control of Pollution Acts (COPAs 1974 and 1989). Under the provisions waste management licences can be obtained. Several offences are created and powers are given to the waste management authorities, including clean-up powers.

Best Practicable Environmental Option (BPEO)

This option provides the best benefit or least damage to the environment as a whole at acceptable cost, in the long term as well as the short term. The concept was developed originally in the 5th Report of the Royal Commission on Environmental Pollution (RCEP) and can be read as a development of the best environmental option concept that links it to economic objectives and takes a long-term approach to environmental solutions.

Following the EPA 1990 were several Statutes on environmental protection, including the Water Act 1989[2] relating to water protection. The most recent example of the protective approach is the Environment Act 1995 (EA 1995).

The Environment Act 1995

The EA 1995 strengthened the regime introduced by the EPA 1990. The following are the more notable aspects of the EA 1995.

- The Act created the Environment Agency, a body dealing with most kinds of pollution that possesses almost the combined power of the other pollution control authorities.

  - The Agency has power to control discharges to, and pollution of, all three environmental media – land, air and water – all within one single organisation.

  - The Agency has the objective of making a contribution to sustainable development.

  - Guiding principles for intervention are proportionality, consistency, transparency and targeting.

  - The Agency has power to appoint its own officers to whom it can confer enforcement powers of, for example, entry, sampling and detention of substances.

  - The Agency has wide enforcement options, among them (in cases of water and waste offences) the power to issue 'works notices', requiring a party to clean up pollution.

  - In determining whether to prosecute, the Agency has regard to public interest and sufficiency of evidence.

- The Act contains provisions on contaminated land, abandoned mines, air quality, a national waste strategy and directions on producer responsibility.

As far as the regulatory framework is concerned, parliamentary intervention was, of course, the most active factor in the development of UK environmental law. Nevertheless, some of the best-known stepping-stones were provided by the common law, especially in the field of torts. These are discussed in Chapter 8 in the general context of environmental liability.

UK Law and Policy

Within the UK much of the environmental legislation and policy is derived from that of the EU as a whole. Environmental protection in the UK has been promoted through a system of licensing and consents controlled by a number of regulatory bodies. The UK has operated a system of IPC for certain industries, which controls discharges to air, land and water of certain substances. Pollution control techniques are operated only where the benefits to the environment outweigh the costs. This system of IPC has had some influence on the recent EC Directive on integrated pollution, prevention and control (IPPC).

Waste management within the UK is based on a hierarchical approach known as the 'waste hierarchy', the main objective being to minimise the production of waste in the first instance. Options for re-use or recycling are explored, with ultimate disposal the last resort. Since 1990 there has been a legal duty of care on all persons in the waste management chain (from producer to final disposer) to ensure that proper handling, transportation and disposal practices are undertaken.

Discharges into water are currently regulated through a system of consents, some of which come within the scope of IPC. The consent system for the protection of water is based upon the requirement to protect the use of the water, for which environmental quality standards have been set. In addition, the ability of the receiving waters to assimilate the discharge should ensure that harm to the environment will be minimal.

As discussed in Chapter 3 in particular, the EA 1995 was introduced to combine the regulatory agencies for IPC, waste management and protection of the water environment. This Act established an Environment Agency which has the power to control discharges to, and pollution of, all three environmental media – land, air and water – within one single organisation.

The introduction of the landfill levy, which is referred to in Chapter 4, demonstrates this policy approach. The range of such mechanisms is set to increase in the near future. While a regulatory regime for environmental protection is in place in many jurisdictions, the EU programme also advocates the adoption of voluntary measures and financial incentives.

The 'polluter pays' principle underpins most legislation, although the principle often has practical difficulties regarding its enforcement.

'Polluter Pays' Principle

The principle was adopted by Organisation for Economic Co-operation and Development (OECD) countries in 1972. It was incorporated in the first Environmental Action Programme of the Commission and is now contained in the EC Treaty, so polluters bear the full cost of prevention and minimisation of pollution, and of remedying environmental damage. This cost should be reflected in the price of goods and services which cause pollution through production, consumption and disposal.

Generally speaking, the business community is unlikely to adopt sound environmental practices voluntarily unless there are commercial benefits. As discussed further in Chapter 10, these benefits are now increasing and coming into sharper focus in view of shifts in business culture over the last decade. The advent of competitive tendering as a common business practice, and indeed a legislative requirement in certain specified instances, means that business practices are subject to both broader and closer scrutiny beyond the core services offered for the particular project in question. The Ministry of Defence in the United Kingdom, for instance, insists on its suppliers achieving the managerial standard BS5750 or the international equivalent ISO 9000. It is probable that in future there will be a similar stipulation to achieve an environmental standard such as ISO 14001, for which the major requirements are presented in Chapter 7.

International Organisation of Standardisation (ISO)

A world-wide federation of National Standard Bodies including the British Standards Institution (BSI) in the UK. It was officially established on 23 February 1947. The aim of ISO is to promote the development of standardisation and related activities in the world with a view to facilitating international exchange of goods and services and co-operation. The work of ISO includes environmental management.

The commercial benefits of sound environmental practice were initially those of enhanced marketability, in the face of growing public opinion in favour of 'environmentally-friendly products'. In addition, there are now concrete commercial opportunities in the growth of an environmentally-friendly market, particularly in the fields of energy efficiency and waste disposal, and in countries which have yet to get their environmental infrastructures fully operational. For instance, there are very significant opportunities in emerging jurisdictions, such as China, India and Malaysia, among others, for infrastructure projects such as construction of water pipelines. Further comment appears in Chapter 10.

European Law

As discussed in Chapter 2, European law has had a tremendous impact on UK law; and continues to do so. One major pillar of European law is the adoption of Directives which are transposed into the national legislation of Member States. The principle behind European law is to ensure that free and fair trade can proceed throughout the EU, on what is often described as the 'level playing field'. As such, the European Commission (EC) Directives seek to ensure common standards. Regulation exists in all Member States to ensure that the movement of goods and services can take place across frontiers without bureaucratic or financial hindrance.

Environmental Co-operation

An interesting aspect of environmental co-operation at the EU level is that 'the UK system', so called, has been virtually imposed on the other Member States. The system relies heavily on bureaucracy, as does the EU system. It builds on a system of licensing and consents controlled by a number of regulatory bodies. Consequently, it gives the relevant decision-making authorities a relatively high degree of discretion. In the Roman-based systems of the continental Member States, the courts take a much more active role in this respect and constantly take account of the discretion exercised by the relevant authorities. The empowerment of administrative - that is extrajudicial - bodies is frowned upon by the courts, and continental states find the constitutional change that is engendered difficult to cope with.

European Union's Fifth Environmental Action Programme

Another pillar of EU environmental law and policy has been action programmes on the environment.

Environmental Action Programme

The European Council approved the First Environmental Action Programme in 1973. Since then four further programmes have been adopted for the periods 1977-81, 1982-86, 1987-92 and 1993-2000. All the Action Programmes provide a policy framework for Community action over the relevant years and indicate new directions for future environmental policy. In addition, they contain specific proposals for legislation that the Commission intends to propose for adoption by the Council of Ministers.

In particular, the concept of sustainability is demonstrated here. Indeed, the aim of sustainable development has generated a variety of programmes and initiatives. In particular, within Europe, the Member States of the EU have adopted an Action Programme on the environment aimed at achieving sustainable development. The programme 'Towards Sustainability' seeks to minimise pollution and to conserve natural resources including biodiversity. This is crucial to Europe and of significance to emerging nations further afield. Since Europe is the main trading partner of many such countries, the EU's Fifth

Environmental Action Programme, covering the years 1993–2000, is very relevant. The programme emphasises the importance of 'shared responsibility', that is, a pluralist approach which involves both the public and private sectors in achieving the aims of sustainable development. Industry, therefore, has a role to fulfil, as referred to again in Chapters 7 and 10.

In addition, the EU intends to introduce a range of economic instruments to curb excessive use of natural resources. Such initiatives include a proposal for a carbon tax that would place a levy on the use of fossil fuels, as an economic incentive to find more energy-efficient techniques and processes. Other examples include a levy on the disposal of waste to landfill sites in order to encourage waste minimisation, re-use and recycling. This type of instrument, which will be of increasing importance, is referred to in Chapters 5, 6 and 10.

Lastly, the Commission is shortly to prepare a new EU strategy for sustainable development setting out mechanisms for integrating sustainable development into all EU policies and identifying sustainable development targets and indicators. In view of the UK's support and its six-month presidency during 1998 this is very pertinent to the present discussion.

International Developments

When considering UK environmental law and policy any practitioner should also be aware of the impact of international legal instruments. As far as the development of international environmental law is concerned, three different stages, in particular, are recognisable:[3]

- The first is the protection of animal species by international treaties. These treaties either concern particular species (eg the Washington Convention 1973) or protect economic interests such as fishing rights.

- The second stage, concerns co-existence, ie the interdependence of neighbouring states from an environmental viewpoint. Cross-border pollution problems and the use of resources in border areas required solutions at the level of equal and sovereign states. The resulting protection of the environment had as much to do with the peaceful demonstration of territorial sovereignty as with the actual environmental problems involved. Only recently did it become obvious that an international, interdependent society of states had to address issues that might not in fact directly encroach upon their sovereignty, but still needed solutions. Examples are the regulation of sovereignty-free areas such as the High Seas, Antarctica and extraterrestrial space. Then came more pressing concerns about noticeable climate change, the publication of scientific data on greenhouse gases and the hole in the ozone layer.

- All the above issues could not be addressed by agreements between neighbouring states; they required stronger, world-wide co-ordination and co-operation. The basis of the third stage – the development of international environmental law – was the United Nations Stockholm Environmental Conference of 1972. At this conference environmental protection was declared a common concern of mankind.

The Importance of International Initiatives

International initiatives and developments have often served as precursors and spurs for national developments. When considering UK law and policy it is therefore appropriate to summarise those which are particularly significant.

The Rio de Janeiro Earth Summit (UNCED)

The fact that environmental protection is a transnational concern comprising many facets was vividly demonstrated by the United Nations Conference on the Environment and Development (UNCED) held in Rio de Janeiro in 1992. The conference suffered somewhat from the sometimes unreasonably high expectations raised by environmental interest groups and media focus on the failure of governments of industrialised countries to accept some of the more far-reaching and expensive proposals advocated by the developing world. Nevertheless, there were significant outcomes which have an international ambit and which, in turn, affect UK environmental law and policy, most notably dealing with:

- climate change;

- resource depletion;

- biodiversity;

- sustainable development; and

- Agenda 21.

The Rio Declaration on Environment and Development

The Declaration is an attempt to set out fundamental principles for the interrelationship of environmental issues and economic development over the coming decades. In the past these interests have often been regarded as incompatible. All states will co-operate in conserving and protecting the Earth's ecosystems, but the developed world in particular is forced to accept a specific responsibility on account of both its pollution record and advanced technology.

Climate Change

It is postulated that the burning of fossil fuels – coal, oil and natural gas – through industrial activity and transportation, plus increased emissions of methane from agriculture and the release of other gases into the atmosphere, have caused a warming of the Earth's atmosphere through the so-called 'greenhouse effect'. This warming is predicted to continue. The best estimates from the world's climatic experts indicate that global temperature could increase by between 3 and 6 degrees Celsius by the middle of the next century. Should this occur, it could lead to greater aridity in some regions, increased flooding and storms in others and general increases in sea levels world-wide.

This, of course, represents an issue of global importance that requires a co-ordinated international response by both government and industry. The Earth Summit in Rio de Janeiro in 1992 presented an opportunity for such a response, and many countries signed up to a treaty that aimed to stabilise or reduce their emissions of the 'greenhouse' gases in the near future. An Intergovernmental Panel on Climate Change (IPCC) was set up and efforts are under way to implement the Framework Convention and to prepare the first Convention of the Parties, particularly as initial commitments are now considered to be inadequate.

The principal aim of the Convention on Climatic Change is to reduce the generation of greenhouse gases. Its detractors made the accurate point that it imposes no precisely quantifiable goal for the reduction of greenhouse gases. The credibility of the Convention was further called into question by the fact that there has been a battle not only between the developed and developing world as to what methods should be adopted to achieve the objective, but also between industrialised countries. The northern European countries have adopted market-based mechanisms to control emissions: in particular a carbon tax. The value of this fiscal control was undermined, however, when it became clear that neither the USA nor Japan, who are major producers of greenhouse gases, were prepared to implement such a tax. The present UK government demonstrated a clear commitment to a tighter regime at the recent meeting in Kyoto, intended to move the process forward. This clearly will have an impact on UK environmental policy.

Kyoto

As a follow-up meeting to UNCED and as the most recent example of international co-operation, the Kyoto negotiations in 1997 were concerned mainly with climate change. The difficulty of achieving international co-ordination was evident from these negotiations. On the one hand the developing countries were concerned that their economies would be held back, while the industrialised nations' advanced technologies would enable them to adjust more easily to the new limits. Therefore, the developing countries successfully stalled most attempts by the USA to pressure them into 'meaningful participation'. The USA was not content that China and other developing countries face few binding limits. Paradoxically, the USA faced criticism from the EU that its proposed limits were too low.

Ultimately a compromise was reached in that:

• the developing countries would face few limits on emissions;

• some countries, for instance Australia, could increase emissions;

• the USA succeeded in writing a trade clause into the agreement allowing countries under their limits for greenhouse gas emissions to sell extra capacity to countries that have reached the limit;

• the EU bowed to US pressure and agreed to lower limits than those proposed.

The outcome of the negotiations will have far-reaching effects that will continue to influence the policies and credibility of national governments. It also affects the stance of the EU who entered the Kyoto talks with the view that emissions of the three main gases – carbon dioxide, methane and nitrous oxide – should be reduced by 15 per cent of their 1990 levels by 2010. Under the Kyoto agreement, however, the EU's target is an 8 per cent reduction of these gases, and also HPCs, perfluorocarbons and sulphur hexafluoride, by 2008-2012.

An interesting comparison can be made with the negotiations for the Vienna Convention on CFCs in 1985. Perhaps surprisingly the roles of the EU and the USA were reversed at that time. During the negotiations, the USA pressed for tighter controls (admittedly in order to make economically viable the unilateral action already taken). The EU was cautious because of fears of the costs involved in the development of new technologies and processes. Only the developing countries took the position that they adopted at the Kyoto Summit and stalled progress in order not to be disadvantaged in commercial terms.

Consequently, the Vienna Convention urged action but did not set firm goals. These were established in 1987 when the Montreal Protocol on Substances that Deplete the Ozone Layer was agreed. It has since been amended several times. It is worth noting that the protocol tries to alleviate developing countries' fears by providing for technology transfers from industrialised nations.

Resource Depletion – Sustainable Development

The world is not an infinite source of raw materials, nor an unlimited receptacle for waste. There are limits to consumption, although they are not yet defined. The industrialisation of the world creates huge demands on natural resources such as timber, minerals, oil and land. For example, overfishing in certain regions is beginning to cause significant problems, and the 'politics' of fresh water grow increasingly complex. Resources are further depleted through sterilisation of land by contamination, pollution of aquatic systems and deterioration in the quality of air.

World trade, which provides both wealth and livelihood, also depletes the resources on which the trade depends. At some stage the limits to growth will be reached. Thus the challenge presented is to achieve 'sustainable development'. It is necessary to ensure that the viability of future generations is not compromised through the actions of past or current generations. It is our moral duty to leave to our descendants a world in a better condition than at present. Mechanisms need to be found that will allow economies to develop while preserving the resources of the planet.

By way of example, the Declaration of Forest Principles recognise the rights of producers to exploit their forests, and that the incremental costs of conservation should be 'equitably borne by the international community'. The principles cover tropical and all other forests.

Sustainable Development: The 'Double Dividend'

The definition which continues to attract the most widespread support was set out in the report of the World Commission on Environment and Development in 1987: 'Our Common

Future'. It was termed: 'a development that meets the needs of the present without compromising the ability of future generations to meet their own needs'.

Central to the issue of international environmental protection is sustainable development as recognised by the proposals emanating from the Rio Conference. Sustainable development may also be defined as reducing pressure on natural resources and optimising the use of human resources. The term 'double dividend' has been coined to describe the dual benefit of sustained natural resources and higher employment. Therefore it is not an academic philosophical concept that exists in isolation from an economic context. Its history is crystallised by key international conferences and the initiatives adopted or nurtured at such gatherings.

Biodiversity

Life on earth is magnificent in the variety of its species. The ecology of plants and animals describes the interrelationship between species. It is beginning to be understood that all animals and plants on the earth are interrelated, and this includes human beings. The enormous diversity of species – or biodiversity – is the underpinning strength of life, enabling all ecological niches to be developed, from the hottest deserts to the coldest polar regions, from the highest mountains to the deepest parts of the oceans.

Diversity as an aspect of the larger environment is a resource to be conserved for its own sake, but on a more selfish level human beings ever-increasingly depend on the diversity of species. Medicines such as cancer treatments are found in species unique to certain regions and new food crops are being developed from wild species found in other areas.

The 1992 Earth Summit introduced a Biodiversity Treaty whereby signatory nations have undertaken to conserve biodiversity within their own territorial limits. This may be achieved through the designation of protected areas and species or through curbs on trade in threatened biological resources such as tropical hardwood timber, rare animals and plants. The first Conference of the Parties was held between 28 November and 9 December 1994, with over 1,000 government delegates and non-governmental organisations (NGOs). The interest in the Convention is, therefore, widespread. Of the 160 signatories, 106 have ratified the Convention and financing mechanisms have been established. The Convention on Biological Diversity contains important provisions relating to the setting up of a network of protected areas and habitat, and species protection of the traditional type.

The Commission on Sustainable Development and Agenda 21

The Commission on Sustainable Development is potentially one of the most important practical results of the Conference. It represents the highest-level United Nations institution concerned with the environment, reporting direct to the Economic and Social Council.

Agenda 21 comprises an enormous shopping list of some 800 pages of necessary measures to harmonise environmental development in the next century, covering such broad and far-reaching issues as changing consumption patterns and promoting sustainable human settlements, with specific reference to the vast and often disorderly urbanisation in Africa and South America.

The principal criticism of Agenda 21 is that it is far too ambitious when viewed against available funds to implement the measures prescribed. The programme has been costed at $625 billion per annum with aid at the time of the Conference running to the tune of $55 billion.

Rio and the UK

The enormous task of transposing Rio's many principles into national and international legislation is gathering pace. For instance, the Conference has served as a catalyst for action not only by EU Member States but also in emerging economies. It inspired China's Five-year Plan, the latest in a series of environmental policy documents, which appeared at the beginning of July 1994, and also Japan's latest Basic Environment Law passed in November 1993. Its influence also extends to India and Malaysia.

The UK government has named three institutions to develop the sustainable development strategy.

The Panel on Sustainable Development

A group of five 'wise persons', chaired by Sir Crispin Tickell, has the task of providing words of warning and encouragement to development about the direction of its sustainable development strategy. The areas under investigation are:

- environmental cost, accounting and pricing;
- transfer of technology to other countries;
- the implementation of an international environmental agreement, taking the Montreal Protocol on the Ozone Layer as an example and, in particular, assessing the evidence that ultra-violet radiation is harmful to organisms;
- depletion of global fishing stocks; and
- the environmental content of the core curriculum for schools.

UK Round Table for Sustainable Development

The Round Table's main function is to oversee the initiatives of all sectors and to feed comments into the other two institutions.

Going for Green

The Going for Green Campaign is aimed at realising the goal of Agenda 21 to empower the individual. The campaign is not intended to rethink everything but rather to work on those areas that need to become environmentally aware.

Going for Green's guiding principles are:

- better resource management;
- reduction of pollution;

- making or keeping a good local environment.

The Going for Green Programme is about enabling, endorsing and acting in the following areas:

- developing a framework;

- setting goals (affordable, achievable and accessible);

- a green code for everyday life; and

- demonstration projects.

It involves public and private policy issues and takes into account the Round Table Committee report under the lead of Sir Crispen Tickell. It includes environmental education and the intention is to go outward to the people and then inward to the government. The campaign aims to seek changes in the above-mentioned areas and it has a cross-party approach.

Implications for Business of Law and Policy

As discussed further, particularly in Chapters 8 and 10, representative business bodies in the UK such as the CBI and ICC have encouraged adherence to environmental standards and the environmental dimension of commerce, as well as to the importance of public awareness. In the development of environmental policy not only should the partnership between government and industry be taken into account, but also the public interest. When advising clients, therefore, there are sensitive, key issues that should be borne in mind by any practitioner which may affect the legal position.

Green Consumerism

It is a fact of life that, though the very act of consuming, people produce waste. As environmental awareness grows, this reality is becoming clearer to consumers themselves. When a link can be established between the actions of the individual and tangible environmental harm, action taken by individual consumers can have a dramatic effect on consumption patterns. These inevitably affect the demand side of the economy, and producers need to adapt to meet changing demands. The 'greening' of consumerism began in just such a manner, brought to light through the impending threat created by CFCs.

The CFC Campaign

Although scientists had been studying ozone in the high atmosphere for many years, it was not until the late 1980s that a link was finally established between the use of CFCs, such as in aerosol propellants and refrigerants, and the observed decrease in the concentration of ozone in the high atmosphere above the polar regions. The 'hole' in the ozone layer presents a direct threat to human health, for instance by creating an increased risk of skin cancer, and indirect threats to humans through destruction of crop species. There is also a threat to the viability of single-cell animals and plants which form the basis of the ecological systems on the planet.

14

Seeing a clear link between their actions as consumers and threats to their well-being, consumers shunned the purchase of aerosols utilising CFCs as propellants. Only as a reactive response did industry switch to non-CFC propellants and eventually world governments signed the Montreal Protocol to curb and eventually ban the production of CFCs.

Therefore, the greening of consumerism did not begin with corporate initiatives. The consumer is seen to be independently powerful, and the corporate sector exists to serve the needs of the consumer. If the consumer wants to buy 'green' products, then industry must provide them if it is to survive.

Waste Management

Green consumerism has manifested itself via cultural changes in the West, although it has moved up and down the political agenda. In many European countries a culture of recycling has existed for some time and many people now regularly make trips to such facilities as 'bottle banks', 'can banks' etc, or participate in municipal collection schemes. They see recycling (and the purchase of environmentally-friendly products) as 'doing their bit for the environment'. In order to broaden the scope of citizens' involvement, the UK government launched its Going for Green Campaign in February 1995, referred to above. As stated, its purpose is to raise people's awareness and responsibility both in their work roles and their private lives. The campaign slogan is 'Going for Green – Making the Difference'.

The principles of waste management have now become clear to the consumer:

- reduce waste production at the outset;

- re-use and recycle where possible;

- recover as much as possible by chemical and physical methods; and

- dispose to the environment using the most appropriate techniques.

As consumerism moves in this direction, industry will have no option but to follow and will have to be advised accordingly.

Transportation Patterns

One further example of green consumerism is the slow move towards a sustainable transportation system. The increase in use of the motor car throughout the world has been rapid. The growth of traffic looks set to continue, although there are glimmers of hope. There is an obvious dilemma in that people want both the freedom offered by a car and a clean and beautiful environment. Paradoxically, the pressures on governments to remedy the situation – particularly in our large urban centres, which have massive traffic densities – are coming from the consumers, the people who are contributing to the cause. Consumerism can, therefore, play a key role in future transport policy and have a major influence. Through a reduction in the dependence on the motor car, there will be less direct air pollution, fossil fuels and other raw materials will be conserved, and towns and cities will be reclaimed by the people who live there. In the UK, the chief executive of

15

the Environment Agency established as a result of the EA 1995, has explained the relevance of an integration of transport policy with environmental objectives.

The Environment as a Business Issue

Responses and Benefits to Business

As is developed later in this book, particularly in Chapter 8, industry is now embracing the environmental ethic for five main reasons.

- *Efficiency.* Environmental improvements often secure financial benefits at little cost. The reduction of through put energy and raw materials in a process will cut costs and cut pollution. It is important to remember that: 'waste is money lost'.

- *Competition.* Environmental improvements may secure a competitive edge. By cultivating a green image, market share can be increased. This needs to be managed; a 'green gloss' will be quickly seen through. A green image needs action and a verifiable system to demonstrate that claims made are truthful. A green image may also help in the recruitment and retention of staff or in attracting inwards investment.

- *Market.* Environmental protection can create a market in itself. The expenditure on environmental protection clearly creates market opportunities in providing pollution-abatement equipment, cleaner technology, recycling systems, clean-up technologies and consultancy services. It is expected that the EU market in environmental protection will reach over $85 billion per annum, and the US market will reach over $100 billion per annum by the turn of the century.

- *Compliance.* Failure to comply with legislation or anticipate national and international changes can be costly. The cost of non-compliance can be high, and failure to keep abreast or ahead of changes in policy at international, national and regional level can cause problems for industry when adjusting to changing circumstances.

- *Commitment.* This is made when concern for the environment within the organisation transcends narrow self-interest and represents the acceptance of the environmental ethic as a moral duty. Once such commitment is established within a business, the workforce will move towards minimising the effect of their activities on the environment.

Stakeholders

As will be seen in Chapters 8 and 10, when considering environmental reporting and interacting with stakeholders it is in the interests of all those with a stake in the company to ensure that environmental performance is maximised. These stakeholders may include:

- customers;

- investors;

- lenders;

- shareholders;

- employees;

- neighbours (human and non-human);

- government.

As noted above, environmental excellence can achieve increases in efficiency through reduction in raw material and energy costs or an increase in market share through appealing to the green consumer. Where these practices occur, profits will increase and stakeholders will see an immediate benefit. Environmental excellence will also reduce waste; hence pollution and the drain on natural resources will decrease. This will benefit stakeholders because liabilities will be reduced, the risk of non-compliance with legislation will be minimised and the overall quality of life and the quality of the environment will be improved.

Health Risks

One of the most contentious liabilities facing industry is the potential effect of its activities on the health of the population, associated not only with the increasingly recognised problem of contaminated land (discussed further in Chapter 4) but also resulting from other industrial activity. In 1984 the accident at the Union Carbide plant at Bhopal killed thousands and adversely affected the health of hundreds of thousands. The directors of the company were indicted for culpable homicide, and these charges stand to this day. Also, accidents at Seveso in Italy and Chernobyl in the Ukraine have highlighted the significant risks involved in industrial processes, not only within the countries where the accidents happen, but also world-wide in terms of loss of business, legal action and loss of insurance cover.

These incidents are extreme cases illustrating the possible consequences of the release of toxic substances into the environment. There are cases where releases of small quantities of a substance over time have had devastating effects on human health. In Japan in the 1950s the slow release of mercury into Minamota Bay eventually led to chronic health problems, with thousands of people contracting Itai-Itai or Ouch-Ouch disease, caused by mercury passing into their brains after eating contaminated seafood.

Therefore, it is essential in any appraisal of the effects of a development, that the potential health risks are investigated and assessed. It is in the interests of businesses involved to ensure that their liabilities are minimised. Many multinational companies have accepted this and now aim to apply the highest standards in all countries in which they operate.

Insurance

Stemming from the above concerns, schemes for insuring companies against environmental damage are becoming available. At present, however, many of them relate to catastrophic, accidental releases only. The insurance market is reluctant to insure a company against long-term environmental damage because of its lack of control and the absence of clarity in the definition of the terms involved.

What is clear, however, is that the world insurance market is becoming aware of its own liabilities and the huge financial costs caused by poor management of environmental risks. The oil spill disaster caused by the *Exxon Valdez* in Alaska, for instance, cost the insurance industry many millions of dollars. The result, of course, is a tightening of the market in terms of increased premiums and restrictions on cover. Insurance companies are also beginning to require that sound environmental management systems are in place and regular eco-audits are undertaken. Further discussion is found in Chapters 7 and 8.

It could be said that in order to protect its own investments the insurance industry is acting as a regulatory authority by refusing insurance schemes where it is not satisfied that liabilities have been suitably managed. One possible way out may be 'self-insurance' within vulnerable industrial sectors to enable business to continue. This would entail members of a particular industry setting up their own insurance schemes by paying premiums into a central pool, which can then be tapped in the event of claims.

An Exemplary Response: The Valdez Principles

These principles were originally devised as a reaction to the environmental disaster caused by the *Exxon Valdez*. They are preventive measures designed to ensure that such a disaster would not recur. Moreover, in view of the issues that are being debated and require urgent attention both at international and national level, they demonstrate a sound starting point for business policy. They are:

Protection of the Biosphere

Protection of the biosphere will minimise and strive to eliminate the release of any pollutant that may cause environmental damage to the air, water or earth or its inhabitants. Habitats in rivers, lakes, wetlands, coastal zones and oceans will be safeguarded and contributions to the greenhouse effect, depletion of the ozone layer and the occurrence of acid rain or smog will be minimised.

Suitable Use of Natural Habitat

Sustainable use will be made of renewable natural resources such as water, soils and forests. Non-renewable natural resources would be made through their efficient use and careful planning. Wildlife habitat, open spaces and wilderness will be protected while preserving biodiversity.

Reduction and Disposal of Waste

The creation of waste, especially hazardous waste, will be minimised and, wherever possible, materials would be recycled. Wastes will be disposed of through safe and responsible methods.

Wide Use of Energy

Every effort will be made to optimise the use of environmentally-safe and sustainable energy sources to meet existing needs. There will be investment in improved energy efficiency and consolidation in operations. The energy efficiency of products produced or sold will be maximised.

Risk Reduction

The environmental, health and safety risk to employees and the communities in which there are operations will be minimised by employing safe technologies and operating procedures and by being constantly prepared for emergencies.

Marketing of Safe Products and Services

Products or services that minimise adverse environmental impact and are safe, as consumers commonly use them, will be sold. Consumers would be informed of the environmental impact of products and services.

Damage Compensation

Responsibility will be taken for any harm caused to the environment by making every effort to restore the environment fully and to compensate those persons who are adversely affected.

Disclosure

Employees and the public would receive disclosure of incidences relating to operations which cause environmental harm or pose health or safety hazards. Potential environment, health or safety hazards posed by operations would be disclosed and no action would be taken against employees who report any condition that creates a danger to the environment or poses health and safety hazards.

Environmental Directors and Managers

At least one member of the Board of Directors will be a person qualified to represent environmental interests. Management will commit resources to implement these principles, including the funding of an office for a Vice-President for environmental affairs or equivalent executive position, reporting directly to the CEO, to monitor and report upon our implementation efforts.

Assessment and Annual Audit

An annual self-evaluation of progress in implementing these principles and in complying with all applicable laws and regulations throughout world-wide operations is advisable for many reasons, particularly in view of upcoming developments. A timely creation of independent environmental audit procedures will be worked towards which will be completed annually and made available to the public.

Practitioners should be aware of the value of voluntary steps in assisting the level of compliance by their clients. As demonstrated in the box below, the experience of major corporations has largely been extremely positive for their competitive, as well as their environmental, performance.

Prevention Better than Cure: The Example of 3M

In 1989 Robert Bringer, Vice-President for environmental engineering and pollution control at 3M, stated: 'We believe very strongly that environmental policy – and by that I mean not just having one, but putting it into practice in all aspects of business – will be the single most important factor for a competitive company in the 1990s and beyond. In short, environmental ethics have to be the most important strategy a company can adopt for its long-term survival.'

3M's managers recognised that the reduction of pollution at source rather than at the end of the production process was the key to such environmental awareness and improvement, and they therefore developed the '3P policy' (pollution prevention pays) in the mid-1970s. Pollution prevention at source depends on four complementary processes:

> *Reformatting products by changing the raw materials involved in the manufacture (eg eliminating the use of solvents or encouraging water-based products).*

> *Modifying the manufacturing process to reduce harmful by-products and implementing a control system.*

> *Redesigning equipment to perform under much more stringent operating conditions and to eliminate as much waste as possible.*

> *Designing for recycling at the very start of a manufacturing process, including recovery of waste materials for re-use or sale.*

3M is still an exemplary case study of a company that has implemented sound environmental management practices as an integral part of its business strategy and in so doing has shown that sound environmental management, far from costing more, has positive financial benefits.

Concluding Remarks

In the light of the developments referred to above, there is no doubt that environmental law and policy in the UK will have a growing impact on business activity. Moreover, environmental management will increasingly be perceived as part of business strategy, regardless of where a company intends to operate, and any practical exportable methodology that can assist will be of benefit to corporate activities. As our environment and economy become increasingly interdependent and as we all work towards a positive future for both natural resources and man-made resources, it is also clear that the heightened awareness of an understanding of the role played by the regulatory, voluntary and economic pressures will be of benefit to all concerned.

---

[1] Study by Cornell University, USA, Prof D Pimental, see *The Independent* 6 January 1998
[2] Eg Water Resources Act 1989, Water Industry Act 1991
[3] Schmidt, Reiner and Mueller, Helmut 'Einfuehrung in das Umweltrecht' (1995) 4th edn, C H Beck

Chapter 2

The Impact of EU Environmental Law

The Background

When the EC Treaty (the Treaty) was originally concluded in 1957 by the six founding Member States, it made no express reference to the environment. Nor were any amendments made in the intervening years to include the environment. It was only when the Single European Act (SEA) was adopted in 1987 that protection of the environment was referred to expressly. Nevertheless, a comprehensive environmental policy was developed in the 1970s by the EC and continued by the EU. In the absence of express powers, this demonstrates that there was an urgent need for such a policy to be developed by the Community and that this need drove the lawyers, administrators and politicians to find, acknowledge and use the implicit powers in the Treaty to protect the environment.

Co-ordinated action on environmental protection began when the Summit Conference of October 1972 launched the first Environmental Action Programme (EAP). Prior to 1972, environmental issues had been raised in relation to the free movement of goods. For example, Directive 67/548 on the Classification, Packaging and Labelling of Dangerous Substances had clear relevance to the environment. In general, however, there was no specific programme to promote environmental improvement.

Even after 1972, progress upon environmental improvement was limited. As with many other areas of legislative change in the Community, it was the SEA that became the catalyst for change. Since then the development of European environmental law has been rapid: for example, in 1992 it became a significant feature of the Maastricht Treaty.

There are two main reasons for the growth of interest in environmental matters. The first relates to competition policy. Increasingly, environmental laws place significant constraints upon industrial activity. Clearly, where one Member State accepts stringent measures of environmental protection, while another makes little attempt to curb pollution, then 'a level playing field' of regulation cannot exist. This would account for why, by 1972, attention was directed at the area of the environment. The second reason relates to the Single Market Programme: the optimism that there would be significant growth across the market led to a questioning of what type of growth was required, and the answer that emerged was that such growth should be sustainable.

It is no longer appropriate to consider the need for environmental protection measures – the necessity is now acknowledged by almost everyone. The more interesting question is why the Community should have played such an active role and continues to do so. Initially, it seems strange that the EU, which was set up as the EEC, is so concerned with the environment. There are, of course, numerous different levels on which environmental action can be taken: local, regional, national, European and world-wide. Although there is much activity at all levels, it is particularly interesting to consider why action at Community level is so appropriate.

The Impetus for Community Action

Nowadays all economic activity – apart from some of the service sectors involving intellectual rather than physical activity – has an impact on the environment. Even farming, which has been traditionally regarded as inherently environmentally-friendly, is now recognised as having a major impact on the environment through its intensive production methods. For example, in certain areas, the application of fertilisers, fungicides and pesticides to the land on a massive scale has led to the saturation of the land with nitrogen and other chemicals. As a result, the usual filtering effect of the water percolating to the water table is no longer effective, and what previously were supplies of water suitable for drinking have become contaminated.

As will be demonstrated in other chapters (in particular, Chapter 10), the converse of the proposition that economic activity has effects on the environment is that measures for the protection of the environment have effects on, and opportunities for, economic activities. Such measures may be taken at all stages of the production, distribution and consumption processes. For example, there may be a ban on the use of certain raw materials such as CFC gases; there may be control of certain production processes that contaminate the environment, such as the sulphate process for the production of titanium dioxide; limits may be placed on the discharge of waste products during the production process; and the finished product may be required to meet certain specifications, for example, gaseous emissions from motor vehicles, the lead content of petrol and the sulphur content of fuel oil.

Clearly, if Member States take action individually on these matters, different norms will be in force in different parts of the Common Market distorting conditions of competition between producers and distributors. For instance, if Member States fix different emission norms for motor cars, not only the circulation of new motor cars for sale in the Common Market will be severely restricted, but also their subsequent circulation when in use. Clearly, there is a need for common action in these cases if the EU is to carry on without compromise.

It may be argued that such common action could be achieved by the traditional inter-governmental route, that is to say by means of international conventions. After all, if all Member States subscribe to the same international obligations a certain harmonising effect will be achieved. However, as recent developments in the Climate Change Convention show, serious weaknesses in the inter-governmental process remain: international agreements are difficult and slow to negotiate; there is no requirement that all Member States conclude the international agreement once it has been negotiated; those Member States which do conclude it may interpret and apply its provisions in different ways; there is usually no proper supervision of the application by the contracting parties of their obligations under international agreements; and effective remedies are usually lacking where a contracting party fails to observe its obligations.

Whereas some of these weaknesses exist at Community level, action by the EU offers considerable advantages over inter-governmental action: there is a permanent executive organ in the shape of the Commission to monitor developments and propose necessary action; even if Community decision-making processes can be slow, they are well established and more coherent and efficient than international negotiations; the Commission is charged with the task of ensuring the proper application of Community law by the Member States; legal machinery exists whereby a common interpretation of Community measures can be secured; and a Member State which fails to apply Community law or applies it incorrectly may have to appear before the ECJ in Luxembourg, and there may also be legal consequences before its own courts, such as actions for damages and impossibility applying national provisions in conflict with Community law.

It can be seen, therefore, that environmental action meets the basic objective of the Community, that is to secure the establishment and proper functioning of the Common Market by reason of the economic and commercial repercussions of the necessary measures. In general, the EU is well placed to take such action by reason of the fact that it can adopt common rules and secure their correct implementation.

Basis for Action: Treaty Sources

Whereas the Treaty of Amsterdam has had some impact upon the numbering of the provisions that are discussed below in order to facilitate an understanding of the chronological developments in this area, the recent changes are referred to in a separate section dealing with the Amsterdam Treaty (see below).

Articles 100 and 235

Even prior to the SEA, which now makes express reference to the environment, a comprehensive Community EAP had been developed because the Treaty contained two general legal bases for action – arts 100 and 235. Article 100 of the Treaty states:

> 'The Council shall, acting unanimously on a proposal from the Commission, and after consulting the European Parliament and the Economic and Social Committee, issue directives for the approximation of such laws, regulations or administrative provisions of the Member States as directly affect the establishment or functioning of the Common Market.'

Where the direct effect referred to could be shown, even if the objective of a proposal was principally environmental, the Commission based the proposal on art 100. This direct effect was relatively easy to demonstrate as regards product specifications because harmonisation facilitated circulation of goods. The effect was rather more difficult to show, but still demonstrable as regards harmonisation of emission norms for industrial processes, because of the effect of harmonising conditions of competition. The direct effect was most difficult to demonstrate, however, in the case of proposals which fixed standards – unrelated to industrial emission levels – and for aspects of the environment, such as water quality standards, air standards and ambient noise levels.

In such a case, resort was made to art 235, also known as a general residuary provision. Article 235 states that:

> 'If action by the Community should prove necessary to attain, in the course of the operation of the Common Market, one of the objectives of the Community and this Treaty has not provided the necessary powers, that the Council shall, acting unanimously on a proposal from the Commission, and after consulting the European Parliament, take the appropriate measures.'

However, in view of the objectives of the Treaty, which refer inter alia to the improvement of living conditions and the harmonious development of the economies of the Member States, and also to the economic effects of all environmental measures, it was usually straightforward to rely on art 235.

Although the practice of basing environmental measures on these two articles has become well established, they have occasionally produced conflict in terms of the legal authority upon which a legislative proposal should be based, rather than providing a coherent juridical basis for Community action. This is also evident in the discussion of art 100A (see below).

Article 130

It was considered by the framers of the SEA that the growing importance of environmental policy deserved express recognition, and that some policy guidelines should be laid down. Accordingly, there are now three articles specifically dealing with the environment: arts 130R, 130S and 130T.

First, SEA produced art 130R, which outlines the principles and broad aims of Community action in relation to the environment. These amendments to the Treaty of Rome came into effect on 1 July 1987. As originally drafted, it defined three broad objectives of environmental policy: to preserve, protect and improve the quality of the environment; to contribute towards protecting human health; and to ensure a prudent and rational utilisation of natural resources.

Article 130R lays down the objectives of Community environmental policy in rather wide terms. It also sets out the principles on which such action is to be based, namely that preventive action should be taken; environmental damage should, as a priority, be remedied at source; and the polluter should pay.

Further provision is made in this article that environmental protection requirements should be a component of the Community's policies; and on the matters to be taken into account by the Community in preparing its action relating to the environment the Council is to act unanimously after consulting the European Parliament and the Economic and Social Committee.

However, since the Council was to establish matters on which decisions may be taken by qualified majority, a rather complex decision-making procedure was provided. This was slightly eased by the fact that the second paragraph of art 130S envisages the possibility of action by qualified majority in certain cases to be specified.

Article 130T goes on to provide that the protective measures adopted on the basis of art 130S are not to prevent a Member State from maintaining or adopting more stringent measures. Essentially, therefore, Community environmental measures form the minimum level. If a Member State wishes to make them stricter for its own territory and in its own economy it may do so, although this way means that its own industry must pay the economic penalty of having to comply with the stricter norms.

Article 100A

Any discussion of legal sources would not be complete without some reference to art 100A, which was also inserted into the Treaty by the SEA to accelerate the harmonisation process that was previously based on art 100. Instead of a unanimous Council decision being required, decisions may be taken on the basis of art 100A by qualified majority in accordance with the co-operation procedure with the European Parliament. In view of the easier decision-making procedure, this legal basis is obviously attractive. However, the question arises as to whether or not it can be used for environmental measures. The same arguments that were used to justify the use of art 100 can be employed here.

Where a measure was necessary to complete the internal market, art 100A of the Treaty empowered the Community to adopt laws concerning environmental protection. The difference between the legislative competence under arts 130, 100A and other Treaty articles is considered below. It is sufficient to note here that where Community legislation was adopted under art 100A powers, it was said that such laws must promote, as a base, a high level of environmental protection (art 100A(3) SEA). This provision is retained following the Treaty on European Union 1992 (commonly known as the Maastricht Treaty), but is extended now to all environmental measures proposed under any other Treaty article. Thus, post-Maastricht, art 130R(2) of the Treaty declares the 'high level of protection' principle to be applicable to all environmental measures, and not merely those necessary for the functioning of the internal market.

The use of art 100A in the way indicated was expressly approved of by the ECJ, as exemplified by the decision of June 1991 concerning the Titanium Dioxide Directive.

Titanium Dioxide Case (Case 300/89, June 1991)

Directive 89/428 was adopted in order to harmonise programmes within Member States on the prevention of pollution caused by waste from the titanium dioxide industry. The proposal was introduced on the basis that it was an art 100A measure. However, the Council then determined that art 130S was the more appropriate legislative basis for this Directive. This required unanimity in the passage of the Directive, which was achieved upon adoption by the Council. The Commission, supported by the European Parliament, nonetheless brought an action before the ECJ seeking an annulment of the Directive. In Commission v EC Council, *the Commission argued that the objective underlying the Directive was the harmonisation of internal market procedures, and not merely the reduction of pollution. As such, it ought to have been adopted under the art 100A procedure. The Court upheld this argument so that the original Directive was annulled. The argument was one of principle. A new Directive, similar in terms to the annulled Directive, has now been introduced based on art 100A.*

One intention of the Maastricht Treaty was to resolve the uncertainty that has arisen concerning the legislative basis for action. Certainly, it would be helpful to know the precise ambit of art 100A, given the wider view of its scope that the ECJ seems to have taken in the *Titanium Dioxide Case*. It must be doubtful, however, whether this has been achieved. It has been argued that since Maastricht there is even greater doubt concerning the correct procedure to be adopted for there is greater complexity of the legal process and, possibly, there is even greater delay.

The Integration of Environmental Principles: Some Jurisprudence

Under the SEA, the importance of establishing a high level of protection under art 100A(3) was obvious when read in conjunction with art 130R(2), which stated that: 'Environmental protection requirements shall be a component of the Community's other policies.'

The significance of this provision can be seen in two cases which relate to waste, and which highlight the conflict that may arise between the principles of free movement and environmental protection. The first case is called the *Walloon Waste Case*, and the second case is widely referred to as the *Danish Bottles Case*.

Walloon Waste Case (Case 2/90, 4 July 1992)

In the ECJ, the Commission challenged a Belgian decree prohibiting the deposit in Wallonia of hazardous waste originating from other Member States. The ECJ found that the decree went beyond the scope of EC Directive 84/631 relating to the control of transfrontier shipments of waste. This was because that Directive did no more than to permit the control of movements of waste, rather than allow a blanket prohibition. However, the Court was required to consider also potential breaches of art 30 of the Treaty and the principle of free movement of goods in relation to the attempt to restrict flows of waste. Waste, especially where it may be recycled or treated, may be considered as 'goods'. Belgium argued that a requirement to protect the environment must be a component of any policy on free movement. The ECJ had much sympathy with this view, and indeed pointed to art 130R(2) of the Treaty. Not only does that provision make it a requirement that environmental protection is a component of Community policy, but it also states that environmental damage 'should as a priority be rectified at source'. The Court translated this into a requirement that the region producing the waste should dispose of it, if at all possible, close to the site of its production. This would minimise the necessity of trans-shipment of waste. It followed that even though the decree was invalid, going beyond the scope of the 1984 Directive, the ECJ would have been reluctant to rule the decree discriminatory on grounds of free movement alone.

Danish Bottles Case (Case 302/86) (1988) ECR4607

Denmark passed an order in 1981 obliging beer and other drinks manufacturers to sell their products using reusable materials. The nature of those materials had to be agreed by a national agency. The order was later amended to allow the use of certain non-approved, non-metal containers, but then a limitation was put on the volume of such non-approved containers that could be used per annum. The Commission sought a declaration that these measures represented a breach of art 30 of the Treaty. In this case, the ECJ acknowledged the potential obstacle to the free movement of goods arising from the particular requirement of the national rule. However, it said that such a rule might be allowed in so far as it was proportionate to the objective of environmental protection which it sought to achieve. Using this important principle of proportionality, the Court determined that the quantity restrictions imposed under the Danish order could not be valid. However, the ECJ were prepared to accept that a requirement for containers to be recyclable could, in itself, be lawful. The significance of this case lies in the Court's acceptance that the need to protect the environment might justify a limitation of the principle of free movement. Environmental protection was described by the ECJ as 'one of the Community's essential objectives'.

In two significant cases involving Italy, heard together in 1979, the ECJ found it necessary to consider the legal basis of environmental provisions prior to the SEA. The cases in question concerned Directives regarding detergents, the sulphur content of fuels (see case 91/79 *Commission* v *Italy* [1980] ECR 1099 and case 92/79 *Commission* v *Italy* [1980] ECR 115).

Detergent and Sulphur Content of Fuels Cases (Cases 91 and 92/79)

The ECJ accepted the validity of the Directives questioned before them on the basis that they have been adopted under Community EAPs. The First EAP followed the 1972 Summit. Thereafter, there have been three other action programmes and, most recently, the Fifth Action Programme. These programmes can be seen as an indication of the will of Member States to further environmental improvement and, as from 1973, they sought to plug the gap in formal legal powers upon which to proceed. In the cases against Italy, the ECJ showed some recognition of this and stated that since the measures had been adopted under Community programmes, and they aimed to further trade by breaking down technical barriers which might have otherwise been an impediment, the Directives should be considered valid. These cases support the law-making power of art 100, as well as the concept of EAPs.

The Maastricht Treaty very much endorses this line of policy from the ECJ by rewording art 130R(2). Rather than describing environmental protection as a 'component' of Community policy, art 130R(2) now reads, 'Environmental protection requirements must be integrated into the definition and implementation of other Community policies.'

It is not easy to explain the precise impact of this change of wording in the absence of the interpretative guidelines from the ECJ. Nonetheless, the concept of integration seems a far stronger tool than that of the 'component' part. Similarly, the mention not merely of 'the Community's other policies', but the definition and implementation of those polices seems to stress the centrality of environmental protection both in the formulation of policy and its enforcement. This change in language sits easily alongside the Fifth EAP. That programme placed great store on the notion of integration of environmental protection throughout Community policy. In certain areas, such as agricultural policy, energy policy and transport policy, one can expect that environmental considerations will have far greater prominence than before. Precisely how, in policy terms, environmental considerations will be taken into account is less than clear. However, where in the future those seeking to protect environmental interests object to elements of such policies, recourse to the ECJ may prove increasingly fruitful in reliance on the far stronger language of the reworded Treaty. This is particularly true in the light of the Treaty of Amsterdam.

Comments on the Reform

The reform of environmental legislation following the SEA in effect introduced dual procedures for environmental action. Where an environmental measure might be said to further the workings of the internal market, then art 100A might be invoked. This would allow qualified majority voting and give the European Parliament a greater say in the content of legislative proposals. Elsewhere, the specific environmental powers under art 130S could be utilised providing that there was a unanimous vote in the Council of Ministers. In this case, the role of the European Parliament would be restricted to an opinion following consultation.

Because of the uncertainties concerning the legal basis for environmental action, the Maastricht Summit sought to address this problem. Broadly, the agreement which was reached at Maastricht was that environmental legislation should proceed by majority voting. Only in five areas of environmental reform under art 130R will unanimity be required. These are: town and country planning; land use (not including waste management); water resource management; issues concerning energy sources and supply; and provisions of a physical nature.

This list is contained within art 130S(2) and seems to suggest, therefore, that unanimity is only required, even in one of the areas listed above, where the measure is introduced under art 130S. Where a proposed measure on, say, land use (or any other topic in the above list) is introduced under art 100A, then qualified majority voting may apply under a co-decision procedure.

Assuming that the proposal is introduced not under art 100A but under art 130S, then if the measure appears in the above list unanimity will be required. This assumes that this list is clear-cut, and that a measure can be readily identified as, say, a 'town and country planning' matter. Doubtless, this itself can be the source of litigation similar to that in the *Titanium Dioxide Case*. Where, however, there is a Directive based on art 130S which does not affect any of the matters in the above list, then qualified majority voting applies. However, this situation is further complicated. As qualified majority voting was extended to environmental measures under art 130S, so too the co-operation procedure under art 100A became part of art 130 procedures for environmental legislation. The co-operation procedure was designed at the time of the SEA to give Parliament a much greater legislative role. It involves the European Parliament in a fuller consideration of the content and status of legislative measures due to a second reading in the Parliament.

The co-decision powers of the European Parliament, introduced by the Maastricht Treaty, therefore extend the democratic input of the Parliament. They are to apply now to art 100A matters relating to the establishment of the Single Market. As suggested above, some of these continue to include environmental laws.

The co-decision process will allow Parliament to veto certain proposals, even where the Council has taken a unanimous view.

The highly complex changes of procedure can be summarised as follows: environmental legislation will be passed under art 130S by qualified majority voting in Council and via the co-operation procedure in Parliament; but in five areas specified in art 130S, there will need to be unanimity in Council (though only consultation in Parliament) if legislation is to proceed under art 130S; however, where a measure relates to the establishment of the Single Market, art 100A should be the basis for action, and this will require qualified majority voting in the Council, and the co-decision procedure in the European Parliament.

The Treaty of Amsterdam 1997

The Treaty of Amsterdam has brought further changes on environmental matters. Sustainable development has become one of the EU's main goals and environmental protection will have to be integrated into all of its policies under the amendments agreed in June 1997. The practitioner should be aware of these changes as well as those of the previous treaties, in particular the SEA and the Treaty of Maastricht. The amendments appear to have reduced the scope for Member States to maintain or introduce national environmental rules for traded goods.

Surprisingly, the makers of the Amsterdam Treaty decided to rename some of the most important articles, consequently potentially complicating matters: art 100A became new art 95; art 130R became new art 174; and art 130S became new art 175. As indicated above, the old article numbers have been used in this discussion in order to avoid confusion.

According to new art 95 (ex-art 100A), there are two possible scenarios: first, under paragraph (4), the Member State that wishes to 'maintain' (usually stricter) existing national legislation on environmental grounds; and, secondly, under new paragraph (5), the Member State that 'envisages' the introduction of new provisions after the adoption of the Community measure based on new scientific evidence and on grounds of a problem specific to that Member State. In both cases, the Member State must notify the Commission of the provisions as well as the grounds for them.

Paragraph (6) introduces a new deadline for the Commission: if, within six (or in a complex case 12) months of the notification, the Commission has not approved or rejected the national provisions, those provisions shall be deemed to have been approved. It is worth noting that under the new art 95, the Commission now has three possible grounds for rejecting the national provisions: they are a means of arbitrary discrimination; they are a disguised restriction on trade between Member States; and they constitute an obstacle to the functioning of the internal market (a new provision).

The status of the national provisions during the six- (or 12-) month investigation period is not clear. Existing national provisions should probably be deemed valid before being found contrary to European legislation. However, arguably, the same is not true for 'envisaged' national provisions.

Article 174 (ex-art 130R) now includes a flexibility provision (in para 2):

> 'In this context, harmonisation measures answering environmental protection requirements shall include, where appropriate, a safeguard clause allowing Member States to take provisional measures, for non-economic environmental reasons, subject to a Community inspection procedure.'

The same provision, though in permissive form, could be found in ex-art 100A(5). It is unclear whether this article impliedly includes a notification provision.

Article 175 (ex-art 130S) now refers to a new, simplified version of the co-decision procedure. The same applies to art 95.[1]

An important change is the replacement of the word 'sustainable growth' in art 2 (Community tasks) with 'sustainable development'. The wording of the Maastricht Treaty regarding the EU goal to promote 'sustainable and non-inflationary growth respecting the environment' was confusing. The new wording is better. It will now be among the main tasks of the Community to promote 'balanced and sustainable development of economic activities' as well as 'a high level of protection and improvement of the quality of the environment'. The amendment has been buttressed by a new provision in art 3(d) of the Treaty that 'environmental protection requirements must be integrated into the definition and implementation of Community policies and activities … in particular with a view to promoting sustainable development'. In a declaration attached to the Treaty, the Commission has promised to prepare 'environmental impact assessment studies when making proposals which may have significant environmental implications'.

Some Conclusions

One obvious desire within the Maastricht Treaty was to resolve the uncertainty that had arisen concerning the legislative basis for action. However, arguably there was even greater doubt in the aftermath of Maastricht concerning the correct procedure to be adopted, and certainly there was greater complexity of legal process, and possibly even greater delay. The Amsterdam Treaty tries to counteract this by imposing stricter deadlines for the Commission. Whilst after Amsterdam it does not seem any easier to decide on legislative bases of environmental action, the layout of the articles has been simplified. And so has the decision process by the adoption of a simplified co-decision procedure.

It is evident from the above analysis that the Community institutions are in any event committed to a programme of environmental protection. Subject to the debates concerning the principle of subsidiarity, it is reasonable to anticipate increasing action on environmental protection in the future. Regulation to date has focused on the prevention of future environmental damage. This has been done largely by standard-setting, the promotion of pollution control technology and the assessment of likely environmental impacts.

More recently, there has been widespread consideration of economic and market incentives towards environmental improvement. Moreover, rather than simply focusing on future developments, the Commission is considering the restoration of existing damage for several reasons. These include the protection of natural resources, the need for environmental safeguards, the competition problems posed by different levels of activity on the part of Member States in environmental restoration and the protection of human health.

Again, economic and social instruments as well as legal measures will be used to achieve these ends, but civil liability systems are also being amended, if only because they form the mechanism whereby responsibility for the clean-up is allocated. The question of historic damage and contaminated land and soil is therefore of particular importance and is discussed below.

Although some may wish to argue that the extension of Community activity into the domestic civil liability laws of Member States goes too far, the Commission can point to its clear legal powers under art 130R(2), where mention is made of: the 'polluter pays' principle; preventative action; rectification of environmental damage at source; and, following Maastricht, the 'precautionary principle'.

Many of these principles are at the heart of civil liability systems: How will the polluter pay? How can future deterioration be prevented? What principle of deterrence is there to restrict future damage and to rectify pollution at source? What rights are there to seek injunctive relief to restrain activity which is feared is causing environmental damage?

The Commission has not been satisfied with the different answers to these questions emanating from different Member States. Rather, it has been seeking to put in place a framework for an EU-wide system of shared responsibility for environmental damage. To this end, a paper on 'Liability for Environmental Impairment' was published. These developments are discussed further below.

National Legislation

Practitioners should be aware that the Directive is the usual legal instrument in the environmental field. In accordance with the Treaty, a directive is binding as to the result to be achieved upon each Member State to which it is addressed. Yet it leaves to national authorities the choice of form and method of transposition into the national system. In addition to the duty imposed by the Treaty, at the end of each Directive there is a provision which expressly requires the Member States to bring into force the laws, regulations and administrative provisions necessary for them to comply with the Directive by a specified date and to communicate the measures in question to the Commission.

Moreover, the Commission has adopted the practice of including a provision requiring the national measures to make express reference to the Directive being transposed, so that the relevant national measures can be more easily identified. The record of transposition of environmental measures by Member States is very patchy. This remains true in spite of these express provisions and in spite of the fact that Member States participate in the negotiation process and their environmental ministers must give their consent before a measure is adopted.

This is all the more surprising since, as described above, until relatively recently nearly all environmental measures had to be adopted unanimously, and, therefore, Member States did not have the excuse that they were outvoted on a matter. Some of the main reasons for this are:

- A lack of proper liaison and communication between the departments of the Member States negotiating the Directives at Brussels and the home departments responsible for their ultimate transposition. On the one hand, this leads to a lack of realism regarding the problems to be faced and the length of time needed to transpose the Directive, and on the other, to a lack of accountability of the department called on ultimately to transpose the instruments.

- A tendency for the Member States to give low priority to the transposition of Directives, especially as this may involve use of precious legislative time and scarce resources.

- A similar tendency where the transposition of the Directive is perceived to be against national interests or those of influential pressure groups.

- A failure on the part of national administrations to understand the necessity for prompt compliance with their EU obligations and a general confusion about the precise nature of their Community obligations.

- Technical and legal problems which arise when the provisions of the Directives are being analysed for the purpose of their transposition.

Various measures are taken to force recalcitrant Member States to conform, including exerting political pressure and mobilising the European Parliament. This latter measure is an increasingly powerful method, as the UK government has found to its cost on several occasions, a particularly good example being the bathing water Directive (see Chapter 5).

Legal and political influence can also be exerted in the case of non-deliberate behaviour on the part of Member States. In this area too there is scope for the services of the Commission to be more active, for proper transposition of environmental rules and standards can be a sensitive and complex issue. For example, the Commission can provide much more contact on a technical level between the services of the Commission and those of the Member States in order to iron out problems of interpretation, remove doubts about the obligations of Member States and achieve a co-ordinated and timely transposition in accordance with the agreed timetable.

Secondary Legislation

There is now a very considerable body of secondary environmental legislation. The principal areas of action and the most important measures in those fields as well as likely developments are:

- general programmes;
- water (both inland and the sea);
- air;
- waste;
- noise;
- chemical and industrial products;
- space development and natural resources;
- flora and fauna;
- nuclear safety; and
- miscellaneous actions.

General Programmes

As indicated in Chapter 1, the EU has proceeded systematically on the basis of general programmes, containing outlines of the orientations of environmental policy to be developed and the areas where priority action is needed. The last general programme to be adopted was in 1993.

Water

As mentioned in Chapter 5, the measures on inland water cover such matters as the quality of surface water used for the production of drinking-water, pollution caused by dangerous or industrial substances discharged into water, the quality of bathing water, the quality of fresh water suitable for fish life, and the protection of underground water against pollution.

In addition, measures deal with the discharge of particular dangerous substances and the urgent problem of the over-use of nitrates in agricultural production. As regards the sea, there are measures controlling pollution coming from land-based sources, decisions on the general protection of the Mediterranean, prohibitions of the discharges of oil and measures on the quality of the water suitable for shellfish.

Perhaps the most important proposal is the Directive on the discharge of waste at sea.

Air

Air emissions present another key area of concern (see Chapter 5). There are measures on gaseous emissions from vehicles (both petrol and diesel engines); the sulphur content of fuel oils; the control of CFCs in the environment and the protection of the ozone layer; the lead content of petrol; the sulphur, lead and particulate concentrations in the air; and gaseous emissions from large combustion plants and municipal waste disposal plants.

Measures for future regulation are given below.

Waste

Waste management is discussed in Chapter 6. There are general Directives on the disposal and treatment of waste and dangerous waste and also a series of Directives on particular forms of waste such as used oil, polychlorinated biphenyls (PCBs), waste paper and drink containers. Other important measures are the Directive on the surveillance and control of transfers of waste across frontiers in the Community and two international conventions on the same issue.

Noise

Noise is an increasingly obvious environmental issue. There are a series of Directives fixing maximum noise levels for such things as motor vehicles, agricultural tractors, earth-moving equipment, subsonic aeroplanes, lawnmowers, domestic apparatus, hydraulic equipment, helicopters and vehicles running on rails.

Chemical and Industrial Products

The key measure in this sector is the Directive on the classification, packaging and labelling of dangerous substances, which has been amended many times already. Other measures concern the biodegradability of products such as washing powders and detergents, precautions to be taken against the risk of major industrial accidents, prevention of pollution by asbestos, and good laboratory practices for the control of chemical products and the export from and import into the Community of certain dangerous chemicals.

Space Development and Natural Resources

The most significant measure is the Directive on environmental impact assessment requiring the evaluation of the environmental impact of substantial public and private developments. There are other measures concerning the protection of our architecture and natural heritage, research into large urban concentrations, and a general system of information on the environment. (See also Chapters 6 and 10.)

Flora and Fauna

There are measures on the protection of wild birds and their habitats and measures protecting other species, such as whales and seals, and the flora and fauna of the Antarctic, the Mediterranean and other oceans generally. There are also a number of international conventions which the Community has concluded, in particular, for the protection of migratory animals and, more generally, for the protection of European wildlife and natural habitats. The most important initiative in this sector is the Directive on the general protection of all wild flora and fauna and their habitats, relating to genetically modified organisms and micro-organisms. Detailed discussion of flora and fauna, as well as the topics that follow, fall outside the scope of this guide.

Nuclear Safety

There are measures fixing norms relating to the protection of the health of the population of workers from radiation, for agricultural products after the Chernobyl accident to the transfer across frontiers of products emitting radiation and for a system of notification and assistance in the case of a nuclear accident.

Miscellaneous Actions

These include measures whereby Member States inform each other and the Community of their initiatives in the environmental field with a view to harmonisation on a Community level, a Community communication setting out the policy on state aid in the environmental sector, an inventory of the sources of information on the environment, a recommendation on how to evaluate the costs of anti-pollution measures taken by industry, a legal basis for financial support for certain environmental actions and a communication on how the protection of the environment can help employment.

One of the most important proposals in this area was the Directive providing for a general right of access to environmental information.

Enforcement Procedures

The Treaty envisages the possibility that Member States will not always fulfil their obligations to the EU and provides a procedure for this – the so-called infringement procedure. Where a Member State fails to transpose a Directive into its national law the Commission will usually be alerted by the lack of action of the Member States concerned their failure to notify the necessary measures of transposition. Complaints from members of the public are another frequent means by which infringement procedures are discovered.

The enforcement procedure is usually commenced by a warning letter. If this produces no satisfactory results the Commission will send a formal letter to the Member State concerned setting out the reasons why it considers that the Member State has infringed its Treaty obligations and asking for the observations of the Member State.

If observations are received, the Commission will examine them before deciding whether to proceed to the next stage, which is to send a reasoned opinion explaining why it considers the Member State has infringed the Treaty and calling upon it to take the necessary action within a given period.

If the Member State does not take the necessary action, or fails to convince the Commission that it is not in infringement, the Commission will start court proceedings. After an exchange of written pleadings, an oral procedure and the conclusions of the Advocate-General, the ECJ will decide whether or not the Member State has infringed the Treaty.

The Commission's policy is to make the infringement procedure largely automatic, so that once there is a suspicion of an infringement or a complaint, the court procedure is set in motion. The result of the automatic infringement procedure is that there are now thousands of cases running and the whole procedure is overburdened.

In addition, the various stages of the procedure may extend over a considerable period – perhaps several years. This can be advantageous in that it enables a settlement to be reached before a case goes to court. It may be that the exchange of letters clarifies issues that had previously been obscure. More often, however, it appears that the threat of court proceedings concentrates the mind of the relevant national administration. In addition, sometimes certain administrations wait until the last possible moment before a judgment of the court is rendered before introducing the necessary national legislation. The disadvantage of the length of time the procedure takes is that the deadline for transposing the Directive has long passed by the time the procedure is completed.

Due to the automatic nature of the infringement procedure there is very little need for the use of the alternative procedure provided by art 170 of the Treaty, whereby one Member State may take another Member State, which it considers to be in breach, before the court.

The Community does not have any direct means to enforce a decision of the court against a Member State. However, where a Member State neglects to apply a court's decision, a second infringement proceeding can be engaged for failure to take the necessary measures to comply with a judgment of the ECJ (art 171).

The procedure, introduced by the Maastricht Treaty, empowers the Commission to recommend in the second action that the defaulting Member State be fined. The court can then impose a fine. Usually this second action is effective. In the rather rare cases where it is not, political pressure has to be brought to bear on the Member State to comply.

In the environmental sector, the failure to transpose is by no means the only basis for enforcement procedures against Member States. The most important other category to mention here is incorrect transposition. This may take several forms.

Examples of Incorrect Transposition

The national administration may try to transpose the Directive by mere administrative practices. Such a transposition is not sufficient according to the case law of the court, since administrative measures can be changed at the whim of the administration and do not provide the necessary legal security. In addition, the transposition may give a particular interpretation to the requirements of the Directive which is inconsistent with the interpretation considered to be correct by the Commission.

Apart from non-transposition and incorrect transposition, there is a third category of cases, where the Member State may simply not enforce the transposed law: this category is 'non-implementation'. This is particularly serious in the environmental sector if the non-enforcement is systematic.

Some Pros and Cons

The decisions of the ECJ in these cases are usually implemented by the Member State concerned, without the threat of further proceedings. There is, however, a problem in the environmental sector, not only due to the huge number of cases which are brought, but also due to the potentially vast number of cases which could arise, particularly with regard to non-implementation of Directives. On the other hand, the correct implementation of these Directives is of basic importance for the protection of the environment and the proper functioning of the Common Market. This is why it has been suggested that the EEA should be monitoring the proper application of the EU's environment norms. As is mentioned further in Chapter 10, however, the EEA's role is that of an 'information gathering' rather than an enforcement institution. Nevertheless, its contribution is important in view of the efforts being made to develop an appropriate strategy which is effective throughout the EU to remedy environmental damage.

Remedying Environmental Damage

One of the key issues facing the EU is that of remedying environmental damage appropriately. The information that has been gathered under the auspices of the EEA was consolidated in the Dobris Report. The results of the Dobris Report (see Chapter 6) have shown a legacy of contaminated land and property that exists in the Member States of the EU. Such land and property can and does pose a threat to human health, the environment and to development potential. The existence of such contamination has led to schemes being set up in a number of countries world-wide to ensure that the risks are dealt with through restoration. The best-known example of such a scheme is Superfund in the USA (see Chapter 4). Other schemes are being introduced in Europe. The French government, for example, has introduced laws on contaminated land that shift the burden of responsibility onto the vendor. The vendor is responsible for returning the site to an acceptable condition, even if the vendor was not the polluter. Similar laws exist in Sweden, Denmark and Belgium.

The development of different systems of liability, civil or criminal, among Member States is likely to lead eventually to distortions of competition and the single market. Against this background, the Commission has spent the best part of the past decade attempting to devise a Community-wide scheme to tackle the problem of historical contamination and trying to resolve the issue of environmental liability.

Environmental Liability

This has been used to describe liability under both criminal law and civil law. In the environmental context, criminal liability usually arises as a result of prosecution by a regulatory body for non-compliance with environmental legislation. Its function is to support regulatory requirements by penalising those who fail to comply with them. Civil liability is the means for charging the cost of environmental damage to those who cause the damage and preventing threatened damage. The limited effectiveness of the civil law systems in achieving the objective has led to consideration of how they may be improved, resulting in the Commission Green Paper, which was published in 1993, on remedying environmental damage, upon which further lengthy research and consultation is being conducted with a view to the preparation of the draft Directive.

The consultation process has revealed a number of the difficult issues that need to be resolved prior to the successful drafting of the Directive. The views of responding national governments and corporations are presented, and they illustrate the broad range of opinions present from country to country and sector to sector. This discussion illustrates well the impact of EU environmental law since the issue of historic damage and clean-up is crucial to all Member States. Moreover, it is particularly topical now that a White Paper is due to be published by the Commission in March 1999.

The Commission Green Paper: The Response to the Consultation Process

The Commission Green Paper on remedying environmental damage was intended to stimulate discussion. It contains no firm proposals, but has an underlying aim of finding the best ways of preventing environmental damage and recovering the cost of remedial action when such action is deemed necessary to prevent damage occurring and its impact on human health.

The Commission received a total of 121 responses to their Green Paper consultation process. The summaries of these responses were given in a document published in mid-1994. Although there were seven classes of respondents, only two are relevant to the theme of this book: national governments and corporations. The matters dealt with are the basis of liability, damage and restoration, joint compensation schemes and the right to bring an action.

Two approaches to civil liability exist: fault-based liability and strict (or no-fault) liability. Liability because of fault requires proof that the liable party committed a negligent or wrongful act that results in damage. Actual physical destruction or gross contamination is generally considered to be damage, but a problem still exists about defining damage for lesser impacts and also defining at what point pollution causes actual damage. Under fault-based liability systems, the party that has suffered the damage will find it difficult to prove that the other party's act was wrongful.

Strict liability eases the burden of establishing liability because fault need not be established. It would still be necessary under this principle, however, to prove that environmental damage had, in fact, been caused by someone's actions. The costs associated with remedying the damage will depend on what environmental media need to be cleaned up and the extent to which clean-up should be undertaken. It is important to ensure that, after clean-up of environmental damage, no unacceptable residual risk to health remains. It is equally important, however, to avoid the high costs associated with excess remediation. The Commission is aware that costs should not be raised to unsustainable levels or that liabilities should not be so excessive that the financial burden on businesses would be too great. Another important issue is deciding what degree of impairment should be taken to constitute damage and, therefore, at what time the need to remedy this damage becomes actionable.

Three difficult questions are raised for deliberation before a decision to opt for a strict liability regime can be taken. The first is defining what activities should be subject to strict liability and what criteria should be used to decide whether certain activities are dangerous, and, therefore, to be covered by a strict liability regime. The second is deciding how to fund the costs of remediation, possibly through joint compensation systems based on charges or contributions from the economic sectors most closely linked to the type of damage needing restoration, or through systems shared with other sectors, or by taxpayers in general. The third is deciding whether civil claims may be made only by the authorities or parties who have suffered damage or by organisations acting on behalf of other interests as well.

Responses of National Governments

Basis of Liability

Seven national governments responded: the UK, Germany, Denmark, Luxembourg, The Netherlands, Portugal and Norway. Only three specified their preference for the basis of liability. The Federal German government cautioned against a strict liability regime for general activities not necessarily involving determined risks. They favoured other solutions for such activities and accepted that such activities would need to be clearly defined. This view was reiterated by the UK government. The government of Luxembourg favoured the introduction of a scheme of strict liability. None of the other governments specified a clear preference for the basis of liability to be adopted.

Damage and Restoration

The national governments that responded to the subject of damage and restoration agreed that the remediation should restore the ecology of the damaged area. The UK government noted that the restoration should be to a similar standard to that prevailing before damage occurred. The Federal German government noted that compensation for environmental damage should be used to actually restore the damaged environment and for no other purpose. Both of these governments stressed the need to avoid excessively costly or otherwise inappropriate technologies that could encourage a restoration out of proportion to the damage caused.

Joint Compensation Schemes

There was general support for the setting up of joint compensation schemes, although it was acknowledged that the US experience demonstrates how difficult it is to ensure that a compulsory scheme is managed efficiently. The 'Superfund' approach, which is referred to in Chapter 4, has been criticised for improving the circumstances of lawyers but not the environment. A number of governments also required answers to questions, such as the type and extent of damage that would require remedying, before they would be prepared to consider to what extent joint compensation schemes could be of use. The government of The Netherlands considered exploring the feasibility of an international fund, rather than assuming that national schemes should be introduced, although the government of Luxembourg considered that a guarantee fund should be imposed on a subsidiary basis.

Right to Bring an Action

Not all of the government responses included an opinion on the issue of the right to bring an action. Both the UK and Federal German governments, however, did respond and both rejected the rights of NGOs to bring an action, arguing that the regulatory authorities already have the powers to prevent pollution and remedy damage to the unowned environment, and that to change these rights would result in overlap and confusion. Of the two other governments to respond, Luxembourg insisted that further attention is required to assess the issue. The government of The Netherlands, in contrast to the German and UK stance, considered that national policy is aimed at increasing the possibility of citizens and NGOs taking legal action against impending environmental damage. The Dutch approach favoured take-away constraints on the right to bring an action by such groups.

Responses of Corporations

Basis of Liability

A total of 14 corporations responded: British Petroleum (BP), Dow Europe, General Electric Company (GEC), Rhône-Poulenc (manufacturing), ECS Underwriting, Lloyd's, Sedgwick, Tellus Corp (insurance), British Gas, National Power, Electricité de France (utilities), National Westminster Bank, Browning Ferris (BFI) and Corning (waste industry). Ten gave an opinion on the basis for liability, with eight opting for a fault-based liability system. Most considered that strict liability is not appropriate for dealing with the majority of cases of impairment to the environment.

Some clearly regulated cases, such as nuclear accidents and oil spills, were considered by British Gas to be suitable for a strict liability regime, provided that an agreed definition of damage and standards of clean-up were laid down. There was a general agreement, when specified, that liability should not be retroactive. The reasons for this included the poor availability and quality of historical data and the problems associated with identifying a single cause or a single polluter.

Of the seven corporations that gave an opinion on the principle of retroactivity, five (British Gas, Dow Europe, National Westminster Bank, BFI and National Power) rejected the concept entirely. Rhône-Poulenc considered that, if the principle of retroactivity were to be applied, then further thought needs to be given on how to approach the subject and Lloyd's considered that a financial cap should be imposed for retroactive clean-up. A number of other corporations, seemingly commenting on the subject of retroactive application of liability, indicated a range of defences that should be available to a targeted facility. These included meeting the established standards of the day (known as the defence of 'state-of-the-art') and compliance with permits the company was operating at the time.

Damage and Restoration

Eleven corporations had a wide range of opinions on the issue of damage and restoration. A common thread was the need to define the terms 'environmental damage' and 'restoration standards'. Another generally common issue related to the level of restoration needed to make the property or land in question fit for a certain purpose, although in these cases there was a general agreement that restoration should ensure that the public health was protected. Words such as 'reasonable' and 'significant' appeared on occasions.

National Power considered that the setting of universal restoration standards would be impractical and that the setting of such standards, in the form of contaminant levels, should be a subsidiary matter. In contrast, Tellus Corp considered that reasonable restoration standards should be set at an EU level to avoid distortion of competition. Along with a number of others, Tellus Corp also expressly mentioned the need to carry out a risk assessment to ensure that a reasonable level of restoration and costs would take place. Electricité de France considered that the Council of Europe Convention's definition of 'environmental damage' was too vague to be practical. It also considered that not all environmental damage needs to be restored.

A number of other responses were given: Lloyd's considered that society should restore damage when a polluter is not traceable; National Westminster Bank suggested that a certificate of compliance should be given to a restored site owner to terminate further liability; and Rhône-Poulenc considered that restoration of all old contaminated sites in the EU would be sufficiently costly to threaten the competitiveness of industry in the EU.

Joint Compensation Schemes

Eight of the 14 corporations commented on the virtues and necessities of joint compensation schemes. In general, they concluded that when a polluter cannot be found, society should pay for the costs of remedying historical pollution and sources of transboundary pollution. There was a measure of disagreement, however, on the means whereby a fund should be levied. Although there was some agreement on the need to levy an industrial company depending on its size and type, BP agreed that a measure dealing with the environmental performance of the sector should also be brought into consideration. Tellus Corp suggested that any scheme should be funded by general green taxes, whereas ECS Underwriting favoured a levy on all industrial sectors in polluting activities. They suggested an increase of VAT on all products or, alternatively, a small percentage load on commercial insurance premiums. Electricité de France, however, suggested that such an approach would be inconsistent with the 'polluter pays' principle.

However the fund is levied, there is clearly a large measure of support for such a fund to deal with historical contamination. Both BP and British Gas stressed the importance of applying the subsidiarity principle, which is referred to below, to the allocation of funds. British Gas considered, however, that in the matter of levying for such a fund, a measure of harmonisation between all Member States was needed. Two of the respondents, National Westminster Bank and Rhône-Poulenc, made a specific point of rejecting the introduction of a general fund such as the US Superfund.

Right to Bring Action

Interestingly, only five of the 14 corporations gave an opinion on this issue, and with one exception, the Dutch company Tellus Corp, all rejected the rights of NGOs to prosecute. Respondents considered that any rights should be restricted to those parties who had suffered losses, or they should belong to the regulatory authorities. Tellus Corp, reflecting the opinions of the Dutch government, gave the opinion that any group has a right to bring an action. The only proviso they presented was that the group must have already been in existence at the time of the incident. Tellus Corp also suggested that the role of the EEA could be developed to enhance the national authorities' role. Only one corporation, Lloyd's, gave a clear reason for restricting the legal role to the statutory authorities. It considered that the involvement of NGOs would lead to costly, vexatious and vindictive claims.

The Position to Date

The Green Paper responses were grouped into seven sectors in all, and the range of opinions and possibilities given by the two selected sector responses gives a clear indication of how many problems still encumber the legislation drafters in Brussels. In the UK alone, the subject of remedying environmental damage was debated at length by the House of Lords European Communities Committee, and resulted in the publishing of a 172-page report on 14 December 1993. This took a much more supportive stance than the government.

The Committee recommended a framework Directive setting out a programme to deal with past pollution. In addition, the Directive should require for future pollution strict liability and a system of financial security from those carrying out potentially damaging operations. The House of Lords Committee accepted strict liability for past pollution where the present owner or operator was responsible in the past and knew, or should have known, that the activities were potentially dangerous. For future pollution strict liability should apply to those knowingly engaged in dangerous or potentially dangerous activity. The defences of force majeure and 'state-of-the-art' should be available against strict liability, but compliance with environmental standards should not be a defence.

The collective opinions in this weighty tome also had to go into the melting-pot in Brussels. By late 1994, the furthest that the Commission had got was to prepare a tender to appoint consultants to look at the intricate details of environmental liability schemes as they operate world-wide. In 1995, the Danish Environment Commissioner again brought the matter forward. Clearly, however, from the responses summarised above, the Commission has had a fine balancing act to perform to establish a plan that satisfies the demands of a wide range of sectors that demonstrate their vested interests in such transparent ways. It is only now that it looks like there will be draft legislative instrument on the subject in the near future.

Legal Basis for Action

As the Commission is now anxious to introduce an EU-wide civil liability regime, largely because, in its view, the varying levels of liability in the Member States affect the competitive nature of businesses, the legal rationale should also be remembered: the Maastricht treaty required the EU to have a policy to protect the environment; the Fifth EAP commits the EU to introducing civil liability at EU level for the year 2000; and a resolution of the EU Council in February 1993 commits the EU to the rapid implementation of the measures agreed at Rio in June 1992, including Principle 13 of the Rio Declaration which requires the development of environmental liability.

Subsidiarity

As has been seen, the Green Paper was merely a consultative exercise outlining the policy issues to be addressed. Having set out the options for dealing with environmental damage, it proposed strict liability rules that might be applied with a system of joint compensation funding financed by the polluting sectors of industry so that the environment can be restored where polluters cannot be found or are not able to pay. As has been outlined, many comments from organisations and Member States were received by the Commission. One major debate that emerged related to 'subsidiarity' and, unsurprisingly, the UK government was one of the respondents to the Green Paper voicing opposition to any action at EU level.

The UK government considered that the common law was adequate to meet EU environmental policy objectives. In addition, the government did not believe that the present distortion of competition argument in the single market was convincing, nor that strict liability should be the only option considered and that compulsory environmental insurance was inappropriate. Moreover, in the view of the government, the joint compensation fund would be ineffective in cleaning up the environment

In the UK, the CBI presented a briefing paper on the topic. It also submitted a detailed report on the Green Paper, recommending a four-step approach: first, the most serious risks must be identified; secondly, the legal position must be clarified (the CBI favours retention of the UK fault-based regime and opposes EU proposals for the harmonisation of strict liability regime); thirdly, the EU should clarify its own approach (it should not use civil liability, a legal regime designed to recompense those who have suffered damage, as an environmental tool); and fourthly, initiatives should be promoted to tackle historical pollution.

Generally speaking, the majority of submissions received broadly supported the options of strict liability and the joint compensation fund favoured by the Commission. On the strict liability side, the debate usually centres around the degree of liability that is most appropriate and which defences should apply: 'state-of-the-art', due diligence or compliance with regulatory requirements. With regard to the joint compensation fund, there have been numerous warnings that the EU should avoid the most obvious and expensive mistakes made by the US Superfund.

As regards the scope of the liability regime, important policy decisions must be made including basic concepts such as the meaning of 'the environment' and the definition of 'damage'. These are vital as they will ultimately set the parameters for rights and remedying in the new legislation. As far as concerns the intent of business, in the UK the CBI set out key points and recommendations in a briefing on the subject which emphasised that commerce and industry want a high-quality environment to improve the quality of life and underpin the competitiveness of Europe in the twenty-first century.

Following the consultation stage, the European Parliament adopted a resolution requesting the Commission to adopt a Directive dealing with environmental liability. In response to this resolution, the Commission commissioned two studies which were, first, a comparative analysis of the rules governing liability for environmental damage in the different Member States and, secondly, a study of the economic impact of the introduction of a system of environmental liability. The two studies will form the basis for a decision by the Commission on what the guiding principle for legislation in the area should be. If the procedure moves on smoothly, the Commission will then adopt a communication on its 'legislative intentions' and draft legislation – probably in the form of a Directive – can be expected at some stage during 1999.

EU Competence

There has been some discussion on how far there is competence in the EU to carry out legislative actions in the environmental area and how far these matters fall within the national competence of the Member States. This doctrine of subsidiarity, which was discussed after the consultation process of the Green Paper, was enshrined in art 3(b) of the Treaty as amended by the Maastricht Treaty. This provides:

> *'In areas which do not fall within its exclusive competence the Community shall take action in accordance with the principle of subsidiarity only if and in so far as the objectives of the proposed action cannot be sufficiently achieved by the Member States and can therefore, by reason of the scale of effects of the proposed action, be better achieved by the Community.'*

Implications for Business

It is evident from the foregoing that the EU environment programme is now solidly based and here to stay. It is already extensive and it will continue to grow. Moreover, the philosophy behind it will come more and more to influence and pervade other policies. The principle that the protection of the environment is part of other policies is written into the SEA and will increasingly become a political reality. In determining the attitudes of industry to this greening of the law and policy, different sectors of industry will have to evaluate their own core interests. In doing so, the essential double nature of environmental policy must be borne in mind.

The first is the element of harmonisation of conditions or competition. The fact that all of

European industry will have to play by the same rules in the Common Market is likely to be a helpful characteristic when evaluating industry's attitude towards environmental policies.

The second is that aspect of environmental policy which relates to more pure environmental objectives. Even here, it would seem that the enlightened industrialist should also have a positive attitude. To the extent that such rules are clearly for the benefit of society, the purely sectorial interests of producers which have been able to profit by a privileged position, especially as regards their waste disposal, must give way to the greater good. While some adjustment will be necessary – and even painful – it can certainly be said that adaptation to progress is a characteristic of modern industry. There will therefore be a challenge to adapt. For this purpose it seems to be essential that modern industry, and its advisers, should be vigilant as regards developments in environmental considerations, particularly at EU level. The reward of such vigilance might well be an ability to take decisions more attuned to the development of policy, thus avoiding costly mistakes and gaining time in which to adapt to the evolving environmental legislation.

Finally, as is also referred to in Chapter 10, there is a very positive aspect of environmental policy for industry insofar as the development of this policy offers an opportunity to industry by creating a range of new needs that can only be satisfied by industry itself. Examples are: three-way catalysers on small vehicles, lean burn engines, substitute products for CFCs in aerosols, new and improved methods of domestic waste disposal, cleaner processes to prevent water pollution, substitutes for lead in petrol and substitutes for a whole range of products, such as pesticides, which have been found to cause environmental problems.

This represents one of the new challenges to industry. In this context environmentalists and industry should be seen as partners playing a reciprocal role in the evolution of EU policy, with the former identifying and analysing problems and the latter helping to find solutions.

---

[1] See art 251

Chapter 3

The Regulatory Framework under the Environmental Protection Act 1990 and Environment Act 1995

Introductory Remarks

When considering this topic, practitioners should be aware of 'This Common Inheritance: Britain's Environmental Strategy' and subsequent reports. Various White Papers have spelt out Britain's environmental strategy. Reference may also be made to 'This Common Inheritance: Annual Report 1997', which reports on the progress made during 1996 to fulfil commitments made in earlier reports. The strategy utilises the various forms of regulation summarised below. As discussed further in Chapter 8, the main cornerstone can be said to be the creation of criminal offences backed up by an enforcement regime and heavy penalties; corporate liability for breach of regulations; and civil liability to ensure the polluter pays for clean-up. (See, for example, s120 EPA 1990.)

Summary of the Statutory Regimes for Environmental Protection

Whereas this chapter concentrates upon the regulatory framework under the EPA 1990 and the EA 1995, it should also be remembered that the statutory regime extends to 'internal' and 'external' regulations.

Internal regulations, that is, those applicable within the workplace, relate to the protection of persons within a workplace or building, or the product or process being carried out. Examples are health and safety legislation or compliance with ISO standards which require the setting up of an auditable system to ensure that the end product meets the specification claimed for it in respect of quality and performance. As will be mentioned in Chapters 7 and 10, the latter often result, in fact, in the reduction of waste.

External regulations, that is, those relating to the immediate environment outside the workplace, fall into three categories: the first two are concerned with discharges from the workplace to any environmental medium – air, land or water – but they operate to limit such discharges in different ways.

As discussed further below, the first category is legislation requiring prior authorisation or site licensing in addition to planning consent for processes which have the potential to cause pollution, or for the deposit of waste to land. In this way, conditions can be attached to such authorisations or licences limiting the levels and types of pollutants which can be discharged. The conditions can also require monitoring of the discharges and entry of the information gathered on a public register. It is important to note that any conditions noted on such licences or authorisations should not duplicate planning conditions.

The practitioner should be aware that the EPA 1990 and The Water Resources Act 1991 (WRA 1991), as amended by the EA 1995, are examples of legislation, breaches of which can lead to a fine of up to £20,000 on summary conviction, or an unlimited fine and/or imprisonment for a term not exceeding two years on indictment. For example, in *NRA* v *Shell (UK)* (1990) Water Law 40, Shell was fined £1 million for breach of legislation.

In addition, in order to emphasise the seriousness of non-compliance, the legislation enables the regulator to take legal action against company directors, senior managers etc where an offence has been committed with the consent or connivance of, or has been attributable to the neglect of, such a person. This is commented upon further in Chapter 8. Fines for environmental offences are increasing. Moreover, the Command Paper, 'Crime, Justice and Protecting the Public', emphasises the need for a realistic fine related to resultant profits or savings from the offence. To date, legal action has, occasionally, been successfully taken against directors, usually where there is persistent breach.

The second category can be described as proactive actions that ensure that environmental effects are taken into account at the earliest stage in respect of new development or in the production process to be used. In planning law, the need for a developer to prepare an environmental statement for certain types of development is well known, and in environmental law an EC regulation established Environmental Eco-Management and Auditing System (EMAS), a community-wide, voluntary, environmental auditing scheme to encourage businesses to demonstrate their commitment to the environment. In return, a successful company will be able to use the official eco-audit logo, the object of which is to encourage customers to buy from companies displaying the logo. Both of these are referred to elsewhere (the EIA in Chapter 6 and EMAS in Chapters 7 and 8).

The third category includes risk pricing and economic instruments, such as environmental taxes, one of the first being the landfill tax (see Chapter 4).

The EPA 1990 and the EA 1995 introduce, essentially, a regime of public accountability for environmental damage. Both Acts address questions of contaminated land and waste regulation, and are a considerable step forward in both of these areas. Whilst the earlier Act indicates the way forward by establishing an Integrated Pollution Control (IPC) system that covers the sometimes overlapping ambits of the different bodies that are involved in pollution control, the later Act goes even further and establishes the Environment Agency (EA), a body concerned with most kinds of pollution. In the following sections the most important aspects of the Acts are looked at in turn.

Environmental Protection Act 1990

The EPA 1990 enables individuals to take an action for damages where an offence under the Act has been committed.[1] For example, s73(6) states:

> 'Where any damage is caused by waste which has been deposited in or on land, any person who deposited, or knowingly caused or knowingly permitted it to be deposited so as to commit an offence under s33(1) or s63(2) is liable for the damage caused.'

The usual defences of volenti non fit injuria and contributory negligence are mentioned in the section. Section 73(6) is an example of civil liability that now extends to many aspects of environmental law. This topic is considered further in Chapter 8.

The substantive provisions of the Act concern contaminated land and waste management as well as the systems of Local Authority Air Pollution Control (LAAPC). Contaminated land is considered in detail in Chapter 4, and waste management in Chapter 6. The pollution control systems are looked at in more detail in the relevant chapter on water and air pollution (see Chapter 5). Therefore, the following sections only provide an outline of the more important provisions:

Integrated Pollution Control

The need for IPC arose out of the recognition that pollution is not usually limited to one medium alone. In the Fifth Report on Air Pollution Control 1976, the Royal Commission stated that:

> 'the reduction of emissions to the atmosphere can lead to an increase in wastes to be disposed of on land or discharged to water. If the optimum environmental solutions are to be found, the controlling authority must be able to look comprehensively to all forms of pollution arising from industrial processes where different control problems exist.'

Following this reasoning, Part I EPA 1990 establishes the IPC system, which is concerned with the most seriously polluting processes regulated by Her Majesty's Inspectorate of Pollution (HMIP). As is seen below, the functions of HMIP have since been incorporated in those of the EA 1995.

Section 6 EPA 1990 prohibits certain processes from being carried on. 'Processes' are described in s1, as 'any keeping of a substance or any activities whatsoever whether on premises or by means of mobile plant that are capable of causing pollution to the environment'. Prescribed processes are not to be carried out without prior authorisation from the relevant authority. Where the process is to be authorised by the EA,[2] it must consider the effect of the process on all environmental media (the 'cross-media effect'). The authorisation must be such that the best practicable environmental option (BPEO) is taken. It is possible for the Secretary of State to intervene by issuing directions on whether or not to grant the authorisation.

By virtue of s2 EPA 1990, the Secretary of State also has the power to issue regulations prescribing other processes and substances. The most important regulations are the Environmental Protection (Prescribed Processes and Substances) Regulations 1991. Generally, the Secretary of State has extensive powers to make plans under s3 and to issue directions under s7. Section 3 is very important in that under this provision, the Secretary of State can make plans in order to comply with EU legislation. All of these powers are in addition to 'list A', a list of prescribed processes that can be found in the EPA 1990.

An application for authorisation must be accompanied by the following relevant information prescribed by Schedule 1 EPA 1990 and the Environmental Protection (Applications, Appeals and Registers) Regulations 1991:

- the name and address of the applicant and/or registered address and number of the company;

- the address of the premises where the process is to be, or is already being, carried on;

- a map;

- a description of the process and the techniques to be used for preventing, reducing to a minimum and rendering harmless the releases into any environmental medium of substances that might cause harm if released;

- proposals for monitoring and details on the release of such substances and its effect on the environment;

- a list of prescribed substances used in or resulting from the process;

- a list of any other substances used or to be used that are potentially harmful if released into the environment;

- details on compliance with any specific conditions and the use of the principle of using Best Available Techniques Not Entailing Excessive Costs (BATNEEC);[3]

- any other relevant information that the applicant wants the authorities to consider.

Note: BATNEEC is a statutory formula used in controlling emissions to the environment which seeks a balance between requiring the use of 'state-of-the-art' technology and processes to minimise emissions, and the cost of doing so. It is an implied general condition of every authorisation granted under Part 1 (IPC) EPA 1990 and air pollution control, that in carrying on a prescribed process BATNEEC will be used for preventing and reducing the release of substances harmful to the environment or rendering harmless any other substances released.

Following receipt of the application, consultation with statutory bodies occurs. Exactly which bodies are consulted depends on the specific case and is specified in the Act. In addition, the public is informed by advertisements in relevant media and is invited to comment on the project.

After considering the application, the EA should decide within four months (or more if the applicant agrees) whether or not to grant the authorisation. The authority is entitled to make the authorisation subject to conditions if it considers that the applicant is able to fulfil them. There is a wide range of conditions that can be imposed. These extend from the compulsory compliance with the BATNEEC principle over compliance with regulations issued by the Secretary of State, to obligations under EU or international law.

Once granted, the holder of an authorisation is entitled to transfer it to another person who wishes to carry on the process. Section 9 requires the new holder of the authorisation to notify the EA within 21 days of the transfer.

Every four years, the EA reconsiders its decision and may take any steps that are within its powers.

The Act itself gave the HMIP certain enforcement powers, which have now been taken over by the EA. These are listed in ss10–14 and s17, and include the following: revocation; variation, enforcement and prohibition notices; and powers to enter property, to examine, to investigate, to seize, to clean up pollution or to prosecute. Against any decisions or actions, there is a right of appeal to the Secretary of State under s15. An appeal must be brought within two months.

Local Authority Air Pollution Control

Processes that are less seriously polluting than those that fall within the IPC ambit are regulated by an LAAPC regime. Since this is discussed in greater detail in Chapter 5, at this point it suffices to point out that a similar system applies to both IPC and LAAPC.

The local environmental health department is responsible under Part III EPA 1990 for preventing and reacting to complaints about statutory nuisances, such as noise, smells or premises in a state 'prejudicial to health or a nuisance'. And under Part I EPA 1990, it is responsible for the authorisation and control of air pollution from waste or hospital incinerators of a certain size, crematoria and scrapyards, to name but a few.

Contaminated Land

Until the EPA 1990 came into force, there was no specific statutory regulation of contaminated land. Liability and responsibility for contaminated land was mainly part of the public health and the planning systems. For the first time, s143 introduced a duty on local authorities (LAs) to compile and maintain public registers of possibly contaminated land. It was as a result of this duty that a highly controversial debate took place resulting in the regime discussed in Chapter 4, and which is still subject to the publication of final guidance.

Part I EPA 1990 concerns the interaction between the IPC and the contaminated land regime.

Part II contains provisions on waste on land, in particular, landfill sites that are contaminated.

Probably the most important provisions in relation to contaminated land are those that allow citizens recourse through the statutory nuisance provisions of s79–83.

Waste Management

As mentioned above and referred to further in Chapter 6, Part II EPA 1990 contains provisions relating to waste on land. An important feature of the provisions is that they iron out some of the mistakes made in the earlier Control of Pollution Acts (COPA) 1974 and 1989.

Significantly, the change of notions from waste 'control' to waste 'management' demonstrates, again, a change in thinking in the same way that the introduction of IPC did, unifying different areas of the same field. The concept of 'waste management' now covers all aspects of waste from production to disposal. This is evident from the discussion in Chapter 6.

Under this system, waste management licences can be obtained (s35) by 'fit and proper persons'. Applications must be made to the Waste Regulation Authority (WRA). The WRA has wide powers to impose conditions on the grant of such licences. Under s69, WRA inspectors have relatively wide powers, including powers to enter premises; to take photographs, measurements, recordings and samples; and to seize objects or substances. As with IPC, appeals can be made to the Secretary of State.

Section 75, as amended by the Waste Management Licence Regulations 1994, provides for a definition of waste. Especially important is the definition of controlled waste to which the EPA 1990 affords a tight regime.

It is noteworthy that s59 gives the waste management authorities the power to carry out immediate clean-up actions. Section 33(1) creates the offences of disposing of, treating, keeping or disposing of controlled waste without a licence, or in a manner likely to cause pollution to the environment or harm to human health. The Act also contains other minor offences.[4]

Section 33(9) contains the available penalties, which include high monetary penalties and also imprisonment (rarely used). Under s157, company directors and managers can be made personally liable for offences by their companies if the offence has been committed with their consent or if they were negligent.

At this point it should be noted that there was a certain interaction between the waste management system and the IPC regime: the EA cannot impose on IPC authorisations conditions that are concerned with the final deposit of waste on land; the EA controls waste production by IPC-regulated companies up until the final deposit when it must inform WRA; and waste disposal facilities other than landfill sites may have to register under IPC. Now, as is seen below, the interaction between bodies and procedures has been streamlined by the Environment Act 1995.

Environment Act 1995 and the Environment Agency

The EA 1995 introduced a new regulatory era. After four years of consultation, this legislation established the EA. This body became operative from 1 April 1996. It has the responsibility for the management and regulation of waste under Part II EPA 1990, including the control of waste carriers under the Control of Pollution (Amendment) Act 1989, both previously the responsibility of the Waste Regulatory Authority (in London the LWRA); for integrated pollution control under Part I EPA 1990 (previously the responsibility of HMIP) and controls over water pollution, flood defences and conservation contained in the WRA 1991 (previously the remit of the National Rivers Authority (NRA)). The EA has a regional structure and London is part of the Thames region.

The following sections are concerned with the establishment of the Agency:

> Part I, ss1–56: on EAs;
>
> Part V, ss108–110: on powers of entry;
>
> Part V, s111: on evidence in pollution offences;
>
> Part V, s112: on false and misleading information.

The main provisions are commented on below.

Former Relevant Statutory Bodies

Before the EA 1995, pollution control was mainly in the hands of the following bodies:

NRA: concerned with the control of water quality in controlled waters, management of water resources, land drainage and defence against flooding , monitoring of water pollution, promoting recreation and regulating fishing.

HMIP: concerned with the regulation of a wide variety of the most seriously polluting processes, often through the IPC system.

LAs: concerned with waste regulation, collection and disposal; with the control of emissions of dark smoke and with the authorisation of prescribed processes.

After the EA 1995, all the functions of the NRA are now covered by the EA, so are the bulk of responsibilities under the IPC system and for waste disposal. In the EA's remit is also the use and disposal of radioactive substances.

It is important to note that the EA is responsible for compiling information and carrying out assessments of the general state of the environment and that certain activities carried out by the new Department of Environment, Transport and the Regions (DETR) have been transferred to the remit of the Agency, including the assessment of chemicals under European law, technical guidance on waste and contaminated land and the co-ordination of the National Rimnet radiation monitoring scheme.

There are additional responsibilities provided for by the Act, in particular, contaminated land and abandoned mines; National Waste Strategy; National Air Quality Strategy; and State of the Environment Reports. These will be considered in more detail below where the Act's substantive provisions are discussed.

Not within the ambit of responsibility of the Agency is the LAs' local air pollution control regime; the emission of fumes, gases, dust, steam or smell from mainly industrial, trade or business premises; and the control of construction noise.

Structure

The EA's structure is separated into eight regions, each headed by a regional general manager: Anglia, South West, Thames, North West, South, North East, Midlands and Wales. The regional boundaries in water management follow existing catchment boundaries of NRA regions. In pollution prevention and control, the regional boundary is the district council boundary nearest to catchment.

Under s108, the EA has the power to appoint officers. These warranted officers include water resource and pollution control officers, bailiffs, pollution inspectors and other enforcing officers from the former constituent bodies of the Agency. For relevant extracts from the 'Management Statement on Guidance for Warranted Officers', see the Appendices.

Aims: Sustainable Development

According to the Act, the main aim of the EA is to make a contribution towards attaining sustainable development. The agency is to do so by goal-setting (eg through good practice guidance), regulation (eg by considering the grant of licences) and the enforcement of prescriptive provisions of the law. For the purposes of this chapter, the most important of these aspects is the enforcement of the law.

Interaction with Planning

There is an important interaction between the planning system and environmental regulation, partly reflected by the express statutory linkage between the need for planning permission from the relevant planning authority before the regulator can authorise the operation of a process or grant a waste management licence. Furthermore, the concept of sustainable development must be considered by regulators when carrying out their functions (s4 EA 1995) and by local planning authorities when drawing up and reviewing development plans and formulating waste plans, as well as dealing with individual planning applications.

The planning system is fundamentally important as all applications for new development will be considered against policies contained in the development/unitary plan for the area, especially as the plan is given a dominance by s54A TCPA 1990. Environmental implications will also be a 'material consideration' and will have to be considered by the planning authority.

Enforcement

Sources

In total, the EA has enforced over 30 Acts and is now the most important player in the pollution control regime. The internal workings of the EA are regulated both by the Environment Acts themselves and by public documents (policy statements and codes of practice).

Principles

Cost-Benefit Duty

The EA must, in the exercise of its powers (as opposed to its duties) take into consideration the cost and benefit consequences of its proposed action, unless it is unreasonable to make such an assessment (s39). This raises the question on how, or whether, the EA will use its powers. Statutory guidance on the application of this duty and on the EA's duty to make a contribution to the objectives of sustainable development have been made under s4 and published by the DETR. In practical terms, any assessment of costs and benefits made by the EA, for example, in deciding whether to take enforcement action, could be subject to judicial review proceedings if the assessment is inadequate.

According to its Enforcement Policy Statement, the EA has regard to several principles, which may be of practical importance to a practitioner and his client in discussions with the EA as to whether enforcement action is required in any given case and, if it is, its appropriateness.

The first principle is proportionality, which involves balancing risks and costs. Whilst specific duties are mandatory, others contain discretionary elements in which principles such as reasonableness and appropriateness determine the proportionality of the EA's actions. The EA will expect that good practice will be followed. Additional methods of balancing risks and costs are the BATNEEC and the BPEO. The latter provides the best benefit or best option to the environment as a whole at acceptable cost, in the long term as well as the short term. BPEO was first developed as a concept in the Fifth Report of the Royal Commission on Environmental Pollution, and may be regarded as a development of the best environmental option concept, which links it to economic objectives and takes a long-term approach to environmental solutions.

The second principle is consistency – the EA will take a similar approach in similar circumstances to achieve similar ends. This is a very general principle, since cases are hardly ever the same because of many variables, such as the degree of pollution, the history of the case and the subsequent risks of pollution. The decision on enforcement action will therefore have to depend on what is referred to as 'sound professional judgement in the exercise of discretion'.

The third principle is transparency. Here the EA's initial approach is to reflect the already publicly available enforcement practices of its constituent bodies and then, eventually, its intention is to harmonise any differences in their respective approaches. Mainly, transparency is concerned with informing relevant persons, for example, licence holders, of what to expect when a warranted officer calls; why the officer intends to or has taken action; and what rights to complain are open to them.

The last principle is targeting. This means enforcing that inspection is directed primarily towards those responsible for or best placed to control activities that give rise to the most serious environmental damage or pollution, or where the hazards are least well controlled.

The principle of proportionality is the most controversial and was debated extensively by the Environment Agency Committee, which was appointed in 1994. The principle is based on ss4(1) and 39 EA 1995, which requires the EA to take into account the likely costs and benefits when considering to exercise any power, or when deciding the manner in which to exercise any such power. Conservation bodies, for instance, fear that the EA will refuse to act whenever it perceives that the cost of action will outweigh the benefit. It has also been pointed out, however, that there is no requirement on the EA to do only beneficial things. Rather, this obligation gives rise to an increased risk of judicial review since it will be relatively simple to allege that the EA had failed to take into account a factor and all too difficult to decide that this is, in fact, the case.

Powers to Obtain Information

The powers of the EA to obtain information are mainly contained in s108 EA 1995. R v Hertfordshire CC, ex parte Green Environmental Industries Ltd (1997) 1 Env L R 114 concerned the issue of a 'request for information' under s71 EPA 1990 by a WRA. Judicial review was sought of the decision to issue the request on the ground that the regulator was using the power to seek self-incriminating information which could be used in a prosecution. The High Court refused to quash the decision but left it open whether the response would be excluded in evidence.

Procedures: How Does the EA Intervene?

Inspection and Entry

Enforcement is largely carried out by inspection. In order to carry out effective inspections, the EA 1995 (Part V, ss108–110) has given persons appointed by the EA a wide range of powers of inspection and entry in order to determine whether any provision of the pollution control enactments is being, or has been, complied with; exercise or perform one or more of the pollution control functions of the EA; or determine whether, and if so how, such a function should be exercised or performed.

The powers are:

- to enter at any reasonable time (or in an emergency at any time and, if need be, by force) any premises which he has reason to believe it is necessary for him to enter;

- on entering any premises by virtue of paragraph (a) to take with him any other person duly authorised by the EA and, if necessary, a constable; and any equipment or materials required for any purpose for which the power of entry is being exercised;

- to make such examination and investigation as may in any circumstances be necessary;

- to direct that any premises be left undisturbed for so long as is reasonably necessary for the purposes of any examination or investigation;

- to take measurements and photographs;

- to take samples of any articles or substances;

- to dismantle, or subject to a test, any article or substances which have either caused, or are likely to cause, pollution;

- to take possession and detain substances;

- to require any person whom the officer has reasonable cause to believe is able to give any information which is relevant to an examination to answer such questions as he thinks fit;

- to require the production of records;

- to require any person to provide such facilities and assistance as are necessary to enable the officer to exercise any of his powers;

- any other power conferred by regulations made by the Secretary of State.

Enforcement Options

Once an inspection has been carried out, the EA officer has a range of enforcement options available in the event of non-compliance. The main options are:

- a warning letter;

- an enforcement notice;

- a prohibition notice (including prevention notices);

- variation or revocation of an authorisation;

- a formal caution;

- in the case of IPC offences, enforcement notices requiring work to be carried out, and prohibition notices forbidding activities;

- prosecution.

Agency *v* Castle Cement Ltd, *Blackburn JJ, 8/11/96 is a recent prosecution brought by the EA. The facts involved the spillage of solvent from a storage tank in breach of the Company's IPC authorisation, which required all plant to be maintained in good order. The warning devices failed to operate. The company pleaded guilty and was fined £5,000 with £4,000 costs.*

In Environment Agency *v* Birchmore (Romney Marsh Skip Hire), *Folkestone JJ, 11/10/96, the offences consisted of repeated dumping of waste despite warnings, failure to register as a waste carrier and breach of duty of care. The accused was bankrupt and offered community service on conviction. He declined and was imprisoned for three months.*

Works Notices

A special regime applies to water and waste. The above notices include 'works notices' requiring a party to clean up water or waste pollution offences.[5] Non-compliance with a notice is an offence, and if a person fails to comply, the EA may still use its existing powers under the WRA 1991 to carry out the work itself and seek to recover the costs. No such works notice can be served where the discharge of the relevant substances was in accordance with the terms of the discharge consent. A right of appeal exists against such a notice (21 days after service of notice to lodge an appeal). Where existing pollution is involved, the EA must be able to show that the person on whom the notice is served did cause and knowingly permit discharge of the substances.

Sampling

As regards the sampling powers of the EA, it should be noted that the Act removes the system of tripartite sampling whereby any effluent sample must be divided into three parts, one of which was given to the defendant, before it could be used in evidence. With variable standards throughout the country and the risk of deterioration of a sample over time, the defendant has lost the potentially important protection of having a sample, which the NRA will rely on in court, independently analysed. The NRA has given the cost of tripartite sampling as one of the reasons for the necessity of a change that the EA has since brought about. It is now also possible to produce in court trace charts from the river monitoring stations without facing legal argument as to admissibility.

Although industry has lost the right to tripartite sampling and will be subject to the service of works notices, it has in exchange gained an extension of the minimum period of consent reviews from two to four years, the removal of objectors' right to request a call-in of consent applications and the suspension of the effect of proposed changes to a consent until the appeal has been determined.

Letters and Notices

The EA has published the 'Code of Enforcement' which is subject to revision periodically and outlines its enforcement practice. It provides guidance to warranted officers when enforcing environment protection and pollution prevention legislation. In compliance with the principles set out in the Deregulation and Contracting Out Act 1994, the Code gives businesses certain rights. These are as follows:

- the right to receipt, at the end of a visit when the officer should explain what further action, if any, is going to be taken, a copy of the leaflet 'Your Rights When Environment Agency Warranted Officers Take Action' (see Appendix 2 below);

- the right to a letter, on request, explaining what needs to be done and why – when warranted officers express an opinion that something should be done – without taking formal action;

- the right, when immediate action is taken, to a written statement explaining why this is necessary (that is, why immediate rather than another course of action is taken, and the consequences of failing to take action);

- the right to a 'minded to' notice, if action is proposed and an enforcement notice is to be issued, letting the operator know what needs to be done in order to comply and within what timescale. There is a period of ten working days after the date of the letter for making representations if it is thought that the proposed action is not justified. The officer and his manager should then take a fair and fresh look at the proposed action in the light of the representations. (A copy of an 'minded to' notice is printed in Appendix 3.);

- the right to be told exactly what rights of appeal the business has when formal action is taken.

Prosecution

Before the actual decision to prosecute is made, the EA's officers will take account of several factors set out in the 'Code for Prosecution Policy'. Where relevant, it will also have regard to the 'Code for Crown Prosecutors'.

Although the factors in the 'Code for Prosecution Policy' are not exhaustive, there are two main criteria: a prosecution must be in the public interest; and a prosecution should only be instigated where admissible, sufficient and reliable evidence exists and it is in the public interest to do so.

The Code describes 'public interest' as consisting of:

- the degree of the actual or potential environmental impact of the act in question on health, flora and fauna;

- the culpability, attitude and motivation of the defendant;

- whether the incident falls within a category of incidents in one of the EA's policies – the factors should then be applied in conjunction with the relevant policy;

- the prevalence of the offence either locally or nationally;

- the attitude of the local community and the effect on the public.

Public interest factors weighing against prosecution are:

*   where there court is likely to impose only a nominal penalty;

*   where the offence arose as a result of a genuine mistake or misunderstanding;

*   where the environmental impact was minor and was the result of a single incident;

*   where the equipment had a latent defect which could not reasonably have been discovered by a competent operator;

*   where the offence was caused by the intervening act of a third party which could not have been reasonably guarded against;

*   where the defendant has co-operated fully with the EA and is able to demonstrate that significant preventative and remedial measures have been taken;

*   where there has been a long delay between the offence and the decision to prosecute (except where the investigation has been complex, the offence has only recently come to light or for some other good reason).

Once it is decided to recommend that it is in the public interest to prosecute or issue a formal caution, the consideration of the evidence for there to be a reasonable prospect of conviction begins.

Other Substantive Provisions

In addition to Part I (ss1–56) and Part V (ss108–112) EA 1995, which are concerned with the establishment of the EA, the Act contains the following important key provisions:

> Part II, s57 – on contaminated land;
>
> s58 – on abandoned mines;
>
> Part IV – on air quality;
>
> Part V, s92 – on National Waste Strategy;
>
> ss93–95 – on producer responsibility.

Each of these key sections is briefly commented on in turn. A more detailed examination of each can be found in the chapters concerned with contaminated land, water, air and waste.

Ministerial Guidance to the EA

The other key part of the general framework is the statutory guidance for the EA under s4 EA 1995, which deals with the contribution to sustainable development that the government expects the EA to make, and also the manner in which it should take account of costs and benefits. The EA has a statutory duty to have regard to the guidance, and the messages in the guidance will help to define a culture for the EA's working methods that will bring benefits for the environment and business.

Briefly, the guidance sets out how the EA can contribute towards sustainable development, first, by taking an holistic approach to the environment, optimising benefits to the environment as a whole, rather than looking at individual parts in isolation; secondly, by taking a long-term perspective, having a particular regard to impacts which may be irreversible, or reversible only at a high cost over a long time scale; thirdly, by paying particular attention to conservation and related issues when considering proposals which are important for biodiversity; and, lastly, by seeking a partnership with business to maximise the cost-effectiveness of investment in technologies and techniques to benefit the environment – the guidance sets out half a dozen ways in which this might be done, including helping businesses to plan for the future.

The government's guidance to the EA includes advice on costs and benefits. It recognises that these cannot always be fully quantified and that there will be circumstances, such as emergencies, in which consideration might be unreasonable. Therefore the EA has been invited to develop advice for its staff on costs and benefit objectives.

In addition to the objectives and the sustainable development guidance, the EA operates within the framework of government environmental policies, such as quality standards, that the EA is expected to deliver. There are specific targets set in the EA's corporate plan. The objectives will also be backed up with actions that ministers will require of the EA, such as a code of practice on the exercise of its regulatory responsibilities. It is intended that this should promote fairness, proportionality, transparency and consistency of enforcement. The code will have to be readily available to regulated organisations and the EA will have to develop procedures for dealing with any complaints of non-compliance. The EA will have to meet the standards of service expected under the government Citizen's Charter, including publishing its own code on openness.

Contaminated Land

In addition to the provisions of the EA 1995, regard must be had to any guidance issued by the EA or the DETR. The latter will mainly affect the definitions and the weight attached to descriptions of relevant factors given in the Act. The first major guidance was published in 1996 and concentrates on the headings of inspection duty, escapes of substances to other land and remediation notices. As indicated in Chapter 4, the intention is that the guidance should be updated constantly. Since, however, the substantive areas relating to the contaminated land regime have yet to be published, practitioners should be aware that any comments relate to the draft guidance.

Generally, the wording of the Act is cautious on the issue of requiring the decontamination of poisoned land. Clean-up is only required in accordance with the intended use of the site. If land, for instance, were to be used for a market garden, it would need much less treatment than land destined to be grassed over or turned into a car park. Remedial action need only be taken where there would otherwise be 'significant harm' and where remedial action would be cost-effective.

Abandoned Mines

Currently, there are statutory protections regarding pollution from abandoned mines. These are to be removed after 31 December 1999, opening up a whole area of potential liability for mine owners and operators. Pollution from mines will, therefore, be an offence unless it is licensed by the EA. It can be said that the problem of toxic discharges from abandoned mines that have been caused through the legal distinction between causing pollution (which is illegal) and permitting pollution (which is legal) has been dealt with by this provision.

The EA deals with discharges from abandoned mines by means of consents. Provided that the consents are complied with, the owners or former operators of those mines will be liable for prosecution and the recovery of costs reasonably incurred by the EA in carrying out any clean-up. The Act also imposes a six-month notice requirement, which came into force in April 1996, on operators intending to abandon a mine, so that measures to prevent pollution can be taken before the mine is closed. The EA 1995 does not assist in clarifying issues relating to already abandoned mines and water pollution issues arising from these mines.

Air Quality

The EA 1995 provides a statutory framework for a new system of air quality control and provides the Secretary of State with very wide powers to make regulations. The new system sets national standards for ambient air quality and reduction targets for nine main pollutants with timetables for achieving these targets. LAs are placed under a duty to review air quality periodically in their areas and create Air Quality Management Areas where quality targets are unlikely to be met. Much of the detailed local arrangement is provided under secondary legislation and government guidance. Further discussion on air emission is given in Chapter 5.

The Secretary of State is also given power to make regulations on the prohibition or restriction of access for vehicles in certain areas. Industrial sites in cities and towns with recurring periods of poor air quality are probably most affected because of increased costs in reducing air emissions and the temporary restrictions on goods delivered by road.

National Waste Strategy

Under s92 EA 1995, the Secretary of State has the power to publish a national waste strategy. The basic objectives of the draft waste strategy are to minimise the production of waste, make best use of waste that is produced and reduce the risk of pollution or harm to human health arising from waste disposal or recovery. Further discussion of waste management can be found in Chapter 6.

The waste strategy is an advisory and non-statutory instrument. Only the so-called Import/Export Plan implements art 7 EC Framework Directive on Waste.[6]

The underlying philosophy of the waste strategy is that waste management options must bear their full environmental costs. The Strategy deals with non-radioactive solid wastes and excludes, therefore, wastes discharged to water or the atmosphere. It includes policies on hazardous or 'special' waste. About 174 million tonnes of controlled waste are currently produced in the UK each year, around 11.5 per cent of this is household waste, 40 per cent is industrial waste and 40 per cent is produced by the construction and demolition industry. Seventy per cent of all controlled waste in the UK is disposed of by landfill.

Producer Responsibility

The EA 1995 gives the Secretary of State power to make regulations imposing 'producer responsibility obligations' on prescribed people for the purpose of increasing re-use and recovery of products or material. The Act also provides for secondary legislation to be introduced to provide a framework for the existing Producer Responsibility Initiative in relation to packaging waste.

Such a strategy will undoubtedly necessitate the increased use of more expensive disposal methods, including incineration and recycling, which, in turn, it is hoped, will prompt the use of processes and techniques that generate less waste. It will be assisted by the rising cost of landfill due to increased regulation of landfill operations and the landfill tax.

Mineral Planning Permissions

New provisions are introduced to bring and keep mineral sites up to current and evolving environmental standards. The cost of upgrading these permissions are, in part, to be met by the industry.

Schedules 1, 3 and 14 EA 1995 provide for an initial review and updating of old mineral permissions phased over six years, and future periodic reviews of all permissions every 15 years.

Reports on the General State of Pollution of the Environment

Reports on the state of the environment are either to facilitate the EA's pollution control functions or to enable it to form an opinion of the general state of pollution of the environment. The EA also has a duty to carry out assessments either generally or site-specifically at the request of the minister to consider the effects or likely effects on the environment of existing or potential levels of pollution. In reporting its findings to the minister, the EA may be asked to identify the options available to prevent or minimise, remedy or clean up the effects of pollution, and the costs and benefits of such options if required.

The practical aspects of the EA's powers can be found in Appendices 1-3.

Concluding Remarks

The EA 1995 sits above and works with the existing legislation concerning the bodies forming part of the EA. Its provisions therefore affected the work, assets, commitments and employees of the whole of the NRA which, as an existing Non-departmental Public Body, had about 7,700 employees in 142 localities; the entire London WRA, a Statutory All-London Regulatory Body with 120 employees in various London offices; the 82 other WRAs, some district and some county councils and groupings of Metropolitan Districts, including about 980 employees in 82 LAs; HMIP, part of the DoE (now DETR), comprising some 430 employees in 16 localities; and other work of the DoE.

Although there is some element of harmonisation of powers, such as the powers of entry for pollution control functions and s108 EA 1995, those concerned with advising the EA ordered or affected by its operations will still need to refer to the WRA 1991, the Land Drainage Act 1991 and the Salmon and Freshwater Fisheries Act 1975, which are the key items of legislation under which the NRA has operated. In addition, Parts I and II EPA covering IPC and waste management licensing remain relevant, as well as the COPA 1974, as amended. A list of enforced Acts can be found in Appendix 4.

---

[1] Section 23(1)
[2] When it falls within list 'A'
[3] Part 1 EPA 1990 on IPC and Chapter 4
[4] Sections 33(5), 44, 60, 63(2)
[5] See s161C WRA 1991, inserted by s162 of Sch 22 of the EA 1995
[6] 75/442/EC, amended by 91/156/EEC

Chapter 4

Contaminated Land: A New Era

Opening Remarks

Until recently, the UK had no law in place requiring contaminated land to be clearly identified by a regulatory agency. Neither was there a law in place requiring an owner or a developer of contaminated land to: delineate the contamination present on that land; evaluate the significance of this contamination; assess the risks it poses to human health or the environment; or clean up the land to an acceptable state.

All this has changed. New powers have been introduced in the contaminated land provisions of the EA 1995. LAs – the Borough and District Councils – who were responsible for dealing with statutory nuisance in respect of seriously contaminated land, have had their powers and responsibilities extended to ensure that they carry out site surveys and identify contaminated land located within their jurisdictions. In certain cases, LAs will also be required to take remedial action to ensure the reduction of unacceptable risks to a tolerable level.

Part IIA EPA 1990 provides a new regime for the control of threats to health and to the environment as a result of the condition in which certain land is found by reason of substances in, on or under it. These polluting substances are contaminating by reason of the significant harm which they may cause or are causing, or as a result of pollution to controlled waters which may arise. In this context, pollution arises from the entry into the water of some poisonous, noxious or polluting matter or some solid waste matter.

Part IIA EPA 1990 is introduced by the EA 1995. The latter replaces and repeals the original proposals in the EPA 1990 that they should be registered as contaminated land under s143. It also repeals s61 EPA 1990, which dealt with fly tipping (the unlawful disposal of waste on land), the provisions of which were never brought into effect.

For the first time in UK law, there is a specific definition of contaminated land and specific procedures for securing remedial action when such land is identified. The operation of the Act will be largely governed by Statutory Guidance to which either LAs or the EA are required to have regard or, in accordance with which, in many important circumstances, they must act. This is commented upon further in Chapter 8 and in Appendices 7, 8 and 9.

The practitioner should be aware that Part IIA and the Statutory Guidance are based on the philosophy of a 'suitable-for-use' approach. The regime only applies when it is necessary to deal with unacceptable risks to health or the environment which arise from the current use of the land in question. Land contamination which might be a risk to uses of land for which planning permission is granted will continue to be dealt with under the existing planning and building control systems. It is anticipated that, wherever possible, remediation will be dealt with on a voluntary basis by an appropriate person as is explained further below, or in conjunction with new development rather than by the imposition of remediation notices under this new regime.

The Statutory Guidance in relation to these provisions is being provided by the EA. Indeed, as the main centre of technical expertise on contaminated land, the EA is empowered to provide guidance and priorities and assist in the drafting of the necessary regulations. The former DoE (now the DETR) which fulfilled these functions, transferred relevant research programmes to the EA. These included the development of guideline concentration values for priority contaminants and the drafting of the framework reports in the 'Contaminated Land Research Series' produced by the Government body. Specified values for a wide range of contaminant parameters will be published as trigger values which, if exceeded, will result in a requirement for further investigation and assessment of the property in question and possible eventual remediation.

The background and approach to the Superfund system that operates in the USA, to deal with the same problem, is discussed.

Remedying Environmental Damage in the USA: Clean-up

Superfund, established by the 1980 Comprehensive Environmental Response, Compensation and Liability Act (CERCLA), imposes a liability for funding the clean up of land which has been contaminated. The liability is retrospective, strict and joint and several. It falls on the present owner of the site in question and the owner of the site at the time the pollution occurred. Where waste is the cause of the environmental damage, liability also falls on the waste generator, the waste transporter and the waste broker. When it is possible to establish liability, the Environmental Protection Agency (EPA) attempts to ensure the clean-up is at the polluter's expense (which may be several parties). If this is not possible, the clean-up is funded by Superfund.

Between 1986 and 1991, the budget for Superfund was $8.5 billion. The money is raised from a number of sources with about half coming from direct taxes on industry, for example, petroleum excise taxes and chemical industry taxes. In practice, liability lawsuits ensure that prosecution and rapid-response clean-up are delayed. Partly because of the high legal costs associated with avoidance of liability, the average cost of a clean-up is currently running at a staggering $29–35 million. One reason for the high cost is that clean-ups are required to reach very high standards.

The EPA has created a list of priority sites and installations throughout the USA using a hazard-ranking methodology. This list, referred to as the Superfund National Priorities List, has some 1,250 sites out of an estimated 35,000 potential Superfund sites reported.

In the US, Court actions involving parties that are allegedly liable also include their insurers, their bankers and the EPA. The UK House of Lords European Communities Committee reported that the number of persons that have been involved in litigation by virtue of Superfund exceeds 14,000. They also reported that, in one single case, the number of insurers involved was over 400. Some estimates put the financial expenditure for litigation associated with Superfund at up to 60 per cent of total costs to date.

Superfund protagonists argue that the system has been successful in that it has raised the level of awareness of industrial companies to the importance of assessing or auditing environmental issues associated with any commercial development or transaction. Antagonists consider that the scheme is too harsh, hence the development of the 'innocent landowner' defence in the 1986 reauthorisation legislation, and that the system is rendering certain activities uninsurable. Others argue that the costs of assuring full clean-up of polluted sites are excessive, that too many resources are being allocated to litigation and that one of the guiding principles of the system – prompt clean-up – is simply not being achieved.

Against this backdrop of more than 12 years of the Superfund regime, the European Commission published its long-awaited Green Paper on remedying environmental damage in May 1993. The paper was intended to initiate responses from interested parties within the Member States during a protracted consultation phase, which was intended to culminate in a conference on the subject and a public hearing in collaboration with the European Parliament. The preliminary consultation phase was completed and the Commission published a document of the summaries of the responses to the paper which have been referred to in Chapter 2.

Council of Europe Convention

In parallel with the developments emerging from the Commission, a Convention on Civil Liability for Damage Resulting From Activities Dangerous to the Environment was adopted in March 1993 by the Council of Europe. The Convention, which was concluded in Lugano, imposes strict liability on those who cause pollution of the environment.

The Council of Europe is a pan-European organisation of democratic states which, with recent additions from Central and Eastern European countries, now includes 27 members, including the EU and European Free Trade Association (EFTA) countries. It remains to be seen how influential the Convention will be on the Commission's evolving policy on civil liability for environmental damage. The Commission attended the drafting meetings for the Convention as an observer.

Seven national governments responded formally to the Commission Green Paper, giving their views on the proposals. Of these, Germany indicated that it would not adhere to the Council of Europe Convention and, further, that it believed that the Commission should not adhere to it either. Conversely, the governments of The Netherlands and Portugal stated that the Commission should adhere to the Convention. Interestingly, the UK government made no comment at all on the Convention in its submission to the Commission on the Green Paper.

The aim and objective of the Convention is to provide adequate compensation for damage resulting from activities dangerous to the environment. These are defined as operations involving dangerous substances likely to pose a significant risk to humans, property or the environment by virtue of their properties and conditions of use. This definition may be qualified by quantitative or concentration thresholds, or restricted to particular risks or concentrations. This appears to be one area within the Convention that is so broadly drawn that much discretion would be left to individual countries, such that it would almost certainly result in widely varying national liability regimes within the EU. Interestingly, four countries abstained on a vote adopting the final text of the Convention: the UK, Germany, Ireland and the former Czechoslovakia.

An operator of a dangerous activity would be liable for damage resulting from incidents at the time the activity was under its control. A separate regime would apply to landfills and other sites for the permanent deposit of waste. Here the operator at the time when damage by waste became known would be liable. The last operator would be liable for any damage that became known after a site closed.

A number of exemptions exist. They provide that an operator would not be liable, first, when damage resulted necessarily from compliance with a specific order or compulsory measure of a public authority and, secondly, when damage was caused by pollution at tolerable levels to be anticipated under relevant local conditions. This might well provide a defence when a business caused damage that was deemed to be acceptable to a regulatory authority. Further means of avoiding liability are provided to operators when the state of scientific and technical knowledge at the time of the incident was not such as to enable the existence of the dangerous properties of the substance to be discovered. Such a means to avoid liability, however, is not provided for operators of waste-management facilities. The existence of such exemptions, uncertainties, and lack of precision seems likely to ensure that a separate civil liability system will be developed by the EU with elements of the Convention providing a means to approach certain issues, such as which activities should be covered. Developments this year should indicate the way forward at EU level.

Background Principles

The UK government has been seriously debating the matter of contaminated land since the mid- to late 1980s, when an all-party select committee deliberated and published a report on the subject. An attempt by the government to introduce a register of land which had been subject to potentially contaminative uses, the so-called section 143 registers (of the EPA 1990), was the first outcome of these deliberations. The proposal to introduce the registers was withdrawn in March 1994, while it was still in the middle of its final consultation process. This followed an outcry, principally from landowners and developers, who quite rightly argued that all land used by industry would be dubbed contaminated, whether it actually was or not.

As has been indicated, being on the register would undoubtedly have impacted adversely on the value of the property. Even if potentially contaminated land registers had materialised in some acceptable format, however, they still would only have represented an information source. No requirements were proposed at that time for LAs to establish the actual state of contamination of identified land, and to determine in which cases the levels of contamination were sufficiently unacceptable as to result in a requirement for remedial action.

The principles upon which the provisions agreed by Parliament are based are as follows:

- remedial action will only be taken on a parcel of contaminated land when the contamination poses unacceptable actual, or potential, risks to human health, to the environment or to property;

- remedial action will only be taken where there are appropriate and cost-effective means to do so, taking into account the actual or intended use of the site (the fitness for purpose or suitable for use concepts);

- remedial actions will be provided such that the urgent and really problematic sites are dealt with in an orderly, controlled and affordable manner;

- a framework of guidance will be provided so as to enable the responsible authorities to proceed with greater confidence in the task of identifying and assessing contaminated land and in determining what remedial steps might be needed.

Identifying Contaminated Land

Contaminated land is any land which appears to the LA, relying on guidance provided by the EA, to be in such a condition that, by reason of substances, that is, priority pollutants, in or under the land: significant harm is being caused; or there is a significant possibility of such harm being caused; or pollution of controlled waters (ground and surface waters) is being, or is likely to be, caused.

'Harm' means harm to the health of living organisms and their ecological systems and, in the case of humans, harm also to property. Harm does not include harm to amenity or offence to the senses of humans. Guidance on this will be issued progressively by the EA.

As is mentioned in Chapter 8, LAs have a duty under the statutory nuisance provisions of the EPA 1990 to arrange (from time to time) to detect any statutory nuisance in existence in their area of jurisdiction. Such nuisances include emissions from premises or from deposits which are in a condition which is prejudicial to health.

Within the provisions of the EA 1995, LAs have their duties extended, and shall cause their areas to be inspected from time to time for the purpose of identifying contaminated land, and enabling them to decide whether the contaminated land is required to be designated as a special site. A special site is land which is causing or could cause significant, that is, 'serious', harm.

Closed landfill sites, particularly those which were in operation before the introduction of licensing in 1976, are likely to be considered special sites, and their location must be notified to the EA. Once a special site is designated, a remediation statement is to be prepared which will specify what actions are required by the appropriate person by way of remediation. The DETR will issue regulations, not guidelines, setting out the criteria to be considered in identifying special sites. The government proposes that prior to the issuing of a remediation notice, except in cases of emergency, a formal consultation procedure is activated with the appropriate person, most probably the owner of the site in question.

As is discussed further below, the LA notifies a person of its intention to serve a notice. The LA has to wait three months before actually issuing the notice itself. LAs must consider the cost of what is likely to be involved and personal hardship before a remediation notice is served.

The Appropriate Person: Who Pays?

The appropriate person on whom the remediation notice for a special site is served is defined as:

> 'The person, or any of the persons, who caused or knowingly permitted the substances, or any of the substances, by reason of which the contaminated land in question is such land, to be in or under that land.'

In any given case, where no such person has after reasonable inquiry been found, or the liability of any such person has been transferred directly or indirectly to the owner or occupier of the land for the time being, or any permission to allow LA access is refused, then the appropriate person is the owner or occupier for the time being of the contaminated land in question. Reference is made to Class A and B (see Chapter 8). Further detail of the allocations of class of persons is referred to in Chapter 9 and the Appendices.

The former (Conservative) government's contaminated-land policy review which led to the Environment Bill proposals was instigated by a general consultation paper entitled, 'Paying for our Past'. Listed in order of priority in this paper were those who, in the government's view, in principle, should be targeted to pay for the costs of remediation. In order of decreasing importance, they are:

- the polluter: the government considered that the 'polluter pays principle' needed to be at the core of any regulatory regime;

- the land owner: the government considered that in those cases where the polluter may be no longer known, or may have gone bankrupt, the owner of the property should be responsible for its condition;

- the lender: the government considered that lenders should not be relieved of all risk in relation to the sums they advance; nor should they be relieved of responsibility where, in exercising their functions, they had caused or contributed to the damage. Some comfort is gained from the opinion that a secured lender executing a charge on the land and taking possession of a site which had previously been the source of off-site environmental damage, will not be liable for the costs of remedying that prior off-site damage. With this knowledge, lenders should be advised to establish the baseline environmental conditions or regulatory compliance of a property or business prior to lending for its purchase or control;

- the public sector: the government considered that responsibility for 'orphan' sites, where the polluter cannot be identified or where an owner or polluter does not have the resources to pay for the clean-up, should lie with the public sector regulators. In these circumstances, spending to clean-up should be taken by the LAs for those instances where taking action will avoid serious risks to health or unacceptable environmental damage.

Although the present (Labour) government has indicated that some of the aspects of the contaminated land regime were too complicated – which has led to further delay in the final publication of the guidance – the main thrust of the policy remains.

Liability could therefore be transferred to a new owner. Liability exists for an owner who knowingly permits the contaminative state of the property to remain without taking any remedial action. It is intended, however, that a person who owned or occupied the land, who could demonstrate that he had not caused or knowingly permitted the contaminants to be present, would not be responsible for remedying the cause of significant harm. On the basis solely of ownership it is intended to limit the requirements of the owner to remedy water pollution. Other powers to remedy water pollution are available to the EA through the WRA 1991. This is referred to further in Chapter 5.

Such intentions raise the interesting question of who pays for remediation in cases where the polluter cannot be found or, indeed, where the owner or occupier simply does not have the resources to carry out remediation. Arguments have been put by bodies, such as the Confederation of British Industry (CBI), that in such cases the responsibility for the clean-up should become a 'social cost'. In these circumstances, and where the public or the environment are considered to be put at unacceptable risk, then it seems likely, in practice, that public money will have to be used. Such actions are likely to only be taken as a matter of last resort and in rather exceptional circumstances.

The former government clearly considered that despite the longevity of Britain's industrial past and despite the fact that roughly nine-tenths of biodegradable waste arisings are disposed to landfills, the majority of contaminated sites which are not deemed special sites can safely be left until they are reused through redevelopment. Redevelopment of such sites would act as the trigger for their remediation. At the time of redevelopment they would be upgraded to a standard where they become suitable for the purpose of the new use. In this way, the problems associated with the setting up and administering of a Superfund equivalent are side-stepped.

Determination of Contamination and Other Guidance

In May 1995, the then DoE published a draft guidance document on the procedure which, in its eventual form, LAs were to use to determine whether land is contaminated. This document did not specify guideline/trigger values for priority pollutants – such values have to be produced either by the DETR or the EA. The 'Determination of Contamination' document introduces the fundamental principles of environmental risk assessment. These principles include the 'source–pathway–target' concept. Specific advice on establishing the nature and sensitivity of each is given.

The LA is required to confirm the presence of substances with a potential to cause harm. This they will do through the commissioning of exploratory surveys or more detailed site investigations. Such investigations will be carried out in cognisance of standard field operating procedures which will specify the number and distribution of samples, the choice of determinants and of sampling and analytical techniques.

The LA will be allowed to use the guideline/trigger values to compare with the concentrations of contaminants found in soil from the investigations. Where actual concentrations exceed the guideline values for key contaminants, this will provide sufficient indication that a significant possibility of harm exists. Following on from this indicative evaluation, an estimation of risk is required for as many plausible source–pathway–target relationships as appropriate. The document provides a series of tables by which the estimated degree of possibility of harm being caused can be correlated with a range of degrees of harm to the areas of concern. These areas are chronic effects to human health, harm to ecosystems and harm to property.

Other guidance as well as regulations will be issued before the new contaminated land provisions come into force, which is unlikely to be before spring 1999. Guidance will be provided, for example, on the matter of who is liable (the appropriate person) and the apportionment of liability. Guidance will also be given on the liability attaching to the most recent person who caused, or knowingly permitted, contamination in the particular circumstances where more than one person had control over the same substances which caused the contamination. It has been indicated that, in such circumstances, the liability will not be joint and several. They have also indicated that 'deep-pocket' persons will not be specifically pursued.

Remediation Notices

In circumstances where a LA has identified land as contaminated, the enforcing authority has a duty to serve on the appropriate person a notice specifying what that person must do by way of remediation and the periods within which he is required to do what is specified. Prior to the service of a notice, there is a three-month period for consultation. A person may volunteer to clean up, and must state their proposals in a statement.

Section 78E(4) and (5) provides as follows:

> 'The only things by way of remediation which the enforcing authority may do … are things which it considers reasonable having regard to (a) the cost which is likely to be involved and (b) the seriousness of the harm or pollution of controlled waters in question.
>
> In determining for any purpose of this part (a) what is to be done in any particular case (b) the standard to which any land or waters are to be remediated or (c) what is or is not to be regarded as reasonable;
>
> the enforcing authority shall have regard to any guidance issued for the purpose by the Secretary of State.'

If, during the three-month period of consultation, the appropriate person has begun a clean-up or has provided the LA with its proposed clean-up programme, the remediation notice will not be served. It is the government that produces regulations, not guidance, to establish the form, content and procedures in respect of these matters and remediation notices in general. Ministers have indicated that in the matter of the form of such notices, they would prefer them to be framed in terms of the objectives to be achieved, rather than the specific works to be undertaken. LAs and the EA retain responsibility for including on a register details of the remedial action taken and the post-remedial condition of the land. In this respect, both are subject to the requirements of the Environmental Information Regulations 1992.

If the cost of cleaning up a site is considered too high in view of the seriousness of the contamination, a remediation notice will not be served. A remediation declaration will then be prepared by the LA specifying details of why and how the site was contaminated and why the remediation notice could not specify remediation actions.

If an appropriate person responsible for an industrial, trade or business premises to whom a remediation notice has been served fails, without reasonable excuse, to comply with a notice, he will be liable, upon conviction, to a fine of up to £20,000 and up to an additional £2,000 for each day of non-compliance. Where the enforcing LA cleans up the land itself, it may recover the costs of this action from the appropriate person in cases where this would not create hardship.

Section 57 EA 1995 introduces a new section to EPA 1990 so that there is now a definition of contaminated land. This is land which appears to the LA to be in such a condition, by reason of substances in, on or under it, that significant harm is being caused or there is a significant possibility of such harm being caused or pollution of controlled waters is being or is likely to be caused.

Harm

Land is contaminated land as defined in s78A(2) where, as a result of substances in it, it is in a condition that significant harm is being caused or there is a significant possibility of such harm. Harm is defined for the purposes of the Act as 'harm to the health of living organisms or other interference with the ecological systems of which they form part and in the case of man includes harm to his property'. Land is also contaminated by reason of substances in it where pollution of controlled water is being, or is likely to be, caused as a result of poisonous, noxious or polluting matter or any solid waste matter entering those waters.

According to the legislation, then, harm can include harm to the health of living organisms, interference with ecological systems or harm to property. What amounts to significant harm will be the subject of detailed guidelines. However, some key principles have emerged which indicate that the harm or interference will have to amount to chronic or acute toxic effect, serious injury or death; irreversible or adverse changes in the functioning of the ecological system; substantial damage to buildings causing them to cease their intended operation; and substantial loss (10 per cent) in value of livestock, crops or land or adjacent land from disease or physical damage or death.

Every LA is required to inspect its area from time to time for the purposes of identifying contaminated land and deciding which land should be designated as a special site for which the EA will be required to take direct responsibility. Special sites are those areas of contaminated land by reason of the condition of which serious harm would, or might be, caused, or serious pollution of controlled waters would, or would be likely to, arise. Regulations are likely to be made to define the different cases and circumstances, areas and localities in which such designations would be appropriate. Decisions to designate a site as a special site will be referred to the Secretary of State who will have overall responsibility in respect of such circumstances.

Significant harm may arise where an LA decides as a result of its inspection and surveys one or more of the following circumstances: the nature and severity of the harm which may arise; the time scale within which such harm could arise compared with the expected life of the development upon it; the vulnerability of those who may be subject to the harm (receptors); the number of people who may be directly affected; and the ease with which harmful effects of pollution may be remedied.

The more immediate the effect of such harm and the greater its severity, the more significant the possibility that the site will be deemed contaminated. The basic approach for the purposes of assessing the significance of the harm and its possibility is by reference to the source of the danger, the imminence of its occurrence, the pathway by which it may operate and the receptors who may be subject to its effects. This is in accordance with the conventional risk-assessment techniques which have been developed over recent decades. Plainly, the possibility of an explosion that would lead to irreparable damage or even death would make the site contaminated.

Where an LA identifies contaminated land, it must take further action. The first step will be for it to notify interested parties, namely, the EA, any occupier or owner of the land together with any other 'appropriate person' as defined in the legislation.

Following the identification of the sites, the LA must decide what steps need to be taken to improve the condition of the site. Further notices will then be served, this time on the appropriate persons, specifying what needs to be done by way of remediation and the time limits within which work must be carried out. In the first instance, the appropriate person will be the person who caused or knowingly permitted substances to be kept on the land which resulted in the contamination. If, after reasonable enquiries, the LA is unable to discover the whereabouts of that person, notices will be served on either the owner or occupier of the land. Where there is more than one appropriate person, the LA will have the discretion to decide the extent to which each of them will bear the liability.

The draft legislation contained a provision to the effect that even if the person who originally caused the pollution could be identified, responsibility for the clean-up would rest with the owner or occupier of land if the LA was satisfied that the intention had been that liability should be transferred. There was a great deal of opposition to this provision, mainly on the basis that the circumstances in which liability could be said to have been transferred were not sufficiently clear. The provision has now been deleted so that original polluters will remain liable. For the sake of clarification, the Act also includes a definition of owner, which is 'a person (other than a mortgagee not in possession) who whether in his own rights or as a trustee for any other person is entitled to receive the rack rent of the land'.

Practitioners should be aware of the circumstances to which the new provisions do not apply:

• Integrated pollution control: no remediation notice may be served where there is power to remedy harm caused by breach of IPC controls.

• Waste Management Licensing: Part IIA does not apply to land where the contamination arises as a result of a breach of condition of a current waste management licence.

• Discharges to controlled waters: remediation notices cannot impede or prevent discharges made pursuant to a discharge consent under the WRA 1991.

• Remediation activities: the carrying out of remediation may require statutory consents of various kinds, including planning permissions and waste management licences (unless exempt).

• Planning: the planning system should deal with risks from land contamination which can arise when a new use is proposed. The system should aim to ensure as a minimum standard that following any change or use of the land permitted by a planning consent, the land ceases to be contaminated land. Part IIA deals only with risks arising from the current use of the land not from its future use permitted by permissions.

• Building control: the building control regime will determine what measures will be needed before development of land affected by contamination can take place.

It should also be noted that the statutory nuisance provisions of Part III 1990 Act will no longer apply insofar as the nuisance is caused by substances in, on or under the land, so that harm is, or may be, caused and do not apply where pollution of controlled water is being, or is likely to be, caused.

In contrast to the draft legislation, the Act now allows for more flexibility in the remediation notice procedure. In particular, before serving such a notice the LA is required to carry out consultations with the owner or occupier of the land which is affected and any other person on whom notice is to be served. Also, having served notice that it has identified the contaminated site, the LA must wait three months before serving a remediation notice. In this way, those who are affected will have an opportunity to enter into negotiations with the LA and also seek professional advice on the condition of the land. A further concession has been introduced allowing the appropriate person to put forward voluntary proposals for cleaning up a site and in such circumstances the local authority can delay the service of the remediation notice for an indefinite period to allow those proposals to be put into effect.

Liability for Other Neighbouring Land

The 1990 Act contains specific provisions identifying the persons that will be liable where pollutants escape outside the boundaries of a site causing harm. As has already been indicated, the appropriate person responsible for clean-up will either be the original polluter, the owner or the occupier. The broad principles are given below.

First, where pollutants escape from a contaminated site (Site 1) on to an adjoining site (Site 2) and the owner of Site 1 did not cause or knowingly permit the pollution, it will not be responsible for cleaning up Site 2. It will be responsible for cleaning up its own site, Site 1.

Secondly, where pollutants escape from Site 1 onto Site 2 and owner 1 did knowingly cause or permit the pollution, it will be responsible not only for the cleaning up of its own site, Site 1, but also for the clean-up of Site 2.

Thirdly, where pollutants escape from Site 1 onto Site 2 and then escape further onto Site 3, the owner of Site 2 will no be responsible for cleaning up further land to which the pollutants have escaped. There is, however, an exception to this: where pollutants had originally escaped from Site 1 on to Site 2, the owner of Site 2 may still be liable if he did not take any action to prevent the further migration of pollutants on to Site 3. This is because where onwards migration of pollutants had been caused or knowingly permitted by the intermediate owner, in this case owner 2, that owner will be treated as the polluter for the purposes of remediation liabilities.

The effect of the third principle will mean that where pollutants escape from Site 1 to Site 2 the owner of Site 2 will not be responsible for any contamination of any other sites which occurred before the date on which owner 2 acquired the land.

Security Matters

There has been much confusion in the past about the question of whether liabilities for clean-up could attach to persons who had taken land as security. As has already been mentioned, by reason of the definition of owner, mortgagees not in possession will not be liable to clean up sites. There is also a specific exclusion in s78(14) of the Act relating to certain persons, such as insolvency practitioners or the Official Receivers. As a result, practitioners are not personally liable unless they take steps which are outside the terms of their appointment and that result in substances that lead to contamination being kept on land.

In practice, in determining who should be exempt from the service of a remediation notice upon them (despite the fact that they may be potentially liable as appropriate persons in principle), the proposed guidance indicates that no account should be taken of the following matters: first, any limitation on the right to take action against an appropriate person as a result of the hardship provisions in s78P, or the fact that an appropriate person is insured or has some other means of transferring his liability. The intention behind these provisions is to avoid the deep-pocket approach that has caused such difficulties in the USA.

Secondly, the LA should have regard to all the relevant information about a potential appropriate person and seek all such information as may be relevant to its decision which can reasonably be made available to it.

Thirdly, having regard to the existing arrangements that may arise between the parties as to their respective liabilities for contamination, the LA should respect such arrangements provided that they have been reached as a result of an arm's-length negotiation and have not been done to evade or avoid liabilities which might otherwise be placed upon them at the expense of the public purse.

The guidance indicates six tests as to the circumstances in which an appropriate person should not be involved in bearing the cost of remediation when otherwise they may be liable.

- Test 1: a person who has provided some financial assistance, guarantee, indemnity, insurance or professional advice or is a landlord, licensor or contractor who has no direct and immediate responsibility for the occupation of the land in question.

- Test 2: where payment has already been made to cover liabilities for remediation, which were sufficient at the date of payment and if they had been carried out would have led to circumstances in which the land would not have remained contaminated. This is a form of no-fault exemption.

- Test 3: where the land has been sold to the current purchaser with full information as to its condition by way of the sale of the freehold or a long leasehold as a result of an arm's-length arrangement without misrepresentation.

- Test 4: where some subsequent chemical or physical change has arisen as a result not of the substance itself, but as a result of the introduction of other substances for which the person is not responsible and did not cause or knowingly permit its introduction.

- Test 5: where substances have escaped from the land on which the substance has been allowed or was caused to be present, provided that the person has not been responsible for the escape to adjoining land and where it can be shown that another person has either caused or knowingly permitted the escape from land A to land B (see s78K(4) and (5)).

- Test 6: the subsequent introduction of new pathways or new receptors as a result of operations carried out on the land, works or changes, or use for which the potential appropriate person was not responsible in terms of causing or permitting.

A failure to comply with a remediation notice without reasonable excuse is an offence.

Exemptions

What is clear and important in the provisions in this new legislative arrangement is that certain persons who may be owners or occupiers are specifically exempt from potential liability. These are people who act in a relevant professional capacity (s78X(4)) and include the following: insolvency practitioners; the Official Receiver; the Official Receiver acting as a receiver or manager; the Special Manager under the Insolvency Act 1986; the accountant in bankruptcy; and any person acting as a receiver or manager under an enactment or order of court.

Procedural Issues

It is possible to appeal against a remediation notice within a period of 21 days beginning with the day on which the notice is served. Despite concerns that the lower courts are not sufficiently equipped to deal with what might be complicated and technical cases, appeals under the legislation will be dealt with by the magistrates' court. The court will have the power to quash, confirm or modify the notice. Assuming that no appeal is submitted and the notice comes into effect, failure to comply with its provisions will constitute an offence. Following summary conviction, a fine can be imposed of up to £5,000 plus £500 for every day after conviction on which the notice is not complied with.

Where the offence related to industrial trade or business premises, the maximum fine will be £20,000 plus £2,000 for every day after conviction on which the offence continues. In addition, if the person on whom the notice has been served fails to comply, the LA can carry out the work itself and recover the cost. In deciding whether to recover the cost, it can have regard to hardships that may be suffered as a result. Furthermore, where the appropriate person is the owner of the land and was responsible for causing the contamination, the LA will have the power to charge interest on outstanding clean-up costs. Any outstanding costs may also be charged against the land.

Under s78N the LA has powers to enter land which is contaminated and carry out works in circumstances where remediation is required and the appropriate persons either cannot be found or have failed to comply with the requirements of the remediation notice.

Where an enforcing authority acts by way of works of remediation as a result of imminent danger of serious harm, or failure to comply with a remediation notice, then it can seek to recover the costs of the remediation works that they have carried out by way of charging orders on the property. There is an appeal to the County Court.

Relevant Factors

Section 78P(2) assists in deciding whether to recover the cost and, if so, how much of the cost which it is entitled to recover. The enforcing authority shall have regard to any hardship which the recovery may cause the person from whom the cost is recoverable and to any guidance issued by the Secretary of State for the purposes of this subsection.

In determining hardship the LA is likely to be advised to have regard to any injustice by the imposition of such costs, undue suffering and anxiety which in the particular circumstances could be caused and any severe financial detriment which would result.

The achievement of what is just fair and equitable should always be the proper approach. It is usually appropriate to recover from those who have caused or knowingly permitted the contamination and those who have done so in the course of business; and those who have caused rather than those who have knowingly permitted contamination or from an occupier or owner in the absence of the original author.

Particular circumstances to which an LA may have regard are if the recovery of the full costs might lead to the closure of a business or would not have fallen fully upon the person from whom the costs are to be recovered, and if the original author had been found. Regard also should be paid to the precautions that were taken before the purchase of the land, and whether the steps that were taken did not and could not have led to an identification at the time of an owner or occupier who had caused the contamination.

Clearly, the LA may think in the circumstances that it is not appropriate to levy the full recovery of costs where the costs are likely to exceed the value of the land. The LA has power as in other statutory provisions to register a charge against the land for the purposes of recovering a full indemnity for the costs they have incurred as a result of the works they have had to carry out.

Registers

Details of all notices served and any appeals will be kept on a public register maintained by the LA. The registers are by no means dissimilar from the contaminated land register which the government was considering introducing a couple of years ago. As has been indicated, one of the concerns voiced against the original proposals was that land would remain on the register even after it had been cleaned up and, as a result, the register would have a blighting effect on the land. It remains the case that sites will stay on the register; however, the effective arrangements mean that any clean-up works which have been done will also be noted. The government's justification for this is that it adopted a 'suitable for use' approach to the control and treatment of existing contamination, that is to say, in determining whether a site needs to be cleaned up and to what extent, regard will be had for the purposes to which the land will be put in the future. This being the case, if details remain on the register of the works which have been carried out on the site, this will alert prospective owners who may wish to put the site to a more sensitive use and which would entail more extensive clean-up works being carried out. This approach also allows for the future assessment of a site where there have been advances in technology allowing for the effects of contaminants to be more clearly ascertained.

Contaminated Land: The Opportunity

Contaminated land could be viewed strictly as a liability. As such, the company may suffer legal penalties, loss of investment, a poor insurance risk or a poor market image. In these circumstances, the contaminated site is a millstone around the company's neck.

However, when viewed as a symbol of past inefficiencies, which the company now wishes to put behind it, a contaminated site may appear as an opportunity for improvement, and even as an asset. Clearly, as it stands the asset has no value (because it cannot be developed or sold in its present state). However, technologies exist for remediation of contaminated sites that will allow the maximum potential of that asset to be realised.

Examples of the positive side of past contamination can be found world-wide. For instance, in South Wales many years of industrial activity (chiefly coal production and smelting) had decimated the environment in some areas, killing all but the hardiest of plants, driving out many of the native animals and affecting the well-being of local inhabitants. However, since the decline of these industries and the development of newer, cleaner technologies, the dereliction has come to an end. New businesses, however, were reluctant to locate to the previously derelict areas for many reasons, including their inability to attract finance because of the liabilities involved in the contaminated ground, and the difficulty in attracting people to live in the area because of potential health risks.

Realising this, industry and local government worked closely together to remediate the contamination. Money was invested to prepare the ground to make it suitable for industrial, retail, commercial, residential and leisure uses. Since the remediation work, South Wales has been subject to rapid growth and the economic benefits to the region are obvious.

Remediation can be applied to discharges to land, air and water. To define the scope of the remediation, it is necessary to undertake an audit of the processes, detailing the releases being made and the environmental effects resulting from these releases. Once the audit has been completed, options for remediation that meet BATNEEC can be examined.

As has also been mentioned, there is an increasing trend away from complete reliance on legislation to achieve environmental protection, and moves towards using economic instruments to drive market forces to act as incentives for cleaner technologies, waste minimisation and national resource conservation. There is no intention to deregulate environmental protection completely. Rather, a balance is sought between regulation and economic instruments to achieve optimum efficiency.

Pricing Mechanisms

Pricing mechanisms attempt to place an economic value on environmental assets that can be accounted for in a cost-benefit analysis. An example is 'contingent valuation', where people are asked to specify their willingness to pay a certain price to safeguard an asset. The value placed upon that asset by virtue of how much people are willing to pay to protect it is used in the cost-benefit analysis of a project that may cause damage to that asset. Other examples include valuing through identification of the costs of reconstruction, or a unit pricing system where individual components of an ecosystem are given unit prices, and the value of the ecosystem is calculated on a bill of quantities.

The use of pricing mechanisms is, however, fraught with danger because many of the assets to which prices are attached are by their nature priceless or not tangible. For example, it is not possible to place a reconstruction cost on a unique and fragile ecosystem if it cannot be replaced. Moreover, how can the spiritual value of a traditional homeland be valued?

Quotas

One mechanism in use relies upon the permitted release of a maximum quantity of a pollutant within a specified area, and the allocation of quotas to allow dischargers to release that pollutant up to the maximum limit allowable. Quotas can then be bought and sold as market commodities, with large dischargers wishing to buy up quotas to allow them to continue to discharge, and smaller companies (where perhaps clean-up is more easily achieved) wishing to sell. The price of the quota will, therefore, be subject to the laws of supply and demand, and (it is hoped) this system will act to restrict discharges and encourage dischargers to minimise their releases.

An example of this is 'air-shed management' where a number of factories within a defined 'air-shed', such as an isolated valley or other area where the air is not easily mixed, are given quotas and a fixed limit is established on the total loading of pollutants into the air-shed. Companies are then allowed to set their own emission levels through the buying and selling of quotas. The quota system can work, although the market in quotas must be strictly regulated to stop abuses such as cornering of the quota market in order to drive out competition.

Levies and Taxes

Much of the discussion regarding economic instruments relates to levies and taxes on the use of raw materials (including energy) or the production of waste. By making it more expensive to purchase raw materials and to dispose of waste products, there is a clear incentive to reduce the consumption of these raw materials and to minimise the quantities of waste produced. This works alongside the development of cleaner technology, by directly encouraging sustainable use of resources and setting up the hierarchy of waste management options from minimisation down to disposal.

An example of this is the carbon tax, where coal, oil and natural gas will be subject to a levy that will encourage the use of non-fossil fuel options, or more efficient use of non-fossil fuel options in the generation of heat and power. In the UK, even in the absence an official carbon tax, there has been a dramatic move away from coal-fired power stations to the more efficient gas-fired facilities, many of which can provide both heat and power. At the same time, there is an incentive to explore non-fossil fuel options such as nuclear, wind, wave, tidal and solar power, although each of these has its own problems. In addition, new fuel technologies are being explored, such as hydrogen-powered vehicles or new battery technology.

Negotiations between HM Customs and Excise and the landfill industry resulted, in November 1996, in the introduction of a landfill levy. The levy was intended to discourage waste producers from disposing of waste to landfill, and encourage minimisation, recycling and reuse. One consequence of this is a move by the packaging industry to restructure and to increase the availability of more environmentally-friendly products.

The key points of the original landfill levy are as follows:

The standard rate of tax will be £7 per tonne. A lower rate of £2 per tonne will apply to 'inactive' waste. This is described as waste which does not decay, give off methane, pollute ground water or contaminate land.

The definition of waste corresponds with that in EPA 1990, as amended. This means that only landfilled waste required to be licensed under the Act will be taxed. Otherwise there are no exceptions.

Tax is imposed on the weight as opposed to the volume of waste. There is no requirement for a weighbridge to be installed on sites that do not already have one. Estimates of conversion volume/weight will be made on a site-by-site basis. Where waste contains added water, for example, to assist with transport or disposal, a discount is available.

The tax does not apply to waste brought to a site merely for recycling. There will be a tax-free zone for such recycling operators.

Mines and quarry waste are presently not controlled by the Act. It is likely that most of this waste will fall within the inactive description and be subject to the lower rate of tax. Alternatively, an exemption from licensing might be achieved.

The government has introduced environmental trusts. Where site operators make payments to these trusts, they will be able to claim a rebate of 90 per cent of their tax contributions, up to a maximum of 20 per cent of their total landfill tax bill.

Lawful site operators have to register with HM Customs and Excise to account for the tax.

Technological Solutions

Minimisation

Highest in the hierarchy of environmental protection measures is minimisation of environmental damage from the outset. This entails minimisation of both the consumption of raw materials and production of waste products. Very often the production of waste indicates the inefficiency of a process, and hence loss of productivity of that process.

A good example is a single-shot metal-plating plant, where the quantities of waste metal lost can be enormous. Clearly, the plant is wasting money in purchasing raw materials that are not used while, at the same time, the metal that is released into the environment causes significant harm to human health and to animals and plants. In addition, wastage of such metals is likely to lead to serious land contamination, thereby increasing liabilities of the industry.

Such problems could be avoided in the first instance through adopting a technology that acted as close to a closed system as possible. Appropriate clean-up technology would allow water and raw materials to be recycled. The techniques to be adopted must, however, ensure the viability of the plant. As such, the saving in raw materials and reduction in environmental damage and liabilities must outweigh the cost of installing and maintaining the cleaner technology.

Best Available Techniques (BAT)

Following on from the objective to minimise environmental harm and resource depletion comes the need to find and implement BAT. In the UK, HMIP has defined BAT for a whole range of industrial processes where significant releases to air, land and water are expected. This exercise was conducted in close liaison with industry.

Implicit within the consideration of BAT is the need to ensure financial viability of the process. Hence BAT is often combined with the principle of Not Entailing Excessive Cost (NEEC) to form BATNEEC. The NEEC suffix allows economic and operational constraints to be applied in the choice of BAT. At the core of the principle is the requirement that the environmental benefits of adopting a particular technique outweigh the financial costs and operating constraints of that technique.

A good example is the application of the EU Directive on the treatment of urban waste water. This legislation, which is referred to in Chapter 5, requires that sewage discharges from large coastal towns and cities be subject to secondary treatment (that is, microbiological digestion of sewage) prior to discharge. This legislation allows an exemption from this level of treatment for discharges into waters considered to be 'less sensitive' only where treatment at the less stringent level can be demonstrated to produce no significant environmental harm.

Accordingly, the principle of BATNEEC is followed, because treating all discharges to the highest standard may not be cost-effective. It is possible that no tangible environmental benefits would result from the application of the highest standards at all locations. If the standards were applied at all locations, the installation of the treatment plant might cost considerable sums of money with little or no environmental gain. For example, a possible saving of several hundred thousands of pounds can be made if the discharge from Hull on the River Humber estuary in England were to be subject to the lower level of treatment without adverse environmental effects.

Remediation

Remediation addresses the problem of what to do when the damage has already occurred. The justification for retroactive action on business grounds is not as clear-cut as for the avoidance mechanisms described above. Remediation can appear expensive without achieving obvious financial benefits for the company involved. However, as is mentioned elsewhere in the guide, when considering the effects of a company's operations on all of its stakeholders, remediation can be seen to be of benefit, and may indeed provide a positive financial gain.

Application of the New Rules

The new provisions on contaminated land are going to introduce wide-ranging liabilities for the owners of problem sites. At the moment it is difficult to determine conclusively how strictly the legislation will be applied and what the basic ground rules will be. For example, in the face of considerable criticism, the former government retained the section in the 1990 EPA requiring the EA to take a cost-benefit approach when dealing with environmental protection. This principle is carried through to the area of contaminated land. As noted in Chapter 3, in essence this requires that remedial action should only be taken in respect of contaminated sites where the contamination poses unacceptable risks to health or the environment and where there are appropriate and cost-effective means available to do so, taking into account the actual or intended use of the site.

The government has also acknowledged the need to take a pragmatic view, since it is clearly not possible to deal with all of the polluted sites in a short space of time. Indeed, in recognition of this, the Act required the designation of so-called special sites which are contaminated sites which may give rise to more immediate and serious pollution concerns.

The underlying purpose of this legislation is to secure the right balance between the remedy of past historical legacies and the future wealth-creating sectors of the economy. It would be neither feasible nor sensible to try to deal with all land contaminated by past activities at once. The wealth-creating sectors of the economy could not afford to do so. The urgent and real problems should be dealt with but in an orderly and controlled fashion with which the economy at large and individual businesses and land owners in particular can cope.

Conclusion

Thus these new legislative provisions seek to achieve a situation where:

- the polluter pays;

- land is rendered in a condition which is suitable for the use for which it is intended;

- sustainable development is achieved by reducing damage from past activities and pollution and by returning contaminated land to beneficial use wherever practicable;

- unacceptable action or potential risk to health or the environment are reduced;

- appropriate and cost-effective means are put in place to take account of actual and intended uses of the site;

- the aim is to improve sites as and when hazards need to be dealt with;

- the private sector can proceed to develop land for beneficial uses without undue economic burdens or disincentives;

- efficient marketing of land which may have been contaminated will arise;

- no unnecessary financial and regulatory burdens are imposed upon those who are entitled to be exempt from them.

How the rules operate in practice will be a true test of the government's commitment to environmental improvement, and whether sufficient background work has been done to pave the way for the new provisions. To date, the government has adopted a hands-off approach, and has consistently taken the view that improvements to polluted sites can be achieved through the voluntary commercial activities of the property sector without the need for direct state intervention. Once again, the government has indicated that these new rules will only bite where there is a failure through other means to deal with threats to health or the environment. While some commentators might interpret this as a further expression of the laissez-faire or deregulatory approach, others may see it as the final warning to the property industry to take the issue of contaminated land seriously before it is forced to do so.

The Future

Many changes lie ahead as the government proceeds with the completion of the new regulatory era in contaminated land. Regulations, guidance notes and framework reports are already appearing, and collectively they will provide greater transparency in the matter of identification and prioritisation of contaminated sites which are to be cleaned up. With the publication of the guidance in final form a new era should begin.

Chapter 5

Water and Air Emissions

Water Pollution

Introductory Remarks

Water pollution offences embrace a wide range of types of pollution. Statutes cover areas as different as the Oil Pollution Act 1971 (consolidating the Oil in Navigable Waters Acts 1955, 1963 and 1971 and the Continental Shelf Act 1964), and the Food and Environment Protection Act 1985. The 1971 Act establishes criminal penalties for contraventions and the 1985 Act provides for a licensing system. There are two aspects that can be found throughout water pollution law: deterrence by criminal sanctions and prevention by (possibly) obtaining a licence prior to operating a polluting process.

Methods of Water Management

In general, there are three methods of water management and protection in the UK. The first is licensing (the operation of the licensing system has been referred to in Chapters 4, 5, 6 and 8). As regards water protection, the licensing system is especially prevalent in the protection of controlled waters.

The second method is through the creation of water-quality levels. These can be aimed at the level of the concentration of substances to be released (known as emission limit values), that is, before the polluting substance is released into the water medium, or it could be aimed at the eventual quality of the medium into which the pollutant substance has been discharged (water quality standards). It has been suggested that the UK traditionally favoured the use of the latter method, because pollutants are dispersed in rivers that, after a relatively short distance, flow into the sea. On the other hand, EU Member States whose geographical position means longer and slower-flowing rivers, are said to have preferred the former.[1] In an interesting development, the proposed new EU framework water Directive, which is referred to below, is to adopt a combined approach of emission limit values and water-quality standards.

The third method of water management is sampling, which applies, in particular, to drinking-water. In the UK, the water companies have a statutory duty to supply water that is 'wholesome'. In fact, the Council Directive on the quality of surface water for drinking 1975[2] only requires that 95 per cent of samples need to comply with the mandatory levels for substances in the water prescribed in the Directive. The 1979 Directive on the sampling and analysis of surface water for drinking[3] prescribes the sampling procedures to be carried out to ensure that water complies with the requirements in the 1975 Directive. It should be noted that more recent UK regulations prescribe a system for classifying the quality of inland freshwaters according to their suitability for abstraction for supply as drinking water.[4] This is the result of wide sampling carried out.

All three of these methods can be found in the regulatory framework.

The Regulatory Framework

The following are the key statutes dealing with water pollution:[5]

Water Act 1989 (WA 1989)

The WA 1989 was mainly concerned with the privatisation of water companies and transferred the functions of the ten water authorities to the now defunct NRA, and to water and sewerage undertakers. The powers conferred by the Act on the NRA are now exercised by the EA.[6] Water and sewerage undertakers retain the functions concerned with water supply and sewerage. The WA 1989 also created the office of Director General of Water Services who, together with the Secretary of State for the Environment, has the role of overall regulator.

The Act was consolidated in 1991 by the principal legislative provisions of the Water Resources Act 1991, the Water Industry Act 1991, and the Statutory Water Companies Act 1991.

Water Resources Act 1991 (WRA 1991)

The main significance of the WRA 1991 is that it extended the functions and duties of the NRA, now the EA.

Role in Water Management (Part II, ss19-81)

In this connection the main functions are to conserve, redistribute and otherwise augment and secure the proper use of water resources; co-operate with the water undertakers for the above; secure a minimum acceptable flow and volume of inland waters; and to manage abstraction and impounding and grant licences or prosecute offenders. (Note: Part V concerns charges made in relation to abstraction and impounding licences.)

Water can only be abstracted for domestic or agricultural or industrial purposes if a licence has been obtained. The requirements for an application for such a licence are set out in ss34-37 and they are considered in accordance with ss38-40. There is a right of appeal to the Secretary of State.

Role in the Control of Pollution of Water Resources (Part III, ss82-104)

In this respect the main functions are to enforce a water classification system and achieve water quality objectives with the powers conferred; prosecute offenders, in particular, those who pollute controlled waters; and prevent and control pollution.

Spillages that threaten to pollute water may provoke actions by the authority (anti-pollution works) to limit or remedy any damage that has already occurred, or to restore water to the quality standard before the pollution. Costs for such operations can be recovered from the polluter (s161), and the authority may still prosecute the polluter subsequent to the prevention action.

Apart from the abstraction and the impounding licences, the other licensing control that the authority has is the granting of discharge consents. Discharge consents are required where trade or sewage effluents are to be discharged into controlled waters. Controlled waters include all inland and coastal waters with the exception of some land-locked inland waters. The authority may attach such conditions as it thinks fit relating to the quantity, quality, nature, composition or temperature of the discharge.

Role in Flood Defence Cases (Part IV, ss 105-113)

To generally supervise all matters relating to flood defence (together with the regional flood defence committees), and miscellaneous functions as to river management and drainage of land.

Enforcement powers (Part V, in particular, ss154-186) include the compulsory purchase of any land which is required for, or in connection with, the carrying out of its functions; the purchase or lease of certain other types of land; the authorisation of certain operations or discharges of water under a compulsory works order; and the exercise of powers of entry.

Role of Informing the Public (Part V, ss207-225)

This extends to various activities, in particular the preparation of annual reports; keeping registers concerning abstraction and impounding licences, pollution control and works discharges; providing maps of freshwater limits, mains, rivers and waterworks; and publishing certain other information. As regards the latter there are certain restrictions on the disclosure of information.

Statutory Water Companies Act 1991

This statute is the second principal Act that consolidates the WA 1989. It is especially important because it provides for a certain continuity between the current water undertakers and the former water companies. Water companies are defined by s38(1) WA 1973 as those companies authorised before the implementation of the 1973 Act, that is, 18 July 1973, by any local statutory provision to supply water, or a company in which the assets of any company so authorised have subsequently become vested.

Section 11(4) WA 1989 imposed on the Secretary of State a duty to ensure that the statutory water companies would become water undertakers. Section 1 Statutory Water Companies Act 1991 removes any constitutional limitations on a statutory water company which might constrain it from carrying out the functions of a water undertaker. The statutory water companies may now also adopt memorandum and articles of association instead of their statutory constitution (ss11-14).

Water Industry Act (WIA) 1991

This statute concerns the regulation of water supply and begins with provisions for the appointment of the Director General (DG) of Water Services.

DG of Water Services

The DG of Water Services is appointed under s1 WIA 1991, and is responsible for monitoring the performance of the water undertakers and sewerage undertakers, to secure economy and efficiency and to protect the interests of others with regard to charging, prices and standards of services. The DG may investigate complaints about water and sewerage companies and adjudicate in some disputes, but usually takes the appropriate initiative himself. This key role is to settle maximum charges levied by the undertakers, having regard to national and EU environmental law.

The DG is head of the independent regulator office OFWAT, and not only does he ensure fair and efficient service by the water industry by means of controlling price increases, but he also oversees the water companies' investment programmes for the charges paid by the customers. Such investment concerns mainly environmental improvements.

The DG and the Secretary of State sometimes have combined powers and duties. Generally, it is the Secretary of State who defines water quality and regulates its use, while the DG mainly oversees the financial side of implementation of the regulations.

In relation to water undertakers, the Secretary of State or the DG has the following powers and duties: either or both shall secure compliance with the conditions of an appointment of water undertakers under Part II (ss18–22) of the WIA. To fulfil this, either or both may make enforcement orders. Civil liability is imposed on the undertakers: the Secretary of State or the DG may seek injunctive relief, or either or both may issue administration orders in cases of insolvency or services default (ss23, 24; note the restrictions in ss25, 26). For the protection of customers, the DG is under the duty to review the activities of undertakers and collect information in respect to them (ss28–30).

Water Undertakers

Most provisions of the WIA 1991 are concerned with the water undertakers – companies appointed to provide a public water supply in a specified area. (Some companies also hold appointments under the same legislation as sewage undertakers; others are water companies with no sewerage functions.)

The purpose of the provisions of the Act is to set a clear framework for the privatised water companies. The water undertakers have the following functions, duties and powers: to maintain an efficient and economical water supply (s37); to ensure supplies of water to premises in the undertaker's area (s37), including a duty for domestic supplies (ss52–54) (breach of the duty is actionable by the consumer; there are also provisions for occasions when the water undertaker may cut off the supply (ss60–63)); to cut off supply or to serve a notice on a consumer requiring action to prevent damage to persons or property or contamination or waste of water (s75); to impose temporary hosepipe bans; to maintain and improve its water mains and other pipes (s37); to maintain constant water pressure at a specified level (ss64–66); and to perform any duty imposed by statute or regulation issued by the Secretary of State, concerning, for example, quality of water (standard of 'wholesomeness') (s68).

The main offences that can be committed by the water undertakers include: supplying water that is unfit for human consumption (s70); wasting, contaminating or misusing water (ss71–73); and/or failing to implement any of the duties imposed (the most important of which are described above).

Sewerage Undertakers

These are companies holding appointment under the 1991 Act and provide public sewerage services in a specified role. Ten companies were appointed in 1989 as successors to the former regional water authorities, to act as both sewerage and water undertakers, although in core parts of their areas public water supply responsibilities may be the function of statutory water companies.

Part IV 1991 Act is concerned with sewerage undertakers. A general duty to provide and maintain a system of sewers and sewage disposal is imposed by s94. The undertaker is under the duty to provide a sewer within six months of a request for domestic sewage purposes. Failure to do so is actionable by the consumer as a breach of duty (ss98, 101).

The undertaker, with the consent of the Secretary of State, has powers of compulsory purchase (s155). In addition, he may fix and recover charges for services provided (s142). A wide variety of further powers to be exercised for the purposes of its functions is listed in Part IV.

Trade Effluents

Special provisions concern trade effluent. The occupier of trade premises has to make an application in accordance with s119 WIA 1991 for consent by the undertaker. The consent may be granted subject to conditions and subject to the powers of variation and revocation.

Sewage Sludge

In relation to sewage, it is crucial to note the provisions of Directive 86/278,[7] which covers the use of sewage sludge. Sewage sludge is solid matter that has been filtered out of the sewage during the treatment works. It contains heavy metals and can also release pathogens and bacteria into the air, which could cause harm to human health. It may be disposed of by tipping at sea, burning or burying, but is often used as a fertiliser on farmers' fields, since it is rich in nitrogen and phosphorus. The Directive provides for the protection of the soil when sewage sludge is used in the environment.

Other regulations were issued by the former DoE in form of the Sludge (Agricultural Use) Regulations 1989.[8] In the same year, the DoE published a 'Code of Practice for Agricultural Use of Sewage Sludge'. These ensure that sewage sludge and the soil where it is used in agriculture are tested for safety.

Liquid Effluent and Nitrates

In relation to the liquid effluent filtered out in the course of the treatment works, the applicable legislative requirements are the Council Directive 91/676 (concerning the protection of waters against pollution caused by nitrates from agricultural sources)[9] and Directive 91/72 (the so-called Bathing Water Directive).[10]

The Agricultural Sources Directive provides for the creation of areas designated for particular protection by reason of their higher vulnerability. Decided in accordance with general Common Agricultural Policy, the UK must reward farmers who take voluntary measures to reduce the amount of nitrate discharges on their land. The Directive's validity is at the time of writing being challenged as contrary to the Community 'polluter pays' principle in the case of *R v Secretary of State for the Environment, ex parte Standley.*[11] The case concerns judicial review proceedings of decisions by the Secretary of State on the application of the Nitrates Directive to the rivers Wavene, Blackwater and Chelmer, and the designation of certain areas of land as nitrate-vulnerable zones. The applicants submit that the Secretary of State misdirected himself as to the proper meaning of 'waters affected by pollution' within art 3(1). Alternatively, the applicants submit that the Directive is unlawful and contrary to Community law in that it breaches the 'polluter pays' principle. The case has been referred to the ECJ.

The WRA 1991 makes provision for the designation of water protection zones (s93 and sch 11) and nitrate-sensitive areas (s94 and Sch 12), apparently a step ahead of the above EU Directive that had been issued at the end of the same year.

In order to understand the applicability of the Bathing Water Directive, it is necessary to understand that liquid effluent is usually treated and then discharged into a river or sea, thereby possibly affecting drinking and bathing water.

All waters (inland and coastal) apart from those for therapeutic purposes, swimming pools etc, or in which bathing is not prohibited and is traditionally practised by a large number of bathers, are bathing waters within Directive 76/160. In the UK, the Directive has been implemented by the growing of consents under the EPA 1990 and the WRA 1991 and in accordance with the Bathing Waters (Classification) Regulations 1991 (SI 1991 No 1597).

Tests under this Directive may, if a result is obtained, lead to the bathing area falling below the standard expected. In 1996, in its Fourteenth Report on the quality of bathing water, the European Commission highlighted the difference in quality between coastal and inland bathing waters. Ninety of the seaside beaches met the minimum quality requirement set in the Directive, but one inland bathing area in three falls short of these standards or is not adequately monitored.

Waste Water

Similarly, the Directive on Urban Waste Water Treatment (Directive 91/27)[12] sets the standards for, and even requires the treatment of, waste water that falls below the minimum level in respect of the treatment of waste water from an urban centre prior to its discharge to a receiving water. For certain marine areas, primary (mechanical) treatment might be sufficient, provided it can be proved that the water quality is not adversely affected.

This Directive also provides for the designation of sensitive areas in which more advanced methods of sewage treatment. An example of an area that is likely to be declared sensitive is an area where drinking-water is taken from surface waters. The deadlines for urban areas to achieve the objectives stated in the Directive depend on the sizes of the agglomerations and the character of the receiving water (from 1998 to 2005). By 1998, any discharge of sewage sludge to water bodies is prohibited.

Drinking-Water

The Drinking Water Directive[13] sets stringent standards for the quality of drinking water. Member States have to monitor drinking-water quality and take the necessary steps to ensure compliance with the mandatory standards. In its annexes, the Directive provides the parameters and parametric values, patterns and frequencies of analyses, and reference methods of analysis. The Directive is regularly brought up to date with scientific progress.

The Surface Water for Drinking Water Abstraction Directive[14] concerns the quality required of surface water intended for abstraction and establishes requirements of certain minimum standards. The UK has implemented legislation under which action can be taken against a body that does not meet the requirements. This Directive will be integrated into the Framework Water Directive (below) and expand its use to include waters not only serving a specific human use.

The quality of water is clearly a sensitive matter. Actions of people affected by substances in bathing or drinking-water may consequently lie against the water undertakers. The reason for the contamination may be failure to implement European Directives, although a recognised difficulty is the proof of a causal link between substance and actual harm suffered.

Drinking Water Inspectorate (DWI)

This is an inspectorate appointed as the 'assessors' envisaged by s86 WIA 1991 to monitor the quality of water supplied by statutory water undertakers and to initiate enforcement action to secure compliance with the legislation. Under s18, the Secretary of State is required to take enforcement action unless he is satisfied that the contravention is trivial or that the company has already given an undertaking to take steps to secure compliance. The DWI is responsible for enforcement action when a water quality standard is breached and where there has been a failure to comply with other requirements, such as sampling, analysis or water treatment. The DWI undertakes an ongoing sampling programme and publishes an annual report.

91

Water Pollution Offences

Offences are mainly created under the Water Resources Act 1991 and can be grouped into four broad categories. The first is where any 'poisonous, noxious or polluting matter or any other solid waste matter enters controlled water' (s85(1) WRA 1991).

In *NRA* v *Egger (UK)*,[15] the court interpreted 'polluting matter' to include matter that is 'capable of causing harm in that it may damage a river's potential usefulness'. In this context, 'damage' was said to mean 'harm to animal, vegetable or other life in the river and/or aesthetic damage'.

The word 'poisonous' was said in *Schulmans Inc* v *NRA*[16] to emphasise the need for scientific proof. In that case, the matter entering the river was fuel oil. The prosecution failed since it was held that there was no evidence of the amount of oil needed to enter the river in order to make it poisonous to fish life. 'Any other solid waste matter' covers discarded waste. Such items need not be poisonous.

The second category is the discharge of sewage or trade effluent into controlled waters (s85(3) WRA 1991). This has been discussed above, but it is worth noting that there are new draft regulations that would enable the EA in these circumstances to prevent or clean up water pollution by serving works notices on the responsible parties. The draft regulations also provide for expedited appeals procedures.[17]

The third category is the emission of matter from a sewer or drain in breach of a prohibition notice issued by the EA, or the emission of sewage or trade effluent from a building or fixed plant on to land or lakes or ponds which are not inland freshwaters in breach of a prohibition notice (s85(4) WRA 1991).

The last category is the obstruction of waters so as to cause or worsen pollution (s85(5) WRA 1991.

A common factor of these offences is that they are committed when someone 'causes' or when a person 'knowingly permits' the pollution to occur. Liability under both aspects is strict and neither fault nor negligence is required.

In a leading case *Alphacell* v *Woodward*,[18] Lord Wilberforce held that 'causing' must involve some active operation or chain of operations that result in the pollution of water. He went on to hold that 'knowingly permitting' meant failure to prevent the pollution from occurring coupled with some knowledge.

Defences

There will be a defence to any prosecution where the polluter's actions have been licenced by a relevant body, such as the EA. There is usually also an emergency defence that protects those who have discharged pollutants in emergency situations, probably beyond the polluter's control, to avoid danger to life or health. According to this defence, the steps taken by the polluter must be reasonably practicable in order to minimise the discharge and its polluting effects. It is also necessary to notify the EA.

Penalties

All these offences carry maximum penalties of £20,000 fine and/or three months' imprisonment on summary conviction, and an unlimited fine and/or two years imprisonment on conviction on indictment. The EA may apply to the High Court for an injunction to ensure compliance.

The European Dimension

It is clear from the above that the majority of new developments in water legislation is European based. Water is also one of the most comprehensively regulated areas of EU environmental legislation.

The Commission's 'Guide to the Approximation of European Union Environmental Legislation' identifies several stages of development. The process was first started at the time of the First EAP (1973) and the Surface Water Directive (1975). It followed the Drinking Water Directive (1980) and water quality standard legislation on fish waters (1978), shellfish waters (1979), bathing waters (1976) and groundwaters (1980). In the area of emission limit value legislation, the Dangerous Substances Directive (1976) and its daughter Directives on various individual substances were adopted. These included mercury (1982), cadmium (1983) and HCH (lindane) (1984).

The next wave of legislation followed a review of existing legislation and an identification of gaps to be filled and necessary improvements. The second wave saw the implementation of the Urban Waste Water Directive (1991) and the Nitrates Directive (1991); the updating of the Bathing Water and Drinking Water Directives (1994 and 1995); an Action Programme on Groundwater and a proposal for an Ecological Quality of Water Directive (now to be replaced by the Framework Water Directive, below); and, for large industrial installations, the Integrated Pollution Prevention Control (IPPC) Directive (1996), which extended to water pollution.

A Framework Water Directive

The most important development is the proposal for a new framework Directive covering all types of waters, from ground to surface waters. The framework Directive is to establish a structure within which the objectives can be better integrated at the national or regional level.

According to its introductory comments it requires: river basin management; an assessment of the characteristics of the river basin; monitoring of the status of surface water and groundwater of the river basin; the establishment of programmes of measures to achieve the objective; the summarising of all the above in a 'River Basin Management Plan'; and public consultation on that Plan.

The objective is, therefore, to establish a framework for ground and surface waters which prevents: further deterioration; protects and enhances the status of aquatic ecosystems; promotes sustainable water consumption based on long-term planning of available resources; and contributes to supplying water of the quality and in the quantity needed for sustainable development.

The Directive would introduce the overall (and arguably very vague) objective of achieving 'good' status in all waters by 2010. The Community territory would be divided into river basin districts as a basis for administrative action. Such action in turn is to be based on administrative structures for each district with a view to producing, by the year 2004, a river basin management plan covering the measures to be taken to attain the objectives set. The Directive would also provide for the designation of specially protected areas (notably for the abstraction of drinking water and bathing).[19]

Three different statuses are envisaged: the first is the status already set for dangerous substances, in terms of environmental quality standards; the second is the quantitative status of groundwaters; and the third concerns the ecological quality of surface waters (in turn divided into physiochemical parameters, biological quality and the physical structure of watercourses). The latter is unprecedented in the UK (except for rivers which are classified in terms of their invertebrate populations).

The Future for Other Directives

Within this framework, which is aimed at environmental protection, other legislative proposals, such as the Drinking Water Directive proposal,[20] which are aimed at consumer rather than environmental protection, are to be maintained. In addition, the Bathing Water Directive remains within the framework.

It should be noted that the Directive on Dangerous Substances has not been dealt with in detail in this chapter. This is because it is due to become redundant once the framework Water Directive, the IPPC Directive and a future proposal for a Directive dealing with pollution from small industries have been adopted and are fully implemented.

The Surface Water Directive is proposed to be repealed once the programmes of measures in the framework Directive are in place. However, the Surface Water Directive's requirements are to be replaced with an obligation to identify all water bodies used for the abstraction of drinking-water, including groundwater, and to establish appropriate environmental quality standards to ensure compliance with the Drinking Water Directive following treatment.

The Fish Water Directive and the Shellfish Water Directive[21] are to be repealed. They only apply to waters which the Member States identify as fish water and shellfish water. They do not, therefore, provide the uniform or universal protection a framework Directive would provide.

It will be appreciated that the Directive is still a proposal and will not be implemented before the beginning of the next millennium. However, during the period of coexistence of the proposal with legislation already in force but destined to be repealed, the preamble asks for a particular effort to be made to ensure coherence of activities. The Commission will, in particular, ensure this co-ordination through a committee set up by the Directive.

Summary of Relevant EU Legislation: The Pre-framework Directive

Control of Substances in Water

Directive on pollution (Dangerous Substances Directive) caused by certain dangerous substances discharged in the aquatic environment:

List 1: particularly toxic substances, which persist over a long period without breaking down or which cause a build-up of harmful substances, for example, mercury and cadmium. These substances should be eliminated.

List 2: substances which should be reduced:

- *Metals such as lead and silver.*

- *Substances which affect the smell of drinking-water.*

- *Substances which affect the balance of oxygen in water.*

- *Discharge limits for specific types of industrial sources of 17 substances on a prohibitory list are fixed through a series of seven daughter Directives and are to be integrated into the IPPC Directive.*

- *There are also environmental quality standards (EQSs) for them.*

- *Discharges to the aquatic environment must be authorised.*

Control for Specific Purposes

- *Wholesome water (duty on water undertakers): in the UK, this is regulated by the Water Supply (Water Quality) Regulations 1989.*

- *Quality of Surface (Drinking Water) Water Directive 1975 sets the categories of drinking water quality.*

- *Directive on the sampling and analysis of surface water for drinking 1979 sets sampling procedures.*

- *Quality of Water (Human Consumption) Directive 1980: all water intended for human consumption (including water in food processes); annexed are guide levels or maximum admissible concentrations.*

- *Note: some limited derogation is permitted to Member States*

Bathing Water

- *Bathing Water Directive 1975.*

- *UK, Bathing Waters (Classification) Regulations 1991*

Fish life

*   *Directive on the quality of fresh waters needing protection or improvement in order to support fish life 1978.*

*   *Directive on the quality required for shellfish waters 1979.*

Other Legislation and Measures

*   *Plant Protection Products Directive 1991.*[22]

*   *Habitats Directive.*[23]

*   *Sewage Sludge Directive.*[24]

*   *Environmental Impact Assessment Directive.*[25]

UK Discussions

In 1997 the House of Lords Select Committee on the European Communities discussed the new draft framework Directive on water resources. It was noted that: it is intended that much of the existing water legislation is to be repealed; a key objective is the achievement of 'good' ecological status of all surface and groundwaters; and the draft Directive seeks to introduce water management to be carried out on a river basin basis with the aim of producing a river basin plan by 2004 in order to then recommend measures to achieve the Directive's objective by 2010.

The Select Committee heard evidence by witnesses who expressed the following concerns:[26] there was a general lack of a clear definition of the objectives that were to be achieved by the year 2010; the need to achieve 'good' status was vague (and, one witness contended, if 'good' in the Directive was the same as the criterion in English legislation, then 42 per cent of UK's rivers would need improvement by 2010); the draft Directive's definition of 'good' gave no leeway for variation in climatic, geographical and ecological conditions across the Community; the EA criticised the premature attempt to establish a single EU-wide water classification system - instead the aim should be a convergence of national systems; the proposals on full cost–recovery charging were either praised as realisation of the 'polluter pays' principle or condemned as not taking into account the economic value of the environment.

Other EU Proposals

In addition to the framework legislation, a new draft daughter Directive, intended as a possible amendment to the framework Directive, would strengthen the EC Commission's role in identifying priority substances and proposing discharge limits and environmental quality standards for them. The proposal is intended to update and simplify the 1976 Dangerous Substances Directive by incorporating the mentioned measures into the framework Directive. The Dangerous Substances Directive could then be repealed.

In addition, for the first time, water pollution from products would be addressed in an EC Directive. In outline the key proposals are: the Commission is to prepare a priority list of substances posing an 'unacceptable hazard' to the environment by 31 December 1998 (the basis of selection for the list is risk rather than hazard); and the Commission is entitled to produce further daughter Directives in order to impose further controls, such as for processes regulated by the IPPC Directive.

Concluding Remarks

In conclusion, it is clear from the above that the EU is the most active player in water legislation. In view of the 1997 developments the practitioner should note that important future changes at European level may be expected and should keep abreast of the proposals.

Air Pollution

Introductory Remarks

At EU level, developments regarding air pollution require constant monitoring, while UK regulations dealing with the control of air pollution can broadly be split into two areas. On the one hand, there is the permitting regime under Part I EPA 1990, and, on the other hand, there are various legal controls on emissions to air, including powers given to LAs to control statutory nuisances. While an overview of the UK legislation is given here, the practitioner should note there are a number of areas that are still under discussion or in progress, for example, the long-awaited regulations setting out air quality objectives to be attained by 2005 that were laid before Parliament in November 1997; a new system for informing the public on levels of air pollution that were launched recently by the Department of Environment, Transport and the Regions (DETR); and the UK's air-quality strategy could be affected considerably by four new air-quality standards currently being considered by the Commission.

Local Authority Air Pollution Control (LAAPC)

The system of LAAPC, introduced by Part I EPA 1990, aimed to provide a counterpart to the 'one-stop shop' approach to regulation of pollution emissions from larger industrial sources under the IPC regime. While IPC covers the larger processes, LAAPC covers a much more numerous and wide-ranging group of industrial processes.

Nonetheless, the two systems have much in common, the main difference being that while IPC takes a holistic approach towards regulating industrial emissions to the environment – in so far as permits are issued covering emissions to air and water and waste disposal, and are issued by the same authority (the EA) – LAAPC covers air emissions only. As is discussed elsewhere, other industrial emissions – water discharges and waste disposal – by smaller industrial concerns are regulated under other statutory provisions, and are regulated by different enforcing authorities. The problem of duplication of controls is also addressed under LAAPC and, in particular, special provisions are made to avoid any duplication of controls that may arise, for example, in relation to waste.[27]

Logically, the permitting of air emissions under LAAPC is dealt with at the local level rather than centrally via the EA, and in this area LAs are responsible for regulating these lesser sources of pollution.

It should be mentioned that LAs regulate emissions to air in a number of different ways, and under a variety of enactments and statutory powers in addition to having similar powers to the EA under Part I EPA 1990. They also have controls over smoke pollution. Furthermore, they have powers to control statutory nuisances, and these may include air pollution-related nuisances.

The IPC/LAAPC system applies to the industrial processes and to the substances listed in the Environmental Protection (Prescribed Processes and Substances) Regulations 1991.[28] Whilst processes which are to fall under the system of IPC are listed under Part A of these Regulations, also known as 'Part A Processes', processes which fall under the LAAPC system are listed under Part B of the Regulations, and are known as 'Part B Processes'.

The LAAPC system parallels the IPC system. Prescribed processes designated for local control must not be operated without an authorisation from the local enforcing authority in whose area they are located. Mobile plant must be authorised by the local enforcing authority in whose area the operator has his principal place of business.

The Environmental Protection (Applications, Appeals and Registers) Regulations 1991[29] set out the procedure for applying for such an authorisation.

Operators of prescribed processes must submit a detailed application for authorisation to the local enforcing authority. The application must be made in writing to the LA and must contain information relating to the process, substances resulting from the process, the techniques employed to prevent or reduce their release, and an assessment of the consequences of such releases into the environment.

BATNEEC

Any permission sought for the release of such substances into any environmental media will be subject to the overriding criterion of whether BATNEEC will be used to prevent or reduce the releases. Therefore, LAs are statutorily obliged to include conditions in any authorisation they issue which are designed to ensure that the process is operated using BATNEEC in order to prevent and minimise emissions of prescribed substances and to render harmless any substance that may be emitted.

These conditions may clarify what exactly are the operator's obligations, for example, in relation to emission limits and monitoring of emissions and exhausts. Conditions must also secure compliance with the other objectives specified in s7(2) of the Act. The conditions imposed may relate to issues such as the number, qualifications, training and supervision of the employees and the design, construction, layout and maintenance of the building.

In addition to any specific conditions included in an authorisation, all authorisations implicitly impose a duty on the operator to use BATNEEC in relation to any aspect of the process that is not covered by the specific conditions. This is the so-called 'residual' BATNEEC duty.

Appeals

Operators can appeal against the refusal of an application, against the conditions included in an authorisation, and against the various forms of notice that may be served by a local enforcing authority. Appeals will not put notices into abeyance, except in the case of revocation notices.

Advertisements

All applications for authorisation (except in relation to small waste oil burners and mobile plant) must be advertised locally and full details (except information that is commercially confidential or would prejudice national security) must be made available so that the public can comment before the process is authorised to start operation or to undergo a substantial change.

Registers

LAs must also maintain registers. These are different from the registers maintained by the EA since, in addition, they contain information about IPC-authorised processes which are operating in their locality. Public registers must be set up by each local enforcing authority giving details of all IPC and local enforcing authority air pollution control processes in its area. These must include specified particulars of applications, authorisations, notices, directions issued by the Secretary of State, appeal decisions and monitoring data.

The information relating to IPC processes will be supplied to LAs by the national Agencies (EA or Scottish Environment Protection Agency) as appropriate. Information is to be kept from the register only on grounds of national security or commercial confidentiality.

Charges

LAs are obliged to levy fees and charges in accordance with a scheme prescribed by the Secretary of State. The scheme is reviewed annually. In addition to the application fee, operators of LAAPC sites must pay an annual fee in respect of each authorisation and a further fee when any application for a substantial variation is made.

Review

As with IPC, any authorisation granted must be reviewed at least once every four years. There are also provisions for the operator to be able to apply for a variation of the authorisation.[30]

Enforcement

LAs have powers of enforcement similar to those which are exercisable by the EA under IPC, to ensure that appropriate standards are being met. In particular, LAs can issue enforcement, variation, prohibition and revocation notices to ensure that appropriate standards of control are met, and raised in line with new techniques and new awareness of environmental risk.

Prohibition notices are a mechanism for stopping a process if there is an imminent risk of serious pollution of the environment.

LAs have powers of entry, inspection, sampling, investigation and seizure of articles or substances which are a cause of imminent danger or serious harm.

Guidance

Government guidance is available to LAs in respect of their powers under LAAPC. This guidance deals with the matters required to be covered in authorisations, and also deals in detail with the application of conditions to authorisations. The Secretary of State's Process Guidance Notes (PGs) have been issued to every local enforcing authority on all the main categories of process coming under local enforcing authority control. These Notes also contain the Secretary of State's views on the techniques appropriate in order to achieve the BATNEEC objective, as well as information in relation to any of the other objectives in section 7(2) of the Act. They are likely to be of interest to operators of prescribed processes as well as to LA. The PGs are intended to cover all the main categories of process prescribed for local air pollution control.

The former DoE issued five general PGs, which explain the main controls and procedures. One Upgrading Guidance Note (UG) has also been issued. There are, in addition, an extensive list of PGs dealing with individual, specific processes.

The Clean Air Act 1993

This Act contains controls on dark smoke from chimneys and from industrial or trade premises, smoke, dust and grit from furnaces etc, smoke-control areas and the collection of information. Provisions in earlier Clean Air Acts relating to statutory nuisances caused by smoke have now been moved to the EPA 1990. Furthermore, the 1993 Act specifically provides that prescribed processes under integrated pollution control are excluded from control under the Clean Air Act.[31]

In outline, its provisions are as follows:

- Part I deals with prohibiting dark smoke from the chimneys of any building, or from chimneys which serve furnaces or fixed boilers or industrial plants, or from any industrial or trade premises.

- Part II concerns the emission of smoke, dust or grit from the chimneys of industrial furnaces and provides that the LA may prescribe emission limits. This part also provides the regulations for the height of chimneys.

- Part III gives LAs (and the Secretary of State) power to declare areas as smoke-control areas so as to abate smoke pollution.

- Part IV provides regulatory controls on the content of fuels.

- Part V deals with the publication of information by LAs and with research and education on air pollution problems.

Clean Air and Statutory Nuisance

The provisions relating to statutory nuisance are set out in Part III EPA 1990. The Act restates and updates the law relating to statutory nuisance. It also contains improvements in the summary procedures for dealing with such nuisances. There is a common factor linking those nuisances listed in the EPA. They must be prejudicial to health or a nuisance. These are alternatives. Nuisance is not defined within the Act and the common law must be called in aid to supplement the statute on this point.[32] Prejudice to health is defined s1(7), and means injurious or likely to cause injury to health. LA environmental health officers are responsible for enforcement.

Whereas statutory nuisance is dealt with in greater detail in Chapter 9, certain points should be mentioned here. Section 79 consists of a list of matters which can constitute a statutory nuisance. The list is an expanded version of the previous statute. It is not an exhaustive list.

Provisions relating the clean air are included for the first time alongside other statutory nuisances, although the Clean Air Act 1993, makes further provision in respect of air pollution.

Section 79(1)(b) provides that 'smoke emitted form premises so as to be prejudicial to health or a nuisance' shall constitute a statutory nuisance. This does not cover smoke from chimneys of private dwellings in smoke control areas, dark smoke from boilers or industrial plants, smoke emitted from railway locomotive steam engines or any other dark smoke from industrial or trade premises. However, the EPA 1990 extends statutory nuisance to cover smoke in domestic premises, such as the weekend bonfire.

The original legislation relating to smoke was prompted not by industrial polluters, but by domestic coal burning. The infamous London smog of 1952 prompted the Clean Air Act 1956 which introduced the present system of smoke control.

Dark smoke and black smoke from industrial premises are now covered by the Clean Air Act 1993. Dark and black smoke are determined by comparison with a shade card known as the Ringelmann Chart, but experienced environmental health officers appear to rely on their own judgement, which is acceptable as evidence in a court.

In respect of private premises only, the emissions of fumes or gas is covered in s79(1)(c). Fumes includes solid airborne matter smaller than dust, and gas includes vapour and moisture emitted from vapour.

Under the former provisions, dust and other effluvia were covered. Smell and steam are, therefore, new (s79(1)(d)) and apply to industrial, trade or business premises. The provisions may have particular application to restaurants and launderettes.

It is a defence to prove that the best practicable means were used to prevent, or counteract, the effects of the nuisance (s80(7)). In the case of premises, dust, steam, smell or other effluvia, accumulation or deposits, animals or noise, the defence is only available where the nuisance arises on industrial, trade or business premises. In the case of smoke, the defence is only available where the smoke comes from a chimney. The defence is not available at all where the nuisance consists of fumes or gases, or any other nuisances declared by any other enactments.

'Best practicable means' covers the design, installation, maintenance and manner and periods of operation of plant and machinery, and the design, construction and maintenance of buildings and structures.

Reasonableness is a factor in determining what is practicable. Local conditions and circumstances can be taken into account, together with the current state of technical knowledge and the financial implications.

The LA has a duty to inspect its areas from time to time to detect any statutory nuisances. If a complaint is made by a local resident, the LA must take such steps as are reasonably practicable to investigate the complaint.

Where the LA is satisfied that a statutory nuisance exists or is likely to occur or recur, then it must serve an abatement notice. This must require the abatement of the nuisance or its prohibition or restriction, and will require the execution of such works, and the taking of such other steps, as are necessary (s80(1)). The notice is to be served on the person responsible or, if the nuisance arises from a structural defect, on the owner of the premises. If the person responsible cannot be found, then it must be served on the owner or occupier (s80(2)).

The EPA 1990 introduces a new right of appeal (s80(3)). The person served has a right of appeal within 21 days from service, to the magistrates' court. The grounds of appeal are circumscribed by the Statutory Nuisance (Appeals) Regulations 1990.[33] This prevents appeals being automatically lodged without any justifiable grounds in order to defer the effect of the abatement notice.

While an appeal is pending the abatement notice may be suspended. In order to prevent this the LA may insert a declaration in the abatement notice that it will remain effective on grounds set out in the regulations.

If the person served contravenes or fails to comply with the notice without reasonable excuse, then a criminal offence has been committed (s80(4)). The LA is not obliged to prosecute for failure to comply with a notice.

However, whether or not they prosecute, the LA may abate the nuisance and do whatever works are necessary (s81(3)). It may recover expenses it reasonably incurs in doing this (s81(4)), although it is often reluctant to do so because of the disputes which arise afterwards about the cost of the work or the efficacy of it, or the need for it.

Section 81A, inserted by the Noise and Statutory Nuisance Act 1993, provides that, where the LA incurs expenses in abating or preventing the recurrence of a nuisance, these may be charged on the property to which they relate.

It remains possible for a private individual who is aggrieved by a statutory nuisance to bring private proceedings in the magistrates' court. The court has power to make an order requiring the defendant to abate the nuisance and carry out necessary works (s82). This will, therefore, continue to be useful where an LA declines to act, for whatever reason. This may occur where the nuisance arises in respect of LA accommodation.

The person aggrieved must serve notice on the person responsible stating the intention to bring proceedings and setting out the matter complained of. This is a new provision. The notice period must be at least 21 days. The person to be served must be the person responsible, unless that person cannot be found, when the owner or occupier is liable.

Costs are no longer at the discretion of the court where the nuisance is proved, but are automatically granted to the complainant. Breach of the order constitutes a criminal offence.

EU Legislation

At the time of writing, the government has launched a consultation document on the Integrated Pollution Prevention and Control Directive.[34] This Directive takes an across-the-board approach to the prevention of industrial pollution covering the various media (air, water and soil). It applies the principle of the best environmental option based on the best available techniques. It sets emission limit values and lays down the general principles governing the basic obligations of operators or persons in control of the installations. In particular, a licence will be required to operate new industrial installations or make substantial changes to existing installations. This will be granted after consultation of the public and, where appropriate, after co-ordinated examination by the various competent authorities.

The Directive lists, in detail, the descriptions to be supplied when applying for a licence and includes provisions for checking compliance with, reconsidering and updating licence conditions. The Directive will enter into force on 10 October 1999, but an eight-year transition period has been allowed for existing installations. A 1997 Commission proposal for a Directive on environmental control of installations not covered by the IPPC Directive aims to extend the principle of integrated pollution control. This, in order to cover a wider group of installations, including small- and medium-sized enterprises, which are not covered by the IPPC Directive.

Generally, before the IPPC Directive's across-the-board approach came into effect, European measures could be classified into different categories: emissions for motor vehicles and diesel engines; protection of the ozone layer; lead in air and petrol; and sulphur emissions.

The measures are either directed are aimed at the control of emissions from industrial plants at controlling individual substances.

Controls on Industrial Plants

In 1984, a framework Directive was introduced concerning air pollution from industrial plants.[35] This established in the EU the concept of authorisations for industrial plants – a system already in operation in the UK. Then, the 1988 Directive on the limitation of emissions of certain pollutants into the air from large combustion plants[36] aimed to control emissions by establishing emission limits for new plants, having regard to the principle of

BATNEEC. This Directive was developed, in part, as a result of the international convention on long-range, transboundary pollution originally agreed in Geneva in 1979 and subsequently amended by protocol.

In addition, in 1989 two Directives were published that concerned emissions from new and existing waste incineration plants.[37]

Controls on Substances

There are Directives which control gaseous emissions from engines. They deal with emissions from motor vehicles, tractors and diesel engines.[38] These Directives adopt the technical requirements laid down by the United Nations Economic Commission for Europe. Relevant requirements cover matters such as the approval of vehicles and the adoption of uniform conditions for the approval of motor vehicle parts and equipment. The directives are extremely technical. By way of example, there are tests relating to the emission of carbon dioxide at idling speed and the durability of anti-pollution devices.

The European legislation does not impose binding requirements on the Member States. The Member States need not adapt their own legislation to take account of the measures in the Directives. However, what they may not do is ban the import of cars and other specified vehicles from other Member States which comply with the requirements of the Directives. This means that if a vehicle is manufactured which complies with the requirements of the Directive, then it is guaranteed freedom of movement throughout the EU. If the vehicle does not comply, another Member State can refuse to import it. This, therefore, is an effective measure for achieving compliance with an environmental standard.

Sulphur in the Atmosphere

There are several ways to control the presence of sulphur in the atmosphere. The aim of the Directive on the sulphur content of liquid fuels is to reduce the amount of sulphur emitted from fuel by reducing the amount contained in fuel in the first place.[39] Almost all organic fuels contain some sulphur. When the fuel is burned it converts the sulphur into sulphur dioxide which, in turn, when it enters the atmosphere, is transformed into sulphuric acid. This is one of the basic causes of acid rain.

Sulphur dioxide in the atmosphere is further controlled along with smoke in Directive 80/779[40] which prescribes air limit values. Evidently the combination of sulphur dioxide and smoke at low levels in the atmosphere is particularly dangerous for people breathing it and can cause lung-related diseases, such as bronchitis and lung cancer. The scientific community, however, has not made it clear as to whether these two substances are synergistic, that is, whether the combined effect of the two is more serious than the effect of each of them taken separately.[41] Nevertheless, this is implemented in the UK by the Air Quality Standards Regulations 1989. This is an area of ongoing discussion and concern.

Lead in the Atmosphere

Lead is controlled in a manner rather like that of sulphur. Limit values are imposed for the amount of lead detected in air[42] and in petrol.[43] The former measure is implemented by the Air Quality Standards Regulations 1989, and the latter by the Motor Fuel (Lead Content of Petrol) Regulations 1981, as amended. The Directive on lead in petrol was amended to introduce the requirement that unleaded petrol should be available on the market.

A controversial proposal was the Directive on the biological screening for lead.[44] The object of the proposal was to screen the population every two years and to set mandatory standards for lead levels in the human body. This proposal was watered down and the current Directive effected two screenings of the population for reference purposes only. In the UK, these took place in 1979 and 1981. Most of the groups sampled met the reference levels in the Directive. These are not the only surveys undertaken in the UK for this purpose, but have contributed more information on the subject.

There are also European provisions level controlling the presence of nitrogen dioxide[45] in the air, and preventing and reducing pollution by asbestos.[46]

Chloroflourocarbons (CFCs)

There have been various measures aimed at controlling the presence of CFCs in the atmosphere. CFCs are a group of stable, man-made, gaseous compounds which became widely used in aerosols, fire protection equipment, refrigerants and air conditioning because they were considered 'safe'. They are also used in the manufacture of polyurethane foam. CFCs are non-flammable and are effective as propellants. However, they are alleged to be one of the causes of the deterioration of the ozone layer, and, as such, have been subjected to international and European controls.

The direction of the controls has been to limit the use of CFCs in manufacturing industries. In 1980, the EU passed a decision which sought to reduce the levels of two particular types of CFCs used in aerosol cans to the level used in 1976.[47] This was allowed by a further decision in 1982,[48] which provided a precise definition of production capacity for the whole Community and a co-operation procedure between the Member States and the Commission as regards information gathering and evaluation.

At this stage, concern about the ozone layer was becoming a matter of international concern and in 1985 the Vienna Convention for the Ozone Layer was negotiated. The problems of trying to operate at international level are clear in the development of this convention as well as in subsequent developments. Clearly, the Third World has been concerned that its developing industrial economies should not be stifled and whilst the industrialised countries had the research and development facilities to develop alternative technologies, such facilities were not available to them. Meanwhile the EU has been concerned about the cost to industry of requiring new processes to be developed. The USA supported a reduction of CFCs on the ground that it had taken unilateral action already and did not wish to be disadvantaged in commercial terms. As a result, the Convention did very little other than urge that something should be done.

In 1987, the Montreal Protocol on substances that deplete the ozone layer was agreed. In total, 132 signatory nations were involved. This Protocol established targets for the reduction and eventual elimination of ozone-depleting substances. It also provided for enabling the transfer of technology between the industrialised countries and the developing countries, and delimits some controls on the trade of ozone-depleting substances. The Community, along with about 50 other parties, agreed the Protocol which has subsequently been amended in the light of advances in technology.

In 1988, the EU adopted a regulation on the depletion on the ozone layer[49] which was replaced and strengthened in 1991 by a further regulation.[50] In some ways, this Regulation introduces measures that are more severe than those agreed in the Protocol. It controls the import and export of CFCs and other ozone-depleting substances; it controls production and consumption in order to phase out these substances; and it deals with management, data reporting and inspection. The 1991 Regulation was amended in 1992.[51] There are also two Council Decisions which allocate import quotas for CFCs and other ozone-depleting substances.[52]

Finally, there is a Directive which deals with the presence of ozone at low levels in the atmosphere which can be a hazard to human health and the environment. The Directive enables the provision of measuring stations and the exchange of information between Member States to enable the public to take precautionary measures.

As was indicated in Chapter 1, virtually the same politics as at the Vienna negotiations determined the negotiations before the most recent agreement, achieved in Kyoto in December 1997. The agreement provides for further cuts averaging 5.2 per cent in greenhouse gases from 1990 levels in the period from 2008–2012. The most notable results were that the USA, the world's largest producer of greenhouse gases, committed itself to cut emissions by 7 per cent; through US pressure emissions trading was introduced (ie the possibility of purchasing another country's quotas); Japan accepted a 6 per cent cut in emissions; Australia is one of only three countries to benefit from a policy of differentiation (which takes account of a country's varying needs) and is entitled to increase greenhouse gas emissions.

The Future for Air Quality in the EU

One of the key areas that addresses many of the concerns of 'sustainable development' is that of future air quality in Europe. A framework Directive on Ambient Air Quality Assessment and Management made its way through the European policy-making system in 1996. The Directive create an EU-wide basis for managing and assessing ambient air quality, including identification of polluted areas requiring particular attention. With this comes an obligation for Member States to maintain good ambient air quality where it already exists, improve air quality where it is poor and provide air-quality information to the public.

Fourteen pollutants will be given safe limits and alert-threshold values: sulphur dioxide, nitrogen dioxide/oxide, black smoke, suspended particulate matter, lead and ozone (all covered in previous EU legislation, and new limits are projected to come in by the end of 1998); carbon monoxide, cadmium, acid deposition, benzene, polycyclic aromatic hydrocarbons, arsenic, flouride and nickel (for which levels will be introduced by the end of 1999).

At the time of writing, a draft daughter Directive containing new air-quality standards for sulphur dioxide, nitrogen dioxide, lead and fine particles has been issued by the Commission: it is the first 'daughter' of the 1996 framework Directive. It demonstrates a cautious two-stage approach because of uncertainties over the sources of pollutants and behaviour.

The levels set will relate to health and environmental effects, and will emerge in daughter Directives to the framework. A common position of the framework was agreed by the Council of Ministers in June 1995. While the daughter Directives are being set, the World Health Organisation (WHO) will be reviewing guidelines on ambient air pollution. These developments highlight the increasing emphasis on public information, as well as the interaction between the environment, health and safety and the need to consider international repercussions.

---

[1] N Haigh 'EEC Environmental Policy and Britain' (2nd edn, 1989), p71
[2] Directive 75/440: OJ 1975 L194/26
[3] Directive 79/869: OJ 1979 L271/44
[4] Surface Waters (Abstraction for Drinking Water) (Classification) Regulations 1996, SI 1996 3001
[5] Halsbury's Statutes, Vol 49 Water
[6] Section 2 EA 1995
[7] Directive 86/278: OJ 1986 L181/6
[8] SI (1989) No 1263. Further reference: House of Lords Select Committee on the European Communities 'Sewage Sludge in Agriculture' (1983) HMSO
[9] Directive 91/676: OJ 1991 L375
[10] Directive 91/72: OJ 1991 L16/29
[11] 7 May 1997, QBD (Potts J); sub nom *R* v *Secretary of State for the Environment, ex parte Metson*
[12] Directive 91/27: OJ 1991 L16/29
[13] 80/778 supra
[14] 75/440 supra
[15] (1992) 4 Land Management [1992] Env LR 130, 209 ENDS Report
[16] (1992) 4 Land Management [1992] Env LR 130, 3 Water Law 72
[17] 4/8/97 DETR
[18] [1972] 2 All ER 475
[19] Commission Communication COM(97)49
[20] OJ C 131, 1995, p5
[21] OJ 1978 L222/1 and OJ 1979 L281/47
[22] Directive 94/414
[23] Directive 92/43
[24] Directive 86/278
[25] Directive 85/37
[26] ENDS Report 270, July 1997, p31f
[27] Environmental Protection (Prescribed Processes and Substances) Regulations 1991, Sch 2, r5
[28] SI 1991 No 472, as amended by the Environmental Protection (Amendment of Regulations) Regulations 1991, SI 1991 No 836 and the Environmental Protection (Prescribed Processes and Substances) (Amendment) Regulations 1992, SI 1992 No 614

[29] SI 1991 No 507, as amended by the Environmental Protection (Amendment of Regulations) Regulations 1991, SI 1991 No 836
[30] SI 1991 No 507 supra
[31] Clean Air Act 1993, s41
[32] *National Coal Board* v *Thorne* [1976] 1 WLR 543
[33] SI 1990 No 2276
[34] Directive 96/61
[35] Directive 84/360: OJ 1984 L188/20
[36] Directive 88/609 OJ 1988 L336/1
[37] Directive on the Prevention of Air Pollution from New Municipal Waste Incineration Plants, Directive 89/369: OJ 1989 L163/32 and Council Directive on the Prevention of Air Pollution from Existing Municipal Waste Incineration Plants, Directive 89/429: OJ 1989 L203/50
[38] See Directive on the Approximation of Laws of Member States Relating to Measures to be Taken Against Air Pollution by Gases from Engines of Motor Vehicles, Directive 70/220: OJ 1970 L76, implemented under the Road Vehicles (Construction and Use) Regulations 1986 and the Motor Vehicle (Type Approval) Regulations 1980. Directive Relating to the Measure to be Taken Against the Emission of Pollutants from Diesel Engines for Use in Vehicles, Directive 72/306: OJ 1972 L190, as amended
[39] Directive on the Approximation of Laws Relating to the Sulphur Content of Certain Liquid Fuels, Directive 75/716: OJ 1975 L307/22, as amended. This Directive was replaced by Directive 93/12: OJ 1993 which sets stricter limits as of 1 October 1994
[40] Directive 80/779: OJ 1980 L229/30
[41] See, for instance, the evidence of Professor Lawther to the House of Lords' Scrutiny Committee on this Directive
[42] Directive on Limit Values for Lead in Air, Directive 82/884: OJ 1982 L378/15, as amended by Directive 91/692: OJ 1991 L377/48
[43] Directive 85/210: OJ 1985 L96/25, as amended
[44] Directive on Biological Screening of the Population for Lead, Directive 77/312: OJ L105/10
[45] Directive 85/203: on Air Quality Standards for Nitrogen Dioxide, OJ 1985 L87/1
[46] Directive 87/217: on the Prevention and Reduction of Pollution by Asbestos, OJ 1987 L85/40
[47] Council decision concerning chlorofluorocarbons in the environment (80/372/EEC): OJ 1980 L90/45
[48] Council decision of 15 November 1982 on the consolidation of precautionary measures concerning chlorofluorocarbons in the environment (82/795/EEC): OJ 1982 L329/29
[49] Regulation 3322/88: OJ 1988 L297/1
[50] Regulations on substances that deplete the ozone layer, 91/594: OJ 1991 L67/1
[51] Regulation 92/3952: OJ 1993 L405/41 and Council Regulation 3093/94: OJ 1994 L333/1
[52] Council decision of 15 July 1991 (91/359/EEC): OJ 1991 L193/42, and Council decision of 5 February 1992 (92/94/EEC): OJ 1992 L35/31 and a Commission decision on the quantities of controlled substances that deplete the ozone layer: 95/324

Chapter 6

Waste Management

The Classification of Waste

Part II EPA 1990 (formerly Part I Control of Pollution Act 1974 and before that the Deposit of Poisonous Waste Act 1972) provides no conclusive definition of the term 'waste'. The EPA 1990 provides in section 72(2) that waste includes: any substance which constitutes a scrap material or an effluent or other unwanted surplus substance arising from the application of any process; and any substance or article which requires to be disposed of as being broken, worn out, contaminated or otherwise spoiled.

The classification of waste is useful for two reasons. First, to determine the controls that are appropriate to deal with it. The more hazardous the waste, whether directly or potentially, the more stringent the controls that are required. Waste which is deadly on contact needs to be more rigorously controlled than waste which is stable and harmless. Dangerous waste should be distinguished from other types of waste.

Secondly, to make an economic distinction as there is an international market for waste. Waste is an economic product which is bought and sold on the international market. It is transported across land and sea and, if hazardous, needs particular care. There is, therefore, a need to have an internationally agreed definition of what constitutes waste which is particularly dangerous as a basis for agreed protocols on packing and management of such waste.

Due to the transboundary repercussions of waste management, this chapter comments on developments at EU and international level, as well as on comparative jurisdictions.

Dangerous Waste

Depending upon the jurisdiction, dangerous waste is may also be termed 'special waste', 'hazardous waste' or 'toxic waste'. In particular, it is useful to compare the approaches in the USA and Europe.

The USA

In the USA, dangerous waste is listed by the US Environment Protection Agency (EPA) and is characterised by such features as its flammability, its corrosiveness, its reactivity or its toxicity.[1]

A US definition was provided by the Resource Conservation and Recovery Act 1976 (RCRA) which defined hazardous waste as a solid waste or combination of solid wastes which, because of its quantity, concentration or physical, chemical or infectious characteristics may cause or significantly contribute to an increase in mortality; or increase in serious irreversible or incapacitating reversible illness or pose a substantial present or potential hazard to human health or the environment when improperly treated, stored, transported or disposed of, or otherwise managed.

Such wastes are then subject to a specific form of management. The effect of the American EPA's method of listing is extremely wide as no thresholds are specified. Therefore, any form of waste containing a listed substance is classified as hazardous waste and treated accordingly, even if the quantity of the proscribed substance is small and causes no damage.

Meanwhile attempts to define the term 'hazardous' or 'toxic' waste by reference to substances or properties have bedevilled the efforts of international organisations. As mentioned below, in 1989 an international convention on the control of the transboundary movements of hazardous wastes and their disposal was finally negotiated and agreed at Basel. This Convention adopted a similar approach to the principles adopted in the USA for the definition of hazardous waste. Annex I of the Convention lists categories of waste which are deemed to be hazardous unless they do not contain any of the characteristics listed in Annex II. There are 18 'waste streams' in Annex I, which include, for example, clinical waste for hospitals, waste from the manufacture of wood-preserving chemicals and waste oils. It also includes a list of key constituents, for instance: mercury, lead and asbestos. These constituents must then possess one of the characteristics contained in Annex III, such as being flammable, explosive, toxic or ecotoxic.

Toxic is defined as having effects if breathed in, eaten or absorbed by the skin, and includes carcinogenicity. Ecotoxic is defined as having an adverse effect on the environment by means of bioaccumulation or by having a toxic effect on biotic systems.

Whereas these definitions are apparently detailed and profound, as in other areas of environmental regulation, in fact a gap between scientific knowledge and environmental regulation exists. This is acknowledged in the Convention itself since not all hazards from waste are fully understood. Moreover, in many areas tests do not exist to assess the potential hazards, and ecotoxicity is a particularly undefined area which depends to a considerable degree not on scientifically-valid tests, but on political pressure.

The Convention also recognises wastes which are not mentioned in its text, but which are accepted as hazardous at national level, as being covered by the provisions of the Convention.

Europe

At European level, the definition of hazardous waste essentially reflects that found in the Basel Convention. The directive on hazardous waste,[2] effective from 31 December 1993, replaced the original 1978 Directive.[3] The Directive, as amended by Directive 94/31, lays down specific rules applicable to the management of hazardous waste. It attempts to establish controls appropriate for the most potentially harmful wastes referred to in Council Decision 94/906. These apply in addition to the general rules on waste management contained in the Waste Framework Directive which is discussed further below. The Hazardous Waste Directive expresses the need to establish a precise and uniform definition of hazardous waste based on experience.

As in the Basel Convention, the Directive cites a list of different categories of waste and wastes with certain constituents, which, if they have certain properties, will be defined as hazardous. The list is more detailed than in the Basel Convention. A further list is to be drawn up which will take additional matters into account in order to provide more detail on the question of determining which waste is hazardous. It is more specific about the origin and composition of the waste and limits values for the concentration of the constituents. This list will prevent waste from being classified as hazardous where only a small amount of the prescribed constituents is present. However, the question of scientific verification remains open, for example, in assessing what makes a waste ecotoxic. Moreover, in view of the sensitivity of the area it may well be that the answer will depend on political prejudice rather than scientific precepts.

The UK

In the UK, hazardous waste and toxic waste are not strictly technical terms in law and dangerous waste is described as 'special waste'. Special waste is waste which 'may be so dangerous or difficult to treat, keep or dispose of that special provision is required for dealing with it'.[4] The current definition of which types of waste fall within this category is generally set out in the Control of Pollution (Special Waste) Regulations 1980. Draft Special Waste Regulations were published by the then DoE for public consultation on 27 May 1995 and came into force on 1 September 1996. These regulations are intended to implement and comply with the Hazardous Waste Directive 91/689 by modifying the Control of Pollution (Special Waste) Regulations 1980.

The Regulations include a detailed guide to the definition of special waste; technical aspects of waste assessment, including the hazard criteria; and the decision-making process on the status of wastes.

A list of substances, such as acids and alkalis, lead and mercury compounds and laboratory chemicals, appears in Schedule 1. In order to be classified as special waste, however, any of the substances must satisfy other specific tests. These tests relate to the effect of the substances on human health: they must be either 'dangerous to life' or they must have a flash point (catch fire or explode) of 21°C or less.

'Dangerous to life' clearly means human life.[5] Reference to human life alone demonstrates the changes that have occurred in the last 15 years. It means that special waste in the UK is currently outdated by reference to its effect on humans and not to the wider environment. The effect on humans is also defined as a direct effect as it is to be tested by its effect if certain quantities are swallowed, inhaled or come into contact with the skin or eyes. This definition is narrower than the definitions at European and international level and requires amendment. Its limited approach contrasts with the general developments in environmental law and policy, which consider broader issues of environmental damage (see Chapter 2).

Mining and Quarry Waste

As can be seen in Chapter 3, this is dealt with generally under other areas of legislation, in particular land-use planning. Nevertheless, the Secretary of State does have power to make this type of waste and agricultural waste subject to the provisions applicable for dealing with general waste.

Radioactive Waste

Although hazardous to humans and the wider environment, radioactive waste is generally excluded from the definitions and controls of dangerous waste as it is covered by its own special provisions.[6]

Other Controlled Waste

In the UK, other waste is referred to as 'controlled waste', that is, that waste which is subject to controls apart from special waste. This includes household, industrial and commercial waste.[7]

Household waste includes waste from domestic premises, caravan sites, residential homes, educational establishments and nursing homes.

Industrial waste includes waste from factories, public transport facilities such as airports and bus stations, and premises used for the provision of public utilities.

Commercial waste means waste from premises used for a trade or business or for recreational purposes.

These definitions may be subject to interpretation by the courts. For example, in the judgment of the Divisional Court in *Thanet District Council* v *Kent County Council*,[8] it was held that seaweed which was collected from the beach by the authority in order to enhance the amenity of the area, and which was dumped on other land, was not controlled waste.

The Regulatory Framework in the EU

When advising on waste management, practitioners must have regard to EU developments in particular. Moreover, when considering waste management, disposal and clean-up, as well as the environmental concerns raised, it must be understood that the regulatory framework, both at the EU and national levels, is still being debated and altered, just as it is in the USA. This is the reason why the description of European common positions and communications, which may be preliminary to the regulatory enactments, is discussed below. The law is in a state of flux and will be influenced by the positions taken in those documents.

Nevertheless, what is clear is that the rules are likely to become increasingly strict. In accordance with the EU's Fifth EAP, covering the period 1993–2000 and entitled 'Towards Sustainability', certainly such strict principles as 'the polluter pays' will be developed further. This principle was adopted by the Organisation for Economic Co-operation and Development (OECD) countries in 1972, and was incorporated in the EC's First EAP. As discussed in Chapter 2, it is now contained in the Treaty of Rome (art 130R (2)).

Under the 'polluter pays' principle, polluters should bear the full cost of prevention and minimisation of pollution and of remedying environmental damage, and this cost should be reflected in the cost of goods and services which cause pollution in their production, consumption or disposal.

These matters are very much part of the wider debate about environmental liability, which includes the problem of 'historic pollution' in relation to contaminated land, and is therefore an important area of future developments to be studied.

The Dobris Report

In order to reach a solution to the growing problem of waste management, proper sources of information and comparative statistics are vital. The European Environmental Agency (EEA) was created, in particular, to be a source of information on the state of the environment in Europe. Its duties are likely to become increasingly significant and are set out in brief in Chapter 10.

In 1993, the EEA published the Dobris Report, a comprehensive report on the state of Europe's environment. The Report combines environmental information from central, eastern and western Europe, and tackles all environmental media. In keeping with the EEA's duties as a gatherer of information, the Report appraises the quality of the environmental data, exposing gaps and monitoring shortfalls. It identifies the most pressing problems without prescribing solutions. The Report covers 46 countries and was commissioned by the European Environment Ministers at Dobris Castle in Czechoslovakia in 1991. When a task force for the EEA was formed in 1993, it inherited the job of producing the report. Its editor believes that the Dobris Report is the most 'objective analysis possible' and should form a 'reliable and rigorous basis for decision-making'.

While it is aimed at policy-makers, the hope is that the Report will also raise public awareness. According to the findings of the Dobris Report, Europe has only 13 per cent of the world's population yet it emits 25 per cent of all greenhouse gases, consumes 40 per cent of all ozone-depleting chemicals and generates 40 per cent of the world's waste. It revealed that relevant data, which spans the period from the late 1980s to 1993, remains patchy in terms of availability and quality throughout Europe.

Waste was one of the key issues among wide-ranging topics addressed, and in the report there is some praise for emission reduction by industry through energy efficiency and waste minimisation programmes, such as in the context of the Aire and Calder Project and its sister and daughter projects in the UK.

EU Legislation

In particular, the EU legislative process relies on Regulations (directly applicable) and Directives (requiring national implementation). The various instruments are referred to in art 189 Treaty of Rome. The choice of instruments has regard to the principle of subsidiarity which is a doctrine embedded in art 3b of the Treaty, as amended by Maastricht which provides:

'In areas which do not fall within its exclusive competence, the Community shall take action, in accordance with the principle of subsidiarity, only if and insofar as the objectives of the proposed action can not be sufficiently achieved by the Member States and can, therefore, by reason of the scale of effects of the proposed action, be better achieved by the Community.'

While there has been considerable debate over the extent of competence of the EU as a result of this doctrine, key aspects of waste management have been developed at EU level. As regards waste, the main instrument that set out EU strategy was the Waste Framework Directive. According to the European legislative procedure framework, Directives set out basic objectives. They are then followed by subsidiary Directives known as daughter Directives, which set out more precisely the objectives which the Member States must achieve.

The Framework Directive

The European regime relating to the control of waste is founded on the 1975 framework Directive on waste,[9] as amended in 1991.[10] This Directive states that its objectives include the protection of human health and the environment and that the recovery of waste should be encouraged. It provides for a system of permits for the treatment, storage and tipping of waste, and the application of the 'polluter pays' principle in respect of costs not covered by the proceeds from treating the waste.

It also advocates the development of measures at national level to prevent or reduce waste, such as clean technologies and the development of products which make the smallest possible contribution to increasing waste or other pollution hazards.

As a framework Directive, this has been followed by a number of daughter Directives dealing with narrower areas. For example, the 1976 Directive on the disposal of polychlorinated biphenyls and polychlorinate terphenyls[11] recognises the special hazards of these materials which are used as insulating material in transformers. They are very toxic and the Directive prescribes particular measures to control their disposal.

Of more general application is the 1991 Directive on hazardous waste.[12] This Directive prescribes more stringent rules for dealing with dangerous waste. It provides for the recording and identification of such waste when it is tipped and sets out rules for the mixing of such waste.

Amendments to the Framework Directive

In March 1991, the Council substantially amended the Waste Framework Directive. As amended, art 1(a) of the Directive defines waste to mean 'any substance or object in the categories set out in Annex I which the holder discards or intends or is required to discard'. There are certain substances and objects, which, if they come within art 2 of the Directive, are excluded from the definition, such as gaseous wastes. Although the term 'discard' is an essential feature of this definition, it is not in fact defined in the Waste Framework Directive. The 'holder' is defined to mean the producer of the waste or the person who is in possession of it. The 'producer' is defined to mean anyone whose activities produce waste and/or anyone who carries out pre-processing, mixing or other operations resulting in a change in the nature or the composition of the waste. The key concept which distinguishes waste under EU law is whether the materials have been discarded by the holder or are intended, or are required, to be discarded.

Outline of the Framework Directive

Article 3 encourages Member States to prevent the production and to recover waste by means of recycling, re-use, or reclamation.

Article 4 requires Member States to 'take the necessary measures to ensure that waste is recovered or disposed of without endangering human health' or the environment. Member States shall also 'prohibit the abandonment, dumping, or uncontrolled disposal of waste'.

Article 5 requires Member States to take 'appropriate measures ... to establish integrated and adequate disposal installations, taking account of the best available technology not involving excessive costs. The network must enable the Community as a whole ... and the Member States to move toward' self-sufficiency in waste disposal. In so doing the Member States must 'ensure a high level of protection for the environment and public health'.

Articles 6–9 require the Member States to create or designate an authority to be responsible for the implementation of this Directive. Such authority shall be required to draw up as soon as possible one or more waste management plans. Such authority will also be responsible for issuing permits relevant to certain activities.

Article 11 allows for exemptions from the permit process and requirement.

Article 15 states that, in accordance with the 'polluter pays' principle, the cost of waste must be borne by the holder of waste, the previous holders or the producer of the product from which the waste came.

Article 16 requires Member States to report to the Commission every three years on the measures taken to comply with this Directive.

The Annexes list the categories of waste, disposal operations subject to permitting procedures and operations which may lead to recovery.

Annex I lists some 16 categories of waste (Q1/Q16). These include production or consumption residues, of specification products, spilled, lost or contaminated materials, products for which the holder has no further use, and contaminated materials resulting from remedial action with respect to land. The final category, Q16, covers any materials, substances or products not contained in the previous 15 categories. A list of wastes falling within the Annex I categories was published in January 1995 and is known as the 'European Waste Catalogue'. This was drawn up by the Commission in accordance with the Waste Framework Directive in order to harmonise nomenclature in the European Communities.

Case Law

The definition of waste has been the subject of litigation in the EU and has various meanings in different states. As has been mentioned above, under EU law a definition of waste was provided by the original Waste Framework Directive. It defined waste as 'any substance or object which the holder disposes of or is required to dispose of pursuant to the National Law in force'. The ECJ joined cases *Vasseso* and *Zanetti*, Cases C-206/88 and C-207/88 and held that under this definition substances or objects which were capable of economic re-utilisation were not excluded from the definition of waste. It also held that it was not a necessary component of the definition that the holder must have intended to exclude all possibility of economic reutilisation of the material by others. These aspects were confirmed in the more recent case of *Tombesi*.[13]

There has been some question over the possibility of citizens' law suits which have led to judicial interpretation in respect of the Waste Framework Directive. In a decision of the ECJ, *Comitato di Coordinamento per la Difesa Della Cava* v *Regions Lombardia* Case C-236/92 (23 February 1994), the court ruled that art 4 of the Framework Directive is not directly effective, thus precluding individuals to file a suit based on it. Yet it should be understood that the opportunity for citizens' suits is still likely to develop in the context of the broader 'environmental liability' regime.

Communication from the Commission: A Community Strategy for Waste Management (1996)

In July 1996 the Commission approved a Communication on a revised waste management strategy. This will place higher priority on producer responsibility and reaffirms commitment to prevention and waste recovery. This strategy must still be approved by the Council of Ministers and the European Parliament, and is expected to be a subject of great debate. Nevertheless, an outline of the Commission position is informative in that it will generally define the terms of reference upon which future changes, if any, will be based.

The Communication establishes as the general objective of the EU's waste management policy the need to ensure a high degree of environmental protection without distorting the functioning of the internal market, with a view to promoting sustainable development. To reach this twofold objective, the Communication spells out the following elements as being of paramount importance: a comprehensive and integrated legal framework and appropriate definitions of waste-related concepts.

The Communication highlights the need for suitable rules and principles: proximity and self-sufficiency, as well as the need for reliable and comparable data.

The Communication confirms the hierarchy of principles previously established that prevention of waste shall remain the first priority, followed by recovery and, finally, by the safe disposal of waste. The implementation of this hierarchy should be guided by considering the best environmental solution, taking into account economic and social costs, generally regarded as a cost-benefit analysis. It is clear that a hierarchical approach to waste management is becoming increasingly recognised. The communication therefore dealt with its components.

The Prevention Principle

As regards the prevention principle, the following measures should be particularly developed:

- the promotion of clean technologies and products;

- the reduction of the hazardousness of wastes;

- the establishment of technical standards;

- the establishment of EC-wide rules to limit the presence of certain dangerous substances in products;

- the promotion of re-use and recycling schemes;

- the appropriate use of economic instruments, eco-balances, eco-audit schemes, life-cycle analysis and actions on consumer information and education as well as the development of the eco-label system.

The Recovery Principle

The recovery principle requires that, where environmentally sound, preference should in general be given to the recovery of material over energy recovery operations. This reflects the greater effect on the prevention of waste produced by material recovery rather than by energy recovery.

Safe Final Disposal

Concerning final disposal, particular care should be taken to avoid as much as possible incineration operations without energy recovery. Uncontrolled landfilling and contaminated sites are two problems requiring special and strong actions at different levels. Further comment on these matters occurs later in this chapter, as well as elsewhere in the text.

Producer Responsibility

The strategy addresses the question of producer responsibility. Producers, material suppliers, trade, consumers and public authorities share specific waste management responsibilities having regard to the life-cycle of a product from manufacture until the end of its useful life. However, it is the product manufacturer who has a predominant role, since it is he that takes the key decisions concerning his product which largely determine its waste management potential. This principle will thus be integrated in future measures, on a case-by-case basis, taking into account the specific responsibilities of the different economic operators.

For example, the automobile manufacturing sector has been selected as a priority sector for the implementation of this principle. This will mean that vehicle manufacturers will have responsibility for their products through to disposal: there are even discussions that this responsibility may be retrospective. It is also to be noted that such an approach, once adopted, is likely to set a precedent for other sectors.

Shipment of Waste

The strategy reaffirms the need for appropriate control of shipment of waste within the legal framework set up by Regulation (EEC) No, 259/93.[14] The trans-shipment of waste is discussed further below in connection with means of disposal. Particular attention is to be paid to achieve the double objective of ensuring a high level of environmental protection without distorting the functioning of the internal market. The appropriate application of the proximity and self-sufficiency principles is needed.

The effects of these principles are that waste must be disposed of in one of the nearest appropriate installations, and waste which is generated within the EU should not be disposed of elsewhere. It should be understood that these principles only apply to waste destined for disposal, not to waste for recovery.

Common Position (EC) No 4/96 Adopted by the Council, on 6 October 1995 with a view to adopting Council Directive No 489 (3/12/96) on the Landfill of Waste

The issue of landfill is another area of grave concern and differing attitudes among the Member States. The Common Position achieved by the Council of Ministers was rejected by the European Parliament and, as a result, the Landfill Directive was set back some time. In March 1997, the Commission adopted a new proposal. Its main aim is to reduce the adverse environmental impact of the landfilling of waste, by setting very stringent standards for landfilling while encouraging waste prevention, recycling and disposal.

The main elements of the proposal are as follows:[15] the setting of quantified targets for the reduction of the proportion of biodegradable waste that is landfilled; the obligation for waste to be treated before it is landfilled; a ban on the landfilling of used tyres; an increase in the cost of landfilling; reinforcement of the general requirements for landfills, in particular, introduction of a minimum distance between landfills and residential areas; and stricter provisions for existing landfills.

It appears that at the centre of the objections to the Common Position is the desire of many remote regions of the EU to avoid any liability under the Directive. The Council of Ministers attempted to meet that objection by providing an exclusion for small landfills in rural areas with a population density below 35 people per square kilometre. This raised concerns that the legislation could seriously weaken environmental protection standards across much of the EU by providing too large a loophole. Nevertheless, those provisions not dealing with liability are likely to be kept in some form or another and, in fact, considerable progress on the draft Directive has been made.

In this context, landfill is the burial of waste in the ground, often in voids resulting from the extraction of minerals. Conditions attached to waste management licences regulate the kinds of waste which each landfill site may accept. This is not only to ensure that special wastes are only landfilled, if at all, at suitable sites, but also to control the generation of leachate and landfill gas. The draft Directive seeks to allow landfills to receive only certain stipulated types of waste and to restrict the practice of co-disposal. It also seeks to raise the standards to which landfills are to be operated throughout the EU. In the past, the Commission has expressed the view that the cost of disposal of waste to landfill is too low compared to other methods of disposal and should be increased. It has also regarded landfill as the last resort in the hierarchy of waste management options.

Recent Developments

Considerable political controversy surround the proposal for a landfill Directive. Ministers had to be pressed by Ms Bjerregaard, as the European Commissioner, not to adopt a formal Common Position on the Directive, since this would have gone against the convention that the European Parliament should first deliver its initial opinion. The Commissioner, angered at how much the Directive was watered down by Ministers, may now look to the European Parliament to press for it to be tightened up again. However, British MEPs, who played a key role in killing off the previous landfill Directive in 1996, may not be so receptive this time.

The Commission had proposed successive reductions of 25%, 50% and 75% by 2003, 2005 and 2010 respectively, all from a 1993 baseline. The Presidency compromise would see these changed to reductions of 25%, 50% and 65%, respectively, probably by 2005, 2008 and 2015 at the earliest. In addition, Member States reliant on landfills for more than 80 per cent of their biodegradable municipal waste would be able to claim further four-year extensions. The baseline year has also been changed to 1995.

Other changes include a weakening of the proposal that all wastes should be treated before landfilling, which will now be required only if environmental benefits would result. And the proposed deadline for upgrading existing landfills to the standards set for new sites would be put back by several years – to eight years after the Directive has to be transposed into national laws, or three years for co-disposal sites. Another essential part of the haggling over the Directive was a relaxation of the proposed controls on waste disposal underground, practised in Germany and Sweden.

Environmental Liability

As mentioned in Chapter 2 the proposed Directive on civil liability for waste was shelved when agreement was not reached and the opportunity was taken to broaden the debate to cover improvement to the environment generally. In March 1993 the European Commission published a Green Paper on remedying environmental damage. The paper served as a starting point in the debate on how to create an environmental liability regime at EU level. The Paper attracted a great number of submissions from Member States, international organisations and interested parties, and led to the commissioning of several studies for consideration by the Commission.

Although the Commission's decision as to the precise legal form and content of any potential liability instrument is not yet known, developments are imminent and a speech by the Commissioner for the Directorate responsible for environmental matters has given some indication as to their likely position. The Commissioner seems to favour action which will specifically tackle the existing environmental pollution problems in Europe, which have been caused both by incidents of gradual pollution and sudden accidents.

The need for such action has been justified according to three main arguments: the implementation of EU environmental principles, the desirability of harmonising Member States' liability laws so as to avoid any possible distortion in the functioning of the internal market, and the need to supplement the existing gaps in the environmental protection regimes of the Member States. The form of future action taken by the Commission is likely to develop around the following conceptual frameworks.

Scope

In contrast to the Superfund approach in the USA, the scope of any liability instrument will be restricted to future environmental damage and the enactment of any measure introducing retroactive liability has been ruled out. It appears that the concept of environmental damage will be defined to include not only the traditional forms of injury to proprietary or personal interests, but also ecological damage.

Nature of Liability

The Commission appears to be strongly in favour of a regime based on strict liability. This regime would not prevent a polluter from relying on the defence of force majeure or the act of a third party. However, it is still unclear whether such liability will be defined by the type of damage caused or by the harmful activity carried out, and whether, within the second category, an exhaustive list of included activities or installations will be provided. The range of available defences, the test of causation and the burden of proof are associated factors which still need to be determined.

Cost of Remediation

The importance of developing clear guidelines which ensure that the amount of damage to the environment, as well as the cost of its restoration, can be adequately assessed in economic terms has been affirmed. Valuation techniques for lost and damaged resources already exist at EU level, having been developed in connection with environmental impact assessment. Any such valuation mechanism should also take into account the relative cost and benefit of restoring the environment in order to avoid disproportionate spending.

Financial Security

The purpose of developing a regime of financial security is to ensure that polluters have the financial means to bear the cost of remedying the damage they cause. The Commission seems to have focused in this regard on voluntary insurance incentives. The provision of a guarantee fund has also been mentioned, as have compulsory schemes, but apparently these ideas have been shelved. Such a guarantee fund would operate at the national or regional level to provide compensation to victims and to restore the damaged environment in an emergency or when the liable party is insolvent or cannot be identified.

Access to Justice

This issue is linked to the broader EU objective of the implementation and enforcement of environmental law as a whole. Certain comments have been made earlier in Chapter 2 in this respect. The inability of the regulatory authorities in the Member States to pursue every case of environmental pollution is one of the reasons for supporting greater access of groups and individuals to the courts. The Environment Directorate-General, DG XI, is still considering whether any provision of access to justice will be confined to facilitating judicial review actions, or will extend to a wider range of remedies and enable groups or individuals without a proprietary or personal interest in the damage to seek injunctive relief, compensation or restoration of the environment.

Ecological Damage

The Commission has emphasised the importance of developing a system whereby the polluter can be held liable for those forms of environmental damage which do not involve any element of injury to either proprietary or personal interests. It is anticipated that provision will be made for extending liability to this type of damage.

The Lugano Convention

The Commission is aware that the 1993 Convention of the Council of Europe on Civil Liability for Damage Resulting From Activities Dangerous to the Environment (the Lugano Convention) contains many of the elements of a comprehensive liability regime. Not only does it establish a no-fault liability regime, but also it gives environmental protection organisations the right to take legal action, and requires signatories to establish a financial security system. Moreover, it is seen as an ideal framework for a common liability regime, not least because it leaves the Member States a great deal of flexibility in implementing measures and authorises them to adopt stricter national environmental measures.

So far, only five states (none of the more powerful members) have signed the Convention. If the Community decides to ratify the Convention, specific EU legislation will be required to apply it within the Community. However, the Commission has so far not disclosed whether or not such a step is likely, although it is well known that some Member States are not in favour of such a move.

The UK

The waste regime in the UK distinguishes between controlled waste and special waste. The regime itself was in a state of flux pending the full implementation of the EPA 1990. Part II of that Act deals with the control of waste on land. The provisions in Part II relating to licensing were originally expected to be implemented by 1 June 1993, but were finally implemented on 1 May 1994.

The Licensing System

The Control of Pollution Act 1974 (COPA) Regime

COPA 1974 originally introduced the licensing system. Licences to deposit waste were available from the disposal authorities subject to a prior grant of planning permission. Conditions could be attached to the disposal licence under the COPA 1974, but the effect of these conditions was limited by the courts. In *Leigh Land Reclamation Ltd* v *Walsall MBC*,[16] it was held that the only time when breach of a condition constituted an offence was when it related to a deposit undertaken in breach of a condition. In other words, a breach of a condition relating to some other matter, such as the provision of eating facilities or sign boards, was not actionable.[17]

However, it was held in the Divisional Court decision of *R* v *Metropolitan Stipendiary Magistrate, ex parte the London Waste Regulation Authority and Others* and the *County Council of the Royal County of Berkshire, ex parte Scott and Another*,[18] that the licence requirement under the COPA 1974 applied to cases where waste was being held on a temporary basis at transfer stations, as well as to situations where waste had reached its final resting place. The Divisional Court considered that the policy of the COPA 1974 was to regulate operations having substantial consequences for the local environment.

The Regime under the EPA 1990

The administration of waste was altered by s30 EPA 1990. The functions of authorities are divided into three parts: regulation, collection and disposal. Much of the change came about through the introduction of competitive tendering. Thereafter, waste disposal authorities awarded waste disposal contracts through competitive tendering and made contracts with waste disposal contractors, who may be private sector companies or companies set up by the LA. An LA waste disposal company must be at arm's length from the waste disposal authority.[19]

The details of the procedure for applying for a waste management licence are set out in ss35 and 36 EPA 1990, and in the Waste Management Licensing Regulations 1994. These Regulations were designed in part to implement the amended Directive 75/442 by creating legally-binding obligations to comply with its fundamental objectives and to observe the priorities it lays down for waste treatment and in formulating waste management plans. The Regulations set out a considerable number of exceptions to the licence requirements, but none involve the operation of a landfill.

Applications are to be made to the EA. Some of the information required to be in the application includes the location of the facility, including any development (existing or proposed) within 250 metres and details of the types and quantities of waste to be received, such as details of the 'processes' to be followed; infrastructure on the site; location and specification of boundaries, fencing etc; pollution prevention measures to be installed; plans for the management of gas and leachate; and plans for restoration.

An application for a licence may be refused if rejection is necessary to prevent pollution of the environment or harm to human health; serious detriment to the amenities of the locality would be caused; and the applicant is not a 'fit and proper person' to hold a waste management licence.

A 'fit and proper person' is defined in s74 EPA which lists the criteria which, if met, may disqualify an applicant for not being a fit and proper person to hold a licence. Grounds include previous convictions for relevant offences, technical incompetence or inadequate financial resources.

If granted, the waste management licence will be subject to the conditions, if any, the EA considers appropriate, including conditions which are to be complied with before the authorised activities begin or after they have ceased. Conditions may relate to waste which is not within the statutory definition of controlled waste. The government may make regulations and give guidance which affects the conditions which the EA insert into licences. Certain requirements under the 1994 Regulations with regard to escaping pollution must be met in order to guarantee compliance with EC Directive 80/68/EEC on groundwater protection. In addition, the EA is obliged to consult the Health and Safety Executive and the district planning authority about the conditions attached to all licences which it decides to issue. It must also consult the Nature Conservancy Council if the site has been designated a Site of Special Scientific Interest (SSSI). They have 21 days to comment on the application, or longer if agreed to in writing.

The EA is under a duty to supervise the licensed activities of landfills to ensure that the conditions of the licences are being observed and that no pollution of the environment or harm to human health is occurring. Under ss37 and 38 EPA 1990, the EA has the power to vary, revoke, partially revoke or suspend the terms and conditions of a licence after it is issued. A public register containing information pertaining to the waste management regime has been created in accordance with s64. This information consists in part of: current or recently current licences; current or recently current applications for licences, transfers or modifications; and applications for surrender of a licence. The register is open to inspection by the public free of charge.

Controlled waste may not be deposited, treated, kept or disposed of without a licence. The licencing method is used as a means of controlling waste. This method has not been changed by the EPA.

Harmonisation Programme

The long-promised harmonisation of waste regulation practices across England and Wales should move closer on the EA's second birthday in April 1998 with the launch of a new licensing package. However, the large volume of technical work in hand is already making the deadline look ambitious and the upgrading of existing licences to meet current standards is some way off.

As has been mentioned, the waste management licensing regime was introduced in May 1994. Two years later, the 83 WRAs charged with its implementation were merged in the new Agency.

The WRAs brought with them 83 different interpretations of the law and standards for waste sites – and a host of differing application forms and procedures for obtaining or modifying a licence. Licensing practices had evolved piecemeal in each authority, but it was not until May 1996 that the Agency began work on developing management procedures, including a library of standard licence conditions to be applied throughout England and Wales.

Implementing a harmonised licensing regime had to wait while the EA developed a management structure to integrate the waste regulation functions and ex-WRA personnel into its 26 areas and eight regions. This process witnessed the departure from the EA of several experienced waste regulators who would have been well placed to develop the new licensing package.

The new package needs to be intelligible to line managers at area and regional level who have no experience of waste regulation, but need to judge what is required of their staff.

The new licensing package, launched for consultation at a seminar in December 1997, comprises a library of standard licence conditions and working-plan specifications; four standard application forms for obtaining, modifying, transferring or surrendering a licence; and a 'process handbook' instructing EA personnel how to manage licensing procedures.

The EA set out a strict timetable to prepare the package for implementation on 1 April 1998, a process which must include staff training for area officers. Work on drafting the library of licence conditions began in May 1997 and has involved collaboration with the Environmental Services Association (ESA) and metal recycling organisations.

The consultation period on the draft library package spanned just six weeks, to a deadline of 28 January 1998. The final draft was to be approved by the EA's national waste regulation group in March 1998.

Offences

A discussion of environmental liabilities and offences can be found in Chapter 8. However, waste management offences are given here.

Section 33(1)(c) EPA 1990

The general offence of depositing waste is contained in this section, which provides that it is an offence to 'treat, keep or dispose of controlled waste in a manner likely to cause pollution of the environment or harm to human health'. A due diligence defence is available to the commission of this offence, as well as the emergency defence and the defence of acting on employer's instructions. Therefore the Act does not follow the precedent for regulatory offences of creating a strict liability offence.

In this context, definitions are again important. The offence created under s33(1)(c) is very broad. 'Pollution of the environment' is defined in s29 to mean the release or escape of the waste into any medium so as to cause harm to man or any other living organisms supported by the environment. 'Harm' is further defined to mean 'harm to the health of living organisms or other interference with the ecological systems of which they form part, and in the case of man includes offence to any of his senses or harm to his property'.

It should be understood that this offence can be committed whether or not the offender has a licence. Whereas the other parts of the section deal with the situation where waste is handled in some way without a licence, or in breach of a condition in a licence, s33(1)(c) creates an offence that is concerned with environmental protection rather than enforcing the licensing regime.

Section 33(1)(a), (b) EPA 1990

The offences in this section replaced the previous offences in s3 COPA 1974. These deal with the liability for the deposit of waste without a licence. The offence in s3(1)(a) COPA 1974 was of causing or knowingly permitting the deposit of controlled waste on land or using plant or equipment for the deposit of waste. In the EPA, the offences have similarities, except for one important difference: s33 refers to *knowingly* causing or knowingly permitting such deposit. The new offence seems, therefore, to incorporate an element of knowledge which was lacking in the former offence under the COPA 1974.[20]

In *Kent County Council* v *Beaney*,[21] the meaning of 'knowingly permitting' under COPA 1974 was considered, and it was held that an inference could be drawn from the particular facts of the case that the respondent knew of the tipping that was taking place on his land.

Interestingly, the 1996 Royal Commission on Environmental Pollution suggested that the system of licensing exemption should be reviewed. The reason for this was concern that higher landfill and effluent charges lead to undesirable land-spreading practices.

The penalties for offences have already been substantially increased: six months imprisonment and/or a fine up to £20,000 in the magistrates' court and two years and/or an unlimited fine in the Crown Court. (In the case of special waste (controlled waste which is dangerous or difficult to treat) the penalty is the same except that the maximum sentence on indictment is five years' imprisonment.) In practice, the EA seems to carry out the prosecution of offenders effectively. For example in July 1997 a Bristol waste operator was jailed for four months and a company was fined £7,500 by West Malling magistrates for five disposal offences under s33(1)(c). Other offences under s33(1)(a), for disposal without a licence, attracted a fine of £16,500 on a Surrey company.

Duty of Care

The duty of care which was introduced by the EPA 1990, in force from 1 April 1992, represented an important and novel form of liability on producers and handlers of waste. Under the previous legislation, liability ceased the moment the waste left their hands. Their liability now extends beyond the moment the waste leaves their control. There are implications for insurance valuations and civil liability in this new duty of care.

When the duty of care principle was first introduced it was understood as extending liability from 'cradle to grave'. In fact, the duty of the waste producer is not as extensive as that. Rather, it is designed to satisfy the European concept that the polluter pays. The producer of waste is responsible for the proper disposal of the waste. This means that the producer must ensure it is transferred to a responsible carrier. The producer can no longer escape liability simply by passing the waste on to anyone else such as a fly tipper.

The duty as spelled out in s34 is to prevent the commission of one of the statutory offences (see above), prevent the escape of waste, make sure it is transferred to an authorised person and ensure that a written description goes with the waste so that others can comply with the duty.

Thus, the provisions focus on the control of waste prior to disposal and the steps to be taken on disposal. Liability after transfer will be limited to failing to take reasonable steps to detect and prevent breaches by the next person in the chain. It is likely, therefore, that a waste producer who complies with the rules of guidance on transferring waste, will be considered to have taken such reasonable steps.

This duty is imposed on all those who import, produce, carry, keep, treat or dispose of controlled waste (s34). This includes special waste. It was implemented by the Environmental Protection (Duty of Care) Regulations 1991,[22] which are supported by a Code of Practice, 'Waste Management: The Duty of Care', and a circular issued jointly by the DoE, the Scottish Office and the Welsh Office, 'The Duty of Care'.[23] The only exception to the duty is in respect of the householder who produces domestic waste from the home.

The circular is directed at waste disposal authorities and offers advice and interpretation of the duty of care. LAs are also waste producers and are also subject to the duty of care. In their capacity as waste collection authorities, they collect, carry or transfer waste through direct labour organisations. Where they award contracts to the private sector, they will not be waste holders. However, they will be subject to the duty of care as brokers. This means that when a LA arranges for the transfer of waste, the correct documentation will have to be produced. The circular contains a suggested transfer form for this purpose, and urges authorities to produce standard documentation.

Note: the term 'duty of care' is a familiar term derived from the law of tort and the famous case of Donoghue v Stevenson. *It is a common law principle which has been adopted by Parliament on previous occasions, for instance, in the duty owed by an occupier of land to visitors to that land.[24] The central idea of the common law principle is that a person owes a duty to take care not to injure others by his acts or omissions. The duty extends down the chain of consumers who do not necessarily need to be connected by contract.*

Nuisance

The tort of nuisance is the remedy most widely used by parties seeking to recover for environmental damage. Nuisance is an act or omission on land which unreasonably interferes with or disturbs another person's use or right of enjoyment of other land. An action under the law of nuisance can only succeed where the plaintiff has an interest in land. It is not, therefore, available to a person who has suffered personal injury, but is not affected as a landowner.

Nuisance may be either private or public. A private nuisance is a wrong only to the owner or occupier of the land affected. A public nuisance is a nuisance materially affecting the comfort and convenience of a class of people, and which is also a criminal offence. With regard to private nuisance, some degree of inconvenience is accepted as inevitable when living in close proximity to others. An interference is only a nuisance if it has been unreasonable in all the circumstances.

In practice, where a person's use or enjoyment of land is unreasonably interfered with, the situation may be more conveniently dealt with under statutory nuisance procedures. The EPA sets out a list of categories of statutory nuisances which may be required to be abated by the service of an Abatement Notice. However, this requires the involvement of the LA and will not permit recovery of compensation for accrued damages.

The Rule in Rylands *v* Fletcher

This case was decided by the House of Lords in 1865 (see Chapter 8), and imposed strict liability for all damage resulting from: a person having brought something on to his land which is not naturally there; which is accumulated there for the defendant's own purposes; and which escapes from its place of accumulation to somewhere outside the defendant's control, for example, toxic chemicals or water held behind a dam.

In strict liability cases, it is no defence to prove that all possible precautions have been taken to prevent damage resulting from an escape. Liability in nuisance has generally been regarded as strict, but it has been constrained by the principle of the reasonable user of the land as a defence. If the user is not reasonable, the defendant who creates a nuisance will be liable for consequent harm to his neighbour's enjoyment of land, even though he may have exercised reasonable care and skill to avoid it. The same is true for *Rylands* v *Fletcher* if the use is held to be non-natural. Similarly, as in negligence, reasonable foreseeability of damage is a prerequisite of liability for damages in both nuisance and *Rylands* v *Fletcher*.

Negligence

Negligence requires proof of fault, that is, conduct falling below a standard that the courts would regard as reasonable. As this is difficult to prove where complex processes are involved, and nuisance often provides an easier route, negligence has not made a substantial impact in environmental matters. To succeed in a claim for negligence, the plaintiff must prove that the defendant owes a duty of care to the plaintiff, the defendant is in breach of that duty and the foreseeable damage to the plaintiff has resulted from the breach of that duty.

The existence of a duty of care depends upon foreseeability. If it was not foreseeable that the defendant's actions would cause damage to the plaintiff, then there can be no duty of care. Foreseeability, in turn, depends on common sense. The general rule is that a defendant will be responsible for any type of physical damage which would have been foreseeable by a reasonable man as being something for which here was a risk, even if the damage would only occur in very exceptional circumstances. It is only the type of damage that must be foreseeable, not the actual damage to the plaintiff.

Disposal Methods

Recycling

In the UK the concept of recycling was put firmly on the agenda in the government's White Paper on the Environment 'This Common Inheritance'. This White Paper set a target of 25 per cent of household waste to be recycled by the year 2000. Britain does, in fact, already have a reclamation industry which has a turnover of several billion pounds per year. However, less than 10 per cent of the household waste that can be recycled is currently reclaimed. The government estimates that 50 per cent of all household waste is recyclable.

Section 49 EPA 1990 imposes a duty on waste collection authorities to investigate what arrangement would be appropriate for dealing with household and commercial waste in their area. They must then prepare a plan setting out their proposals. The object of the government's proposals is to minimise the amount of waste which has to be disposed of by reclaiming and recovering as much of the waste as possible. The Waste Management Paper No 28, 'Recycling',[25] provided further information on this.

In keeping with the philosophy of introducing market forces into environmental regulation, a system of financial credits has been introduced by s25 EPA 1990. The object of this is to encourage the use of recycling as a method of waste disposal. The system involves the waste disposal authority (the body responsible for disposing of the waste) making payments to the waste collection authority (the body responsible for collecting the waste), in respect of waste which they have collected for recycling. The amount paid will, eventually, represent the savings made in the long term by the waste disposal authority in respect of their marginal disposal costs. They will have less waste to take to the landfill site or to the incinerator. If a third party, a charity, for example, collects waste for recycling, then it can receive a payment representing the saving made on collecting the waste and disposing of it. Regulations have been made which provide a method for calculating these costs.[26]

The idea of using financial instruments to encourage recycling is supported by environmentalists. Friends of the Earth, for example, encourages such a method, but it emphasises that it should only be seen as one way to encourage a reduction in the overall quantity of waste produced.[27]

Packaging Waste

Packaging waste is a major contributor to the waste stream and to the problem of litter. The European Commission has issued a proposal for a Directive on packaging and packaging waste. Over a ten-year period, it is intended that 90 per cent of all packaging waste will be reused and, therefore, will not enter the waste stream. In addition, the amount of packaging used should be reduced by the manufacturers. Packaging will bear an UC mark indicating whether it is reusable. Member States will have to institute systems for collecting and sorting such waste.

These policies will clearly have a major impact on the manufacturing industry, as well as on the waste industry. It is worth reflecting that the collapsed 'East' German system of minimal packaging and recycling already had many of the characteristics proposed by this draft Directive.

As has been seen, European policy also advocates recycling as a means of dealing with waste. The Packaging Waste Directive is aimed at this end. In the UK, the Producer Responsibility Obligations (Packaging Waste) Regulations 1997 (SI 1997/648) have been passed, which impose unlimited fines for failure to register and which affect few business sectors. Currently, the government has asked the Advisory Committee on Packaging (ACP) to be involved in a wide review of the packaging regulations during 1998.

The ACP has been asked to report by the end of May 1998. The government will consider representations from other interested parties before going out to consultation later in 1998. The review will have four broad objectives: to determine whether the regulations are adequate to comply with the 1994 EC Directive on packaging; to simplify the regulations if possible, while maintaining the 'shared obligation' approach; to identify the scope for 'increased' recovery and recycling of packaging waste – 'increased', presumably, above the EC targets; and to achieve fairness between sectors in the shareout of recovery obligations, and encourage co-operation along the packaging chain.

The ACP has also been asked to advise on four other issues: the case for separate recycling targets for household and for commercial and industrial waste, and the scope of strengthening LAs' role; the case for new regulatory measures to encourage reuse and minimisation of packaging; the effectiveness of current requirements on evidence of compliance, in particular, the packaging recovery notes issued by accredited reprocessors; and, lastly, how small business might be encouraged to help increase recovery and recycling levels.

Landfill

Several issues regarding landfill have already been discussed under the heading 'Europe' (above). Landfill is the most common method of disposing of waste in the UK. Over 80 per cent is currently disposed of in this way. Since, as will be seen below, landfill sites pose a number of environmental problems, there is increasing pressure to deal with waste in other ways. In a paper on waste strategy for England and Wales in 1996, the government stated that it intended to reduce the amount of waste going to landfills to 60 per cent of the present level by 2005. Accordingly, in October 1996, a new tax on landfill waste was introduced with the aim of shifting the tax burden away from profits and towards the use of resources and pollution, thus providing an incentive to reduce waste.

There are a variety of laws that affect landfills. These can be broken down into two main categories: those that create a planning system which may affect applications for the opening or expanding of landfill sites, and those that govern the management and aftercare of landfill sites. Additionally, there is a new statutory regime for the identification and control of contaminated land (see Chapter 4), with important implications for landowners' potential liabilities.

Regulatory Issues

The pre-eminent statute is the EPA 1990, as amended by the EA 1995. This latest piece of legislation affecting waste disposal in England was designed primarily to rationalise the administration of English environmental laws under fewer regulatory authorities, and provide the statutory underpinning of a national waste strategy to encourage the re-use, recovery or recycling of any waste products or substances.

This was desirable to avoid inefficient duplication of efforts, and promote consistency of standards across the country and across the various media such as air, water and land.

As mentioned earlier, the EA is now the regulatory agency responsible for overseeing landfill sites. The EA took over the functions of the WRAs, NRA and HMIP as of 1 April 1996. Further details of the changes may be found in Chapter 3.

Landfill Sites and Planning Law

Since the issue of landfills is important in the UK and is a controversial issue in the EU, it is important to understand the planning aspects of landfill sites. The planning system plays an important role in environmental regulation, particularly with regard to the location and siting of development. Nearly all development requires planning permission from the local planning authority before it can be carried out. It is necessary to have planning permission for the site before an application for a waste management licence will be granted. Planning permission is generally issued to the owner of the land, whereas a waste management licence is usually awarded to the operator of the waste disposal site.

Local Procedures

The primary sources of planning law are the Town and Country Planning Acts (TCPA) and the Planning and Compensation Act 1991 (PCA). Planning permission is required to begin disposing of waste on land as the deposit of waste materials on land involves a material change of use, according to section 55(3)(b) of the TCPA. The responsibility for planning lies with London Boroughs or Metropolitan Authorities in cities, and is split between District and County Councils elsewhere. All LAs draw up plans which set out their strategy for development in the area, and often include aims for action on the environment. These are called development plans.

One element of a local development plan is a local waste plan. Such a plan contains the LA's waste policies and forms the basis of the consideration of a planning application. It should address the land use implications of the authority's waste policies and the need for waste sites and facilities. Some areas of the country are currently still compiling their local waste plans.

Under s16 PCA, all proposals for creating a waste development, meaning any development designed to be used wholly or mainly for the purpose of treating, storing, processing or disposing of refuse or waste materials, require a newspaper advertisement together with a notice posted at the site or notification of neighbours. The Health and Safety Executive (HSE) and the EA must be consulted in connection with planning applications relating to landfill sites. In practice, planning applications are often the subject of informal negotiation between the developer and the local planning authority where the authority will negotiate some kind of planning gain in exchange for the granting of planning permission. These are called 'section 106 agreements' and are enforceable contracts as against each contracting party but also as against future owners of the land. These types of agreements have been criticised, however, as being prone to secrecy and abuse.

Environmental Impact Assessment (EIA)

The Town and Country Planning (Assessment of Environmental Effects) Regulations 1988, implementing EC Directive 85/337 on the assessment of effects of certain public and private projects on the environment, came into force on 15 July 1988 and applied to all projects for which a planning application was lodged on or after that date. The Directive required the environmental effects of certain large projects to be considered before permission to go ahead with them was granted. It has been incorporated into the planning procedure for projects where planning consent is needed and is dealt with by the LA. There are some projects for which the EIA is mandatory (Schedule 1 projects), including oil refineries, nuclear power plants and incinerators for toxic waste. There are a greater number of projects (Schedule 2 projects), including landfill sites, for which an EIA is required if the local planning authority is of the opinion that they are 'likely to have significant effects on the environment by virtue of their nature, size or location'. Consultation between the developer and the authority to decide if an EIA is needed is usual.

If an EIA is needed, the basic procedure is as follows. First, the developer discusses the scope of the written submission which he is required to make to the planning authority (known as the Environmental Statement) with the authority, so that the full range of issues which need to be dealt with can be agreed.

The developer prepares an Environmental Statement which must identify the direct and indirect effects of the development on humans, plants, animals and other aspects of the environment and the steps that are proposed to avoid, mitigate or remedy these. The developer has to produce a summary of the Statement in non-technical language.

The planning authority must send a copy of the Environmental Statement to various public bodies, usually the EA and the relevant Nature Conservancy Council, and invite their comments. It must also make the Environmental Statement available to the public and receive any comments that they have to make. The developer must also publish notices in the local press and post them on site.

Finally, the competent authority must take into account the Environmental Statement and all the views expressed to it, as well as all other relevant factors in making its final decision as to whether a project should go ahead.

Challenging an Authority's Decision

If permission is refused, or granted subject to conditions which the applicant considers unreasonable, or if the planning authority fails to decide on the application within the eight-week period, then the applicant can appeal to the Secretary of State. The appeal takes the form of a complete rehearing, including the policy merits. Most appeals are decided by written representations to inspectors appointed by the Secretary of State, although either party can opt instead for a public hearing.

A planning authority's decision to grant permission can be challenged only by way of Judicial Review. This of course involves the usual problems of locus standi and costs; and even if successful would in all likelihood merely result in the case being remitted back to the planning authority. Decisions of the Secretary of State can be challenged under s288 TCPA, which has similar requirements to Judicial Review, but only a 'person aggrieved' by the decision can use this provision.

Enforcement

The power to enforce is vested primarily in District Authorities, the London Boroughs, or the Urban Development Corporations, and is entirely discretionary. Most LAs simply do not have enough resources to monitor and enforce every breach of planning control, and most rely on complaints from the general public.

The main enforcement tool is the 'enforcement notice' requiring the owner or occupier of land to take specified steps to remedy the breach. A breach of planning law is not in itself a criminal offence, but the failure to comply with an enforcement notice is. A planning authority may issue an enforcement notice where they consider it 'expedient' to do so, having regard to the development plan and to any other material considerations. There are additional powers to issue stop notices and injunctions to prevent unlawful activity. Notices must specify the alleged breach, the steps required to remedy it, the reasons for issuing the notice and the date on which it takes effect (which must be at least 28 days from the date of service). They can be appealed to the Secretary of State in writing, during which time it is suspended.

Under the PCA, planning authorities can serve a 'planning contravention notice' seeking information relating to the use or occupation of land, or a 'breach of condition notice' for non-compliance with a condition of planning permission. It is a criminal offence either to ignore such notices, or to provide incorrect information in response to a contravention notice. By reason of s196A–C, planning authorities have wide powers to enter land at any reasonable time to see if there has been a breach of planning control.

Under ss191–194 TCPA, if any person wishes to ascertain whether any existing use of land or buildings is lawful, or whether any operations which have been carried out on land are lawful, he may apply to the local planning authority specifying the land and describing the use or operations in issue. If the local planning authority is satisfied on the information provided of the lawfulness of the use or operations, it may issue a certificate to that effect.

The Decision Process

In considering applications for landfill sites, planning authorities should take account of: agricultural land quality; the quality of nearby habitats; the proposed size of the site, which should be large enough to allow for the effective management of the site; and the capacity for environmental improvement of the site when completed.

If planning permission is granted, conditions should be imposed concerning issues such as the area to be filled, the timescale of the operation, the hours of the operation, access arrangements and the volume of traffic, the general nature of the wastes, standards of restoration and aftercare management. There is considerable confusion about the correct extent of the conditions to be placed in planning consents for landfill sites. As a general rule, these should not overlap with the matters which are dealt with under the site licence. There will, however, inevitably be some degree of overlap. Matters properly dealt with under the licensing regime are considered below.

The Problem of Leachates

At its most basic, landfills involve digging a hole in the ground and filling it with rubbish. However, problems do arise from leaching, which is the process whereby liquid seeps through the landfill and takes with it harmful chemicals from the waste. This leachate can leave the land contaminated, and can enter the groundwater supply and get into the rivers and waterways and reservoirs. Another problem associated with landfill sites is the production of gases. As the waste which is buried rots down, it can produce methane gas and carbon dioxide. Methane gas is potentially explosive, and carbon dioxide is a gas which contributes to the greenhouse effect.

The most usual method used to deal with the problems of leaching is the barrier method. This involves lining the site with a barrier to prevent seepage. A barrier may be a natural barrier formed from the rock or other material underlying the site. For example, a layer of clay soil may be an effective barrier for certain types of waste. Alternatively, an engineering solution might have to be sought, such as the construction of a curtain wall out of appropriate materials. This is clearly an expensive solution, especially if it is undertaken as a remedial solution for a site already in operation.

The problem of leaching is of most concern on sites which have taken hazardous waste. As indicated above, by its very nature such waste is dangerous or difficult to deal with. In the UK it is the practice to undertake co-disposal, that is, to dispose of different types of waste in the same landfill site. An argument in support of this method of disposal is that where industrial waste is disposed of with household waste, the latter serves to reduce the concentrations of components leached from the former. In effect, the industrial leachate is diluted. In particular, domestic refuse can serve to neutralise acid wastes and heavy metals which arise in considerable amounts in the UK from, for example, the titanium dioxide industry and metal-finishing processes.[28]

It has, therefore, caused considerable consternation in the UK waste industry that the proposed Landfill Directive advocates monodisposal: landfill sites should only accommodate one type of waste.[29] This consternation has also been expressed by the Royal Commission on Environmental Pollution. As mentioned earlier, the British MEPs have voiced concern regarding some of the recent suggestions to deal with landfill sites.

Under s35 EPA 1990, it is possible for the waste regulation authority to grant licences subject to conditions relating to the care of the site after it has been filled. In addition, under s61, the waste regulation authority has power to enter and inspect closed landfills. Where it considers that these are in such a state as to cause harm to human health or pollution of the environment, it can undertake such work as is reasonable and recover the cost from the current owner of the land.

Under the COPA 1974, there were no such powers as those available under the EPA 1990. Under the COPA 1974, once a waste disposal licence was surrendered, then the waste regulation authority had no further control over the site. Under s39, however, the authority has a choice as to whether to accept a surrender of the licence. It is to inspect the land and seek further evidence from the licence-holder if necessary. The EA is to be consulted about the surrender. If the surrender is accepted, then the waste regulation authority is to issue a certificate of completion which states that the authority is satisfied that the condition of the land is unlikely of cause harm to human health or pollution to the environment.

It can be seen that the provisions under the EPA 1990 considerably enhance the powers to control closed landfill sites. Such sites may cause problems years after they have been closed. The holder of the licence will remain responsible for the site if the authority consider there is any risk to humans or the environment, such as the development of methane gas or toxic leachates emanating from the site. The Act proposes no upper limit to the continuation of such liability.

Incineration

Another method of waste disposal is incineration. On the Continent the reverse is true – incineration is the major form of waste disposal. When waste is burned in an incinerator there are two consequences: gases will be emitted into the air and residues in the form of ash and sludge will be left behind.

Waste incinerators are subject to air pollution control which falls under Part I EPA1990. They are not also subject to the controls on waste disposal under Part II. However, when the residue is discarded, this waste is covered by Part II.

The Royal Commission on Environmental Pollution has published a report called the 'Incineration of Waste',[30] which concludes that under the new system of controls, waste incineration should play an increasing part in a national strategy on the management of waste. As a disincentive to landfill as a method of waste disposal, the Royal Commission recommended that a levy should be applied on all waste disposed of in this way. It also encouraged the use of reclamation of waste.

At European level, the incineration of hazardous waste is governed by a Directive. The government has published a consultation paper[31] on its implementation and proposes to implement the air emission standards in the directive through the IPC system under the EPA 1990. Remarkably, this would tie in IPC with waste legislation.

Transfrontier Shipment of Waste

As is mentioned above, waste is bought and sold on international markets and is shipped around the world, and as such is seen as an economic good. The European proximity principle is applicable to waste and states that waste should be dealt with as near to its source as possible. Moving waste around over great distances – particularly hazardous waste – increases the chance of some environmental damage being caused.

Once waste is accepted as an economic good, then the basic European principle of freedom of movement of goods comes into play. The potential conflict between this principle and the principles relating to the protection of the environment becomes apparent. In the case of the *Wallonia*[32] (see Chapter 2), these issues arose. There was an initial question to be decided as to whether waste which is unusable and non-recyclable and therefore devoid of commercial value was covered by the rules on the free movement of goods. The ECJ held that since the waste was being transported across a border as part of a commercial transaction, it was therefore subject to art 30 regardless of the nature of those transactions.

Reasons for the trans-shipment of waste are likely to be economic. It may be cheaper to dispose of waste by shipping it to a foreign country, even taking into account transport costs, rather than disposing of it at home. This may be particularly apparent when contrasting the cost of disposing of waste in an industrialised country as against a Third World country.[33] Disposal costs in such countries may be cheaper because of the lack of regulatory controls, the lack of enforcement of control or because of a lower standard of technology. However, environmental consciousness in the Third World has been heightened, not least because of some disastrous incidents of waste dumping.

The Impact of the Basel Convention

The Basel Convention on the Control of Transboundary Movements of Hazardous Wastes and their Disposal 1989 controls the import and export of waste to and from the signatory states. In 1995, the convention was modified to impose a more stringent regime. The UK government has supported these further controls and has now implemented them through a recently published policy document. In the same year, the Environment Minister made clear that all exports of waste for disposal are banned, as are most imports for disposal, except where 'exceptional circumstances' apply. Exports of waste for recovery may continue under certain controls, where such exports are to OECD countries. However, exports to non-OECD countries are banned. There is no constraint on imports of waste for genuine recovery operations (including recovery for energy).

In Europe, the existing provision is the Council Directive on the Supervision and Control Within the European Community of the Transfrontier Shipment of Hazardous Waste 1984.[34] This has, as from 1 May 1994, been replaced by the Council Regulation on the Supervision and Control of Shipments of Waste Within, Into and Out of the European Community.[35] The Regulation results from the participation of the EEC in the Basel Convention.

The Regulation provides for a prior notification procedure which will inform the appropriate authorities of the type and method of dealing with the waste. These authorities may then take whatever steps are necessary to protect the environment, which may include objecting to the entry of the waste. The export of waste to other countries is banned unless these countries are EFTA countries and are parties to the Basel Convention. The Regulation deals with shipments of waste between Member States, within Member States and outside the Community.

For shipments within Member States, a system of supervision and control is to be set up and notified to the Commission. The import of waste into the Community is also covered and limited to specific states. In certain cases, waste may pass through the territory of the Community on its way to its final resting place in another country. Such trans-shipment is also subject to a notification procedure and must be notified to the last competent authority of transit within the Community. The Regulation lists three categories of waste: green, amber and red; which are subject to different control procedures. Radioactive waste, to the extent that it is not otherwise controlled, is also included.

In *R v Environment Agency, ex parte Dockgrange Ltd*,[36] the defendant imported a shipment under the green procedure which was subject to less stringent regulation than the red procedure. The EA informed the defendant that, since he was importing a mixture of waste, the material should be treated as 'unassigned waste', thus falling within the red list procedure. The defendant argued that each and every constituent part of the mixture could be identified as one listed in the Regulation for the green procedure. It was held that nothing in the Regulation suggested that waste could not be mixed; the different constituent parts of the mixture would determine which procedure should be followed, unless the mixture itself was mentioned as a separate item in one of the Regulation's lists.

The earlier 1984 Directive on trans-shipment of waste is implemented in the UK by the Transfrontier Shipment of Hazardous Waste Regulations 1988.[37] These regulate the contract for the disposal of the waste, the export and import of waste, the duty of carriers and relevant documentation.

Concluding Remarks

Developments in waste legislation in the UK are affected tremendously by both European and international developments. For example, it has been reported that a UK company has recently been found liable under Superfund. Although by no means a novel clean-up under US legislation, this case has a number of striking features. It involves an English defendant, the polluting activity in question dates back over 100 years, and the interest of the English defendant in the site ceased many years ago. Doubtless insurance archaeologists will be busy tracing policies which may assist to fund the defence, and doubtless insurers and re-insurers will wonder if the trail of long-tail liability for environmental pollution in the US will ever end.

In terms of day-to-day matters, the costs associated with waste and its disposal, as well as clean-up, are increasing. The DETR may be contacted to obtain current details with regard to fees and charges in relation to the relevant activity. Moreover, in general both industry and government have advocated the hierarchy of waste as good for business and the environment as can be seen from dialogue with the CBI and the DTI respectively. Waste minimisation techniques are being applauded, such as in the well-known Aire and Calder and daughter projects. Also, the provisions of the Waste Prevention Bill 1997[38] aims to enable local authorities to make arrangements for reducing, preventing or avoiding the generation of controlled waste. There is no doubt that the regulatory regime will become increasingly strict while the DETR and the EA continue the preparation of a statutory waste management strategy under the EA 1995. Reference may be made to the inquiry into sustainable waste management that is to be launched this year by the House of Commons Select Committee on the Environment Transport and Regional Affairs.

The issues which the Committee intends to address are: the environmental impact of different waste management options and the validity of the waste hierarchy; the environmental validity of current EC and UK targets and the likelihood of achieving them; the impact of recent and proposed legislation, such as the landfill tax and EC Packaging Directive on performance against the EC and UK targets; the role to be played by different waste management options in future UK strategy; the need for additional legislation or alternative policy instruments to achieve a sustainable balance of waste management options; the roles, achievements and policies of the DETR, and the EA, LAs and other public and private bodies concerned with waste management. The Committee will focus its attention on England. However, it says that is will also draw on relevant experience in other parts of the UK and other countries.

Europe

Although the Communication on waste strategy offers few specifics, its proposals are likely to be invoked by the Commission to justify future legislative activity. It reaffirms the EU's commitment to the prevention of waste, and its judgment that landfills should be the option of last resort for waste. The strategy emphasises the need to move towards a 'closed loop' policy for waste substances and products. While consumers and public authorities will bear some responsibility to put this into practice, it is the product manufacturer who has the predominant role.

What is clear from the development in the landfill Directive is that the Commission supports a move to pretreatment of waste before disposal, in order to reduce quantities of waste and/or eliminate dangerous waste. Moreover, the Commission considers that only non-recoverable waste should be accepted in landfills.

It remains to be seen whether the Commission will succeed in setting out a single EC-wide environmental liability system to replace the existing patchwork of different regimes. The Commission is facing serious problems in harmonising the liability regimes of a number of Member States with different legal traditions, and will probably face the opposition of industry. In addition, it has to convince those Member States which interpret environmental matters as falling under national control by virtue of the principle of subsidiarity. This last issue is highlighted by the fact that not all Member States have been in favour of the Lugano Convention which is described above (pp66–69). Nevertheless, despite the obstacles it appears that a single EC-wide system of environmental liability must be anticipated shortly.

---

[1] See JT Smith II, 'The Challenges of Environmentally Sound and Efficient Regulation of Waste – the Need for Enhanced International Understanding' (1993) 5 JEL 91

[2] Directive 91/689 on Hazardous Waste: OJ 1991 L377/20, as elaborated by Council Decision 94/906 22 December 1994

[3] Directive 78/319 on Toxic and Dangerous Waste: OJ 1978 L84/43

[4] Section 62(1) EPA 1990
[5] Part II, Sch II of the Regulations
[6] See the Radioactive Substances Act 1993
[7] Section 75 EPA 1990, the Controlled Waste Regulations 1992 (SI 1992 No 558). For licensing matters only the definitions under the former law apply. See s30 Control of Pollution Act 1974 and the Collection and Disposal of Waste Regulations (SI 1988 No 819). See also Waste Management Licensing Regulations 1994 (SI 1994 No 1056). Note also the Commission's review of the EU Waste Strategy (Com 96 (399)). See also the UK's National Waste Strategy referred to in Sch 2A EPA 1990
[8] [1993] Env LR 391
[9] Directive 75/442: OJ 1975 L194/39
[10] Directive 91/156: OJ 1991 L78/32 and Directive 91/692: OJ L377/48
[11] Directive 76/403: OJ 1976 L108/41
[12] Directive 91/689: OJ 1991 L377/20. This Directive replaces the 1978 Directive on Toxic and Dangerous Waste, Directive 78/319 OJ 1978 L84/43 as from 31 December 1993
[13] *Re Tombesi* [1977] 270 ENDS Rep 43
[14] Amended by Council Regulation (EEC) 120/97
[15] EU Bulletin 3/1997
[16] [1992] Env LR 16
[17] The *Leigh Land Case* was held to have been wrongly decided on another point
[18] [1993] Env LR 417. The Divisional Court held that the earlier decision of the Divisional Court in *Leigh Land Reclamation Ltd and Others* v *Walsall Metropolitan Borough Council* was decided wrongly
[19] DoE Circular 8/91, Welsh Office Circular 24/9; 'Competition for Local Authority Waste Disposal Contracts and New Arrangements for Disposal Operations', and see also *R* v *Avon County Council, ex parte Terry Adams Ltd* (1994) The Times 20 January
[20] See J Bates, UK Waste Law (1992)
[21] [1993] Env LR 225
[22] SI 199 No 2839
[23] 19/91, 63/91, 25/91
[24] Occupiers' Liability Act 1957. See also *Donoghue* v *Stevenson* [1932] AC 562 and *Rylands* v *Fletcher* (1868) LR 3, HL
[25] HMSO Publication
[26] Environmental Protection (Waste Recycling Payments) Regulations 1992 (SI 1992 No 462), as amended by the Environmental Protection (Waste Recycling Payments) (Amendment) Regulation 1993 (SI 1993 No 445)
[27] Friends of the Earth, 'Using Financial Instruments and Other Measures to Reduce Waste and Encourage Re-use and Recycling' (March 1993)
[28] See JR Grownow, AN Schofield and RK Jain (eds), *Land Disposal of Hazardous Waste* (1988), in particular, Chapter 3, p125
[29] 'UK Landfill Practice: Co-Disposal' (DoE 8 September 1993) HMSO
[30] Cm 2181 (1993)
[31] News Release 047/97
[32] Case C-2/90, *Commission* v *Belgium* [1992] OJ C195/9; [1992] 1 ECR 4431; [1993] 1 CMLR 365
[33] See Schmidt A 'Transboundary Movement of Waste under EC Law: The Emerging Regulatory Framework' (1992) 4 JEL 57
[34] Directive 84/631: OJ 1984 L326/31
[35] Directive 93/259: OJ 1993 L30/1
[36] The Times 21 June 1997, QBD
[37] SI 1988 No 1562, and see the Department of Environment Circular 16/89 for advice on the Regulation.
[38] HC Bill 108

Chapter 7

Regulation and Voluntarism: A Balancing Act

Shared Responsibility

In view of the general awareness of the state of the natural world, it is imperative that organisations, both large and small, should focus on their role in the protection of the environment. This focus should exist irrespective of whether or not the companies are involved in a polluting industry or activity, and should transcend compliance.

In its Fifth EAP, 'Towards Sustainability', covering the period 1993–2000, the EU targeted the role of industry in implementing the principle of 'shared responsibility' to achieve improved environmental protection and preservation. The aim is that all organisations should be involved. Indeed, the European Commission has recognised that small- and medium-sized enterprises (SMEs) must be equipped to participate fully in this initiative. Moreover, EMAS exemplifies the need for a practical approach.

These trends and initiatives mean that industry is now required to perform a balancing act between regulation and voluntarism that enables the optimum use of resources. Moreover, advisors should be aware of this requirement. In order to make business more profitable and to benefit society as a whole, organisations should aim to protect the environment by taking account of the highest standards in technology and good management practices. Management theories indicate that this is best achieved by a combination of formal and informal corporate measures, including a comprehensive corporate policy on the environment and follow-up procedures, such as environmental audits.

Currently there are various methods that have evolved relating to the analysis of a company's performance in terms of its environmental performance. There is an ethical link between proper environmental performance and good business performance which is becoming increasingly clear from the point of view of shareholders, investors, banks etc. In order to have a real picture of the assets and liabilities of a company it must be understood that environmental liabilities are very much part of the equation. This factor was very obvious in the debate in the UK over the proposed register for contaminated land. The proposal was, in fact, withdrawn as a result of the lobbying of many property owners who considered that transactions and the market would be blighted as a result. Nevertheless, the debate did raise awareness among companies, especially since it is true to say that most of them are currently holding, or will hold in the future, property that has been contaminated in some way. This means that, especially following the Environment Act 1995, there may well be repercussions for such organisations in terms of the assessment of their balance sheet.

Many aspects of environmental management can affect the finance of a company. At the international level, a recent illustration shows the bad effect that perceived improper environmental management can have on the reputation of a company. When Shell's business ethics in Nigeria became a major concern, its quoted share price fell dramatically and it had to undertake a very expensive, large-scale media exercise to recover the standing of its name. As referred to above, Shell has also suffered the cost of non-compliance by paying the largest national fine of £1 million when sued some years ago; the money came directly from its 'bottom line'.

An enhanced awareness of the environmental aspects of running a business will entail reviewing procedures and processes, not only to make them more environmentally sound, but also to improve efficiency. Businesses across the spectrum have been surprised at the cost-effectiveness of measures to reduce energy consumption and minimise waste generation. The use of low-energy technologies, improved insulation, the plugging of leaks, recycling of materials and energy can all lead to significant savings.

The principle of sustainable development as endorsed by the Fifth EAP should be at the forefront of any corporate environmental policy. This principle recognises that the world's natural resources are either renewable or finite. Renewable resources should be managed in order to provide a continuous stream for ongoing productivity. Finite resources should be used only in the most productive and efficient ways. This will allow time for the development of alternative sources once existing resources have been depleted and/or for the development of comprehensive recycling schemes to renew these resources. In view of the trends and issues referred to in the final chapter, it is clear that practical steps should be taken now as regards sustainability.

The future growth and forward planning of any organisation requires crucial budgeting of available resources, the most important being financial and human resources. Management should consider projections in terms of a 'green budget' in their effort to support a credible environmental protection policy and to maintain a high marketing profile, as well as to attract public support for ongoing activities.

Management standards are an increasing feature of business life. For many companies the quality standard ISO 9000 is now almost second nature. But beyond notions of quality, verifiable standards are being extended into new areas, such as the environment under ISO 14000, which is discussed in detail below. In addition, in one sense EMAS is just another example of this trend, albeit with some novel aspects. It would be prudent for organisations and their advisers to gear up their understanding regarding the role of management systems.

Pathways to Sustainability

Companies which intend to take sustainability seriously should assess their own sustainable goals. These would constitute the long-term vision of the company operating in accordance with sustainability. Environment Management Systems (EMS) can be converted into sustainability management systems to provide clarity about what are sustainable levels for the effect of the company's activities, and to drive progress towards them.

There will be difficulties – the challenge of identifying sustainability goals for a particular company is complex – and in certain cases the 'sustainable level' for an existing process or product may be zero. The implication for the company may be that an alternative process or product will be required on the path to sustainability. Flexibility is a vital element. Existing EMSs may improve current products and processes, but they should also identify environmental problems which can only be resolved by a lateral rethink.

Any company committed to understanding sustainability will not just have an EMS. It will also have a sustainability benchmark against which to test performance and identify the sustainability gap. Unsustainable practices will be highlighted, and major strategic decisions about product substitution or process change will be planned by proactive management.

Regulatory Influences

The EPA 1990 envisaged a comprehensive regulatory scheme of IPC, this principle having since been taken up as 'the way forward' by the EU. Historically, the EPA was influenced by the growing volume of EU legislation on the environment. Since the modifications to the original EEC Treaty (Treaty of Rome 1957) brought about by both the SEA 1987 and the Maastricht Treaty 1992, the institutions of the EU have an express mandate for the development of comprehensive environmental regulations with the support of all the Member States, which has major ramifications for the operation of businesses.

In developing its environmental legislation, the EU has taken into account established environmental protection legislation and policy in the USA. Liability for the clean-up costs of such sites may fall not only on the owner/operator, but also on companies who transported any waste to the site, previous owners of the site, companies whose waste was dumped on the site at any time and even lenders to those companies. As indicated in Chapter 2, in Europe the Commission published a Green Paper on environmental liability in March 1993, which is likely to result in a stricter enforcement regime quite soon.

While the EU is working towards harmonisation within its borders, jurisdictional differences between Member States do still exist, and having separate legal systems, some Member States have imposed stricter standards than those enacted at EU level. The effectiveness of enforcement measures also varies widely. Looking further afield, there is an undoubted need to fulfil international environmental standards in order to compete globally in terms of trade, tenders and the market. As is clear from the discussion regarding ISO 14001, sustainable development requirements have pushed global business towards an enhanced proactive management approach, which is particularly effective in risk management.

Many Third World countries have enacted sophisticated environmental legislation, which will have a significant impact on any business operating within their territories. For instance, India has both environmental auditing and impact assessment regulations in place. Thus it is important for companies not only to be aware of existing regulations, but also of forthcoming regulatory developments and their enforcement.

Higher Standards

From an international point of view, the ideas behind an organisation's environmental policy are vital. At the very least, the aim must be to comply with the minimum standards that have been set locally. Ideally, the standards maintained should be the strictest possible, bearing in mind the cost-benefit ratio. For international companies, a single policy encompassing all the varying requirements found in the jurisdictions in which they operate is an ambitious and potentially expensive endeavour, although the Bhopal incident in 1984 demonstrated that if high standards of management are not maintained, the consequences can be devastating. That particular incident led to US businesses being forced to maintain uniformly strict standards wherever they carry out their operations, irrespective of local regulations. Where financial constraints do not allow such an approach, a single minimum standard to be applied, with stricter standards for those jurisdictions which have enacted such standards, is a viable option for the effective management of an organisation's environmental pollution control efforts. This is true both of the developed and developing world. However, by accepting such standards before they become compulsory, it may be possible to gain market advantage.

Despite some deregulation initiatives, generally the current trend is for increasing implementation of environmental legislation with stronger enforcement and tougher penalty provisions, including criminal fines imposed on those having control of the polluting operation. By way of example, the EPA 1990 strengthened the criminal penalty provisions within the UK and gave sweeping powers to the Secretary of State for the Environment to enact comprehensive regulations for the control of everything from air and water pollution through to litter. The recent re-enactments by the US Congress of the Clean Water Act, the Clean Air Act and the enactment of SARA in 1986 have tightened US federal laws, at the same time imposing stiffer criminal and civil penalties.

Developments in Third World and Eastern European countries are being closely monitored by international organisations, including the UN. The imposition of penalties for environmental crimes, moves by, inter alia, the EU to impose strict liability on companies causing environmental damage, and international monitoring of environmental protection efforts, should all be borne in mind when developing corporate environmental policy.

Practical Repercussions

One of the main reasons legislative developments need to be anticipated is the necessity to budget for capital items, such as new plant and process equipment. It is particularly important to keep abreast of international initiatives which eventually have repercussions at regional and local level. In this way, the business remains competitive by anticipating new measures and acting upon them. This has been especially evident in the refrigeration business with the phasing out of the use of CFCs because of its damaging effect on the ozone layer, for example. One company, Elstar, which supplies refrigeration units to public houses and clubs, announced that it switched its entire production to ozone-friendly chemicals in the early 1990s. It is believed to be the first maker of commercial fridges in the world to switch to gas-cooled cabinets, some four years after the EU agreed to ban CFC's under the Montreal Protocol.

A well-thought-out public relations approach to increase awareness of a company's green credentials is invaluable. In the UK, for instance, the impact of improved environmental performance by organisations such as Marks & Spencer and B&Q has been dramatic. They have effectively dictated environmental management standards to would-be suppliers and, in some cases, have actually sought to assist smaller organisations in their supply chain to meet those standards. Such improvements have thereby extended overseas.

Greenness is often synonymous with quality in the eyes of consumers. Moreover, consumer interest in the environmental performance of a business is no longer limited to those living in the immediate area of the company's activities. As is referred to further below, many companies now publish details of their environmental policy in their annual report. The EU believes that all sectors of society must be made to feel a sense of shared responsibility for the environment, and the drive to increase public access to environmental information is seen as fundamental in this context. The EU's 'eco-labelling' scheme, which is described below, had a similar thrust.

In the UK, the Department of Trade and Industry (DTI) has recommended a 'cradle to grave' approach in relation to product stewardship. This means that the supplier of a product which has the potential for contaminating a site or causing pollution should take responsibility for it by developing environmentally-sound practices covering the use of that product. This applies even when the product is no longer within the supplier's control, for example, when it is being transported, used by the consumer or when it is sent for disposal.

Communication is vital – workers, shareholders, the local community, green action groups and the press should be kept informed of how perceived environmental problems are being solved and, if possible, given a role in helping find solutions. Set against this background, there is a potentially overwhelming array of regulatory and voluntary issues for a company to address.

The Business Bottom Line

As seen above, there is no shortage of reasons why companies should pay attention to the environment. Evidence of continuing enhanced public awareness of the issues, consumer pressure and the interest of other stakeholders, as well as current or potential regulations from the UK, Europe and further afield, are factors that are regularly highlighted in surveys and reports. Often environmental initiatives can save money and improve profitability and competitiveness. This is clear both from the general approach seen in the Aire and Calder Project and from many individual case studies.

The Aire and Calder Project is a well-known example of co-operation, team work and the application of sound environmental management. In the Project, 11 companies along the Aire and Calder Rivers worked together and, in the process, reduced their emissions by 25 per cent and saved £3 million. Good environmental management increased productivity by minimising wastage of materials. Savings were made through the application of technology, good housekeeping or process modification (re-use, recycling etc) and a reduction in the cost of clean-up, especially of pipes. Such advantages do not just have to be in terms of large companies – SMEs can also benefit. A further advantage is the avoidance of aggressive prosecution from, for example, the NRA.

Key success factors in the Project were senior management support, effective project champions, a supportive culture, mutual support and encouragement of the club set up specifically for the project, and consultant input based on knowledge of the methodology.

The goals of the Project were to achieve cost-saving, competitive advantage, compliance and risk reduction through people, systems and technology. People involved no added cost, but led to good housekeeping; systems were a low-cost item; technology was a capital cost. The success of the Aire and Calder projects and the relating projects that it has spawned speaks for itself.

There are many initiatives which have resulted in benefits to the bottom line, new product opportunities or increased market share. For some organisations, improved environmental performance has been motivated by requirements, whether current or anticipated. As mentioned below, there is a huge potential to save by, in particular, good housekeeping, especially in connection with waste and energy issues. Whereas the average pay-back period is often 18 months, which was the target in the Aire and Calder Project, some initiatives involve no capital outlay at all. Moreover, the application of management standards such as ISO 14001 can assist corporate efficiency generally, wherever it operates.

No activity is without some impact on the environment even if it is not subject to laws and regulations. Therefore organisations throughout the spectrum, whether manufacturing companies, retailers, service companies, multinationals or SME's, have issues that they should address in regard to the environment. In addition, the cost-effective objective applies to any business. For many of the companies that do address these issues, it has been made clear that unnecessary costs and wastage occur through inefficient use of energy, water and raw materials, and the final disposal of 'waste' products. Thinking efficiently, thinking quality, looking for new uses for materials previously considered waste, taking ideas from people at all levels in the company, working with suppliers – all these characterise the companies that have put themselves in the leadership division. This is why, for example, the National Westminster Bank has coined the expression 'Good business management equals good environmental management' and vice versa.

The Environmental Balance Sheet

The environmental repercussions of business activity have been considered in a debate that used to be confrontational: economics versus environment. The emphasis of this debate has shifted. If a business operates a manufacturing process or owns, manages, intends to acquire or wants to develop property assets, then the environmental liabilities are increasingly open to question. As discussed in Chapter 9, appropriate due diligence is being carried out increasingly which can affect the negotiations in, and success of, transactions greatly.

Furthermore, largely as a result of the circumstances in the USA where the 'deepest pocket' is found to redress environmental damage, lenders, insurers, investors and employees are now much more sensitive to the problem. This is true whether they arise from historical or ongoing pollution. Such interested parties will scrutinise the health of an organisation's 'environmental balance sheet' much more closely. Unfortunately, as a result of this growing sensitivity, initial estimates for liabilities or potential clean-up costs can be very high. In some cases, as has been seen in the USA, they can also threaten the viability of an acquisition, a divestiture, a development or merger, or the entire business. In addition, as the insurance industry has experienced to its cost, retrospective measures taken in response to enforcement action by a regulator are rarely cost-effective. Further detailed comment occurs in the chapters which follow.

Yet, however extensive or substantial liabilities may be, they become considerably more manageable when quantified accurately after thorough investigation and assessment of the issues or impacts involved. Liabilities can also be contained by a proactive strategy which uses cleaner technology and integrated waste management practices to reduce future pollution, minimise environmental impacts and improve environmental performance.

A carefully monitored and well-reported programme of effective environmental management or remedial action is vital to inspire employees, encourage investors, protect commercial interests and substantially improve the environmental balance sheet of business. Here, ISO 14001, in particular, is playing an increasingly significant role. Proper environmental performance is not an add-on or an afterthought: it requires constant effort, commitment, attention and enthusiasm, in the same way as other key business functions.

Environmental Reporting

This term is generally referred to the reporting of organisations on their environmental performance, typically to shareholders in the annual report, but also by way of separate reports for other groups, such as employees and the general public. It is an essential requirement for registration under EMAS and under the Valdez Principles (see Chapter 1). Organisations and their advisers should be aware of a UK initiative to assist SMEs under EMAS, known as the Small Company Environmental and Energy Management Assistance Scheme (SCEEMAS). More generally, the trend towards corporate openness (see Chapter

10) emphasises the need to be aware of environmental performance. The award scheme related to environmental reporting initiated by the Association of Chartered Certified Accountants (ACCA) is described below.

SCEEMAS

In a bid to enable SMEs to take up EMAS, a new scheme to help smaller companies register under EMAS, SCEEMAS was launched by the government on 16 November 1995. EMAS is a voluntary EC scheme which aims to promote positive environmental management in manufacturing industry, specifying a systematic and verifiable approach by which companies can manage and continually improve their environmental performance (see Chapter 4). SCEEMAS is available to applicants in the sectors covered by the regulation. Companies with fewer than 250 employees world-wide and an annual turnover of less than £16 million are eligible to apply. The scheme has been subjected to continual review, however, since its introduction, and during 1998 in particular, with a view to replacing it with another scheme.

Before a site can be registered under EMAS, the company is required by regulation to set up an EMS and publish a statement covering its environmental performance. The system and the statement have to be checked by an independent verifier. Grants will be paid for one or more of the following stages to allow companies flexibility to decide how much outside help they need to minimise cash-flow problems.

> Phase 1, environmental review: a 40 per cent grant for establishing a register of a site's environmental effects and legislation, drawing up a policy and a programme with objectives and targets to ensure legal compliance and continual improvement in performance.

> Phase 2, management system: a 40 per cent grant for documented procedures, monitoring and internal audits tailored to the site which meet the requirements of EMAS and/or BS7750.

> Phase 3, environmental statement: a 50 per cent grant plus the balance from other stages covering a report on the site's environmental performance, which has been independently validated by an accredited verifier.

The National Industrial Fuel Efficiency Service Ltd (NIFES) was appointed to administer the scheme on behalf of the then DoE (now DETR). In order to launch SCEEMAS, the DoE and the CBI provided a series of road-shows to draw attention to, and enhance understanding of, the scheme.

The feature that sets EMAS apart from other standards is the public statement and the verification process. Although those companies that have committed to EMAS have commented on their long-term commitment, they seem to agree on the value of the public statement for their public credibility Europe-wide. There is no doubt that the credibility aspect is crucial in terms of reporting generally. Guidance on the content of the reports and the methodology of the report has been prepared by the World Industry Council for the Environment and the Public Environmental Reporting Initiative under the auspices of the International Chamber of Commerce (ICC). In addition, ACCA has developed annual awards as an initiative to encourage improvement in environmental reporting standards.

ACCA Awards

Nineteen-ninety-seven was the seventh year of ACCA's Annual Environmental Reporting Awards Scheme. Increased experience, clarity of focus and better produced environmental information systems have led to steady improvement in the quality of company environmental reporting over the years. This has led, in turn, to an increasing quality in those reports submitted to the Environmental Reporting Awards Scheme (ERAS).

Environmental reporting is still voluntary in most countries. This has several consequences. Perhaps the most important is that systematic environmental reporting is still very much a minority 'sport' practised, on the whole, only by the larger companies in certain industries. While the majority of large companies address environmental issues to some degree in their reporting, such reporting is typically superficial and patchy. The submissions to ERAS typically represent the very best examples rather than common practice.

Another consequence is that the voluntary status of environmental reporting produces a bewildering diversity of approaches. According to ACCA, the positive side of this is that it appears to encourage innovation in the range of experimentation that reporting companies undertake. The negative side is that the reports exhibit little standardisation or comparability. This lack of standardisation also means that different reporting organisations place a different emphasis on different aspects of reporting. It may be that there can never be any such thing as a 'complete' environmental report, but most reports to date have tended to have at least one or two glaring omissions.

The most striking general omission from current practice is any systematic attempt to link the economic and financial attributes of the business with its environmental activities (see Chapter 10). This manifests itself frequently in a complete separation of the environmental report from financial statements. It is probable that 'best practice' in environmental reporting will eventually emerge as requiring both an explicit identification of the financial implications of the environmental agenda, and the production, at least in summary, of an environmental report within the annual report alongside the financial statements.

Other significant issues that have to be addressed in developing environmental reporting include: serious consideration of the implications of sustainability for the business (a far from trivial question); systematic focusing on the organisation's stakeholders and, perhaps, their information needs and rights; a systematic analysis of how general environmental reporting will interface with the reporting under EMAS; what the environmental agenda and environmental reporting might mean for the financial markets; and what form of environmental reporting one can reasonably expect from SMEs.

The role of regular environmental reporting is to help a business monitor how it is progressing towards meeting its green policy objectives. Some businesses and organisations – at the larger end of the spectrum generally – go into great detail, producing elaborate and impressive brochures for dissemination to employees, the public and external parties with which it trades or does business. These are particularly representative on the entries to the ACCA Awards. For the typical organisation, though, such lengths may not be necessary –

although they can possibly be very useful in the case of businesses operating in environmentally-sensitive areas, or close to neighbours with which it wishes to stay on good terms.

A regular environmental statement, say, on an annual basis, does help everyone make sure that management (top to bottom and vice versa) remain focused, list the policy objectives, detail the actions that have been taken towards meeting them in the year and, most importantly, list those actions to be taken in the following year. The following environmental statement then records how the company has fared in complying with these.

As businesses increasingly improve their communication both internally and externally, many now produce corporate newsletters, magazines and the like. This type of reporting finds a ready and interested audience. Companies have found it beneficial to publish extracts on company notice boards, as well as interim progress reports throughout the year. It is cost and time effective to try to incorporate the business's environmental objectives into the regulated management reporting systems. Progress towards quality, health and safety and personnel objectives are probably reported already: the environmental ones can simply be added to the list, as recommended by the CBI.

Environmental reporting is becoming more usual as a business practice as pressure for stakeholder accountability and competitive awareness increase. Previously, the environment was only mentioned in a paragraph in the annual report stating that the company was making every effort to 'safeguard the environment'. Just as the public and other stakeholders develop their understanding of environmental concerns, they also increase their demands for information. Companies, especially in sensitive sectors, such as Wessex Water in the water industry, that try to avoid projecting a 'dirty image', discover that admitting a problem is there and showing what is being done to combat environmental damage is more publicly acceptable. As regards the supply chain, suppliers such as B&Q are finding that to retain their customers they either have to accept evaluations and supplier questionnaires, or provide evidence of environmental performance on their own initiative.

The chemical and oil industries were the first to issue annual environmental reports. Soon afterwards, others followed their lead, including pharmaceutical and fast-moving consumer goods industries. Whereas these reports, like environmental statements, vary widely in scope and credibility, certain basic characteristics can be recognised: financially relevant information on liabilities, environmental insurance and environmental expenditures; information on compliance programmes, audit programmes, and accidental oil and chemical spills; and corporate environmental policy and programmes, including environmental goals, public and community relations programmes, environmental innovations and new environmental services.

As organisations – and their advisers – become more familiar with such voluntary steps, there is no doubt that this will, in turn, assist with compliance.

ISO 14001

It should be understood that since environmental issues and problems are generally transboundary, so the most appropriate solutions are transboundary. It is therefore important to explain the role of ISO 14001 which is an international environmental management standard whose recognition is growing rapidly in many sectors of activity, both public and private.

Background to ISO Standards

In 1946, ISO was founded as a world-wide federation to promote the development of international manufacturing, trade and communication standards, thereby facilitating the international exchange of goods and services. The ISO organisation itself is a private-sector, international standard body based in Geneva. ISO has promulgated more than 8,000 internationally accepted standards for everything from paper sizes to film speeds. ISO reviews input from government, industry and other interested parties before it develops a standard. More than 120 countries belong to ISO as full voting members, while several other countries serve as observer members.

In August 1991, ISO established a Strategic Advisory Group for the Environment (SAGE) for the purpose of assessing the need for environmental management standards and to recommend an overall strategic plan to develop these standards. ISO requested SAGE to consider the following issues: the promotion of a common approach to environmental management similar to total quality management standards (for example, ISO 9000); the enhancement of businesses' ability to attain and measure improvements in environmental performance; and the utilisation of international standards to facilitate trade and remove trade barriers.

SAGE was specifically instructed not to consider environmental criteria such as levels of pollutants, health assessments/risks, technology specifications and products/process criteria.

For over a year, SAGE studied the UK's BS7750 and other national EMS as possible starting points for an ISO version. Indeed, the final ISO 14001 standard reflected the conditions of BS7750 to such an extent that companies certified to the UK standard were automatically transferred to the international standard which has superseded the national forerunner.

In 1993, SAGE recommended the formation of an ISO technical committee dedicated to the development of a uniform international EMS as well as other standards on environmental management tools. ISO formed Technical Committee (TC) 207 to develop a series of environmental management systems standards to accomplish the 'standardisation' in the field of environmental management tools and systems.

In June 1993, TC 207 met for the first time in Toronto, where some 200 delegates representing approximately 30 countries agreed to complete a draft of the EMS and auditing international standards. SAGE was officially disbanded. Following an interim meeting 17–20 April 1994 in Surfer's Paradise, Australia, TC 207 met in Oslo, 24 June–1 July 1995, Norway, where 500 delegates representing 47 countries agreed to elevate the EMS and auditing standards to draft international standards with scheduled publications by the end of 1996. By July 1995, TC 207 had members from 63 countries indicating the level of recognition of the need for an international approach.

Six Technical Subcommittees (SCs) and Working Groups (WGs) were created within TC 207, and are currently formulating standards in the following areas:

- SC1: Environmental Management Systems, with the UK as the secretariat, administered by the British Standards Institution.

- SC2: Environmental Auditing and Related Environmental Investigations, with The Netherlands as the secretariat, administered by The Netherlands Normalisatie-Instituut.

- SC3: Environmental Labelling, with Australia as the secretariat, administered by Standards Australia.

- SC4: Environmental Performance Evaluation, with the USA as secretariat, administered by the American National Standards Institute (ANSI).

- SC5: Life-cycle Assessment, with France as the secretariat, administered by Association Française de Normalisation.

- SC6: Terms and Definitions, with Norway as the secretariat, administered by Norges Standerdiseringsforbund

- WG1: Environmental Aspects in Product Standards, with Germany as the secretariat, administered by the Deustches Institut für Normung e.V.

On 17–21 June 1996, TC 207 delegates from 50 countries and ten liaison organisations met in Rio de Janeiro, Brazil, to complete the ISO 14000 drafting process. The main outcomes of the meeting are as follows:

The 14001 and 14004 environmental management systems standards received final approval and were issued by ISO on 1 September 1996.

The 14010, 14011 and 14012 environmental auditing standards are in the final stages of publication and have been overwhelmingly approved by the plenary. These standards were published in conjunction with the 14001 and 14004 standards.

SC1 established a working group to gather information about the implementation of ISO 14001 SMEs. The working group will report back to TC 207 at its next meeting to recommend the direction that the TC should take towards developing the guidance standard 14002 Environmental Management Systems – Guidelines on Special Considerations Affecting Small and Medium Size Enterprises.

SC3 voted to begin work on Type III environmental labels, also known as 'environmental report cards'. These labels are similar to the nutrition panels found on cereal boxes and are intended to provide the consumer with the necessary information when choosing a product based on its environmental impacts.

SC3 also reaffirmed the 14024 Environmental Labels and Declarations – Environmental

Labelling Type I – Guiding Principles and Procedures document as a committee draft, which places it in line for draft international standard status next year. This standard could become the basis for mutual recognition among the 24 environmental labelling programmes currently operating around the world.

SC4 decided to completely revise the existing environmental performance evaluation working draft and perform a line-by-line analysis of all comments received. The final result of several days work was a fifth working draft that reflected major advances in negotiations.

SC6 voted to elevate 14050 Terms and Definitions, to draft international standard status. This document should provide the user of the 14000 series of documents with a single source of terms used in the practice of environmental management.

ISO 14000 Environmental Management Systems Overview

The ISO 14001 standards represent a state-of-the-art, industry-lead initiative that requires corporate policy commitment to continual improvement, compliance with regulations and prevention of pollution. Conformity with these standards can assist an organisation in moving beyond reactive management and into a posture of proactive control of its environmental impacts.

The 14000 documents consist of two main groups of standards: those that evaluate organisational performance and those that evaluate product performance. Within the category of organisational performance, there are three standards: environmental management systems, environmental auditing and environmental performance evaluation. There are also three standards for product evaluation: life-cycle assessment, product labelling and environmental aspects in product standards.

The ISO 14000 series is recognised as the world standard whereby all organisations will be assessed for their commitment to environmental excellence. There are three critical strategic drivers for inclusion of this standard in a company's management system.

First, the 14001 series provides a single framework for strategic environmental management that is not only recognised world-wide, but can be certified by an independent auditing organisation. This means that organisations that adopt the standard will be included in a group of 'world class' organisations that reflect the cutting edge of environmental management. This inclusion will increase the positive public perception of these organisations.

Secondly, the international recognition of the EMS certification will allow organisations to enter markets that require this certification as a condition of doing business. Currently, many governments and organisations, as well as the US government departments and the major US car manufacturers, plan to grant preferred status to ISO 14001 certified companies.

Thirdly, the 14000 series of standards provides an organisational 'blueprint' for strategic environmental management that reflects an internal focus on methods and systems. US environmental regulatory agencies, insurance companies, investors and the public will treat preferentially ISO 14001-certified companies for their proactive management strategies, internal efficiencies and reduced environmental risk.

The Importance of ISO 14000

The importance of this series of standards can be seen from the following:

- *The 14000 series provides a focus on internal management systems and process efficiency rather than specific performance goals or product characteristics.*

- *The systems are implemented by industry itself, rather than an outside regulatory 'command and control' approach.*

- *The standards require policy commitment to continual improvement, compliance with regulations and prevention of pollution so that organisations can move beyond reactive management and control proactively their environmental impacts.*

- *These standards allow for the independent third-party certification of an organisation's EMS (to ISO 14001), which creates both credibility and integrity.*

- *ISO 14001 conformity will enhance an organisation's public image, decrease liability exposure, provide a mechanism for increasing process efficiency, lower operating costs and contingency set-asides, reduce insurance premiums, decrease potential enforcement penalties, and provide for continual improvement of EMS which will lead to improved environmental performance.*

The Goals of ISO 14000: Their Relation to Key Issues

The goals of ISO 14000 are to evolve a series of generic standards that provide business management with a structured mechanism to measure and manage environmental impacts. By way of example, two major themes throughout the ISO 14000 standards have direct application to the contaminated land or brownfields redevelopment process. The first is the desire for consistency in environmental management standards and practices. The idea is that wherever a company may be located, if the programme complies with the standards, its excellence will be universally recognised.

As a result, international standards are being developed for environmental management systems (ISO 14001–14004); environmental auditing (ISO 14010–14013); internal reviews (ISO 14014); environmental site assessments (ISO 14015); evaluation of environmental performance (ISO 14031); product-oriented standards such as environmental labelling, terms, and definitions for self-declaration environmental claims (ISO 14020–14024); and life-cycle assessment (ISO 14040–14043).

These standards are designed to help an organisation establish and meet its own policy goals through objectives and targets, organisational structures and accountability, management controls and review functions, all with top-management oversight. The focus is on management rather than performance standards. As a result, the centrepiece of this section, the 14001 standard for EMS, provides a framework for assessing, managing and reducing the liabilities associated with environmental aspects of operations. Through several key requirements the 14001 standard places environmental management into the realm of strategic decision-making where, from an organisational perspective, more effective decisions for reducing risks can be made.

There are two key areas where these developments can have obvious impact on the value of an organisation, one is in connection with land and the development of brownfields, the other relates to risk management. In the USA, in particular, the question has been posed whether these principles, standards and management guidance assist in the management and redevelopment of brownfields. This is an issue which, following the impact of Superfund, is of crucial importance there and of growing significance in the UK, as well as in the EU generally. (Examples of how the ISO 14000 certification process can bring benefits to businesses, ranging from economic and technological to social and political are discussed below.)

It can be seen that these same ISO 14000 standards, once they are developed and verified, can be a valuable management tool to turn brownfields into fully utilised properties. As is clear from Chapter 5, contaminated land is a very topical subject and urgent solutions to the problems are needed. This discussion considers the benefits of ISO 14001 generally before then applying the standard to the management of brownfields.

Benefits of ISO 14000

Economic

ISO 14000 brings with it increased operating efficiency by reducing costs, waste and energy usage; preventing pollution; substituting less toxic materials; recovering costs through recycling programmes; and eliminating redundant systems.

Companies are seeking ISO certification in response to market pressures and to maintain and expand their current customer base. Many are also reacting positively to the de facto requirement for supplying products and services world-wide with qualified supplier listings. Others are seeking preferred supplier status and an expanded customer base.

On the regulatory side, ISO 14000 has some direct benefits: certification can result in a decreased number of customer, regulatory and registrar audits, as well as reducing the cost of multiple inspections, certifications and product registrations. Faster permitting and reporting processes can also be realised. In the USA companies that develop a fully integrated EMS may be eligible for the reduction of regulatory penalties by up to 95 per cent, whereas companies with no such compliance programmes can face significantly increased penalties. Another important economic benefit feature of ISO 14000 certification is decreased liability exposure leading to reduced insurance rates and better access to capital.

Technical

The ISO 14000 standards are designed so that certified companies improve their environmental performance by preventing pollution and removing systematic causes of non-compliance. Decisions relating to environmental technologies are internalised, leading to a process which can result in more cost-effective and longer-lasting solutions to pollution problems. This process can create technical environmental performance programmes that can become fully integrated to achieve both short- and long-term strategic business objectives. Not only does this process promote world-wide sustainable development, but it also provides a single EMS for global organisations.

Social

Companies that choose ISO 14000 demonstrate a sincere and credible commitment to the environment, satisfying multiple stockholder interests for corporate accountability while promoting a 'good neighbour' policy. An ISO 14000-certified company projects an image of a socially responsible organisation. Businesses are seeking to demonstrate environmental excellence. Those that integrate environmental awareness and ecological responsibilities with daily operations will have a positive effect on the international marketplace and global community.

Political

Certainly ISO 14000 represents a practical means to manage regulatory compliance proactively. It reframes the regulatory context by using a voluntary consensus approach. This consensus will enhance the environmental performance of companies doing business in countries that have weak or non-existent regulatory systems. ISO 14000 provides a common, systematic approach for international organisations working in countries with different regulatory frameworks. ISO 14000 is not a panacea for bad environmental actors, but it can result in superior performance with less regulatory oversight and burdens.

The Use of ISO 14000 to Improve Brownfields Management and Redevelopment Processes

The experience in the USA, in particular, has demonstrated that no country or company with brownfield sites should embark on a brownfields redevelopment programme without seeking a comprehensive and consistent approach to manage the problem. ISO 14000 can improve brownfields decision-making. A country seeking to understand its brownfields problem, or a company that has multiple brownfield properties, can develop a policy statement and environmental objectives and targets. The system can be designed to reduce risk to residents and neighbours using risk-based corrective action standards, and then recycle these properties for future productive use. Risk-based corrective action simply means that the clean-up standard is dependent on the future use of the property. It is well known that, for instance, more stringent standards are used for parks and residential areas than for paved-over factory or commercial sites. In the USA, for example, according to the *Washington Post*, two of the country's largest outlet shopping malls (in Carson, California and Elizabeth, New Jersey) are being built on brownfields that no one would consider for homes. These projects, and others on a larger scale, need careful planning. ISO 14000 can provide the necessary standards for a major redevelopment project.

Practical Steps

A management system designed pursuant to ISO 14001 is an essential first step in providing a framework for solving the brownfields problem. Managers would begin by inventorying and categorising the properties on the basis of location, size, use (present and past), identity of owners and previous ownership, contamination in soil and groundwater, source of contamination (on-site and off-site), cost of remediation, future uses and so on. A brownfields database would be the centrepiece for a management programme that would be developed and implemented to restore properties or sell them off to businesses or venture capitalists. For those properties that would be retained, policy-planners and senior management can use ISO 14001 to guide their decision-making to reduce or eliminate existing liabilities on the property. A liability inventory is commonly performed in this process.

An ISO-brownfields redevelopment programme would have as its goals increased productivity of property, creation of jobs, reduction of costs, wastes, energy usage, prevention of pollution and unnecessary further industrial development and responsible future use of property. Objectives and goals must be clearly articulated by managers who are seeking to develop appropriate standards to revitalise these distressed properties. Partnership joint ventures can be established to foster simpler and more cost-effective solutions to brownfields problems. ISO 14000 provides the foundation for these important business–social–economic decisions to be made.

The USA Experience

In the USA Brownfields joint ventures have been booming in popularity in the last two-and-a-half years. One example is the environmental merchant bank, Landbank of Denver, which has teamed up with Cherokee Industries of North Carolina to make $5–100 million deals either by buying acreage or entering into a risk-sharing joint venture with property owners. Real estate service firms have joined with environmental remediation firms to jointly propose real estate ventures. Atlantic Environmental Services, for example, has teamed up with North American Realty Advisory Services to redevelop old manufactured gas plant properties that exist in over 2,000 locations throughout the USA. In Los Angeles, the California Centre for Land Recycling has announced that it has formed a partnership with the Trust for Public Land to spur redevelopment of brownfields in that state. The Irvine Foundation has agreed to provide $2 million to finance the start-up of that project. For each of these major joint ventures, an ISO 14001 management plan can guide decision-making and encourage the development of a cost-effective, energy-efficient project.

A brownfields redevelopment programme with an ISO 14000 component can also fulfil many business objectives. Experience in the USA has shown that such a programme can prevent redeveloped sites from becoming eyesores again through current or future mismanagement; reassure current owners, developers, lenders and investors that their liability protection will not be compromised by operations of new enterprises; offer a new way for brownfields entrepreneurs to achieve environmental compliance without regulatory interference or control; and convince government officials and the sceptical public that a trade-off for a lesser level of current clean-up for a potential greater level of environmental consciousness in future site operations is worthwhile.

Continuous Improvement

An important component of ISO 14000 is continuous improvement. There is a significant need not to repeat the mistakes of the past. In this context, ISO-brownfields redevelopment and management projects must not only avoid land-use problems that have created industrial waste, but must also improve the future use of the properties. Energy-efficient 'green buildings', open space, conservation easements and other innovative planning techniques make important contributions to the quality of life in communities. Advisers familiar with ISO standards are uniquely qualified to provide sound management advice to create projects that will benefit society in the near and distant future.

Recommendations

Brownfields redevelopment projects should do more than simply foster healthy communities throughout our cities. With careful planning using ISO standards, brownfields can be redeveloped in conjunction with an infrastructure that will conserve environmentally-sensitive areas and reduce urban and suburban sprawl. Projects with sound community planning will attract private-sector financing and expand market resources that are critical to brownfields development.

Carefully planned efforts will undoubtedly attract environmentally-sound industries that will prevent the future spread of brownfields and foster environmentally- and economically-sustainable communities. ISO 14000, used in conjunction with economic planning processes, will permit consistency and conformity with accepted standards to replace the haphazard industrialisation that occurred before people were aware of the devastating impacts of pollution.

The ISO 14000 standards will have a dramatic effect on the way business is conducted throughout the world. If adopted by companies in significant numbers, estimated impacts should be reduced. The ISO 14000 standards can do more than create better business planning in the future. Properly utilised, they can assist countries and companies to remediate brownfields and turn these into productive properties that will be continuously improved in the future.

Managing Environmental Risk: A Systems Approach

More generally, the field of environmental risk management is relatively new and has developed rapidly over the past several years. Until the development of the ISO standards, there has been, however, a significant lack of integration of seemingly dissimilar disciplines into a meaningful context for top-management risk decisions. The more recent broad-based approach, centred on the ISO 14001 standard for EMS, addresses many of the issues that have kept environmental risk management focused on technical rather than strategic issues.

Since the first Earth Day in 1970, the EPA has passed thousands of pages of complex, involved regulations for protecting the environment. These regulations are often difficult to interpret and implement, and have resulted in the new position of 'environmental manager' for any firms that are required to comply with these statutes. Environmental managers have taken on the complicated and difficult tasks of ensuring that their organisations comply with the laws, and that management is not unduly exposed to the risks of fines and/or imprisonment. The data generated as a result of these efforts present an intricate picture of organisational operations, but in most cases are not adaptable to strategic decisions and are difficult to piece together in order to achieve an overall picture of where the firm stands with respect to its environmental liabilities.

While the increase in regulatory requirements has resulted in improvements to specific environmental media such as air, water and land, as well as the clean-up of highly contaminated areas, the overall response of industry has been to merely react to the requirements and attempt to achieve compliance through end-of-pipe solutions. The environmental profiles and risk-related information have been pushed into lower levels of management where the sheer volume of data is often difficult to interpret and manage, and is generally not placed into the context of strategic decisions to allocate precious organisational resources. The end result is that environmental liabilities have been ignored unless they approached extreme levels, at which point top management become involved. However, for many organisations, this is too late and their operational and financial performance suffers as they find themselves trying to quickly fix problems that had taken many years to develop.

As has been seen, the ISO series of standards changes the scenario greatly. The ISO 14001 standard describes an integrated series of processes that are intended to provide organisations with the elements of effective EMSs that can be integrated with other management requirements in order to assist them to achieve environmental and economic goals. These types of EMSs are intended to support environmental protection and prevention of pollution in balance with socio-economic needs.

From a risk management viewpoint, the standard provides a framework for assessing, managing and reducing the liabilities associated with the environmental aspects of operations. Through key requirements, the ISO 14001 standard places environmental management into the realm of strategic decision-making, where more effective decisions for reducing risks can be made. The ISO 14001 standard can be used to integrate the risk and environmental management processes into an effective strategy for identifying, analysing, controlling and reducing environmental exposures.

It is becoming understood more and more that corporations that have achieved ISO 14001 certification will have demonstrated a positive commitment to managing the immediate and long-term impacts of their products, services and processes on the environment. ISO 14001 conformance should favourably impact the cost and availability of environmental liability insurance products. Corporations which demonstrate that they are proactive environmentally should receive favourable underwriting consideration and should qualify for a decrease in premium levels. Several environmental insurance companies have already committed to include ISO 14001 certification as a critical factor in their environmental risk management underwriting processes.

The ISO 14001 process requires that a company conducts internal EMS audits. The results of EMS audits can be used to provide much of the environmental management programme details normally covered in an Environmental Risk Assessment Survey for insurance underwriting purposes.

Key Elements: The ISO 14001 EMS Standard and Risk Management Standard

The ISO 14001 standard for EMSs incorporates the basic principles of systems theory, and outlines an organisational framework for the systematic identification, control and improvement of environmental aspects and impacts. Rather than focus directly on environmental performance, the standard addresses the management systems used to control environmental performance. This is a marked departure from the command and control approach to environmental management. Whereas management is still accountable for attaining emission levels prescribed by regulations and agreements, through an integrated series of management systems, it can actively seek ways to reduce or eliminate pollutants and go beyond compliance.

In particular, corporate management and their advisers should recognise that the standard requires five basic activities that organisations must follow. First, to establish top management commitment to environmental management and promulgate a comprehensive environmental policy; secondly, to develop objectives, targets and a programme to implement the environmental priorities stated in the policy; thirdly, to perform the activities necessary to achieve the objectives and targets, develop documents and records, and train employees in their environmental responsibilities; fourthly, to monitor and measure on a regular basis the performance of the EMS; and lastly, to review the entire set of environmental management activities periodically to ensure continual improvement.

These basic activities comprise the essence of the EMSs required by ISO 14001, and are intended to facilitate allocation of resources, assignment of responsibilities, and ongoing evaluation of practices, procedures and processes to ensure achievement of the environmental policy requirements.

Thus the standard views the organisation from the process perspective, defines the 'big picture' of environmental responsibility through the policy statement and seeks structural solutions through comprehensive monitoring, internal audits and management reviews.

Using ISO 14001 in Practice to Manage Environmental Risks

The ISO 14001 standard for environmental management provides a practical and workable framework for controlling environmental risk. Its focus on continual improvement and prevention of pollution encourages entities to move from reactive risk management and risk financing into comprehensive risk control activities. Following this path, organisations and their advisers assure themselves and their financial partners, including insurance partners, that they are identifying, prioritising and actively managing environmental exposures to lessen the likelihood of loss.

Baseline

ISO 14001 first addresses risk by requiring that a baseline of environmental performance be developed through the identification of environmental aspects and legal and other requirements. These sections of the standard may require performing an initial review, which, if properly structured, can also serve as a risk-assessment tool for determining environmental liabilities. The results of this initial review can furnish top management with a complete picture of organisational processes and their associated environmental impacts. Additionally, the review links legal requirements with these operations so management has a clear understanding of what operations are being performed, what the environmental aspects of those operations are, what regulatory requirements are applicable to each and where the significant risks exist.

The first step to an ISO 14001 EMS is to develop a baseline of existing conditions. This is done by performing a process known as an 'initial review', which provides a complete picture of the organisation's processes, environmental aspects and impacts, and regulatory and other compliance requirements. This baseline provides a factual basis for identifying actual and potential environmental exposures, and builds a foundation for setting an organisation's environmental priorities. Management can integrate these factors into its strategic decision-making process.

The baseline step correlates with the three primary steps of the risk assessment process: hazard identification, exposure assessment and risk characterisation. The 14001 standard requires an identification of environmental aspects and impacts, and a determination of their significance. This review furnishes data that provides input into technical risk assessments, and data upon which management can make various strategic decisions.

The review of conditions and impacts, and the determination of legal and other requirements, are critical to the continual improvement of the EMS. The baseline is important as the first step in setting initial risk management priorities, and is merely the beginning of the risk management cycle.

Policy and Planning

Translating the results of the initial review into a policy statement, objectives and targets and an environmental programme is the second area of potential risk reduction. By requiring top management to set environmental policy, the organisation must clearly delineate its values and priorities, one of which must be a commitment to the prevention of pollution. The policy serves as the background for specific objectives and targets, becoming the compass for managing environmental risk. By committing to eliminate the causes of potential hazards, management launches a process of systematically identifying and reducing or eliminating polluting substances and environmental hazards.

Management can use the policy and the initial review to guide the organisation in its quest to reduce or eliminate liabilities based on the integration of accurate factual information about organisational processes and overall organisational priorities. By following up with a management review at periodic intervals, the standard assures that environmental information within the purview of top management and organisational learning about environmental performance are included in the strategic decision-making process.

In addition, compliance with regulatory requirements becomes merely the minimum and going beyond compliance becomes the accepted way of doing business.

The next phase of an ISO 14001 EMS is to codify the management's environmental priorities in a policy statement supported by objectives and targets. The policy, objectives and targets define the 'big picture' perspective, which provides the impetus for a series of actions to minimise risks emanating from uncontrolled emissions, non-compliance with regulatory requirements, inadequate environmental management practices and uncorrected adverse conditions. This is also the opportunity to prevent losses by removing or reducing the causes of pollution and any 'leftover' liabilities from previous incidents. In addition, identifying impacts on local communities provides the basis for a 'good neighbour' policy and prevention of adverse social impacts.

The policy serves as an organisational 'compass' to provide long-term direction and reinforcement of fundamental values. It is the tool that senior management can use to communicate their vision and the company's direction. Effective environmental policies cover areas of high risk for the organisation, and are derived from the initial review.

A corporate environmental policy addresses the full realm of environmental risks facing an organisation. The policy should cover the following topics:

- minimising risk to employees and communities;

- emergency preparedness;

- complying with regulations and laws;

- defining responsibility and authority for environmental management;

- providing employee education and awareness;

- evaluating the environmental impact of processes and materials;

- reducing, recycling and re-using materials;

- minimising waste and reducing emissions;

- co-operating with regulatory agencies;

- actively participating in public policy development;

- measuring attainment of objectives and goals.

Actions

A third key area of the standard that provides risk-management tools is in personnel management. In the USA, for example, the majority of regulatory non-compliances that have been reported to the EPA have been from disgruntled employees. It would seem, therefore, this area can be particularly troublesome for management. The standard requires that the environmental responsibilities of each employee whose work impacts the environment be defined and communicated, and that they be provided with adequate resources to implement and control the EMS. In addition, employees must be trained and competent, and must be informed about the performance of the organisation's EMS. These actions can serve to increase the satisfaction levels of employees and reduce the likelihood that non-compliances will either exist or be prematurely reported to the regulatory authorities.

Once management has determined its environmental priorities it moves forward to define a detailed environmental programme, including specific structure and responsibilities for achieving its environmental goals. ISO 14001 promotes the idea that minimising environmental impact is the responsibility of each employee. An organisation-wide awareness is created, which in turn is supported by comprehensive training programmes. These actions greatly reduce the risk of unplanned emissions, as well as reducing the risk that an employee will violate the law, knowingly or unknowingly.

Deployment of responsibility for environmental impacts within the organisation is the key issue here. Many organisations have already done this with the ISO 9000 quality management systems standard, as it embraces the principle of making product and service quality the responsibility of those performing the work. By including environmental requirements in each job, management makes each employee responsible for potential emissions to the environment, and supports the employees by providing resources to control and eliminate these emissions. As a result, the risks of unplanned or accidental emissions are reduced because these emissions are routinely controlled by those directly involved in the operations rather than involving external personnel in an oversight control method such as compliance auditing.

Communications

The fourth area of potential risk reduction is in the area of documents and records. By requiring comprehensive document control and record management systems, the standard provides for the gathering and retention of information about the environmental performance of the organisation. This information may be crucial in establishing the position of the organisation should any legal proceedings arise, or should the organisation report its environmental performance to interested parties. Most organisations will find that as they refine and centralise their document and record management systems, duplication and redundancy are reduced, and that needed information becomes more available.

The ISO 14001 requirements for internal and external communications create a positive perception of the organisation and its environmental policies. A dialogue with interested parties can help organisations to deal with emerging issues of concern and demonstrate a proactive stance on the environment. This strategic element reduces the risk of citizen suits and negative customer perceptions, and can give an organisation some 'breathing space' when confronted by a contentious or sensitive environmental issue.

This requirement also affords the organisation an opportunity to address the quality of life issues not normally considered in a technical risk assessment. These issues often reflect the values and social concerns of the community, which can be included in organisational decision-making through an active, two-way communication process involving interested parties. The organisation can use this communication process to address its environmental impacts on diverse groups of people and lifestyles. It can ensure that community perceptions of environmental risks are accurate and undistorted by rumour and/or media. In some cases an organisation may even be able to demonstrate that its environmental protection activities actually save a community money, or maintain and create jobs, both of which cast a positive light on a company and its management.

Information Management

A final area that can improve risk management practices is in the generation of timely and accurate information about the environmental aspects and impacts of organisational operations. The standard requires routine monitoring and measuring of environmental performance, as well as the prevention, detection and correction of non-conformities. Additionally, internal auditing provides management with data about the degree of implementation and effectiveness of the management systems used to achieve environmental performance. These types of data can be tracked, trended and used as the basis for continual identification and reduction of risks. Overall, the 14001 standard fosters better management decisions and a clearer basis for risk reduction because it improves the quality of the environmental performance information that is available to management.

The ISO 14001 ensures the development and implementation of a logical system of process documentation. The requirements for document control assure that management can locate and retrieve the documents necessary for operating the systems, reducing the risk of uncontrolled operations. To further reduce this risk, the standard requires a comprehensive definition and implementation of operational controls to ensure achievement of the objectives and targets. The controls provide direct assurance that operations have been evaluated and that they are being carried out under optimum conditions, and that both suppliers and contractors are involved in responsible environmental management.

The standard requires management to develop and test procedures for emergency situations, which provide guidance for preventing and mitigating the broad range of circumstances that could be encountered during emergencies. These procedures greatly reduce the risk from unplanned events by forcing management to consider the range of probable emergencies and their impact, and to prepare for possible losses in advance of their occurrence.

The 14001 requirements for emergency preparedness and response can assure management that contingency planning and crisis management are integral parts of organisational life, and that any potential impacts resulting from unplanned accidents will be dealt with in an appropriate manner. Crisis management can provide assurance to stakeholders as well that the organisation has planned for unforeseen events and is acting as a responsible citizen, thus reducing the likelihood of citizen suits or poor community relations.

One of the greatest strengths of this standard is its provisions for environmental information generation, retention and evaluation. This information comes from routine monitoring and measuring of operations, corrective and preventive actions and EMS audits. By having access to these different types of information, management can more accurately assess potential and actual risk exposures and can better plan to eliminate or reduce them. The generation of environmental information on a continual basis allows management to stay on top of changing conditions that could result in new or unexpected environmental exposures.

Data quality is a central issue in environmental risk management. Incomplete, inaccurate or incomparable data can greatly distort any type of management decision, which in turn could have serious implications for decisions required by the organisation. The implementation of ISO 14001 highlights any existing gaps in knowledge and data that decision-makers must grapple with as they define and control risks. One of the biggest benefits from an ISO 14001 EMS is the focus on filling in these data gaps in a comprehensive manner. By ensuring that environmental data comes from a broad array of activities and that these activities are related to specific objectives and targets, management assures itself of a high level of data integrity for strategic environmental decisions.

Strategic Review

Finally, the standard contains a provision for a management review of the entire system, in the light of actual performance and external conditions. This builds in an ongoing strategic risk management process, which ensures that both internal and external changes, that could result in changed risk exposures but may have otherwise gone unnoticed, are fully considered and included in strategic decisions. The management review also provides the foundation for continual improvement.

Management review engages strategic planners and top management in the task of evaluating the effectiveness of existing systems and seeking structural solutions for reducing risks and preventing undesirable incidents. This review must consider implicit and explicit issues, intended and desired results, what actually happened as a result of management actions, changes in the organisation, changes in the marketplace and changes in government and communities during the last planning period. The combination of intended results and actual results is what strategic analysts call realised strategy, or what the actual state of the organisation was during the period of review.

For example, although management may enact controls for minimising the release of a certain chemical, the unintended use or disposal of products may have a severe effect on customer perception of the firm as environmentally responsible. During the management review, top management should address the implicit and explicit aspects of this issue to take advantage of the opportunity to build customer satisfaction, and may decide to enact other related actions, such as product labelling, product redesign to remove toxic or hazardous materials, elimination of packaging or developing the infrastructure for product recycling. The management review allows merging of environmental considerations with financial objectives, customer satisfaction criteria, measures of internal management excellence and community activities.

In short, strategic review determines whether the choices and decisions made during the risk management process to control environmental risks worked.

Concluding Remarks

The ISO 14001 standard serves as an excellent environmental risk management framework to ensure that a business systematically evaluates and analyses existing and potential exposures before losses occur. ISO 14001 raises environmental decisions to the strategic realm, where risks can be assessed and long-term resource allocations can be made using a 'big picture' perspective that includes competitive considerations and existing operational priorities. Practitioners should also be aware of the role that the standards can play in enabling their clients to perform the balancing act referred to above in regulation and voluntarism.

By implementing ISO 14001, top management ensures that it is effectively handling its environmental risks and limiting its exposures, addressing structural solutions and reducing the need for excessive risk financing. Environmental loss controls, such as those promulgated by the ISO 14001 EMSs, place an entity in the best position to access environmental insurance or other risk financing vehicles for an acceptable cost. ISO 14001 is truly a systems framework that enables organisations and their advisers to include environmental risk management as a strategy for their future.

Chapter 8

Environmental Liability

Introductory Remarks

The prospect of environmental liability can no longer be regarded as an American scare story. In mid-1991, Mountleigh (a leading property company in the UK) went into receivership with very serious consequences for its financiers. Mountleigh's collapse was linked to its inability to sell a £125m project, the Merryhill Shopping Centre, which was built on contaminated land. The project site had previously been used partly as an industrial tip by British Steel and partly as a landfill site. When the deal failed, the company could no longer continue to service its loan repayments and consequently collapsed.

Another example involved the owners of a successful hotel, funded by a well-known bank, who decided to sell it and realise their profit in the venture. During the negotiations it emerged that the hotel was built on contaminated land – the site of a defunct petrol station. The sale fell through, and due to the environmental and health implications the LA put a closure order on the business.

Clearly, environmental issues are presenting serious liability risks for business and this chapter is intended to set out the basic legal position and to consider the following issues: criminal liability; civil liability; liability of directors, managers and company officers; and lender liability

Criminal Liabilities

In the UK, there are a number of statutes imposing criminal sanctions on those who are in breach of environmental law. The sanctions imposed can be very severe depending on which section of the law is breached and may include imprisonment, unlimited fines and withdrawal of trading permits.

The Environmental Protection Act 1990

Part I: IPC/LAAPC Offences

As has been mentioned in earlier chapters, Part I EPA governs the system of IP, and the related system of LAAPC. These systems require the more polluting industries (defined in Regulations) to be licensed by the EA, or the relevant LA, before being carried on.

Under s23 generally, it is an offence for a person to carry on a prescribed process except under a licence (an authorisation, occasionally referred to as a consent) and in accordance with its conditions; fail to comply with enforcement or prohibition notices served by the regulatory body; obstruct an inspector in the exercise of his powers; or commit deception, forgery etc.

Part II: Waste-related Offences

Part II EPA governs the system of the regulation of waste. Those in the business of dealing with, treating or disposing of 'waste' as defined in the Regulations are required to obtain a licence from the EA. The waste management licensing regime was introduced on 1 May 1994 by the Waste Management Licensing Regulations 1994 (SI 1994 No 1056) (WMLR 1994), and the detailed provisions are to be found in the Regulations. An overview of the waste regulatory regime can be found in Chapter 6. A number of Guidance Notes were published at the same time as the Regulations and have been updated subsequently. Any business and/or its advisers needing to undertake further research in this area should take note of them. Those who produce waste as a by-product of a process or activity must comply with the statutory duty of care in relation to that material.

Under s33 (as amended by Regulations) it is an offence for a person to deposit, abandon, dump or knowingly cause or permit to be deposited, abandoned or dumped controlled waste (now known as 'Directive waste') without, or in breach of, a licence; dispose of or recover (or knowingly cause or permit the disposal or recovery of) 'Directive waste' without, or in breach of, a licence; treat, keep, dispose of or recover 'Directive waste' in a manner likely to cause pollution or harm to health; breach any condition of a waste management licence; or breach the duty of care contained in s24.

'Directive waste' is anything which is discarded, ie abandoned, dumped, disposed of or put in its final resting place, or subjected to a recovery operation without which it is useless.

The offences of 'depositing' or 'causing' (as redefined) will require proof of some positive act on the part of the defendant; 'permitting' is the act of allowing something to occur, once it is known that it is likely to occur, though there is no need to show knowledge of the illegality of the deposit.

Part IIA: Contaminated Land

The new Part IIA EPA, discussed more fully in Chapter 4, contains the contaminated land provisions (ss78A–78YC).

Those sections provide that it is an offence for the person served with a remediation notice by a LA in respect of contaminated land, to fail, without reasonable excuse, to comply with any of the requirements of the notice.

The 'person served' is the appropriate person as defined by Part IIA and GNs, that is the original polluter, or the owner or occupier if the original polluter cannot be found, subject to exclusionary tests in the GNs. These provisions are not yet in force and are unlikely to be published before the spring of 1999.

Part III: Statutory Nuisance

The common law rules on nuisance are supplemented by statute. The legislation aims at passing the control of public health into the hands of the LA administration and to criminalise public health offences. Part III EPA deals with statutory nuisance which came into force on 1 January 1991. The Act restates and updates the law relating to statutory nuisance. It also contains improvements in the summary procedures for dealing with such nuisances. This repeals the relevant sections of the Public Health Act 1936 (ss91-100), and also the Public Health (Recurring Nuisances) Act 1969. It is an attempt by Parliament to introduce a system of integrated pollution control providing for the improved control of pollution arising from industrial and other processes. However, nuisances relating to watercourses, ditches and ponds are still covered by ss259-265 Public Health Act 1936.

Part III EPA covers various issues including litter, abandoned shopping trolleys, waste on land, pollution at sea, clean air, stubble burning, genetically modified organisms, dogs, nature conservation and statutory nuisance.

There is a common factor linking those nuisances listed in the EPA. They must be prejudicial to health or must constitute a nuisance. These are alternatives (*Betts* v *Penge Urban District Council*).[1] There is no statutory definition of nuisance: the common law definition of private or public nuisance applies (*National Coal Board* v *Thorne*).[2] Accordingly, it is necessary to show that the activities constituting the alleged nuisance emanate from one site and interfere with the enjoyment of property owners on another site. Therefore it is an aspect of a property right. A property owner could allege interference with the enjoyment of their properties or injury to their health, especially if supported by professional evidence from a medical expert or from an environmental health officer. They need not establish actual injury if they can show that it is likely to cause injury. This will be sufficient to be prejudicial to health as defined in section 1(7) of the Act where the meaning is stated as 'injurious to health or likely to cause an injury to health'. In fact, the historical origin of statutory nuisances dates back to the Victorian era. However, as seen above, the provisions are now codified in the Public Health Act 1936, which was designed to deal with aspects of public health. Although the commission of a statutory nuisance may involve other aspects of environmental harm, enforcement action will only occur if some injury has occurred or is threatened to people. LA environmental health officers are responsible for enforcement.

Section 79 Offences

This is the most important section, listing activities which can constitute a statutory nuisance. The list is an expanded version of the previous statute. It is, however, not an exhaustive list and the provisions cover:

Section 79(1)(a): Housing Conditions

Where premises are unfit for human habitation, the court may issue an order prohibiting their use for human habitation. However, the general principle of statutory nuisance remains unaltered: 'any premises in such a state as to be prejudicial to health or a nuisance'. This covers extreme dampness and structural defects in properties. In some modern flats the problem of condensation has become particularly acute. By way of example, in *Greater London Council* v *Tower Hamlets LBC*[3] it was held that extensive dampness and mould growth were sufficiently bad in the circumstances of the case to constitute a statutory nuisance.

The person aggrieved must serve notice on the person responsible stating the intention to bring proceedings and setting out the matter complained of. The notice period must be at least 21 days, unless it is in respect of noise, when it can be three days. The person to be served must be the person responsible, unless that person cannot be found, when the owner or occupier is liable. Where the nuisance arises from a structural defect the owner is liable. Costs are no longer in the discretion of the court where the nuisance is proved, but are granted automatically to the complainant. Breach of the order constitutes a criminal offence.

Section 79(1)(b): Smoke

Section 79(l)(b) provides that 'smoke emitted from premises so as to be prejudicial to health or a nuisance' shall constitute a statutory nuisance. This does not cover smoke from chimneys of private dwellings in smoke-control areas, dark smoke from boilers or industrial plants, smoke emitted from railway locomotive steam engines or any other dark smoke from industrial or trade premises. The protection afforded to steam engines was achieved by a steam engine enthusiast in the House of Lords.

It should be understood that the EPA 1990 extends statutory nuisance to cover smoke in domestic premises, such as weekend bonfires, soot, ash, grit and gritty particles. Historically, the original legislation relating to smoke was prompted not by industrial polluters, but by domestic coal burning. In fact the infamous London smog of 1952 prompted the Clean Air Act 1956 which introduced the present system of smoke control.

Provisions relating to clean air are included for the first time alongside other statutory nuisances, although the Clean Air Act 1993, which consolidated and updated the Clean Air Acts 1956 and 1968, and which came into force on 27 August 1993 makes further provision in respect of air pollution. Further comment may be found in Chapter 5. If the smoke emitted from the burning of rubbish is dark smoke, that is smoke which is as dark or darker than shade 2 on the Ringelmann Chart, then an offence has been committed under the Clean Air Act 1993.

There is a defence if the emission was inadvertent or if the defendant can show that he had taken all practicable steps to prevent or minimise the emission.

Section 79(1)(c): Premises

Emissions of fumes or gas are covered in respect of private premises only. 'Fumes' includes solid airborne matter smaller than dust, and gas includes vapour and moisture emitted from vapour. Premises are defined so as to be wide enough to include land even where that land is in a natural state. For instance in *Leakey* v *National Trust*,[4] it was held that a hill which slipped after severe weather onto the plaintiffs land was part of the premises. The defendants were liable in nuisance for failing to prevent the landslip.

Section 79(1)(d)-(f)

Dust and other effluvia were covered under former provisions. The provisions relating to smell and steam are, therefore, new (s79(l)(d)). They apply to industrial trade or business premises. It may have particular application to restaurants and launderettes. Again, the steam rail enthusiast succeeded in excluding steam engines from this provision. Provisions relating to accumulation or deposits (s79(l)(e)) and animals (s79(l)(f)) are repeated from the former Public Health Act.

Section 79(1)(g): Noise

Section 79(l)(g) covers noise emitted from premises so as to be prejudicial to health or a nuisance. This was previously covered by ss58, 59 Control of Pollution Act 1974. Noise complaints received by LA environmental health departments have increased significantly. The courts are prepared to take a pragmatic view. In *Coventry City Council* v *Harris*[5] the Crown Court accepted that a leading brass-band player should be allowed to practice his trumpet in a semi-detached house, but limited it to one hour a day. In *London Borough of Southwark* v *Ince*[6] the noise from the nearby Old Kent Road was sufficient to constitute a nuisance in the light of the Council's failure to insulate the flats adequately so as to minimise the noise.

The noise from dogs could be prosecuted under the same subsection. It might be possible to allege that dogs were kept in such as way as to be prejudicial to health or a nuisance (s79(l)(f)). It was held in *Galer* v *Morrisey*,[7] that an animal could not fall within the section merely because it was noisy, although this was doubted in *Coventry City Council* v *Cartwright*.[8] It may be the case that there are local bye-laws prohibiting the keeping of noisy animals which would provide an alternative cause of action.

Generator noise is clearly capable of falling within this section provided the environmental health officers are able to provide evidence, which may include evidence of a scientific nature such as noise measurements, as to the level and quality of the noise. Vibrations from machinery are also included within the definition of noise (s79(7)).

The increasing concern about noise nuisance is reflected in the implementation of the Noise and Statutory Nuisance Act 1993, which came into force in January 1994. This Act inserted 'noise ... emitted from or caused by a vehicle, machinery or equipment in a street' into the list of statutory nuisances in s79 EPA. It also inserted a new section 80A which deals with abatement notices in respect of noise in the street. The 1993 Act also provides for noise caused by burglar alarms and loudspeakers in streets and it makes it clear that the power of abatement in s79(1)(g) includes the power of LAs to seize and remove equipment which it appears is being used in the emission of noise.

A further Noise Act was passed in July 1996. However, although new noise offences are set out in ss2-9 of this Act, it is only likely to be of limited use as the new noise offences will only apply to areas chosen by the LA (s1). Hence noise control will vary from area to area. It has been reported (*The Times* 7 May 1997) that Tower Hamlets has already decided to adopt the Act.[9] In addition, the Act does not address the problem of cumulative noise incidents and it does not deal with noise affecting or emanating to or from business premises.

Recent Noise Case Law

In *R* v *Tunbridge Wells JJ, ex Parte Tunbridge Wells BC* (1996) Env LR 88, noise from amplified music illustrated further weaknesses. An abatement notice need not contain a date for compliance where the notice merely prohibited the occurrence or recurrence of a nuisance.[10]

Section 80(7): The Defence of 'Best Practicable Means'

It is a defence to prove that the BPM were used to prevent, or counteract, the effects of the nuisance. The defence is limited. In the case of premises, dust, steam, smell or other effluvia, accumulation or deposits, animals or noise, the defence is only available where the nuisance arises on industrial trade or business premises. It is not available in respect of the smoke nuisance as the smoke is emitted from an open site not through a chimney (s80(8)(b)). BPM include such matters as local conditions or circumstances, the current state of technical knowledge and the financial implications. The means may include the design, installation, maintenance and operation of plants and machinery and the design, construction and maintenance of buildings.

It is for the defendant to establish the defence. The standard of proof required for the defence is the civil standard of the balance of probabilities. The defendant must show that reasonable practicable means have been taken to deal with the nuisance. In *Chapman* v *Gosberton Farm Produce Co Ltd*,[11] the defendant had sought planning permission to construct a device which would have countered the effect of the noise coming from his premises. The local planning authority had asked him for further information relating to his application and he failed to comply with this request. When prosecuted for nuisance, he argued that his application for planning permission constituted the BPM to deal with the nuisance. The judge held that as he had not provided the further information he could not rely on the defence. The judge used the term 'reasonable' in relation to the defendant's endeavours, rather than 'best'. However, this case leaves open the question as to whether the defendant could have relied on the defence if he had supplied the further information and his application had then been refused.

Procedural Aspects: s80 and Nuisance Abatement

The LA has a duty to inspect its areas from time to time to detect any statutory nuisances. If a complaint is made by a local resident, the LA must take such steps as are reasonably practicable to investigate the complaint. This double duty will operate to oblige those LAs which had previously declined to inspect council premises to reverse their policy.

The action could be brought by the environmental health officers of the LA. The procedure would initially involve service of an abatement notice in respect of the nuisances. The authority has a duty to serve such a notice where it is satisfied of the existence of the nuisance in that it is continuing or is likely to occur or recur. The notice must require the abatement of the nuisance or its prohibition or restriction and the execution of such works, and the taking of such other steps as are necessary (s80(l)).

It is to be served on the person responsible or, if the nuisance arises from a structural defect, on the owner of the premises. If the person responsible cannot be found, then it must be served on the owner or occupier (s80(2)).

There is, however, some question as to the extent of the duty of LAs. LAs are faced with an increasing volume of complaints in respect of noise, and their ability to bring formal action in all cases may become increasingly limited. There is no reported decision which provides a precedent for the extent of their duty under the EPA. On the other hand there is some evidence of attempts by local residents to oblige LAs to act. The notice should be served on the defendant as the person responsible for the nuisance or as the owner/occupier of the site. As seen below, the defendant has a right of appeal to the magistrates' court against the abatement notice, but if he does not exercise this right, and has no reasonable excuse for his failure to comply with the notice, the LA may bring proceedings for breach of notice. The maximum fine under these circumstances, as the owner of industrial, trade or business premises, is £20,000.

There is also provision for any other affected local resident to institute private proceedings in the event that the LA does not act (82). The application goes directly to the magistrates' court; there is no power for a private individual to serve an abatement notice. In any event notice of intention to bring proceedings must be served on the defendant. In the case of the noise nuisance, this must be three days' notice; in all other cases 21 days.

Right of Appeal (s80(3))

The EPA 1990 introduced a new right of appeal. The person served has a right of appeal to the magistrates' court within 21 days from service of the notice. The grounds of appeal are circumscribed by the Statutory Nuisance (Appeals) Regulations 1990.[12] This prevents appeals being lodged automatically without any justifiable grounds in order to defer the effect of the abatement notice.

While an appeal is pending, the abatement notice may be suspended. In order to prevent the suspension, the LA may insert a declaration in the abatement notice that it will remain effective on grounds set out in the regulations. If the person served contravenes or fails to comply with the notice, without reasonable excuse, then a criminal offence has been committed (s80(4)). The LA is not obliged to prosecute for failure to comply with a notice.

However, whether or not it prosecutes, the LA may abate the nuisance and do whatever works are necessary (s81(3)). It may recover expenses incurred in abating the nuisance (s81(4)), although they are often reluctant to do so because of the disputes which afterwards arise about the cost of the work or the efficacy of it or the need for it. Section 81A, inserted by the Noise and Statutory Nuisance Act 1993, provides that where the LA incurs expenses in abating or preventing the recurrence of a nuisance, these may be charged on the property to which they relate.

In view of the potential reluctance by LAs to proceed, it is important to bear in mind that it remains possible for a private individual who is aggrieved by a statutory nuisance to bring private proceedings in the magistrates' court. The court has power to make an order requiring the defendant to abate the nuisance and carry out necessary works (s82). This will, therefore, continue to be useful where an LA declines to act for whatever reason such as where the nuisance arises in respect of LA accommodation.

Water Pollution: s259 Public Health Act 1936

River quality, insofar as it is in a state that is prejudicial to health or a nuisance, is a statutory nuisance under this section. Thus the local environmental health department has an overlapping jurisdiction with the EA. In practice, it would seem that LAs do not use this provision, appearing to rely on the pollution control officers of the EA to deal with polluted watercourses. This is discussed further in Chapter 5.

Water Resources Act 1991

Pollution Offences

The WRA determines the powers and duties of the EA in respect of water-related issues. Further discussion of emissions to water is to be found in Chapter 5. Briefly, the WRA creates a series of water pollution offences which the EA and others can use to prosecute polluters. As a result of ss85–89 it is an offence for a person to:

- cause or knowingly permit poisonous, noxious or polluting matter or any solid waste matter to enter 'controlled waters';

- reach any prohibition or condition imposed under s86 relating to discharges from a drain or sewer;

- cause or knowingly permit trade or sewage effluent to be discharged into controlled waters or by pipe into the sea;

- cause or knowingly permit trade or effluent to be discharged in breach of any prohibition or condition imposed under s86 from buildings or plant on to land or into lakes or ponds which are not inland freshwaters;

- cause or knowingly permit any matter to enter inland freshwaters so as to tend to impede the proper flow of the waters in a manner leading or likely to lead to a substantial aggravation of pollution or its consequences;

- contravene a prohibition under s86.

Although these provisions seem absolute in their terms the EA has the power to issue discharge consents and, provided their terms are complied with, no offence is committed.

The offence of 'causing' a pollution offence will, again, require proof of a positive act on the part of the defendant.

'Permitting' the offence can consist of merely allowing pollution to occur. This includes not preventing it if it were possible to do so, in actual knowledge of the circumstances, or after turning a blind eye to the obvious, or deliberately refraining from enquiry for fear of the truth.

Practitioners should note a recent case involving the run-off of fire-fighting water into controlled waters, whereby it was held that the site owner caused water pollution rather than the fire service.

There is the additional offence of 'failing to comply with consent conditions'. This offence can be committed by any person who is subject to the benefit and burden of the consent itself, whether or not they own any land or carry on any industrial activity themselves. This was established by the case of *Taylor Woodrow Property Management Ltd* v *NRA* [1994] Env LR D20, where the consent was issued to Company A, but associated Company B was responsible for policing the outfall to the river. Despite not owning the land and not carrying on any activities, Company B was prosecuted successfully for allowing polluting matter to enter waters in breach of the consent.[13]

Ignorance of the law has never been a defence; it now seems that ignorance of the facts is no defence either. Failure to make all reasonable enquiries, and then take steps to stop any pollution from occurring, may therefore be a criminal offence.

Private prosecutions can also be brought under these WRA provisions – the EA is not the only body with power to bring such prosecutions. By way of example, one of the objects of some environmental organisations is to assist in bringing legal action to prevent environmental damages.

Procedural Offences

Under ss161A–161S which were inserted by the EA 1995, it is an offence for the person served with a works notice by the EA to fail to comply with any of the requirements of the notice. The person served is the person who caused or knowingly permitted the polluting matter to be present.

This provision is not yet in force and pressure is being brought for this procedure to be applied by the EA in accordance with principles similar to those imposed on LAs by GNs in respect of contaminated land.

Currently, there is nothing in the new provisions requiring the EA to take specific account of guidance, but there is power for the Secretary of State to make regulations governing form, content and procedure. If similar considerations are not imposed on the EA, the works notice is likely to be much more readily used than the remediation notice relating to contaminated land. It would therefore be a much more important short-term target for attention by lawyers and clients.

Water Industry Act 1991

Discharge offences relating to trade effluent

The WIA sets out the powers and duties of the privatised water companies. Under s118 it is an offence for an occupier of trade premises to discharge trade effluent into public sewers without or in breach of the sewerage undertaker's consents as to the nature and composition, the quantity and rate of the discharge and identification of the sewers into which the discharge can be made.

Public Nuisance

Public nuisance is a criminal offence. It is very broad in scope and enables the courts to categorise as criminal such activities that may not be covered by statute or other common law crimes. Arguably, it could be used as a safety net to deal with assaults on the environment which are not prohibited by statute.

Public nuisance may be defined as an act unwarranted by law or an omission to discharge a legal duty which materially affects the life, health, property, morals or reasonable comfort and convenience of a class of Her Majesty's subjects who come within the sphere or neighbourhood of its operations.

The Attorney-General acting on his own or in realtor's proceedings may seek an injunction to prevent public nuisance. Furthermore, an LA is entitled to proceed in its own name for an injunction on behalf of the inhabitants if they fall within s222 Local Authority Act 1972.

A person who suffers damage over and above that suffered by the general public as a result of a public nuisance is entitled to damages from the party responsible for the nuisance. Such damages may be for personal injury and for pure economic loss.

Defences

There are statutory defences to some of these offences. Regarding waste offences, s33(7) EPA, in particular, contains defences if the defendant can show that all reasonable precautions were taken or he was acting under instruction from an employer or the activities were undertaken in an emergency to avoid harm to the public.

In addition, the new s78M(2) EPA provides that it is a defence to a prosecution for non-compliance with a remediation notice if the offender is able to show that the reason for the non-compliance was that a joint polluter could not or would not pay his allocated share of the cost of compliance.

Section 80(7) EPA provides that it is a defence to a prosecution in respect of a statutory nuisance on industrial, trade or business premises to show that the best practicable means were used to counteract the effects of the nuisance.

Section 87(2) WRA provides that a sewerage undertaker shall not be guilty of an offence under s85 of 'polluting controlled waters' by reason only of the fact that a discharge from a sewer or works in the ownership of the undertaker contravenes conditions of consent relating to the discharge if: the contravention is attributable to a discharge which another person caused or permitted to be made into the sewer or works; the undertaker either was bound to receive the discharge into the sewer or works or was bound to receive it there subject to conditions which were not observed; and the undertaker could not reasonably have been expected to prevent the discharge into the sewer or works.[14]

Sections 88–89 WRA (water pollution offences) contain defences if the defendant can show, in relation to authorised discharges, that a polluting discharge took place in accordance with licence conditions, and in relation to unauthorised discharges, that the discharge took place in an emergency to avoid danger to life or health; all reasonable steps were taken to minimise the harm; and particulars were furnished to the authorities as soon as possible.

Penalties

Depending on the offence and the identity of the defendant, the potential maximum penalties are six months' imprisonment or a £20,000 fine in the magistrates' court; two to five years' imprisonment or unlimited fines in the Crown Court.

Under the new contaminated land provisions, daily default fines are imposed for non-compliance with a remediation notice.

Civil Liabilities

Under English civil law, there is a limit to the remedies available for individuals suffering the effects of environmental damages who wish to take direct legal action. For the most part these arise under common law rules of tort which were developed by judges. From the standpoint of anyone seeking a remedy for an environmental damage these rules might not be altogether helpful, as only those who have suffered direct foreseeable[15] damage to person or property can sue. It will be seen that the class of plaintiff differs according to the category of tort selected. The torts relevant to environmental damage will be examined briefly.

Tort of Private Nuisance

Private nuisance is perhaps the most important form of tort as regards a remedy for environmental damage.

The Tests: Case Law

In order to bring a successful claim for private nuisance the following tests must be satisfied: there must be an actionable interference and the interference must be regarding the use of or some right over, or in connection with, the enjoyment of another person's land.

The nuisance complained of must normally represent a continuing or repetitious problem. For example, the emission of noxious fumes from a factory or the discharge of effluent into a river over a prolonged period of time would be actionable under the heading of private nuisance. The harm complained of must either amount to an interference with the beneficial use of the property, or cause actual physical damage to the property. Not every interference will constitute actionable nuisance. Interference must be unreasonable, since the law of nuisance seeks to balance the rights of the owners of land to use it as they want without interfering with the rights of the owners of neighbouring land. If the defendant's acts are malicious, that is likely to convert interference into actionable nuisance, which might not have been so in the absence of malice.[16] However, if the defendant has an established right to do the actions complained of, malice is irrelevant.[17]

Although it is not necessary to prove negligence in all cases, there must still be some fault on the part of the defendant. This tort is often used in combating noise,[18] interference with rights of light,[19] atmospheric pollution[20] and pollution of fresh water.[21]

Fresh water and atmospheric pollution frequently come from a number of sources. For example, several companies may be responsible for discharging different waste products (mostly chemicals) into the same river. The question of causation can be difficult in practice. However, if it can be proved that nuisance is caused by a plurality of sources, each polluter is liable, even though the level of pollution caused by him does not amount to a nuisance by itself.[22] Despite this, the courts have refused to recognise some forms of environmental damage as falling within the tort of nuisance, for example interference with a view.

One difficulty for claimants seeking compensation for environmental harm is contained in the famous formula of Thesiger J in the case of *Sturges* v *Bridgman*:[23] 'What would be a nuisance in Belgrave Square would not necessarily be so in Bermondsey', also known as the 'Locality Rule'. This policy imperative means that a degree of environmental pollution might be acceptable in one locality but not in another. It is relevant where personal harm is alleged. Then the particular circumstances of the case are taken into account and this includes locality. In cases where damage to property is alleged, the principle does not apply. In *St Helens Smelting Co* v *Tipping*,[24] copper-smelting premises emitted noxious vapours which damaged the plaintiff's trees and shrubs. Since the pollution resulted in damage to property the plaintiff won the action.

The nineteenth-century policy which underlay this decision is clear. Actions in nuisance are primarily concerned with protecting the rights of landowners insofar as those interests include the health and welfare of human beings. They are not necessarily inimical to the interests of the environment. If the environmental damage affects the value of the land it is actionable in nuisance. The individual landowner will pursue the polluter for compensatory damages. The courts do not compensate for damage to the environment per se; there must be a link to the material interests of the owner of that piece of environment. At first sight, it might seem that economic values are attributed to aspects of the environment when in fact the detriment for which compensation is awarded is the damage caused to the property. For example, in the *St Helens Smelting Co* v *Tipping* case, damages of £361 18s 2d were awarded for the damage to the trees and shrubs – a substantial sum in 1865. However, it is worth reflecting on the nature of the landowner's interest. The plaintiff was described as being the proprietor of an estate of great value. The damages reflect the diminution in value of the estate, not the cost of replacing the trees or shrubs.

Another significant case concerning environmental issues is *Halsey* v *Esso Petroleum Co Ltd*.[25] The defendant owned and operated a depot which was used for the distribution of oil. They were held liable in private nuisance for the damage caused by the action of acidic smuts to the plaintiff's laundry, the nauseating smell and noise caused by the operation of the plant and movement of tankers. The character of the locality was relevant in determining liability for the smell and noise since it was a matter of personal discomfort and inconvenience that did not affect property values. This is reflected in the amount of damages awarded: £200. The economic value attributed by the judges to the damage caused to the health and well-being of humans was trivial.

In the *Cambridge Water Company* v *Eastern Counties Leatherwork plc*[26] case, the rights of landowners in relation to water flowing under their land were considered in the High Court and the House of Lords. The case concerned a leak of a solvent, perchloroethene (PCE), from the defendants' leatherworks into the groundwater supply. The leak occurred during the ordinary operations of the tannery on the site during the period prior to 1976 when the solvents were delivered in drums. In the High Court, Kennedy J held that the storage of solvents on the manufacturing premises was a natural use of the land. The judge took into account the benefits to society of the presence of the small works up and down the country with drums stored in their yards. In a manufacturing society the presence of such drums, some of which must inevitably pose a potential hazard, are part of the life of every citizen. The judge stated that while it was foreseeable that some damage would occur from an escape of the contents of these drums, their storage on the site did not constitute a non-natural use of land for the purposes of the doctrine. Likewise, in *WH Smith Ltd* v *Daws*,[27] the Court of Appeal held that sewage which had escaped from a lavatory pipe fell within the exemption of the natural use. In the *Cambridge Water Company* case, in the Court of Appeal, Mann LJ stated obiter that, in the court's view, the spilling of PCE did not amount to an escape. He stated that the rules make a person liable for an escape, but in this case the liability arose because of the action of the defendants in spilling the PCE. The judge suggested that it might have been different if the chemical had got into the groundwater system by leaking through cracks in a storage tank. The rule in *Rylands* v *Fletcher*, which is referred to in Chapter 6 and further below, was not applicable, apparently, in either the High Court or the Court of Appeal, although on different grounds.

The House of Lords accepted that an action in private nuisance to protect such property rights would succeed provided that the damage was reasonably foreseeable. They considered the earlier decision of *Ballard* v *Tomlinson*[28] which concerned the natural rights to receive ground water in an uncontaminated state. An interference with that right, which is a property right, constituted an actionable nuisance.

Natural Rights

There are two natural rights attaching to the freehold ownership of land which are relevant within the context of environmental law. One relates to water and the other to air. The former involves the right to receive water in an uncontaminated state, as was discussed in the *Cambridge Water Company* case mentioned above. The latter concerns the right to receive an unpolluted flow of air through a defined channel. The right to clean water applies to water percolating underneath land or flowing in defined channels (*Ballard* v *Tomlinson* (above)) and the right of a riparian owner to have the water flowing in a state which is not noticeably altered in terms of its character, quality or quantity (*Young & Co* v *Bankier Distillery Co*).

The water itself is not the subject of a proprietary right. The natural right is to take the water. It follows that anyone taking the water must not contaminate it in such a way as to interfere with another's natural right. Accordingly, there is a right of action in nuisance against anyone who is contaminating water which is being used by a property owner as a natural right incident to that property ownership.

There are several nineteenth-century cases besides *Ballard v Tomlinson* which deal with this issue. They consider the question of whether the contamination results from the exercise of a 'natural' right. For example, in *Smith v Kenrick*,[29] the defendant worked his mine in such a manner that the water which naturally percolated in his mine was able to flow down into the plaintiff's mine, which was at a lower level. This was held not to be actionable since he was working his mine in a proper manner and was not negligent or malicious. In *Baird v Williamson*,[30] however, the facts were similar except that the water flowed into the lower mine by the action of the defendant who was pumping it from another source. The defendant was actively controlling the flow of the underground water and was therefore liable for interfering with the plaintiff's natural right. The distinction seems to be that if the defendant's action constitutes a non-natural use, that is if the defendant puts poison into the water or interfered with its natural flow by diverting it, then this is actionable. If, however, the action of the defendant is part of the exercise of a natural right, such as abstracting the water, then it is not actionable. Further discussion of the case law is helpful.

In *Ballard v Tomlinson* the contamination was caused when the defendant put sewage and refuse from his printing works into his well. This contaminated the water in the chalk aquifer and the plaintiff was no longer able to use it for his brewing processes. In the *Cambridge Water Company* case the spillage was accidental and no negligence was established. However, the House of Lords emphasised that, while liability was strict under the tort of nuisance, the damage must have been reasonably foreseeable. On the facts of the case, it was found that the environmental contamination was not foreseeable by a reasonable supervisor. Moreover, in the *Cambridge Water Company* case, as noted, it was argued that the spillage of PCE, which then filtered into the underground water, was a breach of the natural right of the water company to abstract water in the state in which nature had supplied it. This breach was actionable under the tort of nuisance subject to the prerequisite that the damage caused was reasonably foreseeable. This action was, in the opinion of the Court of Appeal, independent of the ordinary law of nuisance. However, in the House of Lords, Lord Goff discounted this approach, holding that the tortious liability in *Ballard v Tomlinson* arose either on the basis of the rule in *Rylands v Fletcher*, or under the law of nuisance. He also held that the rule in *Rylands v Fletcher* was part of the law of nuisance, not a separate tort.

In brief, therefore, both of the so-called natural rights are protected by the tort of private nuisance as property rights. They do not constitute a further level of protection for the environment nor do they further the principle that the polluter should pay. The polluter might be required to pay for the environmental damage but only if that damage constitutes an interference with a landowner's property right and if it was reasonably foreseeable.

The *Cambridge Water Company* Case: Key Issues

It should be noted that in the Cambridge Water Company *case, the plaintiff and defendant were not adjacent landowners as they were in the earlier case of* Ballard v Tomlinson. *In that case the pollutant dissolved into the percolating flows of groundwater and was carried down the catchment at an estimated rate of seven metres a day towards the plaintiff's borehole which was 1.3 miles away. The ability of the hydrogeological inquiry conducted by the British Geological Survey to identify the source was remarkable. Even so, much is left to conjecture because the working scientific knowledge of the action of the contaminant, PCE, is still limited.*

Much of the current scientific knowledge now available has been gained as a result of the scientific inquiry into the Cambridge Water Company *case. The room for dispute over technical matters in cases of this sort is large and a careful preparation of the expert technical evidence will be of the utmost importance. It was found on the balance of probabilities that Eastern Counties Leather plc were at least materially responsible for the concentrations of PCE found in the borehole belonging to the Cambridge Water Company.*

There are various technical questions which are remarkable in this case. Most significant was the ability of the British Geological Survey to trace the source of the contamination. The spillage of the PCE was relatively small (3,200 litres), in relation to the total amount of PCE on the premises (up to 50,000-100,000 litres per year used between the 1960s and 1991).

In addition, PCE is a chemical which evaporates rapidly in air but does not dissolve readily in water. In fact, it might have been expected that most of the spillages would have evaporated before soaking into the ground. PCE is familiar in the domestic context in the form of cleaning agents used to remove grease. The British Geological Survey was able to trace the source of this small quantity of the chemical because of its findings in relation to the structure of the underlying land. It found that the PCE travelled down through the chalk lying under the tannery until it was stopped 50 metres down by a layer of sedimentary rock, a chalk, which was relatively impermeable. Pools of PCE formed at that point and gradually dissolved in the groundwater. Once dissolved it passed along a deep and narrow pathway which found its way to the borehole.

This ability to pinpoint the source of the contamination is an indication that one of the most notable problems of establishing liability, that is, proving causation, may be diminishing given the judicious use of scientific and technical evidence.

Locus standi: *Who may bring an Action?*

Traditionally, only the parties who have interests in land (legal or beneficial) can bring action in nuisance and that continues to be the case.[31] However, there is a quite recent development in this area of law[32] where the Court of Appeal allowed a plaintiff, to obtain an injunction to prevent a new tort of harassment without the evidence of owning an interest in land. It is now widely thought that an occupier without any proprietary rights could bring an action in nuisance provided that there is an actionable interference.

Furthermore, other suitably qualified litigants may be able to bring an action particularly environmental organisations, such as the Anglers' Co-operative Association, whose objects include assisting to bring legal action to prevent pollution. The LA may also bring action as a plaintiff in private nuisance. The exercise of their statutory powers does not exclude the jurisdiction of the court in nuisance cases.[33]

The Tort of Negligence

The Tests

In bringing a successful claim for negligence, all of the following tests must be satisfied according to the classic *Donoghue* v *Stevenson* model: the existence of a duty of care owed by one person to another; that there has been a breach of that duty; and that a foreseeable damage has resulted from the breach.

Negligence, despite its immense value in other areas, has in the past been of limited use in environmental cases, due to the necessity of establishing fault and that the damage caused is reasonably foreseeable. It is normally relied upon where there is no remedy in other torts, such as nuisance and the rule in *Rylands* v *Fletcher*. In English Law, however, the courts will not normally award damages for pure economic loss.[34]

Case Law Examples

Owners of ship repair yards have been held liable to employees for failing to take adequate steps to protect employees against excessive noise in the yards.[35]

A farmer was held liable for spraying insecticide known to be dangerous to bees on oil-seed rape, while the crop was in flower and being worked by the plaintiff's bees, thereby killing them. The advice to farmers from both manufacturers and the government was that the bees should be protected by not spraying during the flowering period and that the insecticide was most effective when spraying took place after the flowering period.[36]

A water authority was held liable in negligence for failing to warn downstream riparian owners of chloride pollution in a river, of which it was aware and which was of a concentration known to be damaging to crops.[37]

However, in *Gunn* v *Wallsend Slipway and Engineering Co Ltd*,[38] no duty of care was established between an employer and the employee's wife who had died from a lung disease brought about by the presence of asbestos dust brought home from the shipyard on her husband's clothes.

The decision to extend the categories of duty of care is a policy issue and one which the courts may be reluctant to make.

Reasonable Foreseeability

The requirement of reasonable foreseeability implies that there must be some relationship between the harm occurring and the harm that was foreseen. If there is a major spillage, such as occurred when the Shell Oil Company discharged fuel oil into the River Mersey, then a reasonable site manager or foreman could have reasonably foreseen some specific environmental damage. It does not require expert scientific evidence to deduce that fish would die and the water would be unsuitable, for example for irrigation purposes or fishing.[39] However, environmental damage may not always be caused by such dramatic spillages or be so clear-cut in its effects. The chain of causation must be established.

If a chemical is spilt over a large number of years in relatively small quantities, the reasonable foreman is unlikely to envisage any particular harm occurring. However, the environmental consequence could be very significant. In the *Cambridge Water Company* case the leakage was caused when the solvents were tipped from the 40-gallon drums into the machinery. It was reckoned that the daily loss of a few gallons of solvent occurred in this way. While the supervisor must have know of the spillages which were wasteful and careless, he could not have been expected to know of their particular behaviour in causing pollution to the aquifers which would be apparent some 30 to 50 years later.

In another recent case, the *British Nuclear Fuels* case,[40] a similar argument was raised in relation to the alleged effect on the genetic make-up of the sperm of a worker within the nuclear power plant at Sellafield and the health of his child. It is reasonably foreseeable that exposure to radioactivity could have both immediate and longer carcinogenic effects on the worker himself. It was arguable that it was not foreseeable that actual harm would be caused to his sperm, even if this had been the cause of the child's leukaemia, which was not proven to be the case.

There are clearly difficulties in establishing an action for environmental damage based on the tort of negligence. Fault liability is justifiable as an action within private law on the grounds that a person should not in general be liable for action except where they could have prevented the damage by behaving with care and without negligence. If a doctor prescribes a drug to which the patient is allergic and the patient as a consequence dies, then it is necessary to establish whether the doctor was negligent in prescribing the drug. The consequence is that one injured person may receive damages, another may not. The philosophical questions relate to the disparity between individuals suffering the same damage but in different circumstances.

For the environment, the questions have similarities. For one case of environmental damage, the polluter may not be liable, for another compensation may be payable. The consequence may be the same, the river may be polluted and the fish killed, but the outcome of that action may be quite different. This belies the general principle that the polluter should pay.

***

The Chain of Causation

The chain of causation must be established between the breach of the duty of care and the harm. Frequently, as seen in the Cambridge Water Company *case, this will involve the use of expert scientific advice. This evidence will normally be couched in probabilities not certainties and the weight of it may depend on the ability of the witness in the witness box. Expert witnesses have special privileges beyond that of the ordinary witness. They may, and should, remain in the courtroom throughout the trial. Their presence is important as they will be able to hear the evidence of the other side, particularly of the other side's experts. They can then brief their lawyer on the weight of the evidence and provide ammunition for cross-examination or re-examination. They are also able to attend the lawyers' conferences before the trial. It is critical that these opportunities are taken to test the strength of the evidence where it depends on scientific proof. If the expert has any doubts or there are any weaknesses in the evidence it is vital they are explored at the pre-trial stage.*

Trespass to Land

A person who is entitled to possession of land may bring an action against any party whose unlawful act causes direct interference with the land. The advantage of this cause of action is that unlike the other torts, there is no requirement for the proof of damage. It is sufficient to prove direct interference on the plaintiff's land. In *Jones* v *Llanwerst UDC*,[41] it was held that where there is a release of solid matter into a river so that it passes downstream and settles on land, the person in possession of that land may bring action in trespass against the polluter.

The question of whether the interference is sufficiently direct to constitute trespass has been raised in several cases. By way of example, two members of the House of Lords in *Esso Petroleum Co Ltd* v *Southport Corporation*[42] have indicated obiter that jettisoning oil cargo from a stranded tanker in a river estuary which was carried by the action of wind and tide to the shore was not sufficiently direct to amount to trespass. An opposite conclusion, however, has been reached in the Supreme Court of Oregon in a case involving the transmission into the air of fluoride particles from the defendant's aluminium reduction plant, which settled on the plaintiff's land rendering it unfit for raising livestock.[43] The cases on this point are not easy to reconcile.

The Doctrine of Strict Liability

In some jurisdictions the problem of strict liability has been confronted by the development of the doctrine in *Rylands* v *Fletcher*. The facts of this case seem to have been designed for environmental litigation. In Blackburn J's judgment in the case, he refers to the person whose grass or corn is eaten by the escaping cattle of his neighbour, or whose mine is flooded by water from his neighbour's privy, or whose habitation is made unhealthy by the fumes and noisome vapours of his neighbour's works. This provides some excellent examples of environmentally damaging activities. The rule provides for the escape of something which is potentially dangerous from land where, as a consequence, damage results. It applies where the object was brought and collected and kept on the land in circumstances where it was not a natural use of that land. The potential danger must have been reasonably foreseeable as the liability is strict, not absolute.

In the UK, unlike other jurisdictions, such as Australia, the development of the doctrine of strict liability has not progressed at the same rate as the tort of negligence. The doctrine has seldom been pleaded and it has been criticised by the Law Commission.[44] Judicial decisions have also severely limited its scope. As noted below, the definition of what constitutes the natural use of land has been surprisingly extensive.

Natural Use of Land

The question to be decided is whether the use is natural or non-natural. The test inadvertently raises some of the same questions which relate to the definition of the word 'environment'. However, it would seem that this factual question is one which will be determined by the judge in the light of human activity. In *Rylands* v *Fletcher* the item was water. Water is a 'natural' commodity, but in this case it was accumulated on the land by the defendants. It did not arrive there by the action of rainfall. It is not the object itself, but the action in bringing the object on to the land, and the consequences of an escape, which are critical in determining liability.

A key issue is whether the escape of hazardous waste from a landfill site or dioxin from a chemical plant be actionable under the doctrines. The first question is whether they constitute a non-natural use of land and the second is whether they are likely to do mischief if they escape. The second question is more easily resolved. The escaped object does not have to be inherently dangerous; water is not, in itself, a dangerous object, but has the potential to cause damage if it escapes, as in *Rylands* v *Fletcher*. Hazardous waste and dioxin are, in themselves, dangerous things, so this requirement is easily satisfied.

As may be seen from the earlier discussion, the decision in the High Court in *Cambridge Water Company* case was in line with past precedents which have restricted the scope of *Rylands* v *Fletcher*. This part of the decision was, however, overruled in the House of Lords. Lord Goff held that the concept of the 'industrial village' and the notion that the advantages of employment for the local community would cause a use to be regarded as a natural or ordinary use of the land were untenable. Although he did not embark on an extensive redefinition of the concept of natural use, he was satisfied that the storage of chemicals in substantial quantities, and their use in the manner employed by Eastern Counties Leather plc, did not constitute a natural use. Indeed, he stated that 'the storage of substantial quantities of chemicals on industrial premises should be regarded as an almost classic case of non-natural use; and I find it very difficult to think that it should be thought objectionable to impose strict liability for damage caused in the event of their escape'. Therefore, had the damage caused by their escape been reasonably foreseeable, Eastern Counties Leather plc would have been strictly liable for the consequences of their escape.

Some Conclusions

Although the House of Lords' decision in the *Cambridge Water Company* case has made it clear that the rule in *Rylands* v *Fletcher* is only an application of the tort of nuisance and is subject to the prerequisite of reasonable foreseeability, it has limited the exception for natural use.

It has been suggested that the decision is a retrograde step for the protection of the environment. Insofar as it limits the concept of strict liability to those who might reasonably have been expected to have foreseen the consequences of their acts, it has had that effect.

Nevertheless, such is the advance in technical knowledge and public awareness of the dangers of pollution to the environment that the issue of what is reasonably foreseeable may not be insurmountable in future cases. For example, the knowledge gained as to the action of organochlorines in underground water as a result of this case must mean that the standard expected of the reasonable supervisor and the working practices adopted must have increased.

The impact of European environmental directives and rules relating to health and safety and the concern amongst the general public about health hazards must have affected the objective standards of knowledge and foreseeability, which affect polluting events which arise in the future.

There are a number of cases where pollution has occurred in the past and land has been contaminated before the activity became unlawful. These cases are known as cases of historic pollution. In the *Cambridge Water Company* case, the House of Lords considered it inappropriate to impose liability retrospectively where it was not so imposed by statute.

The House of Lords was not prepared to extend the rule to cases of extra-hazardous activities. The argument put was that persons conducting such operations should be liable for the extraordinary risks to others involved in such operations. Lord Goff, however, took the view that such a development of the law was a matter for Parliament and not for the judges. It was a situation where Parliament should lay down precise criteria for the incidence and scope of such liability, particularly as Parliament was concerned to establish an extensive statutory regime for environmental liability at that time.

Personal Liability For Directors, Managers and Company Officers

In providing for the protection and clean-up of the environment, there are a number of statutory provisions[45] which actually introduced liability for the corporate body and its directors, managers secretaries and other officers. Whereas the prosecution of corporate bodies for environmental mismanagement is fairly common, personal liability for company officials can no longer be expected to be rare in the light of the developing case law. In this section certain guidelines are highlighted.

Key Provisions and Definitions

The standard provision whereby directors and senior managers may be liable for the acts of a corporate body is as follows:

> 'Where an offence under any of the relevant statutory provisions committed by a body corporate is proved to have been committed with the consent or connivance or ought to have been attributed to any neglect on the part of, any director, manager, secretary or other similar officer of the body corporate where a person who was purporting to act in any such capacity, he as well as the body corporate shall be guilty of that offence and shall be liable to be proceeded against and punished accordingly.'

'Connivance' has been held to imply acquiescence in a course of conduct reasonably likely to lead to the commission of the offence. 'Where he (the director) connives at the offence committed by the company he is equally well aware of what is going on but his agreement is tacit, not actively encouraging what happens but letting it continue and saying nothing about it'.[46]

'Neglect' was considered in *Witherspoon* v *HM Advocate*.[47] 'In considering whether there has been neglect within the meaning of s37(1) on the part of a particular director or other particular officer charged, the search must be to discover whether the accused has failed to take some steps to prevent the commission of an offence by the corporation to which he belongs if the taking of those steps either expressly falls on or should be held to fall within the scope of the functions of the office which he holds.'

'Attributable to' means any degree of attributability will suffice, and in that sense it is evident that the commission of a relevant offence by a body corporate may well be found to be attributable to failure on the part of each of a number of directors, manager or other officers to take certain steps which he could and should have taken in the discharge of the functions of his particular office.

Director, Manager, Secretary or Other Similar Officer

Whilst a company is a legal entity, it cannot perform its roles without the aid of natural persons who act as the 'directing mind and will' of the company, and these statutory provisions seek to make these natural persons to be liable for the acts of a corporate body. By way of example, in *R* v *Boal*,[48] the Court of Appeal considered the scope of s23 Fire Precautions Act 1971, which is in almost identical wording to the standard words set out above. The Court of Appeal held that the intended scope of s23 was to fix with criminal liability only those who were in a position of 'real authority', the decision-makers within the company who have both the power and responsibility to decide corporate policy and strategy.

Director's Duties: An Example

In Armour *v* Skeen,[49] *the Director of Roads of Strathclyde Regional Council, was successfully prosecuted on five charges relating to the accidental death of one of his council employees, his prosecution being based on s37(1) of the Health and Safety at Work Act 1974. At the appeal, Mr Armour conceded that it was his duty to provide the general safety policy for his department and that the facts of the case were sufficient to establish that a statutory contravention had been committed by him in each of the five charges on which he was convicted if he was a person who fell within the categories set out in s37(1). It was submitted on Mr Armour's behalf that since s2(1) of the 1974 Act imposed on the employers, that is, the Council, the duty to ensure inter alia the safety at work of the employees, so far as was reasonably practicable, the members of the Council, who were the policy-makers, were alone responsible for the safety policy and the function of the employees was simply to carry out that policy. There was no duty on Mr Armour to carry out the functions and if there was no duty there was no neglect.*

This submission was not successful. The High Court judiciary held that:

> '... s37(1) refers to any neglect and that seems to me to relate to any neglect in duty, however constituted, to which the contravention of the safety precautions was attributable. That being so, I am satisfied that the 'statement of safety policy' and in particular paragraph 3 thereof, both of which were issued by the Council to inter alia director and departments, and placed on the appellant the duty to prepare, on the bones of these documents the general safety policy in relation to the work of the department. Attention is drawn in the circular to the fact that existing legislation in health safety and welfare would continue to be effective.'

As to the argument that the appellant was not a person within the purview of s37, the Court held that:

> 'There is no question of equipping a Director of Roads with the term 'director', as used in that section. It was said, however, that the appellant did not fall within the class of a manager, secretary or other similar officer of a body corporate or a person who is purporting to act in such capacity. Reference was made to Tesco (Supermarkets) Ltd v Nattrass [1972] AC 1753. Each case will depend on its particular facts, and on this issue will turn on the actual part played in the organisation. Having regard to the position of the appellant in the organisation of the Council and the duties imposed on him in connection with the provision of a general safety policy in respect of the work of his department, I have no difficulty in holding that he came within the ambit of a class of persons referred to in s37(1).'

Mind and Will: Case Law

It appears that for an accused to be a manager within the meaning of the above provisions requires that he has a position of real authority. He must perform a governing role in respect of the affairs of the company rather than merely a day-to-day management function. In fixing criminal (and civil) liability, the court is concerned with the person having the directing mind and will of the company.[50] This is because a company cannot act in its own person but only through the agency of a human being. Traditionally, directors are seen as 'organs' of the company and not 'agents' as they act by virtue of their inherent powers, rather than as someone to whom powers have been delegated.

Different persons may be identified with the 'directing mind and will' depending on the activity in question and the extent of the authority delegated. In *El Ajou* v *Dollar Holdings plc*,[51] the Court of Appeal held that it was necessary to identify the person who had 'management and control in relation to the act or omission in point'. However, the person fixed with liability in this case was still acting by virtue of inherent powers, rather than as an agent. In respect of the relevant act, the officer held responsible took steps without the authority of a resolution of the board, therefore showing that he had the de facto management and control of certain fraudulent transactions. The Court therefore held that the directing mind and will of the company in relation to the relevant transactions were the mind and will of the officer concerned and no-one else.

Company directors are prima facie likely to be regarded as its directing mind and will. In particular circumstances, however, that state is to be conferred on non-directors. As Lord Reid held in *Tesco Supermarkets Ltd* v *Nattrass*:[52] 'The Board of Directors may delegate some part of their functions of management giving to their delegate full discretion independently of instructions from them'. It is clear that labels of 'manager', 'officer' etc do not affect the scope of liability. Lord Denning in *Registrar of Restrictive Trading Agreement* v *WH Smith & Son Ltd* considered ... s15(3) Restrictive Trade Practices Act 1956, which refers to 'a director, manager, secretary or other officer of the body corporate', and stated:

> 'The word 'manager' means the person who is managing the affairs of the company as a whole. The word 'officer' has a similar connotation ... The only relevant 'officer' here is an officer who is a 'manager'. In this context it means a person who is managing in a governing role the affairs of the company itself.'[53]

This decision took a very different approach to that of *R* v *Boal*. It is relevant, however that it was a judgment which was prior to the decision in *R* v *Boal* and that a ruling of the High Court of Justiciary is not binding on Courts sitting in England and Wales.

The Divisional Court recently applied the decision in *R* v *Boal* to a waste management case involving a disposal site manager. In *Woodhouse* v *Walsall*,[54] the manager of a waste disposal site was convicted as well as the company of an offence under the Control of Pollution Act 1974. The Divisional Court held that although the manager had considerable powers and responsibilities, nevertheless he did not have the power and responsibility to decide corporate policy and strategy. The crucial issue (which is clearly a matter of fact and degree) is, therefore, whether a defendant has the power and responsibility to decide corporate policy and strategy. In many cases, it would thus appear difficult to convict a manager below board level.

Moreover, as regards any particular individual, the factors deciding whether he could be personally liable would include his precise role in the organisation, the scope of his duties, the reporting structure and who has real power in decision-making.

Examples of Environmental Offences

The most common circumstances in which an individual is charged with an environmental offence occurs in respect of fly tipping, often carried out by a one-man, 'cowboy' operator. There are provisions which may lead to individuals ending up before the courts. For example, in Merseyside WDA *v* Islam,[55] *Mr Islam, a restaurateur, was found guilty of breach of duty of care in respect of waste under s34 EPA 1990. This requires all those who inter alia produce controlled waste to take all reasonable and applicable measures to prevent fly tipping contrary to s33 of the Act, and to transfer waste only to authorised persons. Mr Islam had paid two men to take his waste away who he claimed had stated they were council workers.*

Where the corporate body goes into liquidation, prosecutions may proceed against individual directors. In HSE and Glasgow City Council *v* McBride,[56] *the city of Glasgow discovered two road tankers holding 36,000 litres of toluene waste on an unlicensed site, the premises of GDP Group, a waste company, at Rutherglen. The company went into liquidation, but charges were brought against its directors under the Health and Safety at Work Act 1974 and for breaches of s3(3) COPA 1974 in respect of unlicensed deposit of poisonous, noxious or polluting waste. Mr McBride pleaded guilty and was sentenced to six months' imprisonment. It is reported as the first case in Britain of imprisonment being imposed on an individual in respect of an environmental offence (3(3) COPA has since been replaced in amended form by 33 EPA 1990).*

Civil Liability: Recent Developments

In view of the evolving personal liability issues, it is useful to consider briefly a related area. By way of example, in *Richardson* v *Pitt-Stanley & Others*[57] the plaintiff suffered an accident in the course of his employment with a company in which his right hand was severely injured. The company had not taken out insurance against liability for injuries sustained by its employees in the course of their employment as required by s1 Employers Liability (Compulsory Insurance) Act 1969. The plaintiff obtained judgment against the company for damages to be assessed, but the company went into liquidation with no assets to satisfy the judgment. The plaintiff then brought an action against the company's directors and secretary claiming inter alia that they had committed an offence under s5 of the 1969 Act by having knowingly consented to or connived at the failure to insure, and that the plaintiff had suffered economic loss equivalent to the sum he would have recovered had the company been properly insured. The judge held that the 1969 Act created civil liability upon directors and other officers of a company not to consent or connive at a breach of the duty to insure. Section 5 of the Act provides that the employer's failure to insure results in the employer being guilty of an offence and was liable on conviction to a fine which now carries a maximum of £1,000 a day. The second part of s5 provides that where the offence has been committed by a corporation:

> '... with the consent or connivance of or facilitated by any negligent on the part of, any director, manager, secretary or other officer of the corporation he as well as the corporation shall be deemed to be guilty of that offence ...'

and shall be liable to the same punishment.

It was held in this case that where there was a breach of statutory duty which involved criminal liability, whether it also gave rise to a civil cause of action, was a question of construction as to whether the relevant statutory provision as a whole – by express provision or by necessary implication – created such civil liability; there was no express provision in the Act creating a civil liability on the part of an employer for the failure to insure. The 1969 Act was intended as a statute within the confines of the criminal law, and not to create civil liability on the part of an employer. Therefore, no civil liability could be attached to either the company or its directors and officers and that the plaintiff's remedy against the company subsisted at common law and under the Factories Act 1961.

Lender Liability and the Environment Act 1995

Introduction

As discussed in Chapter 3, the EA 1995 has a number of primary objectives. First, it created the EA for England and Wales as well as the Scottish Environment Protection Agency (SEPA). The EA is designed to harmonise the former functions of HMIP, NRA and WRAs. It was intended to provide a one-stop regulatory body for industry and complainants, thereby reducing the complications and overlaps which characterised the previous regime. As mentioned earlier, the powers granted to the EA include the power to serve a notice on potential polluters requiring them to carry our works necessary to prevent or clean up water pollution. The EA can also serve enforcement notices for breaches of any conditions on a discharge consent, and it has power to serve remediation notices regarding contaminated land. However, many of the new powers under EA 1995 will be exercised by LAs. Under the new regime, LAs will have a new active role to seek out remediation notices and/or carry out remediation as the enforcing agency, while the EA is the appropriate authority where special sites are concerned. Special sites are land which is so seriously contaminated that it justifies the involvement of the EA itself. These powers, contained in s57 EA 1995, have now replaced Part II EPA 1990, which was complex and proved very difficult to implement. Since this is an area of growing importance, this topic is dealt with in detail and complements the discussion in Chapter 4.

The Guidance: Relevant Remarks

The new scheme of liability for contaminated land provided by EA 1995 is to be supplemented by three levels of Statutory Guidance, which will be provided by the Secretary of State for the Environment. The Guidance will form the basis upon which the interpretation of a number of crucial aspects of the Act will be based. The Guidance will have a statutory effect as secondary legislation and will be put before Parliament for approval under the negative resolution procedure. Without such Guidance, the grounds for certain important matters (including lender liability) will continue to remain unclear.

The Guidance sets out a hierarchy of three levels of guidance: first, guidance with which the enforcement authorities must 'act in accordance', which will have a mandatory effect equivalent to an Act of Parliament; secondly, guidance which the enforcing authority must 'have regard to', that is, which must be taken into account during the decision-making process; and, lastly, guidance which is either narrative or descriptive of the statutory provisions or policy background, which may have the same persuasive influence on the courts as *Hansard.*[58]

The Guidance was expected to be published in April 1996, but due to the nature of the response received after the initial consultation, the government decided to postpone its publication, and early 1999 is currently being suggested as the most likely date. Meanwhile, having regard to previous court rulings on similar issues and the Consultation on Draft

Statutory Guidance (DSG) on Contaminated Land, one can reasonably foresee the possible effects of the Act on the lending and investment industries – which is the purpose of this section.

It is necessary to state from the beginning, however, that there is no specific legislation in the UK imposing liability on lenders for their borrowers' activities. However, there are several indirect ways whereby a bank may become liable for its customers' environmental mismanagement. Unless banks take adequate environmental precautions under EA 1995, there is a real possibility of the emergence of lender liability in the UK.

Comparative Case Law

Developments in the US and Canadian[59] law have led to very high risks being involved in lending to potential polluters. In the USA, in particular, a body of case law has emerged which fosters a degree of predictability as to when a bank may be liable for environmental damages caused by its customers. In two landmark cases, the concept of lender liability clearly emerged, the details of which are briefly discussed below.

In *US* v *Mirabile*,[60] the US Federal Government sued Mirabile, the owners of a contaminated site, for clean-up costs incurred by the US Environment Protection Agency on its land, notwithstanding that the waste was deposited by the previous owner (Turco Coating). Upon bankruptcy, Mirabile joined Turco Coating and their lenders, the American Bank Trust and Mellon Bank, as jointly and severally liable for causing pollution. Mirabile claimed that the banks were participating in the company's activities through their financial support. The banks further joined a Federal Government Agency (the Small Businesses Administrator who possibly approved the project) in the suit for creating the conditions at the site.

It was held by the court that the 'owner/operator' specified by the US Comprehensive Environmental Response Compensation and Liability Act 1990, otherwise known as the 'Superfund' legislation, includes 'anyone who participates in the day-to-day management of the company'. Actual participation in operational decisions of the company is the test; financial participation is not sufficient to attract lender liability. It was further held that the American Bank Trust and the Small Business Administrator did not have sufficient control over the company's activities under this test and they were not liable because they had 'not become overtly entangled in the affairs of the actual owner or operator of the facility'. Mellon Bank, however, was held liable because it was represented on the 'Turco Advisory Board', and one of its officers was involved in the post-bankruptcy oversight of the company.

In *US* v *Fleet Factors*,[61] the Federal Government sought to impose liability on Fleet Factors (a lender) whose activities in a debtor company (SWP) was akin to controlling the company. In this case, Fleet Factors set the price for the company's product, approved the shipment of goods and supervised the office administration, tax forms and redundancy provisions for the company staff. Furthermore, it controlled the access to the company facility and arranged for the auction of its collateral security, which included assignment of the future profit and rights to collect the borrower's receivables.

The court held that while the test for 'control or participation' in management is essentially evidenced by day-to-day participation in the company's operational management, financial control or management would be equally sufficient for this purpose. The US Supreme Court stated that, 'It is not necessary for the secured creditor actually to involve itself in the day-to-day operations of the facility in order to be liable – although such conduct will certainly lead to the loss of protection'. In this case, the court held that Fleet Factors had participated in the management of the company by conducting the activities stated above. Therefore, the meaning of 'control or participation' under the US law is defined by reference to the degree of financial control and participation over or in the company's affairs.[62]

The emergence of the lender liability concept in the US has led UK banks to condemn any suggestion of importing US-style lender liability for environmental damage into the UK. The industry is understandably wary of being connected with environmental mismanagement by their customers. There is no doubt that a different stance would increase the industry's risk exposure and, consequently, affect its profitability. Therefore, during the preparation of the Environment Bill (now EA 1995), the banking industry lobbied the government to provide the lenders with an exemption clause. The government responded by repeatedly stating that it had no wish to prejudice the normal commercial activities of financial institutions, and that it would not consider a lender to be liable merely by virtue of making a loan that enables industries to conduct their businesses. The government's position will ultimately be in the Statutory Guidance, which is still in its draft form. Unfortunately, however, the government has until now refused to make an express provision to exempt lenders who take actions that are designed simply to preserve the property when the borrower becomes insolvent.

General Grounds for Liability

Under EA 1995, two classes of person may become liable for contaminated land: those who cause or knowingly permit pollution (Class A liability group), and those who are the owners or occupiers of the contaminated land (Class B liability group).

Class A Liability Group: 'Causers'/'Knowing Permitters'

Section 78F(2) EA 1995 defines the appropriate person as:

> 'any person or any of the persons, who caused or knowingly permitted the substances or any of the substances, by reason of which the contaminated land in question is such land, to be in, on or under that land'.

Causing Pollution

There have been a number of cases where the meaning of 'causing' has been discussed[47]. *Alphacell* v *Woodward*[63] involved the settling tanks of a paper factory which overflowed into a river, due to no fault of the company. Consequently, the polluting elements in the trade discharge was above the level permitted in the consent. The House of Lords held that there was no need to prove fault or negligence on the part of the defendants. It was sufficient that the company carried out the activities that resulted in a prohibited act, that is, causing pollution. Lord Wilberforce stated that 'causing ... must involve some active

191

operation or chain of operations involving as the result of the pollution of the stream; ... In my opinion, 'causing' here must be given a common sense meaning.'

It is also possible for two or more parties to cause pollution, for instance where the company employs the services of a contractor whose incompetent work causes the pollution.[64] This will also be the case where there is a cumulative effect of pollution emanating from two different sources which can no longer be identified. It should be noted, however, that liability may be avoided on the ground of third-party intervention, for example, trespassers.[65]

Can a Bank Cause Land Contamination?

Generally, banks do not consider themselves as eligible for the Class A liability group. Nevertheless, in recent years banks have become more aware of the environment and how it may affect industry. Consequently, considerable efforts are now being made to develop an appropriate strategy to deal with environmental risk factors, especially ways in which banks may be protected from environmental liabilities that may arise when enforcing securities.

The government, wishing to assure lenders of its protection, opined in the DSG[66] on the issue of 'causing' and 'knowingly permitting', that:

'... there is no judicial decision which supports the contention that a lender, by virtue of the act of lending the money only, could be said to have 'knowingly permitted' the substances to be in, on or under the land such that it is contaminated land'.

Despite such assurance from the government, it is important to note that there is no guarantee that banks will not incur liability on these same grounds. It should also be noted that the existence of an exclusion test for those providing financial assistance (as we will see later) could prove that the government holds the view that banks may be deemed to have 'caused' or 'knowingly permitted' pollution. Moreover, the DSG suggests that liability may arise where the bank has permissive rights over the land to prevent pollution occurring or continuing. It follows, therefore, that lenders may be deemed to have 'caused' or 'knowingly permitted' under certain circumstances. One of the grounds upon which such liability may be based is 'shadow directorship'.

Shadow Directorship

A shadow director is defined in s251 Insolvency Act 1989 as:

'... a person in accordance with whose directions or instructions the directors of the company are accustomed to act (but so that a person is not deemed a shadow director by reason only that the directors act on advice given by him in a professional capacity)'.

Section 251 is generally understood as absolving professional advisers, such as accountants and solicitors, from being deemed to be shadow directors. It could be argued that banking is a profession and, therefore, exempted from being a shadow directorship. However, this argument may be difficult to sustain in the light of current developments in company law. For example, the authors of *Palmer's Company Law*, at para 8.003, have opined that defining shadow directorship is one of the most difficult areas of modern company law, and 'in the case of insolvent companies it might be argued that a bank had become the shadow director of a company to which it had lent money in the context of a closely monitored rescue package'. Furthermore, in *Re A Company, ex parte Copp*[67] it was held that a bank is capable of being a shadow director if it interferes with the management of the borrower company. In *Re Hydrodam (Corby) Ltd*[68] 'shadow directorship' was defined to include anyone who does not claim or purport to act as a director, who may, as a matter of fact, deny the responsibility of being a director, but who, however, 'lurks in the shadows, sheltering behind others who, he claims, are the only directors of the company to the exclusion of himself'.

In practice, the most obvious situation in which a board become accustomed to follow the direction of an outsider (apart from its solicitors and accountants) is one where there will be a penalty for non-compliance. In such situations, banks can be vulnerable. In *Re A Company, ex parte Copp*, Knox J suggested that when a borrower company is in financial difficulties, pressure from the bank commissioning a report on the company affairs and insisting that its recommendations be followed, may suffice for the bank to be liable as a shadow director. Hence, controlling or participating in the management of a customer's business will be prima facie evidence of 'shadow directorship'.

Furthermore, there is also a complementary argument that those who hold equity stakes in a customer's business and, who consequently control the majority or a substantial number of shares in that company, may also be liable for the company's environmental performance. This argument is based on s157(2) EPA 1990, which provides that where shareholders are involved in management buy-outs this may also give rise to environmental liability if they become involved in the management or control of their customers' businesses.

The liability of a 'shadow director' may be both criminal and civil and may arise in relation to any matter for which a director of the company itself could normally be liable. If a bank is considered to be a shadow director, it may be relatively easy to establish its liability for 'causing' environmental damage, since the directors are deemed to be the agent of the company in law.[69] Moreover, in the UK there are a number of items of environmental legislation which impose liability on company directors and officers of the company who consent to or connive at an environmental offence.[70] The issues of 'consent' and 'connivance' relating to a corporate offence was discussed in *Huckerby* v *Elliot* in which it was held that:

> '... it would seem that where a director consents to the commission of an offence by his company, he is well aware of what is going on and agrees to it ... where he connives at the offence committed by the company he is equally well aware of what is going on but his agreement is tacit, not actively encouraging what happens but letting it continue and saying nothing about it'.[71]

Lenders can avoid liability as shadow directors by not stepping outside the ordinary banker–customer relationship and by avoiding taking control or being seen to be controlling the management of the company's business. For example, lenders should avoid a direct commissioning of reports (especially environmental reports). It will be sufficient for banks to indicate to borrowers the need to commission a report and to follow its recommendation as a condition for granting a loan facility. Difficulties may also arise where the security of future profits and rights to collect the book debts, as this may lead banks (in certain circumstances) to make executive decisions. A proper wording of the contract may help in avoiding such complications.

Can Banks 'Knowingly Permit' Land Contamination?

The phrase 'knowingly permit' has also been subjected to a number of judicial interpretations. In *R* v *Thomson*,[72] a case which involved a drug deal, it was held that adding 'knowingly' before an offence of 'permitting' is superfluous because knowledge of some kind is an essential element of permitting. In *Vane* v *Yiannopoullos*[73] it was held that for 'knowingly permitting' a liquor sale offence, a deliberate disregard of events would be sufficient for liability and that actual knowledge is not necessary. This same principle will apply in a civil action for nuisance.[74] Conduct, such as deliberate failure to make appropriate investigations (because it is better not to know) is often regarded as constructive notice, thereby making the defendant liable. Therefore, if all that is required to be liable for 'knowingly permitting' is to 'turn a blind eye', there may be serious implications if a bank does not make reasonable and necessary enquiries about a borrower's environmental activities in certain circumstances.

In water pollution offences, however, it has been held that 'knowingly permitting' requires both a sufficient knowledge of relevant facts by the defendant and also the power to control or prevent the activity that led to the 'permitted activity'.[75] This principle is being adopted in the DSG, as stated above. Therefore, the test for knowingly permitting pollution will be twofold, that is: does the bank have sufficient relevant information on the customer's environmental practice?, and, Does the bank have the power to control or prevent pollution? If the answer to the questions are in the affirmative the bank may be liable.

It is standard practice for lenders to require information about a customer's activities in order to assess risk elements before decisions are made, and this practice can be expected to continue. However, the extent to which banks make environmental enquiries of borrowers could potentially give rise to one of the ingredients of the 'knowingly permitted' offences. Therefore, the way in which information is obtained and how it is used may come to play a very important role.

In addition, lenders tend to include appropriate convenants, warranties and indemnities in loan facilities, so as to be protected from certain liabilities. In such cases, due attention must be paid to the drafting of these convenants, as poor drafting may give rise to the second element of the offence of 'knowingly permit', that is, power to control or prevent pollution. For example, a lender becomes aware through environmental investigations that a borrower has a licence to deposit controlled wastes on land subject to certain conditions. The lender, wishing to be protected against clean-up liability, decides to include an environmental clause in the loan document stating that: 'If the company is in breach of the "environmental licence" affecting the property or its value, it shall be lawful but not obligatory for the lender to take steps and execute such work as is necessary at the company's cost.' In such circumstances, it could be argued that the lender has the power to control or prevent pollution, thereby opening up the lender to the liability of 'knowingly permitting'. A more appropriate clause would ensure that the lender could not be seen as having power to prevent pollution. It could provide, for example, that the lender has the power to increase the interest rate of the loan by, for example, 0.5 per cent for every week that a breach of the licence condition persists. Such a clause may still exert a form of 'control' on company activities, but it will be interesting to see how far English judges would go in finding that control existed in such circumstances. However, in the USA, such clauses have generally protected lenders.[76]

Three circumstances could give rise to liability. First, where banks do not make appropriate enquiries which may amount to a breach of a due diligence exercise when making out a loan to members of certain industries, such as chemical industries. For example, enquiries should be made as to whether the company has appropriate 'environmental licences' for the discharge of its production wastes.

Secondly, where the borrower company has violated an environmental convenant in the loan/debenture agreement and the bank fails to enforce the convenant, or where the loan/debenture agreement includes a clause granting the bank an actual or discretional authority enabling it to intervene in the customer's activities, but it fails to do so.

Lastly, where a bank appoints a receiver to enforce security and it later refuses to supply funds necessary to avoid or abate pollution in the borrower's premises.

However, without a clear judicial decision it is difficult to know precisely when a bank will actually be held as 'knowingly permitting'. Clarity in this area of law would be of immense benefit to industry.

Exclusion of a Class A Liability Group

A number of exclusion tests in Chapter IV, Part E DSG are particularly relevant to lenders. It follows, therefore, that being identified as a member of the Class A liability group does not expressly impose remediation liability. Under the relevant tests (particularly test 7), a whole list of financial activities which may otherwise lead to lender liability, such as making grants and loans, withholding loans, providing credit facilities and indemnifying a person in respect of liability and damage, may be specifically excluded.

One worrying factor in the exclusion test, however, is the provision which states that 'after the tests have been applied, and any exclusions made, there will always be one member of the liability group left to bear responsibility for each significant pollutant linkage'.[77] There will be considerable problems in working our the practical application of this clause, since any exclusion would depend on whether there is someone else left in the group to bear the clean-up costs. This may lead ultimately to the US 'deep pocket' situation, where the party with the most funds is responsible for the clean-up costs – the very result the government is trying to avoid. An example would be where all other persons in the group have been excluded under the appropriate tests except an insolvent company and its bank.

Class B Liability Group 'Owner/Occupier'

Section 78F(4) EA 1995 further states that:

> 'If no person has, after reasonable inquiry, been found who is by virtue of subsection (2) above an appropriate person to bear responsibility ... the *owner or occupier for the time being* of the contaminated land in question is the appropriate person' [emphasis added].

Where the party who caused or knowingly permitted land contamination cannot be found after reasonable inquiry, liability will fall on the owner/occupier. The DSG, in trying to clarify the circumstances that will trigger Class B liability, that is, 'if no person ... has been found', implies that someone or something has to be in existence to be found. Therefore, at Chapter 4, para 24, the DSG states that, 'A natural person would therefore have to be alive, and legal persons must not have been wound up or dissolved.'

How Can a Bank's 'Ownership' of Contaminated Land Arise?

'Owner' is defined in s78A(9) EA 1995 as:

> '... a person (other than a mortgagee not in possession) who, whether in his own right or as trustee for any other person, is entitled to receive the rack rent of the land or, where the land is not let at a rack rent, would be entitled if it were so let'.

In English law, a mortgagee does not incur ownership by virtue of holding a legal interest in land. However, liability may arise where a mortgagee acquires or take steps to acquire the beneficial interest. Following from the above provision, clearly mortgagees will be caught by this definition in the following circumstances: those who have repossessed a borrower's property, and those in the situation where a borrower voluntarily delivers up possession of the property.

A lender who has taken an assignment of rents or a repayment of a loan assigned to it and arranges for the payment of those rents to be paid into a controlled account may also be exempted if (and only if) it is not deemed to be in possession. Questions may be asked as to whether a lender receiving rack rent of a property can, nevertheless, still be 'mortgagee not in possession' since the case law[78] has always equated receiving rack rent with 'possession'. It would appear that lenders receiving rack rents are exempted from ownership liabilities as 'mortgagees not in possession' only if there is a specific assignment of such rents in the legal charge and notice of this has been given to the tenants. Therefore, attention must be given to the drafting of security documents if lenders are to benefit from the statutory exemption.

How Can a Bank's 'Occupation' of Contaminated Land Arise?

Lord Denning stated in *Newcastle City Council* v *Royal Newcastle Hospital*[79] that occupation is a matter of fact and that it exists only where there is a sufficient degree of control. In *Wheat* v *Lacon & Co*[80] an occupier was held to be a person who had a sufficient degree of control over premises to put him under a duty of care. What constitutes the concept of 'sufficient degree of control' is not clear, and it may be that each case will be decided on its own facts. Nevertheless, the degree of control may be sufficient if the occupant ought to realise that failure on his part to use due care could result in injury to a person on the premises. Therefore, where a lender forecloses on its security, eg by sealing off the premises or being in actual occupation, it may be liable.

Furthermore, a bank many be liable in occupation if it interferes with a receiver's function. In English law, a receiver is the agent of the company and not the debenture holder who appoints him, except where the debenture terms state to the contrary. However, if the creditor interferes with the function of the receiver, it becomes liable for whatever the receiver would normally be liable for. If a bank enforces its security, and interferes with the receiver's functions or fetters his discretion by exerting undue pressure on him, such interference may make the receiver the agent of the bank, and the receiver then becomes liable.[81] Consequently, if a receiver is in occupation of the property, the lender is, of necessity, also in occupation.

Insolvency Practitioner's Exemption

As indicated in Chapter 4, s78X(3)–(5) EA 1995 absolves insolvency practitioners who are acting in the relevant capacity from personal liability for remediation costs. However, practitioners may be personally liable where the contamination of land results from an act or omission which it is unreasonable for insolvency practitioners to make. It is unlikely that insolvency practitioners will fall foul of this standard because, clearly, most are accountants, and waste management is not generally their area of concern.

Concluding Remarks

Until recently, banks were thought largely to be unconnected with environmental issues, but this is changing very quickly. Recent research[82] has shown that banks are becoming increasingly aware of environmental issues, and are consequently adjusting their outlook and practices in order to take necessary precautions to avoid potential risks of environmental liability. However, the law is still not clear on what precisely would lead to environmental liability for lenders. The government's attempt to clarify the rules and introduce a more comprehensive regime to allocate responsibility for the clean up of contaminated land is now to be found in EA 1995 and the DSG. Whether these complex pieces of legislation will clarify the law is not certain. What is now clear is that, under the new regime, determination of liability will be very complicated, and there is much prospect of litigation. The courts may have to judge each case on its own facts, but it should be clear that there is no guarantee that banks will not be made liable under the new regime.

The banking industry may become a soft target for the clean-up tasks because it is perceived as one that can foot the bill; banks should now, therefore, be making efforts to avoid such liabilities. The new regime does not pose a threat of direct liability to banks, but there are a few hidden pitfalls, which can be circumnavigated by banks with a little advice.

Furthermore, borrowers are also becoming increasingly prepared to comply with lenders' environmental criteria, and in some cases borrowers actually expect to undertake some remedial work at the outset before loan facilities are approved, according to recent research.[83] Therefore, banks should not be inhibited by the fear of losing customers if environmental enquiries are made.

Finally, the prospect of lender liability in the UK has recently been illustrated by a case involving Midland Bank, which repossessed a property that had been used as a waste-tyre dump.[84] The bank failed to notice the waste-tyre deposit at the time of repossession, but when the waste regulation authority served it with a clean-up notice (as the site owner), the bank entered into negotiations with the authority and decided to clean the site at the estimated cost of above £30,000. Whilst this is the only example of lender liability to date, it can no longer be assumed that such incidences of liability will continue to be rare. Moreover, more generally there is no doubt that the environmental liability regime – at national, EU and international levels – with become stricter and will therefore affect an increasing number of parties.

---

[1] [1942] 2 KB 154
[2] [1976] 1 WLR 543
[3] (1983) 15 HLR 57
[4] [1980] 2 WLR 65
[5] (1992) 4 Land Management and [1992] Env LR 168
[6] (1989) 21 HLR 504, CA
[7] [1955] 1 All ER 380
[8] [1975] 1 WLR 845
[9] (1997) The Times 7 May
[10] (1996) Env LR 88
[11] [1993] Env LR 191
[12] SI 1990 No 2276
[13] [1994] Env LR 320
[14] See *NRA v Yorkshire Water* [1995] 1 AC 444
[15] On the problems of forseeability and remoteness of damage *see The Wagon Mound (No 1)* [19961] AC 388; *The Wagon Mound (No 2)* [1967] AC 617 and generally Winfield and Jolowecz 12th ed, pp120–147
[16] *Christie v Davey* [1893] Ch 316; *Hollywood Silver Fox Farm v Emmett* [1936] 2 KB 468
[17] *Bradford Corporation v Pickles* [1895]AC 587
[18] For example, *Halsey v Esso Petroleum* [1961] 1WLR 683 and [1961] 2 All ER 145
[19] For example, *Colls v Home and Colonial Stores Ltd* [1904] AAC 179
[20] Ibid
[21] For example, *Young & Co v Bankier Distillary Ltd* [1893] AC 698
[22] *Blair v Deakin* (1877) 57 LT 522; *Pride of Derby v British Celanese Ltd* [1952] 1 TLR 1013, 1023 (Harman J). Although the principle was applied to only to pollution, it would seem to be of general application
[23] (1879) 11 Ch D 852, 865
[24] (1865) 11 HLC 642
[25] See no 18 above
[26] [1994] 1All ER 53
[27] (1987) 2 Environmental Law (No 1) 5
[28] (1885) 29 Ch 115 and see also *Young & Co* no 21 supra
[29] (1849) 7 CB 515
[30] (1863) 15 CB (NS) 376
[31] *Malone v Laskey* [1907] 2KB 141
[32] *Khoransandji v Bush* [1993] CA
[33] *Lloyds Bank v Guardian Assurance plc* Lexis 17 Oct 1986; cf. *Budden v BP Oil* [1980] JPL 586 (negligence)

[34] *D & F Estates Ltd* v *Church Commissioners* [1988] 3WLR 368 (HL). However, there may be circumstances where damages for pure economic loss may be awarded, for example, in cases where there is close proximity between plaintiff and defendants: *Junior Books Ltd* v *Veitchi Co Ltd* [1982] 3 WLR 477 (HL)

[35] *Thompson* v *Smiths Ship Repairers (North Shields) Ltd* [1984] 1 QB 405

[36] *Tutton* v *A D Walter Ltd* [1985] 3 WLR 799

[37] *Scott-Whitehead* v *National Coal Board* (1987) 53 P &CR 263. The implications of this decision regarding the liability of water authorities was analysed by Stephen Tromans [1987] Conv 368 at 373

[38] (1989) The Times 23 January

[39] *Pride of Derby Angling Association* v *British Celanese Ltd* (1953) 1 Ch 149; (1953) 1 All ER 179

[40] *Reay* v *British Nuclear Fuels plc* and *Hope* v *British Nuclear Fuels plc* 1990 R No 860 H No 3689 (unreported)

[41] [1911] 1 Ch 193

[42] [1956] AC 218 at 242 (per Lord Radcliffe) at 244 (per Lord Tucker)

[43] *Martin* v *Reynolds Metals Co* (1959) 342 P 2d 790; *McDonald* v *Associated Fuels* [1954] 3 DLR 775

[44] Report of the Law Commission on Civil Liability for Dangerous Things and Activities, Law Com No 32

[45] Such provision is to be found in the EPA 1990, s157, (and the Waste Management Licensing Regulations 1994), the WIA 1991, s210; and the WRA 1991, s217. It is also to be found at s37(1) Health and Safety at Work Act 1974 which as the principal statute applied to breaches of health and safety regulations may give rise to prosecution of directors and managers in a wide variety of circumstances. See also s158 EPA which makes a person liable for an offence committed by another person where it is due to their act or default

[46] *Huckerby* v *Elliott* [1970] All ER 189, 194

[47] [1978] JC 74, 78

[48] [1992] 3 All ER 177

[49] [1977] 1 RLR 310

[50] *Lennards Carrying Co Ltd* v *Asiatic Petroleum Co Ltd* [1915] AC 705, dictum of Viscount Haldane LC at 713

[51] [1994] 2 All ER 685

[52] [1971] All ER 217

[53] [1969] 3 All ER 1065, 1069

[54] [1994] Env LR 30

[55] [1992] ENDS Rep 34

[56] [1992] ENDS Rep 42

[57] [1995] 2 WLR 26

[58] *Pepper* v *Hart* [1993] 1 All ER 42

[59] *Panamericana De Bienes Y Servicos* v *Northern Badger Oil & Gas* (1991) 81 DLR 280

[60] 15 Env Rep (Environmental Law Institute) 20 992 (ED pa 1985)

[61] *US* v *Fleet Factors Corp* 901 F 2d 1550 (11th Cir 1990)

[62] On 30 September 1996, the Asset Conservation, Lender Liability and Deposit Insurance Protection Act 1996 was passed in the USA. The new Act has now amended the definition of 'owner/operator' of the previous regime, and now affords better liability protection for lenders and other fiduciaries

[63] *Alphacell* v *Woodward* [1972] AC 824, HL; *NRA* v *Yorkshire Water Services Ltd* [1995] Env LR 119, HL

[64] *Wychavon* v *NRA* [1993] Env LR 330; *CPC (UK)* v *NRA* [1995] Env LR 131, CA

[65] *Impress (Worcester)* v *Rees* [1971] 2 All ER 357; *NRA* v *Wright Engineering Co* [1994] Env LR 186

[66] DSG, Ch 4, para 16 (note that this provision in the DSG is written in italics as it has no legal force)

[67] [1989] BCLC 13

[68] [1997] BCC 161

[69] *Ferguson* v *Wilson* (1866) LR 2 Ch App 77

[70] WRA 1991, s217; EPA 1990, s157; Consumer Protection Act 1985, s21; Control of Pollution Act 1974, s87

[71] [1970] All ER 189

[72] (1976) 63 Cr App R 65

[73] [1965] AC 486

[74] *Sedleigh-Denfield* v *O'Callaghan* [1940] AC 880

[75] *Price* v *Cromack* [1975] 2 All ER 113

[76] Elizabeth Armstrong (former environmental risks manager at Fleet Factors Bank) at the Conference for Environmental Risks and Liability for Managers in London, 6–7 November 1996

[77] DSG, Ch 4, para 46 and 47. It may be argued, however, that the exclusion of some activities of the financial institution is itself a strong indication that lenders may be rightly held to have 'caused or knowingly permitted' contaminants on land

[78] *Horlock* v *Smith* (1842) 11 LJ Ch 157

[79] [1959] 1 All ER 736

[80] [1966] AC 522

[81] *Standard Chartered Bank* v *Walker* [1982] 1 WLR 1410; *Downstairs Nominees* v *First City Corp* [1992] QC 295

[82] UNEP Global Survey, 'Environmental Policies and Practices of the Financial Sector 1995; Environmental Impacts and the Role of Banking in Europe' [1996] 5 EELR 252; 'Policing the Environment: Private Regulation and the Role of Lenders' [1996] 4(6) Env Liab

[83] [1996] 4(6) Env Liab 117

[84] (1995) 241 ENDS Report 44; [1995] 6 ELM 105

Chapter 9

Environmental Risk Management and Due Diligence

Introductory Remarks

Discussion in the earlier chapter has shown that environmental regulations now cover comprehensive areas of business activities. These may be categorised as: air and water pollution; hazardous and special waste; toxic substances; planning; pesticides and herbicides; radioactive substances; employee protection; biotechnology; statutory nuisances; marine pollution; environmental information; and health and safety matters.

There is no doubt that there are many types of liability and responsibility associated with these activities since environmental law is increasingly having impacts on business transactions. Specific strategies have now been developed to avoid or mitigate these consequences. Indeed, in the same way as any business transaction is automatically considered from the tax angle, it is now imperative also to carry out a comprehensive environmental investigation as a matter of good business practice. Any practitioner should bear this in mind when advising clients.

Transactional Tools

In corporate transactions, such as the acquisition/disposal of corporate assets and mergers, certain tools are employed in order to discover and make adequate provisions for potential environmental problems.

Pre-contract Enquiries[1]

The most useful initial means of creating an environmental picture of the vendor company or business is to make appropriate pre-contract enquiries in the form of an environmental questionnaire. This serves as a prompt to identify and perhaps assess the existence of circumstances which, either individually or in conjunction with other similar or linked claims, could lead to environmental liability. The acquisition or disposal of corporate assets requires a rigorous assessment of the vendor company's environmental position. Information needs to be gathered to enable the purchaser to decide on the environmental warranties and indemnities that may be required.

The environmental questionnaire would normally contain a full set of specific questions, answers to which may give an indication as to whether the land or adjoining property is contaminated nor not and whether other environmental concerns are present. A sample questionnaire may be found in Appendix 7.

The following types of environmental liabilities should, for example, be disclosed in response to the questionnaire:

*   liabilities which are historical, existing or potential;

*   liabilities which concern civil matters such as damages or injunctions or personal injury claims relating to industrial diseases;

*   compliance/regulatory matters including liabilities which concern criminal matters such as fines, prosecutions or enforcement actions;

*   liabilities which reveal capital or revenue cost, whether of a compulsory or voluntary nature.

In addition, the environmental questionnaire will be directed at specific sites which are to be acquired and in this regard the following matters should, for example, be covered: liabilities relating to existing sites, closed sites and operating sites; leased sites which are no longer owned or operated by the company; sites which may have been used by former owners; and closed operations and practices.

It is advisable to ask the vendor to go back as far as possible – at least 15 years, and more where earlier liabilities or incidents of which the vendor is aware should be disclosed. The vendor company should also be asked to give an indication of significant changes or new issues of which it is aware and which may emerge between the date of their response and the proposed date of completion.

The subject matter of the environmental questionnaire should cover:

*   details of monitoring and reporting procedures of the vendor company within its own organisation – this should reveal actual and potential problems;

*   details of monitoring and procedures for reporting accidents or incidents; details of any environmental audit carried out – both internal and external;

*   whether the vendor is aware of any health and safety matters affecting its business, plants or sites or industrial diseases caused by its business or operations which could result in environmental liability;

*   pending or threatened litigation matters;

*   questions concerning disposal of waste produced or otherwise handled by the vendor company;

*   any internal guidance on landfills or other guidance relating to storage management and handling of waste, whether on- or off-site;

*   details of any known or suspected cases of contamination of land, water or air;

*   clean-up obligations in relation to contamination;

- detailed questions should be asked of the relationship with regulatory authorities and related expenditure;

- details of any litigation with neighbours;

- details of environmental liabilities which have or could be incurred under contract, for example, by way of indemnities or warranties given by the vendor company.

Industrial sites and their associated activities and sites used for waste disposal or waste disposal practices themselves are particularly high risk when considering environmental liabilities. The site-specific environmental questionnaire should accordingly concentrate on such matters. This would include detailed information on:

- the operations and activities of the vendor company and whether they caused (or may cause) harm to human health;

- discharges or releases into the air, water and land which could cause environmental liabilities;

- materials and chemicals used, stored or disposed of at the site;

- the vendor company should be asked to check that all conditions relating to permits licences and consents used for the business are being complied with and whether they may be revoked.

Sometimes it will be possible to issue a single questionnaire if the size and complexity of the assets/shares being acquired are relatively small. The enquiries should cover:

- the property and its historic uses;

- waste-disposal policies of the company;

- usage of storage tanks on or under the property;

- regulatory compliance and notices;

- civil liability; insurance policy on the property;

- health and safety issues;

- the historic uses of the adjoining land.

Replies to pre-contract enquiries will often indicate that there are environmental concerns that require immediate attention in the transaction.

Various matters that might cause concern are discussed below by way of example. In addition, suggested guidance is given, although, of course, any practitioner should decide on the basis of the particular circumstances of the case in hand.

The Product and Raw Materials

Although the vendor may well have a product which does not itself appear to cause pollution, the production process should be checked as it may do so. For example, toxic materials may be used as part of the manufacturing process. In such a case the purchaser is advised to request sight of the environmental policy adopted by the vendor, require information as to how it is implemented and enquire how the vendor company monitors compliance with its own policy.

In addition, it is important to carry out investigations relating to the process and previous use of the site.

The purchaser needs to find out from the vendor whether the process may cause emissions which could impose environmental liabilities. In addition, previous processes need to be checked. Although they are no longer used, they may lead to current or future liabilities. Checking out the previous use of the site might alert the purchaser as to the possibility of the land being currently contaminated, with all the attendant costs for clean-up that this could detail.

Waste Disposal

Whenever waste is being stored, transported or disposed of, the purchaser must be aware of its waste management responsibilities under the waste management regulations. These are referred to further in Chapter 6. The vendor should also be aware of its waste management activities and any problems in this connection in order to be in a position to respond to the purchaser's queries.

Environmental Consents and Licences

The purchaser should ask to see all environmental consents and licences which are necessary for the business being acquired. In this context, it is particularly important for the purchaser to check carefully the conditions which attach to them and also to take a view as to whether or not these conditions are being complied with, as current liability may arise out of a previous breach of conditions. Sometimes, the regulatory authority which has granted a licence may review it, so it is crucial to check whether such a review is taking place. In addition, the purchaser should ask to see copies of correspondence between the vendor company and the regulatory authorities in order to consider what local opinions there are about the industry being carried on by the vendor company.

Site Inspection

It may also be useful for the purchaser to visit the site: he may well discover issues that may trigger off environmental enquiries. For instance, there is potentially a significant risk to groundwater pollution caused by discharge or loss of fluids to groundwater. This may manifest itself in cracked concrete or soakaways.

Other significant potential risks for which inspection should be made relate to the position of drains and the route of rainwater run-off, local subsurface hydrogeology and uses of groundwater.

The results from the site visit may lead to the appointment of a specialist to carry out these site inspections and to report to and advise the purchaser.

The vendor would be advised to limit his liability by imposing a financial limit and a time limit on his liability in respect of the warranties or indemnities and demanding that the vendor should control the conduct of any claims which may be made. Replies to pre-contract enquiries will often indicate that there are environmental concerns that require immediate attention in the transaction.

Searches

In addition to making these pre-contract enquiries, it is now common practice for the purchaser to commission an environmental search report. This often identifies the historical uses of the land and the adjoining properties for up to 150 years previously. This may be obtained from certain public registers, such as ordnance survey maps, which are often available in the relevant LA offices. The planning history of the site should also reveal any potential problem areas as far as the use of the site is concerned.

Where the land is found to have had contaminative uses in the past and there is no evidence that satisfactory remediation has been carried out on the site, then there may be need for a full environmental audit on the site. This would serve to determine the extent of contamination and the appropriate method of remediation.

Environmental Audit

In today's climate of increased environmental awareness, a company or lending institution involved in a company takeover or merger will ignore the environmental profile of the companies involved at its own peril. Where a comprehensive pre-contact enquiries and search report show that the land had been used for contaminative purposes in the past, the purchaser has to commission relevant consultants to carry out an environmental audit, having regard to costs and the probability of the anticipated risks vis-à-vis the intended use of the property.

There are environmental audits of varying degrees of sophistication which help to ascertain the effects of previous uses and recommend a cost-effective remedial strategy and possible alternative uses of the land. It could also be used to ensure that environmental risks are taken into account and evaluated at the stage at which their importance to the transaction can be recognised and the information used with maximum effect. Since environmental audits have become increasingly important as regards corporate activities and transactions, the background to the development of auditing, as well as its current role, is detailed here.

Environmental Auditing and International Standards

The 1990s have been hailed as a decade of environmentalism. In 1990 there was an accent on increased environmental awareness, access to environmental information and implementation of sound environmental principles.

Both legislative and economic incentives have placed the environment high on the agenda for businesses and government bodies, as well as consumers, shareholders, investors etc. Some organisations have been aware of this trend and have reflected it in their growth from the beginning; others have taken it on board at a later stage. There have been some that have taken their environmental responsibilities very seriously over the years, aware of the fact that the combination of green concerns and business objectives is a must for business.[2] This has been demonstrated in the ways that they do business as well as their approach to transactions. For example, the chemical industry has been conducting environmental audits for several years; the Chemical Industries Association has a well-established set of guidelines.[3] It is true to say that many believe that commerce can and must grow alongside an expansion in environmental awareness.

The environment is a transboundary, global concern and much of the push towards the 'greening of business' has come about through national initiatives of different jurisdictions where the competitive edge has been noted as well as through regional initiatives of the EAPs, both as regards legislative and market-based tools. As has been discussed in Chapter 7, what has emerged as a particular area of concern is that of sound environmental management. The EU's Fifth EAP[4] emphasised the importance of 'shared responsibility' for the environment which involves all sectors of society, public and private sectors, organisations and individuals alike. While accepting the importance of the regulatory approach, this EAP has highlighted a more creative approach to environmental management through the integration of voluntary mechanisms, financial incentives and central funding. Taking up the thread of the 1987 report of the World Commission on Environment and Development, 'Our Common Future' (the Brundtland Report),[5] the need to protect the environment and preserve it for future generations has been worked upon to take account of the key role that business must assume so that the concept that the 'polluter pays'[6] is complemented by the notion that business can profit positively through an enhanced environmental sensitivity.

While the several hundred legislative instruments dealing with the environment that have emanated from Europe still have a major part to play in protecting the environment, there is no doubt that economic instruments and financial incentives have a useful role in co-ordinating the partnership between the public and the private sector.

In this discussion, it is intended to consider environmental auditing in the light of the need for enhanced environmental awareness and improved environmental management standards, nationally and internationally, bearing in mind the emphasis on corporate responsibility that is vital to sustainable development and having regard to the need to be proactive.

Role and Objective of Environmental Auditing

Environmental Audits are a relatively recent development and their use, which may have a variety of purposes, is still gaining acceptance. Nevertheless, some do see them as the best tool for bringing about environmental reform of industrial practices. This may be true provided that they are one of several mechanisms in a much larger scheme aimed at significantly improving a company's environmental performance and making the results of that performance regularly and readily available to the public. In the USA, the US EPA, the courts and some states have all sought in one way or another to find a future for environmental audits. Under the general EPA Policy on Environmental Auditing,[7] no company is forced to conduct an audit while the EMAS[8] has also left the choice of environmental auditing to the companies or organisations who wish to participate in the scheme. Yet it is also true to say that there can be a real pressure on companies to undertake environmental audits both in respect of their success in the market place[9] and in respect of the success of individual transactions.

The process of environmental auditing was first developed in the US in the early 1970s as a method for an organisation to confirm that it was complying with legislative requirements. Specialist environmental auditors checked compliance and examined sites or plants that were being bought or sold to ensure compliance with, in particular, the Superfund legislation.[10] Following the disaster in Bhopal in 1984 and the liability issues raised for Union Carbide, companies became anxious to ensure that their overseas subsidiaries fulfilled similar standards as their Parent Company and US multinationals began auditing overseas. This brought the practice to Europe where it has assumed a different role largely because environmental liabilities have been less severe. Environmental auditing was considered a way of making a company greener and demonstrating publicly that environmental responsibilities were being taken seriously. More recently, in the US, organisations have considered environmental auditing as a means to protect themselves from criticism, as well as a marketing support, rather than simply a defence against legal liability. Meanwhile the ongoing discussion in Europe in connection with extending liability to circumstances of impairment or damage to the environment[11] has emphasised the role of environmental audits in due diligence exercises.

Basic Objectives

The basic objectives of an Environmental Audit are to check a company's performance against its objectives and policies; report to management on any environmental concerns with suggestions for modifications or improvements; propose programmes for future environmental activity; check compliance with company-wide or other standards, legislative requirements and regulations; specify steps required to achieve total compliance; and recommend action for risk management.

For example, by taking a 'cradle to grave' approach an audit can monitor emissions and discharges, waste and recycling efforts, with cost-effective results that can improve both 'the bottom line' and achieve quality management in economic and environmental terms. In addition, the Audit can be a monitoring exercise to verify training, health and safety and environmental procedures; check the adequacy of record-keeping; provide a satisfactory database for use for any of several purposes; and comment upon an analysis of information produced.

A further objective is to test the validity and quality of the audit management system in place and the adequacy of audit protocols, procedures and compliance manuals, as well as to review any contingency plans. Environmental audits are often seen as management tools which are an aid to the framing of appropriate policies to support marketing, and as indicators of the efficiency of the company's environmental policy. For instance, at the time of insurance review they may be helpful in obtaining satisfactory insurance arrangements, while compliance audits assess general compliance with existing and proposed regulatory standards, corporate standards and good practice. In addition, as seen below, they perform a useful role in transactional due diligence.

While environmental audits, and their results, have been voluntary rather than mandatory, EMAS, for example, does require the independent scrutiny of the environmental impact of a company's activities and does result in a public environmental statement. Similar guidelines were developed through BS 7750.[12] In the UK, both initiatives are beginning to have an effect on the level of corporate green activity.

Corporate Environmental Performance Reporting

The EU's Fifth EAP[13] has recognised that many of the present-day environmental issues and threats to the world's ecological balance are posed by current trends in political, economic and social life and it is, therefore, necessary to bring about substantive cultural change in these areas, which requires a more flexible, imaginative approach to environmental management than has been previously adopted. The underlying principle behind this approach is that, by increasing public awareness about the environmental performance of organisations, pressure will be exerted on those organisations to ensure that their performance is 'acceptable' to the public. For example, in the USA the Valdez Principles,[14] which were evolved following the environmental accident in March 1989, caused by the spillage from an oil tanker, the *Exxon-Valdez*, in Alaska, heralded a way forward for 'socially responsible' companies. The clean-up of the Alaska coastline by the company concerned, Exxon, has, to date, cost over $1 billion, consumed thousands of man years of managerial effort and embroiled the company in over 150 complex lawsuits which, depending upon their outcome, could add hugely to the total cost.

Among other things, these Principles called for an environmentalist on each corporate board and an annual public audit of a company's environmental progress. The message that was sent was that eco-responsibility would be good for business. Leading corporate managers called for 'corporate environmentalism' in the USA and, for example, the head of Pacific Gas & Electric stressed the importance of a dialogue with environmental groups and others as a way forward in an openness that was good for business.[15] This could be seen in the context of corporate environmental policies, published commitment to environmental performance and environmental performance reports. A significant incentive has been the emphasis on freedom of access to information which was embodied in the Directive on freedom of access to information adopted in June 1990.[16]

In the UK, companies in different sectors, such as Wessex Water in the water sector, has been particularly alert to the opportunities involved in being open in their dealings with the environment. Wessex Water, which conducts 40 environmental audits a year, has used the findings for public consultation. In the management's view, environmental auditing saves money and time, after the initial investments. The company launched sewage week in 1993 to open its doors to the public. Such organisations have, in fact, seen that a positive approach to environmental awareness is good for business. It has become increasingly recognised that for environmental reporting to be meaningful, it should be done on a site-by-site basis rather than by providing overall statistics relating to environmental data, such as emissions of different types.[17] This is especially true bearing in mind the possibility of a director being buttonholed and made personally liable for any statement made in an environmental report.

Need for International Co-ordination

There is no doubt that in order to improve the environmental performance of companies and to maximise the effect of this improvement, there should be worldwide co-operation by business to uphold the concept of sustainable development. This is the case, whether in developed or developing regions. Areas as diverse as business investment in Eastern Europe and the development of corporate policy in Japan[18] and India[19] have relied on environmental auditing.

In order that more businesses should join this effort and environmental performance should continue to improve, the ICC established a task force of business representatives to create a business charter for sustainable development. This comprised 16 principles for environmental management. It was formally launched in April 1991 at the Second World Industry Conference on Environmental Management (WICEM 2) in Rotterdam. The last of these principles was:

> 'Compliance and Reporting: to measure environmental performance; to conduct regular environmental audits and assessments of compliances with company requirements, legal requirements and these principles; and periodically to provide appropriate information to the Board of Directors, shareholders, employees, the authorities and the public.'[20]

The charter was one of seven projects by European and North American Business Leaders at the Bergen Conference, 'Action for Common Future', in May 1990. This conference was generally regarded as the main follow-up event to date for the Brundtland Report.[21] The Bergen Conference brought together at ministerial level the 34 Member Countries of the UN Economic Commission for Europe (ECE), including Canada, the USA and the Soviet Union. Non-governmental groups also took part, and the 'Industry Agenda for Action' was endorsed by business leaders at the Bergen Industry Forum and centred around the preparation of the charter and of the auspices of the ICC. The charter was adopted by the ICC Executive Board on the 27 November 1990.

The aims of the charter are worth citing:

- to provide guidance on environmental management to all types of business and enterprise around the world, and to aid them in developing their own policies and programmes;

- to stimulate companies to commit themselves to continued improvement in their environmental performance;

- to demonstrate to governments and electorates that business is taking its environmental responsibility seriously, thereby helping to reduce the pressure on governments to overlegislate and strengthening the business voice in debate on public policy.

Many companies see the charter as a major response to governmental and activist pressures for environmental 'codes of conduct'. In addition, the ICC definition of environmental auditing has been accepted generally as:

'... a systematic, documented, periodic and objective evaluation of how well environmental organisation, management and equipment are performing with the aim of helping to safeguard the environment by:

facilitating control of environmental practices;

assessing compliance with company policies which would include regulatory requirements'.[22]

EU Eco-management and Audit Regulation

EMAS, which was adopted in June 1993 and due to take effect in 1995, began as the draft Eco-audit Directive, which proposed mandatory annual audits by large manufacturing firms. It was aimed at major processes as a complement Eco-labelling which was a scheme concerned with products. As such, EMAS was designed to monitor the end of the pipe and reduce the polluter's impact of large, individual facilities or sites along strictly drawn guidelines. While it still remains more suitable for this in view of its site-based approach, a voluntary 'management systems approach' was proposed during negotiations, and the resulting Regulation establishes a voluntary scheme within which participating companies must establish an environmental management system. The Regulation was extended to enable Member States to include sectors such as the distributive trades and public services on an experimental basis and the negotiations also dovetailed the efforts of the British Standards Institution (BSI), which had been evolving the Environmental Standard BS7750,[23] which was intended to comply fully with the EMS requirements of EMAS. BS7750 and the Regulation draw parallels with BS5750, EN2900 and ISO9000 quality systems and the related audit protocols.[24]

Under EMAS, a verifier will review an organisation's environmental impacts, procedures and targets in relation to its environmental policy and EMAS, and the process leads to an independent verification statement which is required to confirm compliance with the Scheme.

ISO Standards

The UK was the convenor of an ISO International Electro-technical Commission (IEC) working group on environmental management with regard to a draft International Standard. The working group was set up under the aegis of the strategic Action Group on the Environment (AGE) which was established jointly by the ISO and the IEC in 1992.[25] The intention was to design an ISO Standard from the outset, and a draft document was submitted to the representatives of the working group in June 1992. The New Technical Environmental Committee (which reflected that of BSI) was based upon an official proposal to produce international standards on EMSs, environmental auditing, environmental labelling, environmental performance evaluation, an industrial mobility plan for the development of industrial standards and life-cycle analysis.

The objective was to produce an ISO Standard some one or two years after the revision of the BS7750 Standard, and the establishment of certification bodies in 1994, provided that there should be agreement on the production of an international standard. The intention was to evolve a systems approach embracing an environmental management system, health and safety management system and a quality management system.[26]

Accreditation of Auditors

The question of accreditation of auditors is crucial to the value of environmental auditing. To date, the UK appears to be ahead in framing an appropriate procedure. In late July 1993, to avoid duplication of effort, the UK government finally proposed that the National Accreditation Council for Certification Bodies (NACCB) should establish a single unified accreditation programme for BS7750 certifiers and verifiers under the EMAS. EMAS provides that companies wishing to act as accredited verifiers must have personnel with qualifications, training and experience in environmental auditing methods, environmental issues and legislation, as well as technical knowledge of the industry concerned. The Regulation also requires a competent body to be set up to accredit verifiers. While still at the discussion stage opting for a single accreditation system comment was made that the UK government in effect committed itself to a path down which NACCB (now UKAS) had to make sure those accredited meet the competence requirements of EMAS.[27] Subsequent discussions and developments both at the EU and international levels, in the context of EMAS and ISO 14001 respectively, indicate a trend toward compatibility of the schemes.

Scope of Audits

It is useful to consider the scope of the audits as they have evolved by looking at the broad range of services that has developed and been offered by environmental consultants. Briefly, audits can, as noted, be transaction-based, site-specific or more general. The broad range of issues affected by environmental auditing has evolved rapidly in recent times.

A complementary development to the growth of environmental auditing has been a huge expansion in the environmental consulting field. Eco Tech, a British Consultancy, estimated that there were nearly 16,000 environmental firms in Europe five years ago.[28] One of the first in the field was Environmental Resources Management (ERM) which has provided a helpful guide to the basic types of audits available,[29] as follows:

Corporate audit programmes: to assist international corporations in the development of company-wide monitoring.[30]

Due diligence audits: to assess potential liabilities[31] and to provide key information for negotiating parties prior to the transfer of a site as environmental liabilities can have significant impact on the value of a company's assets. The audits frequently save considerable amounts of money by helping to reduce a site's asking price or in securing warranties to cover future environmental expenditure.

Waste audits: to assess all aspects of waste management from the on-site storage of materials to off-site disposal by licensed operators as required by new, more stringent legislations.[32] Waste audits can identify opportunities for cost savings through recycling or resource recovery.

211

Health and safety audits: to adjust working practices in response to new legislation such as the European Health and Safety Management Regulations and the UK's Control of Substances Hazardous to Health (COSHH).[33] Health and safety audits in the UK and throughout the world are used to assess compliance as the basis for ongoing training and improvement programmes and may be integrated into a health safety and environment management approach.[34]

A general example of a site audit could include site setting and location, site history, management systems, raw material storage and manufacturing processes, emissions (liquid, air, noise), waste, health and safety, building materials, energy, security, fire precautions and pest control.[35]

Disclosure and Liability Under Audits

While the US deliberately avoided any public disclosure requirement as part of the EPA policy on environmental audits,[36] EMAS referred to a 'true and fair' disclosure of 'the environmental issues of relevance to activities at the site'. Nevertheless, it must be recalled that this disclosure requirement only comes into play if a company voluntarily chooses to participate in the Eco-audit Scheme.

In particular, in the UK, the audit will disclose legal risks and liabilities for which, as a matter of English Law, no privilege will apply. The wide scope of the audit under EMAS, for example, will tend to destroy the cornerstones of privilege where the dominant purpose of the audit was to obtain legal advice. This will, of course, vary according to the particular jurisdiction when undertaking a global audit.

There has been some concern that by undertaking an audit and having results published a company may find itself vulnerable to attack by voluntary groups and enforcement agencies. Nevertheless, having regard to the general trend in favour of openness, it would be preferable on balance to select the more open approach with regard to environmental matters.

Likely Future Developments

There is no doubt that environmental auditing can assist in the achievement of the goal of 'sustainable development'. To be fully effective, however, a proper international standard will be necessary. One suggestion would be to look at the best features of the methods in Europe and the USA.

It has been stated that EMAS is ahead of the EPA Policy on Environmental Audits in its approach as a market model and its objectives, the improvement of environmental performance beyond the minimally required level together with broad validated public disclosure. There is provision for review within the regulations which is likely to be involved to make the scheme compulsory. In the USA, it has been mentioned that the EPA Policy requires updating since it does not properly reflect the status of environmental audits and public disclosure requirements provided in other US laws and policies. While the EPA Policy is piecemeal, the US approach does have strength in that companies with poor environmental track records have to conduct audits and to disclose results.

Therefore, a 'Euro-USA' proposal should be considered for the future: first, EMAS would serve as the basic 'block model', applying its comprehensive, integrated and standardised approach, including public disclosure requirements; secondly, authority to compel an environmental audit would be added to EMAS and be required by any organisation that is engaged in a significant violation of a material environmental standard; thirdly, further provision would be included to make the absence of positive effort a factor to be weighed in assessing criminal and civil liability – EMAS would be specifically identified as a preferred type of positive effort; fourthly, a 'prevention test' would be added to determine corporate officer liability, either as a supplement or alternative to the 'positive effort' provision.

If this proposal were to be implemented globally, it would bring about a practical hybrid that would merge both the regulatory and the voluntary mechanisms. With the basic 'block model' in place, it may not be long before corporations are required to undertake and publish annual environmental audits[37] in addition to financial ones, and that for public sector works such audits became a pre-tender requirement.

Problems of Conducting an Environmental Audit

Three problems are encountered:

First, time pressures. It is frequently the case that there is simply not time to carry out as comprehensive an environmental audit as the case may justify. In the case of a facility which is likely to be a major polluter, it may be appropriate to advise the parties to alter the timescales to enable a proper investigation to be carried out.

Secondly, access to information. Although the position is improving in the UK, there are only restricted rights of access to information. There are not the sort of 'public disclosure' requirements that one finds in some US jurisdictions. English law grants the public access to environmental information largely via a number of public registers, including: s34 Town and Country Planning Act 1971, Registers of Planning Applications and Decisions; s117 Water Act 1989, Registers of Discharge Consents etc; s6 COPA 1974, Register of Waste Disposal Licences; s14 Food and Environmental Protection Act 1985, Registers of Licences for Depositing Substances at Sea.

Since most of the registers do not contain monitoring data, it is not possible to tell simply from looking at them whether the operator is acting in compliance with his licence. However, the nature of the registers is changing. In 1984, in its Tenth Report, the Royal Commission on Environmental Pollution recommended that:

> 'There should be a presumption in favour of unrestricted access for the public to information which the pollution control authorities obtain or receive by virtue of their statutory powers, with provision for secrecy only in those circumstances where a genuine case for it can be substantiated.'

In line with that approach the more recently established registers do contain more information. For example, the registers under the Water Act 1989 do contain details of water samples taken and at the second reading debate of the Environmental Protection Bill, the then Environment Minister, Chris Patten, announced that the registers to be set up under that legislation would reveal 'raw data' – emission monitoring results etc – and it has been made very clear in a recent government GN that the ability of operators to withhold information from the registers on the grounds of commercial confidentiality would be very restricted.

At the end of 1992, a European Directive granting the public access to environmental information came into force, standardising practice across the Community. These are now implemented by regulations in the UK. Moreover, recent proposals indicate that the practitioner should advise increasingly on the importance of openness.

Thirdly, hostile takeovers. The ability of a purchaser to carry out an environmental audit is severely constrained in the case of a hostile takeover. One is more reliant in that situation on information to be gleaned from public registers, with all their limitations. In any event, in a hostile takeover, the question of risk-shifting is less of an issue. Information about a poor environmental record on the part of the tendering company can be used by a 'target' company to its benefit. Identifying poor environmental practices may help to sway shareholder opinion.

Contract Stage: Techniques of Risk-Shifting

The results of the pre-contract enquiries, the search reports and the environmental audit then become essential tools for negotiating the contract and other transactional documents. The vendor may also be required to disclose potential liabilities at this stage.

The exercise of allocation of risk will involve the following matters: negotiating warranties and indemnities, considering whether insurance is obtainable to provide cover for the relevant risks, requiring remedial work to be carried out by the vendor before completion, incurring potentially considerable costs for clean-up, and civil liability may be owed to adjoining owners.

Where environmental problems have been discovered, appropriate techniques should be devised to shift the risks to the opposite parties. Here are variety of methods that can be employed.

Warranties and Indemnities

Information obtained as a result of the environmental audit will enable warranties to be specific, dealing with the problems identified and to represent that no further problems remain undiscovered.

Given that contamination could be accidental or gradual, toxic or simply extensive, the warranties and indemnities might be worded to cover all such types of contamination.

It is in order to protect the purchaser against environmental liabilities against which he may not be aware that the purchaser requires warranties from a vendor covering the company itself (in the case of a share purchase) or the assets in the case of an asset purchase of the business. When the warranties are checked, existing and potential problems will come to light, thereby enabling information about the company or the business being purchased. This, in turn, will enable negotiations to take place on the significance of these matters on the proposed purchase. Besides being a mechanism for finding out information, the warranties are used as a basis for deciding whether it should be the vendor or the purchaser who accepts the risks of undisclosed environmental liabilities in the transaction.

This will be a matter of negotiation between the parties and will include a financial assessment of the consequences of accepting the risk. Where warranties are given, those giving the warranties accept the risk in relation to the subject matter covered by the warranty. Where, however, warranties are either not given or limited by conditions, it is the purchaser who accepts the risk of environmental liabilities which are not disclosed.

Remedy for Breach of Warranty

If the vendor gives a warranty about a particular matter, he thereby accepts the risk of the particular matter not living up to the warranty. The purchaser can then claim damages for any loss resulting from the breach of warranty. The purchaser's claim is limited in a number of respects.

First, the purchaser is under implied legal duty to mitigate the loss which he has suffered as a result of the breach of warranty. Second, the purchaser cannot receive compensation for losses which are too remote. Third, warranties should disclose such matters as permits, licences, authorisations, consents and any other approvals which are necessary to ensure compliance with environmental legislation. It is essential to have this information about the business of the company which is being carried on. This information would also assist the purchaser in assessing what the compliance costs would be. Fourth, breach of environmental legal requirements (including licence conditions). Any processes for manufacturing products should be carried on by the vendor company in compliance with the legal requirements, so that any breaches can be addressed through the warranties and the disclosure letter. It will then be a matter of placing a value on any known breaches and adjusting the price accordingly. This would relate to such matters as discharges to air, water and sewers, storage and disposal of waste, noise, and odours.

Environmental Indemnity

The purchaser usually tries to obtain an indemnity from the vendor in respect of any environmental liability incurred by the purchaser for breach of the warranties.

This would cover such matters as: fines or penalties in respect of any breaches which took place before completion; liability to third parties because of the state of the property before completion or the business operations of the vendor; the cost of clean-up action payable by the purchaser in respect of matters arising before completion; and the cost of measures taken to prevent or mitigate risks to human health or safety, property, air quality, surface or underground water or soil – where any environmental problems have arisen before completion.

Much to the purchaser's chagrin, the vendor will seek to place a financial limit on his exposure, and time for which the purchaser can claim. This could be problematic because environmental problems which arise today could have been caused by activities and operations dating back scores of years. Hence, a ten-year environmental indemnity may not be as useful as it appears. This means, for instance, that if the problem is discovered 11 years after completion, the purchaser would be liable. Hence the importance of a vigorous environmental due diligence which should assist in focusing on the problem areas and assessing compliance and remediation costs.

It should be borne in mind that the value of an indemnity is only as good as the solvency of the company which provides it. Sometimes it may be appropriate for the parties to split their respective liabilities under the indemnity, so that the vendor will indemnify the purchaser to the extent only of, say, 80 per cent of the total liability, with the purchaser bearing the remaining 20 per cent. As with so many other matters in this area, much will depend upon the negotiating strengths of the respective parties.

Where an indemnity has been given under the contract, the purchaser should be able to make a successful claim. If, however, any financial or time limit has been placed on the indemnity, then the claim will be subject to those limitations. For example, a vendor company may give a warranty to the effect that it has not received any clean-up notice relating to pollution from which it appears that it is alleged to be in breach of the vendor company's waste management licence. If, after the purchase has been completed, it turns out that a notice, for example, an abatement notice had, in fact, been received prior to completion, the purchaser would have a claim for damages resulting from the breach of warranty. His loss – which he has to quantify – will be limited to any financial cap or time limit which may have been imposed.

Negotiating the Cost

The practitioner should note some of the key options as follows: an outright reduction in the purchase price – possibly to reflect all or part of the cost of the remedial programme; the devising of a formula whereby the purchaser assumes an increasing proportion of the contingent risks, for example, the vendor may assume 80 per cent of the risk in the first year and then later reduces proportionally to say 0 per cent in the tenth year; requiring the seller to put the deficiency right as a precondition to proceeding with the contract; using the information acquired on the property as a bargaining chip in relation to other unrelated aspects of the deal; a shift from the acquisition of shares to an acquisition of specific assets so as to reduce the degree to which environmental risks are inherited.

Insurance Cover in Acquisitions and Mergers

One of the key areas of environmental risk management is negotiating and validating aspects of transactions such as acquisitions and mergers.

When considering the environmental liabilities that arise following an acquisition and the associated insurance protection, a number of factors need to be considered, among which are the nature of the transaction, the terms of contract conditions, the past activities of the business and the availability of the insurance history.

Existing insurance policies may be a valuable asset of an acquired company, in relation to the latent risk represented by environmental exposures. The potential cost and availability of insurance in the future may also be a consideration, particularly if an acquisition represents a move into a new area of business.

In the USA, the identification and analysis of past-liability insurance policies to determine what cover they may provide for damage that comes to light either now or in the future is becoming routine. It is often referred to as 'insurance archaeology'.

It is also an important issue in the UK. Until recently, the main focus has been the employer's liability risk. Companies may be acquired which have liabilities which go back many years in respect of the latent injury to employees. It has, in some cases, been necessary to try and trace the employer's liability insurance history for a period of perhaps 30 or 40 years to identify the insurers on cover when the injury occurred. It may be anticipated that a similar situation will arise in relation to environmental damage. As has been indicated earlier, the process is quite likely to bring to light a complicated and perhaps uncertain situation.

Some general observations can be made concerning pre-existing liability policies in an acquisition. First, the question of access to previous policy coverage only arises if the legal entity that was insured under the original cover is transferred. If assets only are transferred, there would be no rights to any previous policies. The issue of past cover might still be relevant in relation to any indemnities given by the vendor.

Second, where the subsidiary of a larger corporation is purchased, that subsidiary may have participated in a group insurance arrangement. It may not have had direct control. The subsidiary may be legally entitled to an indemnity as a named, insured body on the policy. However, unless the insurer is dealt with in the purchase agreement there can be difficulties. The vendor may be obstructive when it comes to obtaining access to the insurance documents or to the insurers.

Third, liability policies may have aggregate limits. These may be exhausted by other subsidiaries in a group arrangement leaving no cover. The existence of an aggregate limit may also mean that the original parent company is reluctant to assist in pursuing a claim under the policy as it will reduce the cover available to it.

Fourth, it may be that the liability covers for the purchased company are on a 'claims made' basis. The existence of policies in earlier years would not then be relevant. To continue cover arrangements would have to be made to continue, the 'claims made' basis or to purchase retroactive occurrence cover perhaps within the purchasing company's programme.

When examining specifically the cover that may be available for latent environmental damage, an unclear and possibly complex picture may emerge. Even assuming that the policy history can be established, together with the precise details of cover, it is quite probable that the cover will vary from year to year, becoming more restrictive. There may even be periods of claims made to cover. Practitioners need to review the situation in detail. For example, in the event that claims do subsequently arise it may be difficult to demonstrate that the damage was caused during the currency of past policies. There may be disputes with insurers in relation to interpretation of some of the restrictive clauses.

Whilst past insurance policies may undoubtedly represent a valuable asset, they cannot possibly be a substitute for a full assessment of the environmental risks associated with a proposed acquisition. It also has to be recognised that in many situations it may be difficult to establish the scope of past insurance cover at an early stage in a transaction.

Remedial Work

As has been indicated above, the potential exposure of a purchaser or a vendor to environmental liability could be minimised by either party agreeing to undertake the remedial work. Indeed, a vendor may well decide to carry out this work in advance of putting the business up for sale, if only to make it easier to sell.

The Impact of Environmental Law on Mergers and Acquisitions (M&A) Practice in Europe

A recent study indicates that the business community in Europe does not yet seem to be fully aware or convinced of the importance of environmental issues to M&A practice. On the question of whether the environmental performance of potential M&A partners was considered by the companies interviewed, the answers differed widely by country. For instance, whereas all French companies thought environmental issues to be material, 82 per cent of the UK companies involved stated that they did not consider environmental issues of potential M&A partners. Even in countries like Denmark and The Netherlands, where environmental issues are generally perceived to be of great importance, only 50 per cent of the companies interviewed indicated that environmental compliance is relevant to M&A practice.

Environmental law problems can also operate as genuine obstacles to the successful closing of a deal. This is notably the case if the purchaser must obtain a number of new environmental permits in his own name because the permits issued to the seller of the facilities cannot be transferred to the buyer in view of their personal or intuitu personae character. This problem is of great practical importance because in certain EU countries (notably Germany), it can take a long time to obtain environmental permits since they are issued after a protracted procedure in which all interested parties can inject their comments. The question of whether permits are transferable is intricate because it involves concepts of administrative and civil law which typically intersect and, at times, clash.

Unlike in the USA, in Europe there is no standard system of environmental clearance of M&As existing as of yet. For example, New Jersey's Environmental Clean-up Responsibility Act (ECRA) provided that a site should be acceptably clean before being sold, transferred or closed. The New Jersey Department of Environmental Protection (NJDEP) set up standards for in-depth review of facilities and properties to achieve ECRA compliance. Clearance can be obtained by submitting to the NJDEP either a clean-up plan or a negative declaration that no discharge of hazardous substances has taken place. The ECRA is a very efficient instrument because, if its provisions are not complied with, the transferee or the NJDEP or both can void the transaction.

To a large extent, the subject of M&A is still governed by the respective laws of the individual Member States of the EU. This is particularly true in the light of the subsidiarity principle. Mainly, there are two points to consider here: the allocation of liabilities between the seller and the purchaser, and the transferability of permits.

The Allocation of Environmental Liabilities

As has been mentioned earlier, there are two types of environmental liabilities relevant here: 'civil liability', which comprises liabilities based on both contractual or tortious theories, and 'public liability', which encompasses criminal as well as administrative sanctions. For both types of liabilities, the following question must be addressed: Which contractual party, that is, the seller or the purchaser, should bear the liabilities originating before a given corporate transaction took place?

The Transfer of Civil Liabilities

As far as the EU is concerned, in the *Welded Steel Mesh* case the EU Commission addressed the question relating to the problem of allocation of liabilities for infringements of EU competition law. The Commission stated that:

> 'For the application of the competition rules of the EEC Treaty to undertakings, this raises the question whether an undertaking existing after restructuring can be held liable for the involvement of a predecessor in the restrictive agreements.'

The Commission has ruled that the national laws on changes in the organisation of a company are not decisive facts and that the question of an undertaking's identity is to be determined according to the following rules of Community law:

> 'If the undertaking which committed the infringement continues in existence it remains liable in spite of a transfer. On the other hand, where the infringing undertaking itself is absorbed by another producer, its responsibilities may follow it and attach to the new or merged entity.'

Therefore, it is arguable that as a consequence of a merger operation a company acquiring all of the assets of another company is entitled to all of the contractual rights and debts/liabilities of the acquired company. It becomes automatically and exclusively vested in the acquiring company even if these debts exceed the assets.

By way of comparison, it is interesting to note the position in other jurisdictions. For instance, the legal position in Belgium is that of a 'general successor'. This means that the position of the acquiring company is comparable to that of a physical person inheriting the entirety of the estate of a deceased person. It has also been ruled that the acquired and acquiring company are jointly liable for the debts of the acquired company. It has been declared that, according to the Belgian law of contracts, a company cannot fully transfer its debts to another company. It has been noted that the acquired company remains liable for its debts during a period of five years from the date of publication of the act of closure of the winding up of the acquired company (art 178 Co-ordinated Laws on Commercial Companies).

It is generally accepted, however, that the consequences of this operation should be largely the same as the ones attributed to mergers. The acquiring companies are general successors to the divided company and are held, on the basis of the terms of division, to all of the liabilities of the latter company. The question whether the divided company remains jointly liable with the recipient companies for its debts during a period of five years from the date of the closure of its winding up has not yet been settled, but should in principle be answered negatively. In view of the uncertainties still existing in Belgian law, it is necessary, in order to achieve the result of a true merger operation, to provide for an express contractual clause to the effect that the seller will be indemnified and held harmless by the buyer for all liabilities and costs related to old environmental burdens.

It should be noted that in Member States such as Germany, where the Third EEC Directive on Mergers has been implemented, it is clearly established that old environmental burdens are taken over by the acquiring company. A company would, however, not be liable under German law if it acquired the polluting company from a trustee in bankruptcy or if the polluting company's activities were stopped and other activities, unrelated to the element of the environment damaged by the predecessor, were undertaken on the site.

Transfer of Assets

Here again, it is useful to compare the position in various Member States. In Belgium, for instance, the sale of the entirety or a group of the assets of a company is characterised as the sale of a 'fonds de commerce' (handelsfonds), that is the sale of a factual entity comprising all material and immaterial goods which are useful to the sound organisation and functioning of a company or a branch thereof. It follows that a sale of assets does not entail that the debts of the seller, including old environmental burdens, are transferred to the purchaser. This is a logical result because the seller does not, in contrast to a merger operation, cease to exist as a consequence of the deal. As a result of an assets transaction, the purchaser only becomes the successor to certain rights of the seller but not the latter's general assignee.

The seller of land who knows that certain dangerous substances are present on the land will, of course, try to negotiate a disclaimer of his warranty for hidden defects. It is, however, well established in Belgian law that the seller who has such knowledge will not be able to invoke the disclaimer.

In Belgium, the companies involved in an assets transaction can request the approval by the creditor of an old environmental debt to a novation. If this is not feasible the parties can resort to a so-called 'imperfect delegation' of liabilities. An imperfect delegation is an agreement whereby the creditor (obligee) agrees that a new party, the delegee, becomes jointly liable with his old debtor (delegator-obligor) for the debts of the latter party. The figure of the imperfect delegation can be an appropriate instrument to avoid the possibility that a creditor of the seller would, at a later point in time, resort to remedies which could jeopardise the deal. One such remedy is the so-called actio pauliana. This remedy is predicated on collusion between the seller and the buyer. The creditor must prove that the buyer was aware of the 'abnormal character of the deal', that is, that the buyer understood that the possibilities for the creditor in question to obtain payment would become less certain as a consequence of the deal. If the creditor is successful, he can disregard the transaction and obtain payment out of the proceeds of the assets transferred to the buyer.

The creditor can also seek the judicial annulment of the decision of the general shareholders' agreement of the acquired company whereby it is decided that the company sells all its assets, is liquidated and wound up.

Evidently, these remedies will be of a particular importance if a substantial asset or the vast majority of assets is transferred and the acquired company is nothing more than a shell wherever the transaction occurs. In Germany, paragraph 419 of the Bügerliches Gezetzbuch provides that a company which acquires all or nearly all of the assets of another person becomes jointly liable with the seller for all the debts of the latter which antedate the transfer of assets. It can, therefore, be said that German law provides for a system of 'imperfect' delegation by operation of law.

In The Netherlands, no imperfect delegation by operation of law exists for a total transfer of assets. It should, however, be mentioned that the Dutch courts have held that a company which acquires substantial assets from another company and thereby unfairly reduces the possibilities for the creditors to obtain full payment of their claims, commits a tort and may consequently be liable to satisfy past claims of the acquired company.

The Dutch courts deem it unacceptable that a successor of a polluting company would be able to profit from an illegal act. A newly established company whose personnel were closely related to that of the company whose assets it acquired was found to have profited from the prejudice to the interests of the creditors and was, therefore, held to be jointly liable with the acquired company towards the latter's creditors. The court held that a newly established company should not be allowed to hide behind its formal legal independence, lest it commit an 'abuse of corporate law' ('misbruik van vennootschapsrecht').

The Responsibility for Public Liabilities

Public liability arises as a result of the infringement of public rules or of conditions attached to a permit dealing with the protection of the environment. This ground for liability encompasses both criminal liability and liability for administrative action and sanctions.

For example, under Belgian law, persons who believe they have suffered damages from an act which constitutes a breach of criminally sanctioned environmental law could initiate a criminal procedure by lodging a complaint in conjuction with an intervention as a 'civil party' in which they generally ask for nominal financial compensation. The advantage to the injured party of following this course of action is that the public prosecution has no option but to open the case. The fault, once established in the criminal proceeding, will automatically also be conclusive evidence for civil purposes of a breach of the duty of care, which is one of the essential elements of a negligence suit. It should indeed be emphasised that in Belgium, in contrast to the more restrictive principles prevailing in the UK, The Netherlands and Germany, the plaintiff does not have additionally to prove that the law sought to protect the interest in which the plaintiff was prejudiced.

As a general rule, corporations are not criminally liable under Belgian law. The regions have no competence to deviate from this widely disputed principle. It should be noted that a limited number of exceptions to this rule exist, such as liability under the law dealing with groundwater. However, corporations are liable for administrative sanctions. In addition, most environmental laws provide that a corporation is liable under civil law to pay the fines which were judicially imposed on its agents or on its employees acting within the scope of their authority.

It is clear that the reorganisation of a company has no impact on the criminal liability of the persons who committed the infringements. A criminal sanction is always of a strictly personal nature.

Administrative Sanctions

Generally speaking, these are enacted by public authorities on the basis of police powers expressly granted to these authorities in statutory instruments and without prior judicial intervention. The civil or administrative courts can, at a later point in time, review the legality of these unilateral administrative acts.

Unusually, the administration will only resort to clean-ups if the polluter has previously refused to remedy the situation himself. The authorities prefer to engage in this dialogue because most clean-up operations lead to protracted judicial proceedings. In the Flemish region of Belgium, for instance, it has been estimated that a forced clean-up is, on average, five times as costly as a voluntary clean-up. Polluters typically refuse to pay the difference.

For instance, in The Netherlands it is well established that companies, as a general rule, are liable to pay the costs of clean-up operations unless they can prove that they were not negligent in any way, and that the public interest is so closely related to the administrative action that, also taking into account the extent of the costs of the operation, the recovery of the costs has to be considered to be manifestly unreasonable.

The Dutch authorities have been particularly active in recovering the costs of clean-ups from polluting companies. Even by the middle of 1989, for instance, 500 million guilders were recovered from the private sector in an ambitious plan to improve the quality of the soil. Problems nevertheless exist if the polluting company no longer exists or if it has gone bankrupt. In The Netherlands, no rules seem to have emerged as of yet to deal with this problem. Commentators have suggested that this vacuum is a major obstacle to clean-up operations.

On the other hand, in France the following administrative policy has been fashioned with respect to recovery of clean-up costs for waste pollution by companies which were subject to a corporate reorganisation. First, the administration has a wide discretion to recover costs jointly or successively from either the last company effectively operating on the site or from the owner of the facility or land. Second, as a general rule the administration chooses the last operator of the facility as the responsible person. A sale of the facility will not limit the administration's right to recover the costs from the last operator. Contractual indemnification may, of course, be provided for between seller and purchaser. Third, if, however, the responsible person was also the owner of the polluted site, the purchaser of the site will be liable for clean up vis-à-vis the administration. Evidently, the French administration has been very successful in recovering the costs of its clean-up action from polluting companies.

In Germany, a clear tendency exists in the policy of LAs to hold the present owners of the site, rather than the person having immediately caused the water and soil pollution, to be liable for clean-up actions. The authorities favour the selection of the present landowner because the latter is in control of the site. This enables the authorities to eliminate the hazard quickly and effectively. In German law, a basic distinction is made between liability for the condition of a site ('Zustandshaftung') and liability ensuing from certain conduct ('Verhaltenshaftung'). Common to both kinds of liabilities is the general rule that a liability cannot be transferred if it is specifically attached to unique features or characteristics of a given person, in other words if the liability has a personal or intuitu personae character.

A further distinction is made with respect to liability for the condition of a site ('Zustandshaftung'). If damages or hazards have taken place prior to the sale of the assets, no police action being undertaken at that point in time, the purchaser of the assets will be liable. If, however, the police action took place prior to the transfer of the asset, a purchaser will be liable if he acquired the asset in the context of a merger or any other transaction involving a universal succession to the rights of the seller ('Gesamtrechtsnachfolge'). A purchaser will, however, as a general rule, not be liable if he merely acquired a limited number of rights ('Einzelnachfolge') from the seller. An important exception to this rule is constituted by s419 Bürgerliches Gezetzbuch, to the effect that if a purchaser acquires all or nearly all the assets of another person, he will also become liable for police actions which took place prior to the asset transfer.

There are also two kinds of public liability for conduct ('Verhaltenshaftung'). If certain illegal conduct took place prior to the transaction but no actual police measure was taken at that time, the local authorities have, as stated above, a wide discretion to select the liable person. In such a case the present landowner will normally be held liable. By contrast, if the police action took place prior to the transaction, the liability for this intervention will be transferred to the purchaser if he is a general successor to for impact in case of a merger. No liability will vest, however, in the purchaser of a limited number of rights of the seller. The liability to pay for the costs of a clean-up action follows the rules on Verhaltenshaftung.

The Transfer of Environmental Permits

It is interesting to practitioners to have an overview of the German, French and Dutch law dealing with the transferability of environmental permits fines. It would take too long to analyse the situation of every single environmental permit in those countries. The emphasis will therefore be laid on the most important permits.

Germany

On the whole, in Germany a high degree of co-ordination between the different kinds of permits exists. The Bundesimmissionsschutzgezetz ('BlmSchG') of 15 March 1974 provided for a 'comprehensive environmental permit', that is, a permit dealing with practically all environmental hazards which also excluded the application of laws imposing other environmental permits. It should be noted, however, that the draining permit of the

Wasserhaushaltsgezetz of 27 July 1957 ('WHG') must be obtained independently from the permit under the BLmSchG. While the WHG provided for a general principle of transferability of the draining permit, the situation with respect to a permit obtained under the BlmSchG is more complex.

In the absence of any specific provisions regarding the transferability of permits, the general principles of administrative law are, therefore, applicable. A permit under the BlmSchG typically provided for two different kinds of conditions: conditions attaching to the facility ('dinglichkeitlicher Verwaltungsakt') and conditions pertaining to the reliability ('zuverlässigkeit') of the person operating the facility ('personbezongener Verwaltungsakt').

At first sight, the conditions of reliability to be met by the operator of the facility seem to cause problems with respect to the transferability of the permit granted under the BlmSchG. The traditional view in German literature is that if elements of personal reliability are taken into account in granting a permit, the permit has a strictly personal character and cannot therefore be transferred to another person or company. In recent literature it is, however, generally accepted that the traditional doctrine is too restrictive. The correct view seems to be that a permit remains valid after a merger or assets transaction. The authorities could, however, revoke the permit under s21(1) BlmSchG if the new persons operating the facility do not meet the conditions of reliability on which the permit was issued.

France

The French legislation has its origins in Napoleonic law, that also lies at the heart of the Dutch 'Hinderwet' (cf below) and the Belgian legislation on hazardous facilities (cf above). In France, a limited number of enlisted hazardous facilities must either obtain a permit (facilities of the first category) or be notified to the public authorities (facilities of the second category). If a licensed or notified facility is taken over by a new operator, the licence or notification inures to the benefit of the new operator or his representative, but either of these persons must submit a formal declaration concerning this modification to the préfet within one month of the commencement of activities.

It is important to note that French law does not consider the change in ownership of the facility to be important but rather the substitution of the actual operator of the facility. This principle is in conformity with Belgian case law, mentioned above, on the transferability of operating permits to the effect that the permit is an accessory to the facility and, therefore, inures to the benefit of the person actually controlling the facility.

The Netherlands

In The Netherlands a wide range of permits dealing with various environmental hazards exists. In contrast to the situation prevailing in Belgium, the procedural rules applicable to environmental permits were harmonised in The Netherlands by the 'Wet Algemene Bepaligen Milieuhygiëne' (WABM) of 13 January 1979. While the law provides that the authorities can, upon request, decide to deal within one procedure with different kinds of permits, this system of co-ordination has only been used in a limited number of cases.

For the purposes of this discussion two important environmental permits which are unanimously considered to be transferable are detailed below.

First, the law on hazardous facilities ('Hinderwet') provides that a series of activities which could have a detrimental effect on the environment must obtain a permit to conduct such activities. It is a well-established principle that no new permit must be obtained if the licensed facility is transferred, provided that the facility did not stop its activities for a period of three years.

Second, the law on air pollution ('Wet inzake de luchtverontreiniging', commonly referred to as 'LUVO') requires that a limited number of facilities that emit polluting substances into the ambient atmosphere must obtain a permit to this effect. Article 20, para 2 of the LUVO expressly states that the benefit of the permit inures to the person actually receiving the permit as well as to his assignees.

Outstanding Issues

An overview of existing legislation dealing with environmental problems facing M&A practice in Europe has demonstrated that a very fragmented and ad hoc response is given to these issues in the different Member States.

Post Responsibilities

With respect to the issue of old (civil or public) environmental burdens, a consensus seems to be emerging that merger effects a shift of these burdens to the acquiring company, while a sales of assets does not result in a transfer of the said liabilities. However, numerous exceptions and caveats do apply. In addition, the question should be squarely addressed, both for civil and public environmental liabilities, whether an acquiring company can reasonably be held to be liable for old burdens of a predecessor if there is no functional or economic continuity between the original infringer and the undertaking into which it was merged. It is, therefore, interesting to note that in recent German literature the thesis was advanced that a company would not be liable for pollution perpetrated by its predecessor if it had not itself engaged in any activities hazardous to the same element of the environment, for instance water. It is advisable, therefore, that this approach should be considered in any given matter in which an acquiring company is faced with potential exposure to old environmental burdens.

It has been proposed that the acquirer should only be liable if it is established that he carried on or adopted the polluting conduct as his own. As in the UK, the following factors should be balanced in order to determine whether the acquiring company can reasonably be held liable for such environmental damage:

- Does the acquiring company engage in activities similar to the ones of its predecessor?

- Does the acquiring company use the facility for activities which are potentially hazardous to the same element of the environment, eg water?

- Did the acquiring company know or should it reasonably have known about the damage?

- Did the acquiring company take adequate precautions to stop the damage from occurring?

- Did the acquired company stop its polluting activities a material period of time before the transfer of the facility?

Due Diligence

It has to be conceded that the problem of transfer of liabilities will, in the majority of cases, be dealt with by the parties involved in a business transaction. The problem will then consist of detecting potential environmental risks in due time. Adequate due diligence can, however, only be properly organised if companies which are targeted by an M&A operation carry out regular audits of their environmental performance and have, therefore, some understanding of their legal exposure. Environmental auditing or management can be defined as:

> 'The managing of the company in its entirety (management, staff and employees) of all those aspects of the company's activities which tax the environment. An environment management system is nothing else but a collection of control, monitoring and feedback instruments which restrict, as far as possible, the degree to which company activities impact the environment.'

Whilst it is true that audits normally have a strictly internal character, it may be in the interest of the targeted company, especially in the context of a merger, to communicate information concerning environmental compliance to the other party. The EMAS regulation is relevant in this respect. Another initiative at the EU level which could have a substantial impact on due diligence in Europe is the Directive on the Freedom of Access to Information on the Environment. This Directive, which came into force on 31 December 1992, provided for a right of access to information on the environment to any natural or legal person without their having to display an interest. The Directive will be an important tool in due diligence because it pertains, inter alia, to data of a factual or legal nature concerning:

> '... public or private projects and activities likely to damage the environment, or endanger human health and plant or animal species, in particular as regards emission, discharge or release of substances, living organisms or energy into water, the air or soil and the manufacture and use of dangerous products or substances'.

It should also be mentioned that the term 'information held by the public authorities' refers, inter alia, to 'information supplied by people other than the authorities themselves', when the body receiving the information had the right to obtain it itself or to demand transmission of that information in exercising its legal powers. Finally, it does not seem likely that the new EEA will be subject to the Directive on the freedom of access to information on the environment. The European Parliament, in its amendments to the Commission proposal on the establishment of the EEA, advocated, by contrast, that the information held by the Agency would be freely accessible.

The problem of transferability of environmental permits has resulted in the same reactive, ad hoc and fragmented approach throughout the EU as the one noted with respect to the problem of allocation of environmental liabilities. As yet, no EU initiatives seem likely to remedy or alleviate this highly impractical situation. The only means to remedy this lack of coherence would be to grant extensive powers of enforcement, implementation and supervision to the EEA, as requested by the European Parliament. At present, and as indicated in Chapter 10, the Member States do not, however, seem to be prepared to endow the EEA with such powers.

Insurance

Opening Remarks: The UK

There can be no doubt that environmental risk and its associated liabilities represent one of the most high-profile and onerous exposures faced by most businesses in the UK today. This is so whether one is looking at the current operations of the company or is concerned with what may have happened in the past. No-one is immune, whether a chemical company, a retail business that erects property on what transpires is contaminated land or the holding company which acquires a subsidiary with hidden environmental problems. The legal framework which surrounds this issue is complex, rapidly changing and, in many areas, uncertain. Indeed, some insurers would argue that in the USA, for example, the only certainty is the uncertainty and capriciousness of the legal system.

When discussing environmental risk and legal liability it is easy to become too general and not focus on the precise issues involved. Here the relevant question is the insurance of legal liabilities that may arise from the release of contaminants into the environment. Such releases may happen very quickly, for example fire or explosion in a chemical storage facility which may result in immediate death or injury or damage to property. They may, on the other hand, be slow and insidious. An undetected leak in an underground storage tank may release contaminants over a very long period, perhaps many years. The resulting damage may occur gradually over that time and again may not manifest itself for many years. The nature of this pollution risk creates problems for the insurance industry as well as the insured.

This section outlines the operation of liability insurance in relation to environmental risk the insurance market in the UK with reference to Europe and the USA, and gives a view of future developments. An understanding of the issues involved is important for the practitioner, both in assessing what coverage may or may not be available now, but in many cases identifying the scope of past coverages, may be of vital importance. It must be understood that, whilst insurance is a valuable tool, it has in this area severe limitations and must be ancillary to the management of risk.

Basic Background

Insurance is a mechanism for the transfer of defined risk. An underwriter in return for a premium promises to provide an indemnity to the insured in the event of certain contingencies. Insurers have, since the last century, issued public or general liability policies to businesses. A typical public liability policy promises to indemnify the insured in respect of legal liability which he may incur in the course of business relating to injury or damage caused to people or property. Among other things, it would exclude damage to the insured's own property and damage deliberately caused.

Until fairly recently, most such policies almost certainly would contain no reference to environmental damage or pollution. There are two basic alternative forms of such policies. The 'occurrence' form and the 'claims made' form.

The 'occurrence' form responds to injury and damage occurring during the policy period irrespective of when the claim may be made by the third party. The 'claims made' form responds to claims by third parties which are forthcoming during the policy period. The injury or damage may have occurred before the current policy period but may not have become apparent. This may be subject to a retroactive date. Claims in respect of injury or damage occurring before this date would be excluded.

The occurrence wording has been – and continues to be – the usual form for public liability policies in the UK and most of Europe. Claims-made forms have been used for some risks particularly in relation to some chemical and pharmaceutical exposures. Also, a number of years ago there was a general move by the insurance market towards the claims-made form but this was not sustained.

Some Concerns

The occurrence form of policy, combined with gradually operating environmental damage or pollution, has caused major difficulties for the liability insurance industry, particularly in the USA. Policies have been called on in relation to damage that has manifested itself 20 or 30 years after they were written. In addition, insurers may have insured the same risk for a period of many years. Due to the fact that damage may well have occurred in each of the policy years and the interpretation put on the word occurrence by courts in the USA, insurers have been exposed for the full limit of the policies written in each of the number of years. All of this is in relation to a risk that insurers may not have foreseen and for which they may not have charged a premium.

Restrictions

The first response of insurers was to restrict coverage for risks in the USA using clauses such as the one that follows:

'This Insurance does not cover any liability for:

Personal Injury or Bodily Injury or loss of, damage to, or loss of use of property directly or indirectly caused by seepage, pollution or contamination, provided always that this Paragraph (1) shall not apply to liability for Personal Injury or Bodily Injury or loss of or physical damage to or destruction of tangible property, or loss of use of such property damaged or destroyed, where such seepage, pollution or contamination is caused by a sudden, unintended and unexpected happening during the period of this Insurance.

The cost of removing, nullifying or cleaning-up seeping, polluting or contaminating substances unless the seepage, pollution or contamination is caused by a sudden, unintended and unexpected happening during the period of this Insurance.

Fines, penalties, punitive or exemplary damages.

This clause shall not extend this Insurance to cover any liability which would not have been covered under this Insurance had this Clause not been attached.'

This form of words was intended to remove the coverage for injury and damage caused by gradually occurring contamination. It started to be applied to some policies in the early to mid-1970s. Unfortunately, from the point of view of insurers, these clauses have suffered sustained attack in the courts in the USA, and have been interpreted in some jurisdictions as still including gradually operating contamination.

Exclusions

The insurance industry responded by introducing an absolute exclusion of such damage along the following lines:

'This Insurance does not cover any liability for:

Personal Injury or Bodily Injury or loss of, damage to or loss of use of property directly or indirectly caused by seepage, pollution or contamination.

The cost of removing, nullifying or cleaning-up seeping, polluting or contaminating substances.

Fines, penalties, punitive or exemplary damages.'

Developments

By the early to mid-1980s in the USA, there was a situation where the insurance market had suffered catastrophic losses arising from pollution claims going back over many years and where they felt the legal system was not allowing them to write even a limited form of cover for suddenly occurring events.

Another major issue in this jurisdiction was the cost of cleaning up the insured's own property. As with policies issued in the London market, policies in the USA exclude damage to the insured's own property, but again, those insured have sought to involve insurers in the face of clean-up orders from the US EPA. However, there exists a situation where coverage for damage caused by contamination, whether gradually operating or sudden, is not available under general liability policies in the USA.

The situation in the USA has had a considerable influence in the UK and Europe in two ways: the insurance industry is world-wide and many European re-insurers have been affected by the problems directly; and the problems in relation to the environment in the USA alerted insurers to the type of problem they may face in Europe.

In the early 1980s in the London insurance market many insurers started to restrict coverage on the basis of the first clause shown above.

General Liability in the UK

In most cases, the general liability policy will exclude damage caused by gradually occurring pollution. It is still, however, possible in some cases to negotiate the omission of this restriction perhaps for the first £10 million of the indemnity limit. This would generally be the case only on risks where the underwriters perceive the exposure to be very low or for large insurance buyers with substantial liability programmes. Many large insurance buyers may be carrying their own risk at the primary levels of a programme, either self-insured or using a captive. If the captive is providing some degree of cover it is sometimes possible to negotiate with excess carriers to obtain coverage.

If the company has a subsidiary in the USA covered under the programme, there would be an absolute exclusion of claims caused by both gradually operating and sudden pollution for that subsidiary. This obviously represents a severe restriction and may in some circumstances go further than the insured might expect. The form of exclusion used may remove cover for immediate damage caused by, for example, poisonous gas released in an explosion. In some circumstances, it may be possible to negotiate cover for such damage following identified and defined events, for example, fire, explosion and overturning of vehicles.

Some of the mutual excess facilities, such as X/L, provide some cover for sudden events resulting in environmental damage if the damage manifests itself and is reported within a short period, perhaps seven or 14 days. These facilities are generally on a claims made basis. They do, however, offer at least some cover which is not otherwise available for companies based in the USA.

In summary, when looking at the general liability insurance programme for any company, it is important to try and structure it in such a way as to achieve the maximum cover for environmental risks that the market is prepared to give, and in the London market there is still some degree of flexibility.

Environmental Impairment Liability Cover

As the availability of cover under the general liability form for environmental damage has become restricted, the insurance market has responded to some extent by offering environmental impairment liability as a separate policy.

This form of cover is normally on a claims made basis which avoids the insurer exposing more than one year's indemnity limit to latent claims and enables him to reassess the past exposure at each renewal. Environmental impairment liability policies will almost always be written on the basis of site surveys giving the underwriters a much more detailed view of the risk and its past history. The cover may include some degree of own site clean-up.

The first widely available cover was introduced in the mid-1970s in the UK, but it did not achieve a high take-up at that time. This was probably for a number of reasons, but principally the then lack of restrictions on most general liability policies and the low profile of environmental issues generally combined with the cost of site surveys and the cover itself.

In the USA in the early 1980s, a number of insurers entered this market but were quickly overtaken by the rapidly escalating problems in this area, particularly including the environmental legislation introduced at about that time. Most of the facilities closed within a relatively short time with large losses. Currently, in the USA there are a small number of facilities in existence, most with capacity below $5 million.

However, in the UK and Europe, it is likely that this form of cover will develop and represent at least part of the way forward in meeting the increasing demand from insurance buyers. An example of a recent initiative in the UK is that undertaken by the Chemical Industries Association and Willis Wrightson. They have developed an environmental impairment liability facility specifically for members of the Association. The leading underwriter is Swiss Re, who have developed considerable experience in this area over the last 10 to 15 years. The necessary environmental surveys are carried out by Hinton & Higgs.

The principal features of the scheme are:

- claims-made policy form;
- coverage for environmental impairment resulting in:
  - death, bodily injury or disease to any person;
  - damage to property;
  - impairment or diminution of or other interferences with any right or amenity protected by law;
- three-year policy period;
- £5 million each occurrence limit, £10 million the aggregate;
- site specificity.

This facility represents a step in building long-term confidence between insured and insurers in what is now and will continue to be a difficult area. Other initiatives are being prepared for industries which are at the front line of environmental exposures.

Pool Arrangements

An alternative to the conventional insurance arrangements which have made some limited headway in a number of European countries are insurance pools. These are basically groups of insurers providing environmental impairment liability on a co-insurance basis. The members reinsure one another and deal with underwriting and claims handling through a committee. As there are currently main pools in for example Italy, France and The Netherlands, the limits available are relatively low.

The Future Role for Insurance

The current situation is perhaps not encouraging from the point of view of the insurance buyer faced by increasingly onerous environmental exposures. The insurance market has rapidly retreated from an area that has caused it catastrophic losses in the USA, and which it fears will cause losses in Europe, certainly on the basis of current policy forms and underwriting methods.

However, there are ways forward, as indicated by the initiatives that are already being undertaken. Capacity for the risks involved can be rebuilt using all the resources of the insurance market which, after all, is in the business of taking risk and is looking for new, long-term sources of premium.

The claims made form will be the basis of cover and careful underwriting based on surveys of most risks will be essential. A responsible and long-term approach by both insured and insurers should enable a viable market to develop with available capacity increasing as experience and confidence grow.

The conventional insurance market will not be the only approach. Industry mutuals will almost certainly have a part to play, and pool arrangements may develop further in Europe. It may be that mutuals and pools become involved in providing catastrophe protection in excess of primary placements with conventional insurers.

Insurance in this field, however, can only follow good risk management practice by the potential insured. There has to be recognition by the insured that the exposures exist and must be managed and, finally, he must be prepared to pay the appropriate premium.

[1] See appendices for sample pre-contract enquiries

[2] For general further reference see Spedding, Jones and Dering *Eco-Management and Eco-Auditing Environmental Issues in Business* Chancery 1993; J Porritt *Where on Earth Are We Going?* BBC Books 1990

[3] See the CIA 'Responsible Care' Guidelines. See also 'Responsible Care' Report May/June 1993

[4] 'Towards Sustainability: A European Community Programme of Policy and Action in relation to the Environment and Sustainable Development', Vol II Corn (92) Final, 27.3.92

[5] World Commission on Environment and Development 'Our Common Future' Oxford University Press 1987

[6] See also Alexandre Kiss and Dinah Shelton, *International Environmental Law* Transnational Publishers Inc and Graham & Trotman Limited 1991 (pp66, 78, 81 and 85), Frances Cayncross *Costing the Earth* The Economist Books 1991, pp93-106

[7] 51 Fred Reg 25,004 (July 9, 1986)

[8] Council Regulation No 1836/OJ 1993 L 168/1 29.6.93

[9] See case studies in no 1 above. Also see eg Arthur D Little, *Environmental Auditing: An Overview*, Centre for Environmental Assurance Cambridge 1989. See also Arthur D Little, *Benefits to Industry of Environmental Auditing* prepared for Environmental Protection Agency, National Technical Information Service August 1983, and Prizner 'Trends in Environmental Auditing' 20 Env LR 10179 May 1990

[10] See particularly 42 USC paras 11001-11050. This is often referred to as Title III of SARA (Superfund Amendments and Re-authorisation Act 1986)

[11] See The Green Paper on Environmental Liability Com (93) 47

[12] See Spedding, Jones and Dering, no 2 above, Chapter 4. BS 7750 has now been superseded by ISO 14001 discussed in detail in Chapter 7 above

[13] See no 4 above

[14] See Porritt no 2 pp147–149

[15] See for example the 3M Approach, ibid pp141–143

[16] Directive 90/313 OJ 1990 L158/56

[17] See for example Wessex Water Environmental Performance Report 1992/1993. See also Wessex Water plc Environmental Charter. Another example in the chemical sector is 'BP Chemicals: The Facts' 1992 Update

[18] See *Social and Environmental Auditing* Vol 13 No 3 Spring 1993

[19] See Environmental Rules Notification No GSR 442(E) 19 May 1993

[20] See ICC Business Charter for Sustainable Development 1990

[21] See no 5 above

[22] See International Chamber of Commerce 'Environmental Auditing' Publication No 469 Paris, France 1989 p6. See also International Chamber of Commerce 'Guide to Effective Environmental Auditing' Publication No 483 Paris, France (1991)

[23] See Spedding, Jones and Dering no 2 above pp60-66. Note that BS5750 was designated CEN 29,000 in the European context of the CEN.CENELEC Rules and had close links with the ISO 9000 Standards. Note also the ILO Auditing Experience Paper 4. Sands 'Lessons Learned in Global Environmental Governance' World Resource Institute 1990 pp33–34. Note also the impact of ISO 14001 now

[24] Ibid Chapter 5

[25] Ibid Chapter 4

[26] Companies have sometimes integrated their approach to environment, health and safety by establishing an HS&E Department which is perceived as part of an overall quality management system. See, for example, 'Health Safety and the Environment: A Statement of BP's Policy' 1993

[27] See ENDS Bulletin December 1993

[28] 'Environmental Firms Clean Up: The Environmental Audit' ERM 1993

[29] 'Quality Management through Environmental Audit' ERM 1993

[30] Ibid. Project Examples: ERM worked with British Gas to develop a comprehensive environmental audit programme designed to audit 4,000 facilities world-wide over a three-year period. For ARCO Chemical, ERM provided team members for audit programmes throughout Europe, the Far East and Australasia

[31] Ibid. Project examples: Eastern Europe investments in new facilities. Major projects include the audit of 27 heavy-manufacturing facilities in the Czech Republic, carried out at Skoda plants on behalf of the International Finance Corporation

[32] Ibid. Project example: US multinational Allied Signal commissioned ERM to assess over 60 waste-handling sites in the UK, Ireland, France and Germany. The programme was designed to identify potential liabilities in respect of waste disposal and to ensure that operators measured up to the highest standards

[33] Ibid. Project example: ERM carried out a series of audits in the UK on behalf of the Clydesdale Bank covering issues such as indoor air quality, the risk of diseases such as legionella and staff health generally. Overseas, the group has completed audits for General Electric at plants in Europe, India and China. Areas covered included emergency response procedures, exposure to chemicals and fire protection

[34] See, for example, J Elkington (ed) *Sustainability Limited: The Environmental Audit*, 1990

[35] The author has evolved certain headings relevant to small- and medium-sized enterprises for an environmental audit programme package which includes emissions, pollution-control equipment, product management, waste, transport policy, public relations, task allocation, human resources, management of change, facility changes and emergencies

[36] For liability reporting see Archer, McMahon and Crough 'SEC Reporting of Environmental Liabilities' 20 Env LR 10105 1990

[37] See no 19 above and the Regulations referred to in India. Also see Sands in no 23 above. See also Spedding, *International Environmental Policy and Management* (Business and the Environment Practitioner Series) Stanley Thornes 1995 (ISBN: 0 7487 2132 0)

Chapter 10

International Environmental Law and the International Agenda: The Future

Transboundary Trends in Environmental Standards

Shared Responsibility

Certain trends and issues should be mentioned to demonstrate the extensive nature of potential future developments in environmental law and management. There is no doubt that there will be several areas to watch at national international and European level which will impact upon how an organisation and its advisers should consider its response to regulatory and voluntary matters. This is quite clear from the concept of 'shared responsibility', which has been highlighted by the current EAP, 'Towards Sustainability'. This concept promotes the partnership of government and industry as a team working together, and proposes that the way forward for the implementation of improved environmental standards will be through a mix of the regulatory, the voluntary and economic instruments. This fact, along with the concern that there should be a level playing field in terms of international trade, has meant that there is an ongoing comparative exchange of information both by government and by industry as regards both compulsory and voluntary standards.

The earlier chapters have covered a variety of themes and issues facing business as it heads towards the twenty-first century. This chapter speculates upon what the increasing concern over environmental issues and the growing volume of environmental regulations world-wide would mean for companies in terms of legal, financial and other risks as well as business opportunities.

Environmental Eras

The development of the environment debate might best be described in terms of eras, the first era being the awakening of public 'environmentalism'. In particular, this was influenced by figures such as Rachel Carson, author of the seminal environmental publication, *The Silent Spring*, and by events such as the Love Canal incident (which led to the creation of the US Superfund regime), Chernobyl, Bhopal and the *Exxon Valdez* disaster.

The next era was the realisation by politicians and policy-makers that environmentalism was a force to be reckoned with and was having a significant effect upon public concerns over government policies. The apex of this era was the 1992 United Nations Conference on Environment and Development (UNCED/the Earth Summit/the Rio Summit), which resulted in several treaties being signed, including the Convention on Climate Change, with its major ramifications for economies and businesses world-wide. Perhaps to the surprise of the more cynical observers, the Earth Summit produced genuine progress, although the recent follow-up summit in December 1997 at Kyoto was an altogether more disappointing extension to the Rio process.

The latest era appears to be characterised by the growing realisation by both the business community and the environmental NGOs that partnership and dialogue is the key to finding acceptable solutions to the world's environmental problems, not least because it is industry which largely has the means to deliver the required improvements.

Sustainable Development

The notion of sustainable development at the very least stretches to the concept of balancing economic growth with environmental protection. Consequently, as has been indicated in earlier chapters, the role of industry in delivering economic growth ought to be at the centre of the debate on sustainable development.

Inevitably then, sustainable development presents both risks and rewards for business, and to the extent that the business community fails to take on board the new sustainability–oriented market regime, the twin risks of increasing regulation and declining markets may well be the reward for failing to react promptly to this new challenge. Whereas this may be considered a rather simplistic way of looking at the issues, at least it has the merit of highlighting, at the macroeconomic level, the serious challenges which business is now facing. Indeed, one might say that the environmental issues now facing us are so serious that a major change in business outlook and practice will be required by industry world-wide: 'business as usual' is not an option – the concept of sustainable development continues to evolve and will continue to impact on economic activities.

World Trade

Institutions in the public and private sector are also aware of the need for dialogue on sustainability, as has been evidenced in recent talks of the World Trade Organisation (WTO). It is clear from the WTO talks that progress on an environmental understanding is crucial. Indeed, the harmonisation of environmental standards may also occur informally as foreign regulatory models are voluntarily adopted. For example, many developing countries today may admit imported chemical products without national evaluation if the product was duly licensed in the country of origin, thereby relying on the presumed effectiveness of foreign controls. On the other hand, several European countries have borrowed from US Federal or California State standards to update their national legislation, for instance, on automobile emissions. Meanwhile India, for example, has taken on board BS7750 as their own Indian (BIS) Environmental Management Standard prior to the implementation of the ISO 14001 standard.

Trade and the Environment

Another growing consideration in terms of environmental performance relates to the global market. On the one hand, as noted, there seems to be a vast and expanding environmental technology business; on the other hand, there is some debate as to how far the imposition of environmental standards can create a distortion in the market or at the minimum prevent a level playing field.

Environmental Impact Assessment: Implementation from the USA to the UK

The vivid illustration of the exchange in environmental requirements at the international level is in the implementation of EIAs. As most organisations and their advisers should be aware, this is the technique and process for gathering information on the likely environmental effects of a proposed development or activity. In order that any adverse effects can be addressed and, where practicable, minimised in the plans, this should be properly carried out whilst the project is still at the design stage.

The EIA was pioneered as an approach in the USA where it was made mandatory for major construction projects by, or financed by, the federal government. Subsequently, it was adapted by the EC and was enacted in 1985 in Directive 85/337. In the UK, the implementation of the Directive is principally by the Town and Country Planning (Assessment of Environmental Effects) Regulations 1988 (SI 1988 no 1199) as amended for England and Wales. There are similar regulations for Scotland and Northern Ireland, and numerous other related regulations, mostly concerned with categories of projects covered by the Directive but which are not subject to the standard planning consent procedures in the UK.

It is true to say that one legislative innovation that has spread widely is the EIA procedure that was first introduced by the US National Environmental Policy Act 1969. The process that has been explained above is mandatory for major projects in the UK, that is, those listed in Annex 1 to the 1985 EU Directive and Schedule 1 to the UK's 1988 Regulations. Annex 2 of the Directive (Schedule 2 to the 1988 Regulations) lists a further group of projects for which an environmental statement may be required by the planning authority (subject to appeal) if it is considered that the project in question would be likely to have significant effects on the environment due to factors such as its nature, size or location. Essentially, the assessment procedure consists of the developer submitting an environmental statement to the relevant authority. Statutory consultees also receive copies. The authority may seek further information and must lay the statement open for comment by the public before determining any application for planning consent for the project. A developer may offer an environmental statement even though it cannot be legally demanded and this may have procedural and other advantages for them. There is formal guidance on the procedures in the then DoE circular 15/88 and in an explanatory booklet 'Environmental Assessment – A Guide to Procedures'. There is an international regime for environmental impact assessments for projects likely to have significant transboundary effects. This has been agreed recently, but still awaits implementation. It is known as the Convention on EIAs in the Transboundary Context.

Although attempts to internationalise the procedure through a treaty have been slow, the EIA is now a well-known legal term not only in English-speaking countries, but also in French-, Spanish- and German-speaking countries. Indeed, it is part of the usual practice in the implementation of public and private projects in many parts of the world for an assessment to be made along a recognised procedure, and it is certainly part of corporate environmental management strategy where companies are investing overseas.

EIAs are increasingly relevant to the provision of aid. Very often, aid organisations will stipulate environmental safeguards on projects and programmes. They will often require environmental appraisal of the plans prior to awarding money. Similarly, stemming from the Earth Summit, the Global Environment Fund (GEF) has been established under the World Bank, with the specific aim of stimulating development, but with the overriding objective of protecting and enhancing the environment.

Project Sustainability: Practical Costing Implications

Related to the topic of EIAs is that of project sustainability. The implications of sustainable development are potentially wide-ranging for activities carried out by organisations. The principle does not imply avoiding all exploitative projects, such as mining or hardwood timber-felling. Nor does it require projects to continue indefinitely. The following are some of its more certain operational implications that have been outlined in the form of recommendations.

First, avoid damage to critical natural capital, such as biodiversity and the ozone layer, and be wary of starting processes that are irreversible.

Second, where possible, put economic values on environmental costs and benefits as a reminder to decision-makers that these resources are not free, with the aim of moderating the use of environmental services.

Third, in certain cases, 'internalise' the costs of a project to the environment, either by requiring compensation to be made (to society or to parties damaged) or by building a 'compensatory project' into the scheme being appraised, for example, planting trees to replace those that have been felled during road building.

Fourth, for man-made and non-critical natural capital, aim to recover at least the initial capital by the end of the project. For man-made capital, for example, a steel mill, this entails applying certain rules, namely, fully recovery of the initial cost of the project over the life of the scheme, leaving the original outlays for reinvestment or redeployment in the future. For renewable natural capital, for example, agriculture, forestry and fishing, it implies maintaining the resource and limiting exploitation to a minimum.

Lastly, in project design, and as part of project negotiations, aim to incorporate many of the environmental costs (and benefits) as possible through the adjustment of actual prices, taxes and subsidies. This is another example of the attempt to 'internalise' such costs, and take the analyst into the realm of policy dialogue and conditionality.

There are many other practical implications of sustainable development, especially in the areas of national and international policies, which are referred to further below.

Pollution Taxes

As mentioned in Chapters 1 and 4, the concept of a pollution tax or financial charge prorated to the volume of pollutant emissions has spread throughout Western and Eastern Europe, as well as the USA. The basic idea is to levy a disincentive charge on specified economic activities, depending on the extend of the environmental harm, and to earmark the proceeds of the charge for specific counter-measures in the form of 'effluent charges'. Moreover, the general concept of the 'polluter pays' principle is seen to exist in different contexts in many jurisdictions, despite varying interpretations. In the UK, the landfill levy has been introduced as a form of economic disincentive to the use of landfill.

Environmental Labelling: Enhanced Public Awareness

More recently there has been a debate over the 'environmental label' which, as mentioned earlier, is a system of product labelling and licensing which has been introduced in areas as diverse as Germany, Japan, Canada and Norway. In view of the European scheme,[1] as well as the information exchange role of the EEA, there will be some effort to avoid unfair trade practices in connection with such labels. It has been mooted that arrangements for the mutual recognition of national environmental labels, possibly including harmonised standards and procedures of product selection and identification will become necessary. Simultaneously, the role of the non-governmental bodies and the likelihood of complaints as a result of enhanced public information will be another trend that should be watched.

One of the forums available is the European Court of Human Rights in Strasburg. For example, an important judgment in the Court has confirmed that governments may be liable for environment pollution as a breach of the European Convention on Human Rights. The judgment in the case of *Lopez Ostra v Spain*, Council of Europe 9/12/1994 confirms that liability under the Convention may arise where public authorities fail to protect an individual's home or private life from pollution caused by others, and may also be liable for pollution which they directly create. This could include noise from military airfields etc. The case has shown that it is not a sufficient defence to demonstrate that the state has a legal regime controlling environmental pollution if effective enforcement cannot be proved as well. The facts of the case concerned a family that suffered pollution from the leather tanning industry. The claim was that the LA had been inactive in dealing with pollution and failed to strike a fair balance between the competing interests of the individual and of the community as a whole. The case shows the importance of transboundary legal procedures.

In the *Lopez Ostra v Spain* decision, the applicants succeeded where the individual in the British case of *Power and Rayner v UK* (1990) 12 EHRR 355 failed. In that case, the British government was able to show it had achieved the fair balance notwithstanding that there was pollution. The court had taken into account the expenditure of more than £30 million in the provision of noise insulation. Both decisions illustrate the importance of a 'fair balance'.

Environmental Auditing

Many transnational corporations – some partly in response to the Bhopal incident – now carry out regular environmental audits to ensure that regulatory requirements and long-term environmental liability, such as legal waste disposal duties, are actively reflected in their subsidiaries' balance sheets. Since the executive board of the ICC adopted its 1988 position paper on environmental auditing for business organisations, reflecting the experience in countries and companies where the practice was already well established, the impetus for the taking up of environmental auditing by government and industry alike has developed. This has sometimes been referred to as the 'eco-audit trail'. It is yet to be seen how far and how quickly the related initiative of 'environmental reporting' will be developed globally.

Throughout the operation of any business, there will be the need to demonstrate to regulators, investors, lenders, shareholders and consumers the ability of that company to meet the demands placed upon it for environmental protection.

Whereas in the past the term 'audit' has referred to ensuring financial probity in business, the term is increasingly being applied in the field of demonstrating environmental probity. For example, the environmental audit is already part of jurisdictions as far apart as India and the USA. The eco-audit is seen as an essential tool to allow the management of a company to be appraised of its continuing environmental performance. The eco-audit will provide a verifiable trail of the environmental performance of a company, from the production of the raw material for its products through the manufacturing process, to the distribution, use and ultimate disposal of that product. This life-cycle or 'cradle to grave' approach demonstrates the commitment of that business to considering the environment in all of its activities.

Recent developments, recognised in countries as far flung as Canada and India, include schemes for eco-labelling. Aimed at allowing the consumer to make an informed choice when buying products, the schemes specify the environmental performance of items.

However, a fundamental difference remains between the more limited scope of auditing as an internal business management technique and the idea of public review. The latter emerges as the key element of the international environmental audit procedures, which, for example, have been followed by the International Labour Organisation (ILO), or in other periodic audits of compliance with agreed upon international standards that are well established. Inherent in these is public disclosure as a means of ensuring democratic control over the implementation of agreed upon international standards.

At the international level, it has been mooted that it may be time to envisage a global auditing body that would periodically evaluate the performance of states and organisations in complying with their international obligations. This is in view of the evident need to make global environmental controls preventative rather than corrective. There is certainly an argument for more imaginative approaches to compliance control in the field of standard setting and regulation that will require further co-ordination within the United Nations family of organisations. Those companies – and advisers – that gear themselves up at both compliance and voluntary levels and recognise the value of improved environmental performance in the global market place will have a definite advantage against this background, both in private- and public-sector concerns.

Investment: The Role of Audits

The market for capital also has its green fringes, with the evolution of banks and finance houses that will only lend money to countries or companies with good environmental credentials. As well as a sound financial return on the loan capital, lenders are increasingly watching to see safeguards placed on the environment. In the past, many lenders have 'had their fingers burned' by lending money for unsuitable projects, only to see enormous amounts of money written off as bad debts. The links between sound money and sound environment are becoming better understood, and lenders are becoming increasingly wary unless their concerns can be allayed. An example is the National Westminster Bank's policy, 'Good Environmental Management Equals Good Business Management'. Indeed, the use of preacquisition and predivestiture environmental audits in company transactions is now common policy. Often, these environmental audits are conducted at the instance of the venture capitalists, who use the results to negotiate price reduction, warranties or indemnities. Sometimes environmental liabilities can stop a transaction proceeding.

Information technology

The advancement of communication technology has brought a greater social responsibility. News, whether good or bad, travels instantaneously around the world. Irresponsible political, religious and business leaders are made to answer for disreputable deeds sooner than ever before. Society is no longer in the dark and demands a certain level of responsibility for the institutions. Such accountability has carried over to certain aspects within the context of human rights and the environment. These issues had seemed to spill over into most areas of society. Business people realise that creating a profit without regard to the environment or people is a losing gamble. There is a necessity for a holistic approach to corporate management. This pertains to businesses of all sizes and regardless of the sectors with which they are dealing. There is a specific need for environmental management.

Mismanagement

The world's worst chemical disaster was caused by a gas leak at the Union Carbide plant in Bhopal, India. The incident killed more than 3,000 people and cost the US group which owned the plant over $470 million in punitive expenses. In addition to monetary losses, all Indian assets in the company were seized and it was forced to leave India at a time when this market was most attractive to investors. The chief executive officer of Union Carbide has described the incident as one of his greatest lessons. It set the organisation on a new course of enhanced environmental awareness world-wide.

As the world becomes a smaller place in which to conduct, good environmental management is becoming related to good business in general. Studies have shown that the cost for creating an environmental management plan and implementing it are nominal compared to the cost of clean-up, law suits, restructuring facilities, potential sanctions and a loss of reputation in the eyes of colleagues and customers. If a sustainable plan is well researched and implemented from the start, overall effects will enable a business to prosper regardless of where it intends to operate.

The EU Agenda

EU Businesses and International Competitiveness

It should be recalled that Member States are not only required to implement environmental policy with regard to each other, but also they are required in the Treaty to co-ordinate what is called a 'common commercial policy' towards non-Member States. Traditionally, the EU has had special tariffs and commercial preferences established for various countries which had former links with the Member States. In a similar fashion, it is foreseeable that EU-based business people will be required to meet the standards recognised in the EU wherever they are responsible for production and employment. It is already true to say that multinational companies have found it advantageous to operate to a similar standard world-wide.

Within Europe however, public perception – particularly in the UK – has often been that the EU tends to harmonise legislation at the European level merely for its own sake. To be fair to the European Commission and other EU institutions, there is often a justifiable, economic reason for harmonising legislation which is not readily apparent to the more vociferous critics of European integration.

Nonetheless, despite the fact that harmonising legislation across the EU may well be justified in many instances, EU policy-makers should remember that it might well be possible to achieve the same aim through non-legislative means, particularly the voluntary approach. In fact, several sections of European industry are currently in discussion with the European Commission over the possibility of implementing 'voluntary agreements' instead of further regulation covering that particular section of industry.

The key issue though is whether at EU level there is an appropriate mechanism to ensure that balanced, 'sustainable' solutions are reached which can garner the support not only of industry and the so-called Brussels bureaucrats, but also the public whose concerns often led the politicians to legislate at EU level in the first place. EU treaties, particularly the latest Amsterdam Treaty, do attempt to address this issue by making explicit reference to sustainable development and the need to include environmental considerations into other areas of EU policy-making and legislation. Whether in practice this will succeed is, however, another matter.

The principle of subsidiarity that is that decisions should be taken 'as closely as possible to the citizen' may present a way forward. However, environmentalists are still suspicious of how subsidiarity is actually being implemented, not least because it is also by using 'subsidiarity' (see below) that some sections of industry and some European politicians believe that Europe can 'deregulate' in the environmental field by giving back to the Member States the power to set their own environmental standards.

Industry's main complaint has been against the practice of harmonising environmental standards upwards by introducing legislation which takes an 'unreasonably high' baseline for compliance. Despite the level playing field concept, which is the benefit that harmonisation is supposed to bring, the business community does not generally accept the level playing field argument as a valid rationale for raising the lowest standards within the EU up to the level of the highest. Conflict arises however, because some EU politicians and policy-makers, and many environmentalists, see things otherwise.

This latter group are joined by some sections of industry (albeit largely restricted to those selling environmental technologies and services) who argue that setting higher levels of compliance and thereby raising environmental standards actually increases industrial competitiveness and stimulates growth in new markets, such as the environmental technology and services sector. Indeed, there is a very credible viewpoint held by some that without high environmental standards being set through regulation, businesses generally do not improve their environmental performance of their own volition.

However, the most recent thinking appears to be that business will respond more favourably to market-based solutions than to increasing regulation since these market-based solutions provide the necessary economic incentives for companies to become more environmentally responsible. Conversely, regulation is somewhat a blunt instrument and there is gathering evidence to suggest that the 'command-and-control' approach to regulation is slowly going out of favour with European politicians and policy-makers.

Amongst all of this, competitiveness remains the key issue. It is true that excessive regulation can impose an inequitable burden on 'local' businesses as against foreign competitors, and in view of the increasingly global nature of the marketplace, this is a crucial concern. However, it is not only over-regulation which is the concern; also at issue is the lack or unevenness of enforcement of environmental regulation in certain countries. Lax environmental policies may provide advantages for local businesses as against foreign competitors who face a more stringent – and, therefore, more costly – regime at home. On the other hand, this does not explain the continued competitiveness and export success of companies from heavily regulated countries such as the USA (although US companies may not see it that way!).

Subsidiarity

The doctrine of subsidiarity has been embedded in Article 36 of the Treaty as amended by the Maastricht Treaty. This provides:

> *'In areas which do not fall within its exclusive competence, the Community shall take action, in accordance with the principle of subsidiarity, only if and in so far as the objectives of the proposed action can not be sufficiently achieved by the Member States and can therefore, by reason of the scale of the effects of the proposed action, be better achieved by the Community.'*

European Environment Agency

Organisations and their advisers should be aware that in terms of European developments there is no doubt that the EEA has a real potential to contribute to the debate on environmental management. The Council adopted Regulation 1210/90 to establish the EEA and the European Environment Information and Observation Network in May 1990. This entered into force when, in October 1993, following a protracted dispute, it was finally decided that the EEA headquarters would be based in Copenhagen. The official opening took place on 31 October 1994. The EEA was established so that 'objective, reliable and comparable' information can be provided to the EU and Member States to enable appropriate measures to be taken to protect the environment, and the implementation of such measures to be appraised.

The aim of the EEA Regulation is also to provide the public with more information about the state of the environment and to supply any necessary technical or scientific support. An illustration of this was the publication of the Dobris Report which was referred to earlier.

The EEA Regulation

The EEA Regulation sets out in detail how the EEA is to operate. It has a separate legal personality and is governed by a management board composed of representatives from each Member State, two representatives from the Commission and two scientific representatives designated by the European Parliament. There will also be a scientific committee. The EEA Regulation lays down detailed provisions for the EEA's financing, which is also open to non-EU Member States in certain circumstances.

The EEA is to establish an information network composed of national information centres, and co-ordinate and assess information provided by the network. In addition, it will provide the EU and Member States with the information needed to adopt and implement appropriate environmental policies and to promote techniques for forecasting and assessing their environmental impact. The EEA's remit includes the promotion of the exchange of information and technologies to prevent or reduce environmental damage. ITs focus will be on air and water pollution, soil pollution, land use and natural resources, waste management, noise pollution, hazardous chemical substances and coastal protection.

As part of its remit, the EEA will also consider cross-boarder environmental issues, liaise with international environment agencies, such as the UNEP, and also other environmental bodies such as the EU Environmental Research and Development Programme. Member States are responsible for organising the liaison between the national authorities and the EEA. Information held by the EEA may be published and made available to the public in accordance with rules laid down by the Commission, provided that the information is not confidential. A report on the state of the environment will be published every three years.

It is important to remember that the principle of sustainable development will influence European policy as a matter of priority for government and industry. The EEA has published a report, 'Environment in the European Union (1995)' – report for the Review of the Fifth EAP. This has found that while the EU is making progress in reducing certain pressures on the environment, this progress is still not sufficient to improve the general quality of the environment and even less to progress towards sustainability.

In the initial discussions about the EEA, certain enforcement duties and other responsibilities were considered. It is possible that the powers of the EEA will be expanded to include the monitoring implementation of EU environmental legislation and providing environmentally friendly technologies and techniques, although there are still some aspects of institutional overlap still exist.

The UK Agency: Some UK Initiatives

Royal Commission on Environmental Pollution (RCEP) Study on Environmental Standards

It is clear that the defining of appropriate standards is vital to the success of sustainable development, as well as proper environmental management. In the UK, the RCEP invited comments for a study, which was launched at the end of 1995, to determine whether a 'more consistent and robust basis' can be achieved for environmental standards. The study has apparently been prompted by the increasing amount of environmental legislation and numerical standards, generating concerns from business that over-stringent standards may impose cost penalties which are out of proportion to the benefits obtained. Another factor has been the growing concern over the impact of a number of toxic chemicals in trace quantities whose targeted control is not adequately achieved. This reflects the on-going debate on costs and benefits and the concern that the ends should justify the means in both environmental and business terms. The study serves as a good illustration of the need for government and industry to work together to influence environmental policy.

According to its mission statement, the RCEP believes that the establishment of the environment agencies under the EA 1995 will lead to more consistent and sustainable standards. It intended to review the basis for regulatory standards and targets in the UK, EU and internationally, taking into account the views of a wide range of interested parties. Accordingly, it is inviting views for its new study as to whether a more consistent and robust basis can be found for environmental standards. The position was set out in the briefing for views as follows:

'The past twenty years have seen a considerable expansion of environmental legislation and policies. Increasing use has been made of numerical standards concerned with emissions, exposures, intakes, and concentrations of substances in the environment. Such standards have been set using various approaches by many different bodies - global, European and national - with the aim of protecting both human health and the natural environment.

It has recently been argued that some standards now being set are so stringent that the costs imposed on society will be out of proportion to the benefits obtained. Others argue that some forms of pollution, for example, prolonged exposure to very low concentrations of certain substances, especially in combination, are not being taken seriously enough.

The creation of new environment agencies responsible for regulating most forms of pollution makes it timely to try to establish a consistent and sustainable basis for standards. The recent transfer of responsibility for the Health and Safety Commission and Executive to the former DoE has highlighted the relationship between pollution control and standards for occupational health.

The Royal Commission's study will compare the methods and procedures adopted in arriving at standards for all types of pollution and for all aspects of the environment. The term 'standards' means standards contained in law, for example, emission limits or environmental quality standards, and also non-statutory protocols, guidelines and targets, and criteria used in deciding individual cases. The study will examine what happens at European level, in other major countries, and in international organisations, as well as in the UK. It will also cover related issues about the approval of chemicals and the regulation of contaminants in food. The Royal Commission will focus in particular on different types of scientific evidence, the ways in which these are utilised, and the potential for resolving present uncertainties through further research.

As part of the study, views are now being sought on a number of issues. The Royal Commission wants to obtain input from all types of organisation and from the general public, based on the widest possible range of situations. Those submitting evidence are asked to describe the experience on which they are drawing. There may be legitimate differences in the approach to standard setting according to the context.'

In view of the discussion of regulations case law and policy, as well as standards, in the earlier chapters it is useful to refer to the key questions that the RCEP has raised.

The General Approach to Environmental Standards

- What should be the purpose of setting standards? How successfully do present standards achieve that purpose?

- Is the level at which standards are set at present (global, European, national or local, or by individual regulators) appropriate?

- What should be done to make the standard-setting process more explicit and transparent? What role should scientific experts have, and how should they be chosen? At national level, what role should ministers and government departments have? Ought there to be a greater role for the courts, or new forms of quasi-judicial regulatory hearing?

- What role should quantification of costs and benefits play in setting and revising standards?

- How adequate is present scientific understanding of toxicity, ecological tolerance and environmental processes as a basis for setting numerical standards?

- Where scientific opinion and public perception are in conflict, what weight should each carry in setting standards and in determining the best practicable environmental option? Should attempts be made to modify public perceptions through education and information? Should the scientific community take more account of social preferences and sensitivities?

- What is the best way of making allowances for uncertainties? When, and how, should the precautionary principle be applied?

- What relationship should be sought between risks from pollution and levels of risk in other contexts?

- How should priorities be determined within pollution control?

Specific Factors in Standard-Setting

- How should standard-setting make allowances for natural variation in exposure to the same hazards?

- In setting standards, what significance should be attached to particular vulnerability or susceptibility on the part of certain individuals, groups or species?

- How valid is the concept of 'critical loads' and where can it be applied?

- What should be the relationship between standards for exposure of the general public and standards for occupational exposure?

- In what ways can standards best be set to encourage innovation, particularly investment in cleaner technologies?

Implementation and Review of Standards

- What are the advantages and disadvantages of standards which are not legally binding?

- In what circumstances could economic instruments (such as levies and tradable permits) or voluntary measures provide a satisfactory replacement for government-defined standards?

- How far do limitations on the detail or precision with which measurements can be made constrain the effectiveness of pollution control? What are the prospects for overcoming such constraints?

- What should be the relationship between numerical standards for particular substances and what is overall the best practicable environment option (as defined in the Royal Commission's Twelfth Report)?

- What is the most effective way of linking standards for environmental quality, or critical loads, to standards for emissions or products?

- What further provision is needed for keeping standards up to date?[2]

The practical issues raised by these questions are of interest to business and practitioners, particularly as they demonstrate a move towards being protective of the environment in the manner discussed in Chapter 1. There is no doubt that accountability for environmental damage will be increasingly significant.

Environmental Reporting

As regards the related matter of reporting, it has already been mentioned that an effective system requires communication between an organisation and its stakeholders to build on the expectations and to explore opportunities created by the changes made. It has largely been as a result of the ACCA and its awards that the UK has pioneered some developments. The production of regular reports on the progress of the system is not essential for corporate success, but it does provide a good focus for the work. For example, BP has stated:

> 'We see great benefit from reporting environmental performance. It provides an internal focus, brings business benefit, enhances reputation and gives us a dialogue for partnership building. In the long term it protects our licence to operate. (Source: 'Setting the Standard' CBI (1995).)

As was indicated there is an ongoing debate to reach a common approach to environment reporting. In particular, here again, ACCA in the UK is concerned with this. When offering guidelines, for example ACCA has emphasised the inclusion of some comments on sustainability, stakeholder communication, site-level reporting, financial implications and independent verification.

In addition, the Intergovernmental Working Group of Experts are working on this at international level and has produced some useful points in its recent report, some key aspects of which appear below.

Introductory Points of the Intergovernmental Working Group of Experts[3]

Environmental accounting practices are being actively developed on a world-wide basis. This report reviews developments in four areas: financial accounting, cost accounting, accounting for physical flows and environmental reporting.

In so far as environmental issues have a financially quantifiable effect and can be captured within established, generally accepted accounting principles (GAAP), then a measure of consensus on practices in the area of financial accounting is gradually being achieved. In the field of managerial accounting, current efforts are directed mainly at the issue of full-cost accounting. They typically fall into two categories: recommendations for more detailed conventional cost accounting, and recommendations for the internalisation of external costs.

More progress is being made on the former than the latter. In the area of environmental reporting, there is great variety of progress in terms of the format and content of reports and the conclusion that is being drawn that greater encouragement needs to be given to achieving comparability.

Recent Developments in Environmental Reporting

New developments in environmental reporting include, first, the sectoral benchmarking of environmental performance. In the UK, for example, the chemicals industry produces an annual report called 'Indicators of Performance'; given the number of free-standing environmental reports issued by companies in sectors such as oil, gas, petroleum, chemicals, water and telecommunications, there is obviously scope for greater experimentation in this area; and, second, the construction company-specific indices of environmental performance, for example, Novo Nordisk (Denmark), Rhône Poulenc (France) and Danish Steelworks (Denmark).

Managerial Environmental Accounting: Some Problems and Solutions

Improved internal costs allocation of private environmental costs is the most appropriate starting point for most entities.

Internalising external (societal) environmental costs poses severe problems for entities because of measurement and valuation problems on the one hand, and national and international competitiveness on the other. Experimentation at the corporate level is likely to be the most productive way forward. Environmental considerations should play a major part in all investment decisions.

At least one major research project into full cost accounting is under way in Canada, and several North American companies are undertaking testing. There may be scope in comparing the environmental accounting methodologies being developed in corporate North America with the experiments taking place in Europe.

Trends in Environmental Reporting

The communication of environmental liability, risk and performance data is now practised by a significant number of international companies. There are clear regional and philosophical differences in current environmental reporting techniques.

Despite the growth in disclosure practices there are no authoritative non-financial disclosure standards and, therefore, little comparability.

Environmental reporting goes largely unattested. Where some form of attestation takes place it is generally unique and cannot be compared. The role of the accounting profession in the environmental attestation process is ambivalent.

It is still difficult to identify the 'drivers which prompt environmental information disclosure'. It is likely that environmental reporting will continue to assume different formats, such as consolidated performance reporting, site-based reporting, staff reporting or financial statement-based reporting. Environmental reporting frameworks may be developed from each and all of these stakeholder groups.

A number of relatively similar environmental reporting frameworks have been developed. This is another area where International Standards of Accounting and Reporting (ISAR) might consider developing core guidance.

Given the world-wide interest in the financial aspects of corporate governance, ISAR should consider ways of developing the theme of environmental governance.

There is no doubt that developments in this area have demonstrated a useful dialogue between government and industry in order to achieve the goal of improved environmental performance.

The Environmental Industries Commission (EIC)

Another illustration of the partnership between government and industry was the launch in 1995 of the EIC. In a message to the EIC, the Right Honourable Michael Heseltine MP, President of the Board of Trade, said:

'There is a significant and growing international market for environmental technologies and advisory services and I very much hope that the new Commission can make a contribution to promoting UK interests in that market in an effective and appropriate way. I hope that your launch event is a success.'

The EIC's principal stated task is to lobby the UK government to support through the introduction of economic instruments, strict enforcement of existing legislation and the enactment of technology standards in line with government practices in other countries.

In addition to a full-time lobbying team, the EIC has a number of politicians, industrialists, trade union leaders, environmentalists and leading academics on its advisory committees. According to its original mission statement set out below, the EIC has emphasised that it is the organisation that will lead the British environmental industry to have a meaningful dialogue with the government to promote British suppliers of environmental technologies and services and will organise an effective public relations campaign to make sure this happens.

According to the EIC the environmental industry is a developing market and the world-wide market for environmental technology and services will grow up to 50 per cent by the year 2000. It has been estimated that the size of the environmental market up to the year 2000 will be £140bn in the UK, £850bn in the EU and £1,000bn in the USA. There is a huge opportunity for British business to tackle the market leaders: Germany, Japan and the USA.

As a lobbying organisation, the EIC has stated that it ensures that British companies not lose out in the world-wide market place. In other countries, the environmental industries sector has been involved with their governments in structuring and influencing regulation and fiscal support, and the EIC intends to be the body to represent the supplier of environmental technologies and services in terms of the UK market.

The EIC's Mission and Objectives[4]

The EIC's mission is to promote the international competitiveness of the UK's environmental industry. We therefore work to:

1   *Identify the barriers to growth facing the British Environmental Technology industry.*

2   *Promote awareness through PR of the commercial and environmental benefits of environmental technology and win general support for a favourable legislative and fiscal framework.*

3   *Lobby for UK and EC Government support through tighter enforcement of existing legislation and enactment of technology forcing standards and the introduction of economic instruments (eg Tax relief and R & D funding).*

4   *Support export initiatives to boost British companies in the growing world market for environmental technology and services.*

5 *Provide an effective link for British environmental technology and services companies with the UK's research organisations.*

6 *Provide Campaign Client Members with information on UK and EC environmental legislation and on funding available for environmental R & D, market opportunities, and facilitating the exchange of information and experience between members through newsletters and briefing notes.*

7 *Schedule an education programme on a commercial basis, targeting mainstream industry to promote the use of environmental technology.*

8 *Collaborate with other national and international organisations.*

The Future Market Place

As the world becomes a 'tighter' market and businesses expand, it is essential for managers and investors to be sensitive to other local concerns. Issues of culture, family, politics and religion affect businesses and their negotiations, and must not be ignored if the host and guest business people are to keep integrity and mutually benefit from development and industry. As has been mentioned earlier, concern for the environment was thought of as a side issue to many aspects in society. Currently, there is a trend towards a more holistic approach to many areas which is to welcomed.

Strategy

For companies who are just beginning to address these issues, to diversify or to invest in foreign markets without a clear environmental policy, seeking professional advice may be the recommended measure. This can assist a company in formulating a management system that is specific to the needs of the business and the desired community. The steps that have been referred to in earlier chapters include an environmental policy which assists prevention and proper planning, leading to an audit and then a clean-up as an aftermath.

Companies should consider the various standards which may be adopted and achieved voluntarily. They should, of course, also consider national regulation, international treaties such as GATT regarding world trade and regional Treaties such as the European Union under Maastricht. The necessary co-operation exists between all entities to enable the creation of checks and standards.

Environmental Payback

Respect for our environment, both ecologically and culturally, has a payback for a business. It means that employees retain integrity working for a responsible business, governments are open to accommodating incoming business and that natural resources are protected rather than exploited.

The Future

There is no doubt that environmental management will be perceived as part of business strategy, regardless of where a company intends to operate, and that any practical methodology that can assist and be of benefit to corporate activities.

As our environment and economy become increasingly interdependent and as we all work towards a positive future for both natural resources and man-made resources, it is clear that the heightened awareness of an understanding for the role played by the regulatory, voluntary and economic pressures will be of benefit to all concerned, particularly bearing in mind the competitive aspects that increasingly emerge.

When companies become more 'green' and consider preventative measures concerning the environment, then business activities become more efficient because of forethought. Not only is there an emphasis on payback within the short term but, in the long term, the market place is opened out to enable bottom-line success on a broader plane.

There is no way that a business can justify environmental irresponsibility in the light of well-known benefits to society, profit, reputation and development. Having regard to the impacts of information technology the holistic approach to all facets of industry is not a trend: it is a necessity.

Today, the more enlightened businesses and their advisors are realising and capitalising upon effective environmental management as an integral part of their overall business planning. Realising that a stronger pay back comes when companies are socially responsible to both people and ecology, these businesses are voluntarily implementing action to prevent disasters and abuse of the environment. This voluntary approach has also become important in developing jurisdictions, though regulation may lag behind.

Often in the past, no preventative measures were recognised. Most 'measures' had been by way of sanctions after some sort of disaster or crisis caused by ignoring or abusing the environment. However, this is changing, and these enlightened leaders of industry are also seeing an advantage in developing their products and technology with the environment as one of the priorities. These companies represent the future, a future where businesses are going beyond compliance towards a new age in which environment and the marketplace go hand in hand.

---

[1] It should be noted that it has proved very slow and complicated to develop and may not continue
[2] RCEP Briefing Paper (1995)
[3] Intergovernmental Working Group of Experts on International Standards of Accounting and Reporting, Geneva, 6–8 December 1995; Background Paper on Current Developments in Environmental Accounting
[4] EIC Mission Statement 1995

Appendix 1

The Environment Agency: Enforcement Practice Guidance For Warranted Officers

Introduction

1   This is general guidance on the procedures to be followed by Agency warranted officers when enforcing environment protection and pollution prevention legalisation[1] in line with the principles of the Agency's enforcement policy.[2] Complementary guidance for more specific regulatory activities will be prepared in due course.

2   *Important Note*

This guidance does not weaken the environmental protection afforded by the relevant Acts and their Regulations. It does not affect a warranted officer's duties and powers to take immediate enforcement action against businesses and individuals, or to require them to take immediate remedial action, in any case where it appears to warranted officers to be necessary to take such action or impose such a requirement.

3   The guidance does not apply to prosecutions. In considering prosecutions, warranted officers should refer to guidance given in the Agency's Enforcement Policy Statement until the comprehensive prosecution policy for the Agency has been prepared.

4   The Agency's policy gives business the following rights:

a   the right to a *letter*, on request, explaining what needs to be done and why – when warranted officers express an opinion that something should be done – without taking formal action;

b   the right to a *'minded to' notice* and an entitlement *to have its point of view heard* by the Agency *before* formal action is taken;

c   when *immediate action* is taken, the right to a written statement explaining why this is necessary (ie why immediate rather than another course of action, and the consequences of failing to take action); and

d   the right to be told exactly what rights of *appeal* it has when formal action is taken.

These rights reflect the principles set out in the Deregulation and Contracting Out Act 1994.

Enforcement Practice

5   The following are, in the Agency's view, the key elements of good enforcement practice, which must be applied.

6   At the end of a visit, warranted officers should explain what further action, if any, they are going to take and give information on the rights to: written confirmation of suggested remedial action, make representations, appeal or complain. The information should be confirmed at the same time by the provision of the leaflet, 'Your Rights When Environment Agency Warranted Officers Take Action'. The leaflet may also be used to provide information to businesses, individuals or their representatives on the action required of them.

Letters

7   If warranted officers intend or are asked to write they should do so as soon as practicable and should say when a letter can be expected. Letters should make the status of the advice clear. Where a letter requires remedial action it should set out what needs to be done, why, within what period, and what law applies. It should be explained that there are ten working days to make representations to the warranted officer's manager if it is thought that the action required is not justified.

8   Warranted officers should not take formal enforcement action during the ten working days period for making representations beginning on the date of the letter – unless immediate action is justified by the risk.

Enforcement Notices

9   If a warranted officer intends to issue an enforcement notice, an operator has a right to know and to understand what needs to be done to comply and within what timescale. Unless immediate action is necessary, the opportunity should be given to make representations to the warranted officer's manager if it is considered that the proposed notice should not be issued, or should be changed.

10   Warranted officers should discuss with the operator what the breaches of the law are and the action which will be needed to comply. As well as complying with any statutory provisions, warranted officers should give the operator a written summary covering: the reasons for the proposed notice, what constitutes the failure to comply with the law, outlining what needs to be done to comply and by when – together with the leaflet explaining business' rights. The summary must be enough to enable the operator to make representations. By way of example reference can be made to Appendix 2.

11   The operator has ten working days – from receiving written notice of the intention to issue an enforcement notice a sample of which is at Appendix 3 – to make representations to the warranted officer's manager if it is thought that the requirements should be changed or the notice should not be issued. Warranted officers and their

managers should take a fair and fresh look at the proposed action in the light of representations.

Immediate Action

12 Whenever warranted officers need to take immediate enforcement action, they should provide a written statement as soon as practicable explaining the reasons. Prohibition notices should include such explanation where they do not already do so.

13 In the case of their power to 'seize and make safe' warranted officers should send a written explanation as soon as practicable.

14 Immediate action should, where practicable, be discussed with operators at the time and the views expressed taken into account.

Appeals

15 Warranted officers must give an operator written information on how to appeal when issuing notices, explaining the grounds, how, where and within what period an appeal may be brought, and, where applicable, that action on an enforcement notice is suspended while an appeal is pending.

Monitoring

16 The Agency will introduce systems to monitor that a leaflet has been provided to every operator they visit, that where warranted officers intend to issue enforcement notices they confirm their intention in writing, and that any representations are properly considered.

17 The Agency's Board and Executive will ensure that this guidance is applied fairly and effectively.

Start date

18 This guidance will be adopted forthwith.

---

[1] See Annex 1
[2] See Enforcement Policy Statement PGSO1

Appendix 2

The Environment Agency: Your Rights When Agency Warranted Officers Take Action

The Environment Agency's Enforcement Policy Statement sets out the principles to be followed in enforcing environment protection legislation.

If a warranted officer

- *intends to take immediate action*, for example by issuing a notice prohibiting a certain action, you have *a right to a written explanation as soon as practicable* of why this is necessary. Prohibition notices normally include such explanation;

- *tells you to do something,* you have a *right, if you ask,* to be given a letter explaining what needs to be done, when and why. On receipt of the letter, you have ten working days to make representations to the warranted officer's manager. You may be asked to agree to a shorter period as an alternative to taking immediate action;

- intends *to issue an enforcement notice,* you have *a right to a written explanation of what is wrong, an outline of what needs to be done, and by when.* You have a right to have your point of view heard by the warranted officer's manager if you consider that the notice should be changed or should not be issued. You have ten working days in which to make representations, which will be considered on a fair and fresh basis.

When a notice is issued you will be told in writing about *your statutory right of appeal* and given the appropriate form to use to appeal. You will be told:

- how to appeal;

- where and within what period an appeal may be brought;

- the grounds upon which an appeal may be brought; and

- where the law requires it, that the action required by the notice is suspended while an appeal is pending.

The procedures and rights outlined above provide ways for you to have your views heard if you are not happy with the warranted officer's action. If these procedures have not been followed, you should let the officer's manager know.

You can speak or write to the warranted officer's manager who will investigate your grievance and tell you what is going to be done about it. Experience has demonstrated that most grievances will be settled in this way, very often immediately. If you are not satisfied that your grievance has been handled in accordance with this procedure, you can contact the Agency's Regional General Manager or write to the Chief Executive at the Agency's headquarters (see address below) who will see that your complaint is followed up promptly and fairly. You can also write and ask your Member of Parliament to take up your case with the Agency or with Ministers. Your MP may also ask the independent Parliamentary Commissioner for Administration (Ombudsman) to review your concerns.

The Regional General Manager for your region can be contacted at:

[address]

What is the Environment Agency?

The Environment Agency is responsible for the enforcement of certain environmental protection legislation: the main instruments are set out in Appendix 4. It is a non-departmental public body with a board appointed by the Secretary of State for the Environment or the Minister of Agriculture, Fisheries and Food or the Secretary of State for Wales. It adopts, across all its functions, an integrated approach to environmental protection and enhancement which considers the impacts of substances and activities on all parts of the environment, taken as a whole and on natural resources. Its functions include:

*   regulating industrial processes with the greatest pollution potential;

*   regulating the keeping, use and disposal of radioactive material;

*   regulating the treatment and disposal of controlled waste;

*   preserving and improving the quality of rivers, estuaries and coastal waters;

*   acting to conserve and secure proper use of water resources;

*   supervising all flood defence matters;

*   maintaining and improving salmon, trout, freshwater and eel fisheries;

*   issuing angling licences;

*   conserving the water environment and promoting its use for recreation; and

*   maintaining and improving non-marine navigation.

How can you find out more about how the Agency's functions are enforced and about environment protection legislation generally?

Information and advice, including what individuals and businesses must do by law, can be found in the publications of the former bodies which have been brought together in the Agency or from: The Environment Agency's local office at:

[address]

or

The Environment Agency's HQ at:

Rio House, Riverside Drive, Aztec West, Almondsbury, Bristol BS12 4UD

Telephone 01454 624400; Fax 01454 624409

Appendix 3

Sample Enforcement Notice

To:

[The name, address and, when appropriate, other relevant details of the person/business/ activity to whom/which this letter is given, for example, the type and location of the regulated activity, the environmental licence reference number and the relevant legislation.]

I intend to issue an enforcement notice because:

[A simple explanation of what is wrong and why it is a failure to comply with the law.]

The notice will require you to:

[A statement of the standard(s) to be achieved, and by when, plus, where applicable, an outline (covering all main points of substance) of the possible means of achieving it (them).]

If you consider that I should not issue such a notice, or that its requirements should be changed, you should telephone, write, or make an appointment to see me or my manager. Otherwise you will receive the notice in not less than ten working days. If you would like anything explained in more detail or further discussion please contact me by telephoning [warranted officer's telephone number].

My manager is:

[Name, address and telephone number.]

Signature

[Warranted officer's signature.]

Date

[The date of preparation of the notice.]

Office address:

Appendix 4

The Environment Agency: Enforced Acts

Each Act has associated Statutory Instruments, Orders and the like – these are not listed.

Water Management

Water resources

Water Resources Act 1991
Water Industry Act 1991
Water Resources Act 1991
Water Industry Act 1991
Salmon and Freshwater Fisheries Act 1975

Pollution Regulation

Discharges to water

Water Act 1989
Environmental Protection Act 1990

Flood Defence

Water Resources Act 1991
Land Drainage Act 1991
Land Drainage Act 1976
[Flood Defence byelaws]

Waste Regulation

Control of Pollution Act 1974
Control of Pollution (Amendment) Act 1989
Environmental Protection Act 1990

Fisheries

Diseases of Fish Act 1937
Sea Fisheries Regulation Act 1966
Salmon and Freshwater Fisheries Act 1975
Wildlife and Countryside Act 1981
Diseases of Fish Act 1983

Salmon Act 1986
Water Resources Act 1991

Integrated Pollution Control

Environment Protection Act 1990

Radioactive Substances

Radioactive Substances Act 1993

General

Environment Act 1995
European Communities Act 1972

Navigation

Water Act 1989
Water Resources Act 1991
Land Drainage Act 1976
Sea Fish Industry Act 1951
Pilotage Act 1987
Harbour Docks and Piers Clauses Act 1847
Anglian Water Act 1977
Upper Medway Navigations and Conservancy Act 11 and 14
Southern Water Authority Act 1982
Thames Conservancy Acts 1932, 1950, 1959, 1966, 1972

Recreation

Water Resources Act 1991

Conservation

Water Resources Act 1991

Appendix 5

Local Authority Air Pollution Control

Is the process prescribed?

Yes:

Part I, EPA 1990

If authorisation is needed LA must impose BATNEEC conditions

Separate powers of enforcement officers mainly under:

PACE 1974

EPA 1990

HSWA 1974

Has there been a breach of an authorisation or condition or is a breach anticipated?

Yes: enforcement notice

No: does the process involve an 'imminent risk of serious pollution' to the environment?

If yes: prohibition notice

NB: LA must maintain registers of all authorisations of processes granted in their local area under Part I of the Act

Yes:

Part III, EPA 1990

S79 EPA 1990: statutory nuisance

What kind of emission?

Smoke

Fumes or gases

Dust, steam, smell or other effluvia (only from industrial, trade or business premises)

LA may serve abatement notice

Or individual may make a complaint to a magistrates' court under s82 EPA 1990

No:

Clean Air Act 1993

Part I: prohibition of dark smoke from several types of chimneys or any industrial or trade premises.

Defences:

Defendant acted inadvertently

Defendant used all practicable steps to minimise pollution

Part II: LA's power to prescribe emission limits of smoke, dust or grit from chimneys or industrial furnaces

Regulations for height of chimneys

Part III: LA's power to declare 'smoke control areas'

Part IV: control of the content of fuels

Part V: Publication of information by the LA

Research and education on problems of air pollution

Air pollution caused mainly by traffic fumes kills 24,000 Britons prematurely each year.

A Government Report (by Committee on Medical Effects Air Pollutants – a government advisory body) on 'Quantification of the Effects of Air Pollution on Health in the UK' (January 1998) says pollution has three effects:

First, any chemicals, such as sulphur dioxide and ozone, act as irritants to the bronchial tubes of the lung. Some, such as nitrogen dioxide and ozone, release substances that damage the lung's lining.

Secondly, together, these cause inflammation, irritation and make the lung less efficient at fighting infection.

Thirdly, particulates, the tiny particles produced mainly by the burning of diesel fuel, are the most dangerous to health.

Source: *The Independent*

Appendix 6

Code of Practice
Waste Management: The Duty of Care

The Code of Practice provides guidance on how to discharge the duty of care imposed by s34 EPA 1990. If a waste producer is taken to court for failing to comply with the duty of care, the Code can be used in evidence. It has the same status as the Highway Code in a traffic case. So its contents are critical to the waste industry. If waste producers fail to follow the guidelines, they are exposing themselves to prosecution.

The Code gives step-by-step advice and is divided into six sections:

Waste Producer is to Identify the Waste

Every person who handles the waste must be provided with a description of the wastes so they know how to handle it. They should know its components in enough detail to know, for example, whether it can be safely transferred from one vehicle to another, what containers are appropriate and whether it can be mixed with other waste.

Duty to Hold Waste Carefully

All holders of waste must keep it safely while it is under their control. They must also ensure it is in a fit state to travel. Under the new system, the holder has responsibility for seeing the waste safely on its journey. The liability may not be 'cradle to the grave', but is more extensive than before when it ceased once physical possession had passed.

Check the Transferee

Under the Controlled Waste (Registration of Carriers and Seizure of Vehicles) Regulations 1991, a comprehensive system of registration of carriers of waste was introduced from 1 April 1992. Registration may be refused if the carrier has been convicted of an offence connected with waste management and the authority think it would be undesirable.

Fears have been expressed that many small firms will be unaware of the new requirements. As some recognition of this, the government granted carriers of construction waste an extra two months (until June 1992) to apply for registration. The scrap metal industry were also concerned about the imposition of the duty of care and were given extra time to accommodate new arrangements. There are also some exemptions such as British Rail and charities.

Subject to that, holders of waste must ensure that the carrier is registered and is suitable for carrying the particular type of waste.

The government envisaged that the rules would be enforced mutually by all the holders of waste. As one holder was required to check the credentials of the next holder in the chain in order to satisfy the duty of care, this was perceived as creating a mutual enforcement society.

Check the Transferor

The transferee of waste must check that waste is not received from a source which is apparently in breach of the duty of care. The transfer note must be properly completed and the registration of the carrier delivering the waste should be checked. This means that a carrier without proper registration should be turned away; hence the concern in the industry that the new rules have not percolated through the numerous small firms and one man operations engaged in carrying waste.

Checking the Destination of the Waste

There is no specific duty on a waste producer to audit the final destination of his waste. However, there is some encouragement for such a practice in the Code which states that such an audit and periodic site visits would provide evidence that an attempt had been made to prevent subsequent illegal treatment of the waste.

The waste manager should have a look to see that it appears to match the description. The practice of undertaking full checks on the composition of samples of the waste is encouraged.

Expert Help and Advice

Finally, the Code refers to the availability of advice from waste consultants and emphasises the primary responsibility of waste holders to discharge their duty of care.

Who Must Exercise the Duty of Care?

All persons who import, produce, carry, keep, treat or dispose of controlled waste, and persons having control of such waste as brokers, owe a duty to take care that an offence is not committed. There is no precise definition of 'broker'. However, the Code states that a waste consultant who is directing the eventual destination of the waste may be caught by the duty.

The operator is also under a duty to ensure that the waste carrier who delivers the waste to the site is registered in accordance with the Control of Pollution (Amendment) Act 1989.

The law requires that all reasonable precautions and all due diligence have been exercised. The offence is criminal, but not absolute. If all reasonable steps have been taken to prevent an escape causing damage, then no prosecution will succeed. A trade practice or custom may be evidence of what is reasonable. On the other hand, a court may decide that a custom of the trade is a bad practice.

Appendix 7

Pre-contract Environmental Enquiries

In typical conveyancing transactions, having obtained the Property Information Form (PIF) from the vendor's solicitor, the purchaser's solicitor should consider the extent to which environmental issues should be raised in property transactions. Examples are:

First, *enquiries and additional enquiries*. Replies to the normal pre-contract enquiries may indicate that there are environmental/contaminated land concerns present, in which case further enquiry should be pursued along the lines referred to in Appendix 8. The model pre-contract environmental enquiries include a full set of environmental questions, the answers to which may give an indication as to whether the land or adjoining property is contaminated or not, and whether other environmental problems are present. A positive response to any of these questions should lead the purchaser to consider the need for more specific investigation and inquiry, for example, a site investigation.

Second, *searches*. In addition to local and other searches, where appropriate (especially in commercial property transactions), the purchaser's solicitors should commission an 'environmental search report'. This often presents the historical uses of the site for up to 150 years previously. Where the land is found to have had contaminative uses in the past (such as those listed in Appendix 9) and there is no evidence that satisfactory remediation has been carried out on the site, then there may be a need for a full environmental assessment/audit of the site. As noted in Appendix 8, this will assist in determining the extent of contamination and the appropriate method of remediation.

Third, the *contract*. The results of the pre-contract enquiries and environmental report or audits then become an essential tool for negotiating the contract and other transactional documents. The need for appropriate environmental covenants, warranties and indemnities is becoming an essential part of property transactions.

B1.1 Standard Pre-contract Environmental Enquiries

Enquiries

1   Is the property affected by any substance likely to cause nuisance, pollution of the environment or harm to human health? If so, please give details.

2   Has any structure on the property been constructed in the whole or part on reclaimed, filled in or built up land, or is the vendor aware of any potential future cause of

267

subsidence land erosion or similar problems which may affect the property or any structure?

3   Is the vendor aware of any ground surface movement, escape of gas or other similar indicator which might indicate earlier disposal of waste?

4   Is the vendor aware of any contamination or pollution of the soil on the property and/or the water on or running through or under the property?

5   Has the vendor, or to his knowledge any other party, carried out at any time on the property any manufacturing or other process or extraction of minerals? If so, please give details. If not, are there current proposals to do so?

6   Please confirm that no poisonous, noxious or polluting matter or any solid waste matter within the meaning of these words in s161 WRA 1991:

a is in or on the property; and

b has entered into any stream or controlled water or underground water from the property (either directly or indirectly).

7   Does any drainage from the property discharge into a watercourse?

8   Has the property or any part of it been included in a litter control area designated under section 90(3) EPA 1990 or is the vendor aware of any circumstance likely to give rise to such a designation?

9   Is the vendor aware of any contamination on neighbouring properties which could affect or spread to the property? If so, please supply full details.

10 Has the vendor had cause to complain about the state or condition or the manner of use of any adjoining or neighbouring property? If so, please give details.

11 Has any land within 300 metres of the property been used for keeping, treatment, storage (whether permanent or temporary), disposal, deposit, burial or incineration of any form of wastes as defined within s75 EPA 1990? If so, please provide details.

12 Is the vendor aware of any proposals to carry out any of the activities referred to in (11) above on any land within 300 metres of the property? If so, please provide details.

13 Is the vendor aware of any migration of gases normally associated with landfill operations that may be migrating (whether vertically or laterally) under, in or through the property from neighbouring land? If so please give details.

14 Please give details of any notice and/or notification of infringement (formal or otherwise) of current effect given to the vendor or its predecessors by any regulatory authorities in relation to the property and/or activities on the property and of relevant penalties or appeals.

15 Is there any reason why any authority (for example, Local Authority, Environment Agency) might inspect the property or take any steps in relation to the property to

avoid or minimise pollution of the environment or harm to human health, or any indication that it might do so? If so please give details.

16 Please give details of any discussions or negotiations with any relevant body with respect to the grant, revocation, renewal or variation of any contract, agreement, consent, licence or arrangement relating to matters of environmental concern.

17 Please give details of any contract, agreement or proceedings in respect of any contract, agreement, consent, licence or arrangement relating to matters of environmental concern.

18 Has any past or present use of the property resulted in any contamination or pollution of the soil on any neighbouring land or of any water standing on or running through that land (whether a natural or man-made water course or by percolation)?

19 Please provide all information in the possession of the vendor as to any use of the property by the vendor and all previous owners and occupiers of the property which could have resulted in ground or water contamination (for example, the use, manufacture, handling or storage at the property of any hazardous substances which are subject to special regulations made pursuant to the Health and Safety at Work etc Act 1974, the Environmental Protection Act 1990, or any other similar legislation now in force.

20 Are there any actual or potential claims, actions or proceedings or threatened litigation by the vendor in respect of the contamination of or damage to the property by reason of the release, escape, discharge or emission of any substance from neighbouring or nearby properties, or any process or other activity on such properties?

21 Are there any actual or potential claims, actions or proceedings or threatened litigation against the vendor or any circumstances known to the vendor likely to lead to action in respect of the contamination of or damage to the neighbouring property by reason of the release, escape, discharge or emission of any substance from the property, or any process or other activity on the property?

22 Except as answered already, have there been any complaints about environmental matters relating to the property from local residents, members of the public, pressure groups or occupier of neighbouring properties? If so, please supply full details and state what consequent action has been taken by the vendor, the regulatory authorities and/or complainants.

23 Has any complaint been received regarding noise, smells, emissions or other nuisances emanating from the property?

24 Is the vendor aware of any proposals or circumstances which might give rise to the termination or revocation of any contract, agreement, consent, licence or arrangement, relating to matters of environmental concern?

25 Have there ever been any disputes or complaints (whether formal or otherwise) made by any person or relevant authority regarding the use of the property or any building

or plant or machinery at the property relating to noise or vibration other than under the provisions applicable to statutory nuisances?

B1.2 Additional Environmental Enquiries

B1.2.1 Industrial Properties

Enquiries

The Property

1   Is any underground or surface water abstracted on or for the benefit of the property? If so, please provide copies of any licence and confirm the vendor has complied with all conditions relating to the licence.

2   Have any steps been taken to revoke, suspend or vary such licence/consents? If so, please give details.

3   Is there an air conditioning system at the property? If so:

4   Is there a planned routine maintenance programme for any cooling tower and other parts of the system?

5   When was the system last inspected (and did this inspection include testing for legionella bacteria)?

6   Has the operation and maintenance of the system been approved by the Health and Safety Executive and/or the Environment Health Officer?

7   Please supply copies of the vendor's records of the above routine maintenance and of the cleaning chemicals and dose rates used and the dates of treatment.

8   Has there ever been an outbreak of legionella or humidifier fever or other associated health problems within the workforce or other occupiers of the property?

9   Please provide details of any of the following which are on, in, over or under the property:

a genetically modified organisms (as defined in s106 EPA 1990);

b polychlorinated biphenyls (PCBs), asbestos or other toxic substances on the property.

10 To the vendor's knowledge, do any of the transformers or electrical equipment at the property contain polychlorinated biphenyals (PCBs)?

11 To the Vendor's knowledge, are any of the following substances used or contained in any equipment on the property: CFCs, halons HCFCs, carbon tetrachloride, 1,1,1, trichloroethane, methyl bromide. If so, please specify the type and quantity, the equipment in which it is used or contained and whether any contracts have been entered into to substitute another substance.

12 Have any of the following substances in pure, compound or derivative form been used in any works of construction, alteration or addition to any buildings erected on the property:

  a lead or any materials containing lead which may be ingested, inhaled or absorbed, except where copper alloy fittings containing lead are specifically required in drinking water pipework by any relevant statutory requirement;

  b urea formaldehyde foam or materials which may release formaldehyde in quantities which may be hazardous;

  c materials which are generally comprised of mineral fibres, either man-made or naturally occurring, which have a diameter of three microns or less and a length of 200 microns or less or which contain any fibres not sealed or otherwise stabilised to ensure that fibre migration is prevented;

  d other substances generally known at the date hereof to be dangerous or deleterious or likely to affect the health of occupiers of such buildings?

13 If so, please supply full particulars including details of any action taken in relation thereto and copies of relevant correspondence with professional consultants.

14 Does the whole or any part of the property comprise a landfill site? If so, what measures have been taken to close the landfill?

Waste Disposal

1 Is the vendor aware of the presence/ storage/burial/disposal of any waste in on or under the property? If so, please specify the type of waste, whether it is industrial, commercial or household waste and specify whether it is special waste within the meaning of s62 EPA 1990.

2 Has the property ever been used for the deposit, keeping, storage, treatment or disposal of controlled waste as defined in s30(1) COPA 1974 and s75 EPA 1990 or any special waste or any polluting or hazardous substance ever been deposited or disposed of on the property (whether deliberately or accidentally)?

3 How is commercial waste or trade effluent disposed of? Please provide a copy of any Agreement relating to such disposal

4 Please confirm that no radioactive material or waste has been dealt with on or from the property.

5 Are there any discharges made to controlled waters as defined in s104 WRA 1991? If so, please supply a copy of the appropriate discharge consent pursuant to Part III WRA.

Storage Tanks

1 Are there any storage tanks, pools, pits or bunds on the property (whether active or inactive or above or below ground)? If so, please specify whether the storage tanks contain any material or are empty.

271

2   If they contain any material, please specify the nature and quantity of the contents. If not, when did they last contain materials?

3   Have there been spillages or seepage from such tanks before or during vendor's period of ownership of the property?

4   What is the current condition of the tanks and what facilities exist for inspection?

Regulatory Compliance/Notices

1   Please supply full details of all hazardous substances (as defined pursuant to the Planning (Hazardous Substances) Regulations 1992 (P(HS)R) on, over or under the property, which exceed controlled quantities, including the quantities present and their precise location.

2   Has any offence been committed under the P(HS)R?

3   Please supply copies of all Hazardous Substances Consents (including deemed consents) and copies of the applications therefore. Please confirm that such consent relates exclusively to the property.

4   Please supply details of any appeal lodged with regard to an application for Hazardous Substances Consent.

5   Please supply details of any revocations, modifications or refusals of Hazardous Substances Consents and/or their conditions.

6   Please supply a copy of any consent under Regulations 3 or 5 Notification of Installations Handling Hazardous Substances Regulations 1982 (NIHHS).

7   Have there been any sales of or changes of control of any part of the property to which any Hazardous Substances Consent applies? If so, please supply a copy of any application made for the continuation of a Hazardous Substances Consent after any change of control or ownership of the property and the resulting modified (or revoked) consents.

8   Has any Hazardous Substances Contravention Notice been issued? If so, please supply full details and the result of all proceedings and appeals.

9   Are there or have there been on the property any substances controlled by the Control of Substances Hazardous to Health Regulations 1988 (COSHH)? Please supply a copy of the most recent COSHH assessment carried out and confirm that all recommendations arising from the assessment have been implemented and have been regularly maintained and reviewed.

10   Does the Radioactive Substances Act 1993 (RSA) apply to the property or has it ever applied?

11   Please list any registrations of substances kept on the property under s1 RSA.

12   Has there ever been any uncontrolled disposal breakdown or decay of any radioactive substances in the property?

13 Has any authorisation been granted under s6 RSA for the disposal of radioactive waste as defined by s18 RSA on the property?

14 Is the site within a consultation area for planning purposes of any other site under CIMAH, NIHHS or the RSA?

15 Please provide details of any failure to comply with above requirements.

Civil Liability

1   If the purchaser's environmental consultants indicate that there have been breaches of any environmental requirements and that remedial action is required to be taken, please confirm that the vendor will be responsible for the costs of such action including consultant's fees.

Environmental Audit

1   Please supply details of any reclamation or detoxification or clean-up works of which the vendor or the registered proprietor is aware which have at any time been carried out on the property or any adjoining property.

2   Please give full details of any of the following in relation to the property:

a   any environmental audit of the property which has been commissioned, or;

b   any environmental specialist appointed;

c   any monitoring sampling or assessment undertaken.

3   With reference to any such audit or report:

a   was it instigated as a result of any request, notice or intervention by any proper authority, statutory or regulatory body?

b   did the results reveal the need for further action to protect the environment or human health?

c   please provide details of any action requested and action carried out;

d   is there any cost analysis of any proposed action not yet carried out?

e   are there any existing conditions at the property which require further action?

Insurance/Indemnity

1   Please give details of any insurance policy covering the property or any part of it relating to the environment impairment.

2   Please supply full details of any current insurance against environmental liabilities in respect of the property together with details of all claims (whether settled, refused or outstanding).

3   Has any claim been made or is any claim contemplated on any policy of Insurance kept by the vendor or of which the vendor is aware in respect of any damage occurring to

the property or to any adjoining or neighbouring land or to air or water and arising from a release on or from the property of any substance which is capable of causing pollution of the environment or harm to human health or any other living organism supported by the environment?

4   Does the vendor have the benefit of insurance in respect of the previous or current use of the property? If so, and if so required, would it be possible for the purchaser to take over the policy on exchange of contracts?

5   Has cover against any environmental risk ever been refused?

Health and Safety

1   Please advise whether the provisions of the Health and Safety at Work Act 1974 and also similar legislation have been observed and complied with so far as the property is concerned.

2   Please advise whether the fire escape arrangements have been approved by the Local Authority. If so, please provide evidence such as the Fire Certificate.

3   Has the vendor received or is the vendor aware of any proposal or circumstances which may lead to service of any notice under the Health and Safety at Work Act 1974?

B1.2.2 Business and Offices Users

Enquiries

1   Is there an air conditioning system at the property? If so:

2   Is there a planned routine maintenance programme for any cooling tower and other parts of the system?

3   When was the system last inspected (and did this inspection include testing for legionella bacteria)?

4   Has the operation and maintenance of the system been approved by the Health and Safety Executive and/or the Environmental Health Officer?

5   Please supply copies of the vendor's records of the above routine maintenance and of the cleaning chemicals and dose rates used and the dates of treatment.

6   Has there ever been an outbreak of legionella or humidifier fever or other associated health problems within the workforce or other occupiers of the property?

7   To the vendor's knowledge do any of the transformers or electrical equipment at the property contain polychlorinated biphenyls (PCB's)?

8   To the vendor's knowledge are any of the following substances used or contained in any equipment on the property: CFCs, halons HCFCs, carbon tetrachloride, trichloroethane, methyl bromide? If so, please specify the type and quantity, the equipment in which it is used or contained and whether any contracts have been entered into to substitute another substance.

9 Have any of the following substances in pure, compound or derivative form been used in any works of construction, alteration or addition to any buildings erected on the property:

a lead or any materials containing lead which may be ingested, inhaled or absorbed, except where copper alloy fittings containing lead are specifically required in drinking water pipework by any relevant statutory requirement;

b urea formaldehyde foam or materials which may release formaldehyde in quantities which may be hazardous;

c materials which are generally comprised of mineral fibres, either man-made or naturally occurring, which have a diameter of three microns or less and a length of 200 microns of less or which contain any fibres not sealed or otherwise stabilised to ensure that fibre migration is prevented;

d other substances generally known at the date hereof to be dangerous or deleterious or likely to affect the health of occupiers of such buildings?

10 If so, please supply full particulars including details of any action taken in relation thereto and copies of relevant correspondence with professional consultants.

11 Is the vendor aware of the presence/ storage/burial/disposal of any waste in on or under the property? If so, please specify the type of waste, whether it is industrial, commercial or household waste and specify whether it is special waste within the meaning of s62 EPA 1990.

12 Has the property ever been used for the deposit, keeping, storage, treatment or disposal of controlled waste defined in s30(1) COPA and s75 EPA or any special waste or any polluting or hazardous substance ever been deposited or disposed of on the property (whether deliberately or accidentally)?

13 How is commercial waste or trade effluent disposed of? Please provide a copy of any Agreements relating to such disposal.

14 Are there any storage tanks, pool, pits or bunds on the property (whether active or inactive or above or below ground)? If so, please specify whether the storage tanks presently contain any material or are empty.

15 If they contain any material, please specify the nature and quantity of the contents. If not, when did they last contain materials?

16 Have there been spillages or seepage from such tanks before or during vendor's period of ownership of the property?

17 What is the current condition of the tanks and what facilities exist for inspection?

18 Please supply full details of all hazardous substances (as defined pursuant to the Planning (Hazardous Substances) Regulations 1992 (P(HS)R)) on, over or under the property, which exceed controlled quantities, including the quantities present and their precise location.

19 Has any offence been committed under the P(HS)R?

20 Please supply copies of all Hazardous Substances Consents (including deemed consents) and copies of the applications therefore. Please confirm that such consent relates exclusively to the property.

21 Please supply details of any appeal lodged with regard to an application for Hazardous Substances Consent.

22 Please supply details of any revocations, modifications or refusals of Hazardous Substances Consent and/or their conditions.

23 Please supply a copy of any consent under Regulations 3 or 5 Notification of Installations Handling Hazardous Substances Regulations 1982 (NIHHS)?

24 Has any Hazardous Substances Contravention Notice been issued? If so, please supply full details and the result of all proceedings and appeals.

25 Are there or have there been on the property any substances controlled by the Control of Substances Hazardous to Health Regulations 1988 (COSHH)? Please supply a copy of the most recent COSHH assessment carried out and confirm that all recommendations arising from the assessment have been implemented and have been regularly maintained and reviewed.

26 If the purchaser's environmental consultants indicate that there have been breaches of any environmental requirements and that remedial action is required to be taken, please confirm that the vendor will be responsible for the costs of such action including consultant's fees.

27 Please supply details of any reclamation or detoxification or clean-up works of which the vendor or the registered proprietor is aware which have at any time been carried out on the property or any adjoining property.

28 Please give full details of any of the following in relation to the property:

 a any environmental audit of the property which has been commissioned, or;

 b any environmental specialist appointed;

 c any monitoring sampling or assessment undertaken.

29 With reference to any such audit or report:

 a was it instigated as a result of any request, notice or intervention by any proper authority, statutory or regulatory body?

 b did the results reveal the need for further action to protect the environment or human health?

 c please provide details of any action requested and action carried out;

 d is there any cost analysis of any proposed action not yet carried out?

e are there any existing conditions at the property which require further action?

30 Please give details of any insurance policy covering the property or any part of it relating to the environmental impairment.

31 Please supply full details of any current insurance against environmental liabilities in respect of the property together with details of all claims (whether settled, refused or outstanding).

32 Has any claim been made or is any claim contemplated on any policy of insurance kept by the vendor or of which the vendor is aware in respect of any damage occurring to the property or to any adjoining or neighbouring land or to air or water and arising from a release on or from the property of any substance which is capable of causing pollution of the environment or harm to human health or any living organism supported by the environment?

33 Does the vendor have the benefit of insurance in respect of the previous or current use of the property? If so, and if so required, would it be possible for the purchaser to take over the policy on exchange of contracts?

34 Has cover against any environmental risk ever been refused?

35 Please advise whether the provisions of the Health and Safety at Work Act 1974 and also similar legislation have been observed and complied with so far as the property is concerned.

36 Please advise whether the fire escape arrangements have been approved by the local authority. If so, please provide evidence such as the fire certificate.

37 Has the Vendor received or is the Vendor aware of any proposal or circumstances which may lead to service of any notice under the Health and Safety at Work Act 1974?

B1.2.3 Residential Enquiries

Enquiries

1 Is the vendor aware of any past use of the property which might have given rise to any contamination or pollution of the land?

2 Please confirm that no domestic or other waste, toxic or any other dangerous substances have been stored on, buried or disposed of in or under the property.

3 Please confirm that there have been no breaches on or in connection with the property of the provisions of the Environmental Protection Act 1990 or any other environmental legislation relating to land contamination.

4 Please confirm that there have been no breaches on or in connection with the property of the provisions of the Water Resources Act 1991 or other legislation relating to water.

5   Is the vendor aware of leakages from gas pipe or other emissions from or into or relating to the property?

6   Is the vendor aware of any asbestos in any part of the property or in any fixtures and fittings? If so please supply full details including the type of asbestos, its location, amount and condition and the steps which have been taken (if any) to remove it or ensure that it does not cause a hazard to human health.

B2.1 Environmental Search Report

This report is based on the historic use of the land. This information could be obtained from a number of public registers, such as Ordnance Survey maps, registers of waste disposal site licences, Planning Registers, and surveys of derelict and despoiled land. Many environmental services companies compile available information and adapt for the specific use of their clients. It normally would take between seven to ten days to complete a search, an additional fee may be paid for a quicker service.

Such a search report is a due diligence exercise that should be taken on all commercial property transactions, including mergers and acquisitions and disposal of assets. This is all the more important as solicitors may be liable in negligence for not making adequate investigation on the properties.

The cost of the report is less than £300 (VAT inclusive). This appears to be good value for money, especially as the incurable liability may be substantial when such exercise is not undertaken. Where the initial report presents reasons to worry, a more comprehensive report may be commissioned.

There may be problems, however, where there is illegal tipping of contaminant on a site which is unknown to the landowners and the relevant authority, and hence cannot be covered by the report. Perhaps this may be deemed a latent defect on the property, which the vendor is not reasonably expected to know about.

B2.2 Environmental Assessments and Audits

Environmental audits are a review of performance of a company over a range of environmental criteria. If a purchase of domestic property or a lease of a tenth-floor office suite is proposed, it is unlikely that an environmental audit would be appropriate. Audits are expensive particularly if they involve scientific analysis of soil/ground water sample from the site.

Audits are likely to be important in transactions where it is known that: the land has been subject to some past or present industrial activity or other use which could have given rise to contamination; the transaction involves the acquisition of a business which has a significant environmental law compliance component; and where the amount involved is sufficient to justify the considerable expense.

Greater importance is attached to the environmental audit as a tool for assessing risk and liability for a purchaser, vendor or lender. The key matters which an audit will seek to identify when used in transactions are: the nature and the extent of any existing contamination on the site (including its sources and possible migration); the presence of any hazardous materials or substances on the site which may give rise to future contamination; and the different methods by which the site may be cleaned up.

Who Can Rely on the Report?

There may also be problems on the issue of who can rely on the environmental search report and environmental audits. In *Caparo* v *Dickman* (1990) AC, it was held that an investor cannot rely on an auditors' report which was published for another purpose. So who can rely on the report: purchaser, vendor, investors, lenders, lawyers? This is an area to watch for obvious reasons.

Appendix 8

Property Acquisition: Purchasers' Considerations in Carrying Out a Detailed Environmental Site Investigation

Introductory Remarks

Some background information on what a pre-acquisition environmental audit should achieve is set out below, together with the areas of potential liability any purchaser should be aware of when considering whether to purchase land which may be contaminated.

In deciding to commission such an audit (a Phase 2 audit) the objectives of any purchaser are: to identify accurately the environmental risks in a transaction; assess the chances of those risks turning into costs or liabilities; and apportion and allocate those risks in the light of that assessment.

Reasons for an Audit

The use of environmental audits is likely to increase in view of the contaminated land regime in the EA 1995. In any event, environmental audits or site investigations are important in property transactions where it is known or suspected that: the land (and possibly any neighbouring land) has been subject to some past or present industrial activity or other use which could have given rise to contamination (particularly where there are local sensitive receptors); and where the amount involved is sufficient to justify the considerable expense.

Source, Pathway, Target

In this context environmental liability essentially arises when have three factors are present. These are: a 'source' (ie polluting / dangerous substances); a 'pathway' (surrounding circumstances enabling these substances to move eg leakages and underlying strata types); and a 'target', that is, potential sensitive receptors which could be damaged by any pollutant (for example groundwater).

If a primary indication of the existence of these factors is given in a Phase 1 audit, a Phase 2 audit should enable more precise clarification of the degree to which these concerns should be taken into account in deciding whether to proceed with any acquisition.

Information Obtained

A detailed environmental audit should provide all of the information a prudent purchaser requires, including details of:

- the physical extent of any contamination;

- the seriousness of the contamination;

- the materials which have contaminated the site;

- claims and potential civil claims by neighbouring landowners;

- claims and potential claims by the regulatory authorities under the WRA 1991, the EPA 1990 and EA 1995;

- prosecutions under environmental licences that are in place and whether the site is in compliance;

- any recommendations for remedying problems, taking into account any limitations and providing an assessment of the costs of such options.

Assessing the Risk

Assessing the risk of potential problems caused by the existence of contamination is the final element of the investigation exercise.

First, an assessment of the likelihood of the risk occurring should be made (this can only be properly addressed with scientific and technical advice and therefore should be made within the context of a Phase 2 audit); and, secondly, the consequences of such a risk becoming an event need to be examined. There may well be an environmental risk which is relatively small, but the consequences of that risk becoming an event may mean a multi-million pound compensation claim. This is where the review of any potential legal liability referred to below becomes important. Thirdly, it is important to attempt to assess the timing of the risk so that medium- and long-term costs may be anticipated.

A Purchaser's Legal Liability for Potentially Contaminated Land

Whereas the general legal position has been referred to in more detail as regards the main provisions, an overview is useful for an understanding of the purchaser's position.

Common Law Liability

Nuisance

A purchaser may be liable in nuisance if he permits an unlawful interference with another person's use or enjoyment of his land, where such interference is unreasonable in all the circumstances. This may be the case even where you are not the party originally responsible for causing the nuisance when you can be taken to have 'adopted' the nuisance, that is, by failing to remove the contamination. Damage might have been caused to a neighbour's land by contaminants having migrated on to that land or substances may have polluted a local watercourse (including groundwaters), in which case a person entitled to abstract from such watercourses may suffer damages.

A purchaser may also be liable in negligence, although for such a claim to succeed it would be necessary to show that as a purchaser: they owed the third party a duty of care; that they were in breach of that duty; and thereby caused damage to the third party, such damage being a reasonably foreseeable consequence of that breach.

Statutory Liability

Liability for Statutory Nuisances

A statutory nuisance can arise where premises (including land) are in such a state so as to be prejudicial to health or a nuisance. This could include contaminated land and may also include any accumulation or deposit of materials.

In the first instance, the LA would serve an abatement notice under s80 EPA 1990 on the person who is 'responsible for the nuisance', that is, the person whose act or default or sufferance the nuisance can be attributed to, or, if that person cannot be found, then the owner or occupier of the premises or land will be the person served with such a notice. If the nuisance is due to a structural defect it is the owner of the land against whom the LA will bring proceedings.

In addition to the LA, any person aggrieved by a statutory nuisance may bring a complaint in the magistrates' court where an order may be made requiring the defendant to abate the nuisance, prohibiting the recurrence of the nuisance or imposing a fine. A defence to such proceedings can be claimed where the defendant can prove the best practicable means were used to counteract the effects of the nuisance.

Any expenses reasonably incurred by a LA in abating or preventing the recurrence of a statutory nuisance may be recovered from the person who caused the nuisance. Whilst a new owner may not have actually caused the nuisance, the default of such person in failing to remove the cause of the nuisance may be sufficient to render the new owner liable. It would therefore be important for any new owner to take steps to remove any potential contaminative/nuisance-creating substances. Failure to comply with an abatement notice can result in the imposition of a fine of up to £20,000 where the offence relates to trade, industrial or business premises.

Occupier's Liability

A purchaser may also be liable to visitors under the Occupier's Liability Act 1957 if he fails to take such care as, in all the circumstances of the case, is reasonable to see that the visitor will be reasonably safe in using the premises for the purposes for which he is invited or permitted by any occupier to be there. The Occupier's Liability Act 1984 imposes a liability on occupiers in respect of trespassers in certain circumstances. These provisions are probably only really of relevance where the land in question is heavily contaminated.

Liability in Respect of Land in an Adverse Condition

Under s215 Town and Country Planning Act 1990, a LA may serve a notice on the owner or occupier of land which it considers is in such a condition that the amenity of its area is adversely affected by that land. The notice may require steps to be taken to remediate such condition and failure to comply can result in the imposition of a fine of up to £1,000.

By virtue of s219 of the Act, if the necessary steps are not taken then the LA may do so and recover the reasonable costs of so doing form the person is then the owner of the land.

Liability for Water Pollution

Under s85 WRA 1991, a purchaser of land may also be found to be the person who 'caused or knowingly permitted pollution to enter controlled waters', for example, watercourses and groundwater. The purchaser may be held to have 'knowingly permitted' such pollution by failing to take measures to stop contamination migrating into such watercourses where they were aware that such a potential may exist. Commission of such an offence can result in a fine of up to £20,000 or imprisonment or both.

Under s161 of this Act, the EA can carry out any necessary work to prevent or clean-up pollution of controlled waters and reclaim its expenses from the person who caused or knowingly permitted such substances to be present on the land. Again, a purchaser may also be potentially liable for such costs.

Liability for Waste

A new owner may be liable for any waste deposited or placed on the land without the requisite licence if he permits such waste to remain there, in which case he would be liable to a fine under s33 EPA 1990 of up to £20,000 or to imprisonment for up to six months.

Furthermore, s34 of this Act imposes a duty of care on various classes of people (including 'keepers' of waste which could be construed as including a new owner of land on which such waste is present) to take all reasonable steps to prevent the escape of waste from his control or from that of any other person, for example, tenants. Failure to comply with this duty of care is an offence punishable by a fine which can be unlimited on indictment.

Liability for Contaminated Land Under the EA 1995

This new statutory liability regime is in respect of land which LAs consider to be contaminated. Such land will be in such a condition by reason of substances in it that either significant harm is being caused or there is a significant possibility of such harm being caused or pollution of controlled waters is being or is likely to be caused, as shall be determined in accordance with guidance to be issued shortly.

Once such land has been identified (or is determined to be a 'special site' (where 'serious' harm or pollution is being or may be caused, in which case the EA becomes the relevant regulatory authority), the relevant authority will serve a 'remediation notice' on the 'appropriate person' requiring the site to be cleaned up. In the first instance, such a person will be the person who 'caused or knowingly permitted' the substances which are causing the problem to be present on land. A new owner could potentially fall under the category of 'knowingly permitting' where he is aware that there may be such substances present on the land.

If no such person can be found, then the owner or occupier for the time being is the appropriate person. Therefore, if the vendor was not the 'appropriate person' (by virtue of not having caused or knowingly permitted the contamination) in the first instance, the new owner may be liable in such a case where the 'polluter' cannot be found. Guidance is to be issued which should clarify more precisely in what circumstances an 'appropriate person' will be identified. It is for this reason, amongst others set out above, that it is only prudent for a purchaser to ascertain more precisely whether the land is in such a condition that a remediation notice may be served on him so that steps may be taken to ensure that any liability remains with the vendor by whatever means can be negotiated.

Failure to comply with a remediation notice results in the imposition of a fine of up to £5,000 (plus a daily fine) and up to £20,000 where the offence relates to industrial, trade or business premises.

Liability is also to be imposed in respect of off-site contamination (contamination which has migrated to neighbouring land) in certain specified circumstances. In addition, the LA may itself carry out the remediation where the appropriate person fails to do so within the specified time or where there is an imminent danger of harm being caused.

Finally, the cost of remediation may be claimed from the appropriate person and may be secured as a charge on the land if there has been a failure to pay the relevant authority.

Personal Liability of Directors and Officers

It should not be forgotten that directors and officers of companies may suffer personal liability for criminal offences committed by their company. The EPA 1990, the WRA 1991 and the relevant provisions of the EA 1995 all provide that where an offence under these Acts is committed by a corporate body which can be proved to have been committed with consent or connivance of, or to have been attributable to, any neglect on the part of any director or other similar officer (or a person purporting to act in that capacity), he shall also be guilty of such an offence as well as the corporate body.

Practical Strategy

On ascertaining more precisely what the risks are, various options can be taken by a potential purchase including: claiming a reduction in the price to cover the cost of clean-up and any potential claims; carving out any particular problem area in the site concerned; withdrawing from the acquisition; requiring rectification of the known problems by the vendor prior to purchase; and negotiating warranties and indemnities. Although these have not been very common in commercial property transactions, they are being used increasingly to allocate risk and are recommended in property deals where the activities on the site may have adversely affected the condition of the land.

Concluding Remarks

Any practitioner should note the importance of the due diligence activities referred to above, which can have evident financial implications for any client in transactions.

Appendix 9

Schedule of Contaminative Uses

Introduction

This list was originally compiled by the former DoE as one of the tests to be used in determining what goes into the register of land subject to contaminative uses. Although, the proposal for such a register was officially abandoned in 1993 and its statutory framework (s143 EPA 1990) was repealed by the EA 1995, the list remains a useful indicator as to whether one should embark on an environmental investigation or not.

Notes:

'Contaminative use' is defined as any use of land which may cause significant harm or risk of significant harm being caused on the land by reason of substances in, on or under the land.

The titles of the main profiles relevant to each description of use are given in brackets.

DoE Consultation Paper May 1991

Agriculture

- Burial of diseased livestock (profile: to be determined)

Extractive Industry

- Extracting, handling and storage of carbonaceous materials, such as coal, lignite, petroleum, natural gas, or bituminous shale (not including the underground workings) (profiles: coal mines and coal preparation plants; oil refineries and petrochemicals)

- Extracting, handling and storage of ores and their constituents (profiles: mineral workings; mineral processing works)

Energy Industry

- Producing gas from coal, lignite, oil or other carbonaceous material (other than from sewage or other waste), or from mixtures of those materials (profiles: gasworks and coal carbonisation plants; oil refineries)

- Reforming, refining, purifying and odorising natural gas or any product of the processes outlined above (profiles: gasworks and coal carbonisation plants; oil refineries)

- Pyrolysis, carbonisation, distillation, liquefaction, partial oxidation, other heat treatment conversion, purification, or refining of coal, lignite, oil, other carbonaceous material or mixtures and products thereof, otherwise than with a view to gasification or making of charcoal (profiles: gasworks and coal carbonisation plants; oil refineries; coal mines and coal preparation plants)

- A thermal power station (including nuclear power stations and production, enrichment and reprocessing of nuclear fuels) (profiles: power stations; radioactive materials; asbestos works)

- Electricity sub-station (profiles: power stations; electrical equipment)

Production of Metals

- Production, refining or recovery of metals by physical, chemical, thermal or electrolytic or other extraction process (profiles: metal processing; heavy engineering)

- Heating, melting or casting metals as part of an intermediate or final manufacturing process (including annealing, tempering or similar processes) (profiles: metal processing; heavy engineering; miscellaneous (High Street) trades)

- Cold forming processes (including pressing, rolling, extruding, stamping, forming or similar processes) (profiles: metal processing; heavy engineering; electroplating and metal finishing)

- Finishing treatments, including anodising, pickling, coating, and plating or similar processes (profiles: metal processing; heavy engineering; electroplating and metal finishing; miscellaneous (High Street) trades)

Note: Metals are taken to include metal scrap.

Production of Non-metals and their Products

- Production or refining of non-metals by treatment of the ore (profile: mineral processing works)

- Production or processing of mineral fibres by treatment of the ore (profiles: mineral processing works; asbestos works)

- Cement, lime and gypsum manufacture, brickworks and associated processes (profile: mineral processing works)

Glass-making and Ceramics

- Manufacture of glass and products based on glass (profile: glass manufacturing)

- Manufacture of ceramics and products based on ceramics, including glazes and vitreous enamel (profile: to be determined)

Production and Use of Chemicals

- Production, refining, recovery or storage of petroleum or petrochemicals or their by-products, including tar and bitumen processes and manufacture of asphalt (profiles: oil refineries and petrochemicals; mineral processing works; drum and tank cleaning)

- Production, refining and bulk storage of organic or inorganic chemicals, including fertilisers, pesticides, pharmaceuticals, soaps, detergents, cosmetics, toiletries, dyestuffs, inks, paints, fireworks, pyrotechnic materials or recovered chemicals (profiles: bulk inorganic and organic chemicals; fine chemicals; fertiliser manufacture; pesticides; pharmaceuticals; textile and dye industry; paint and ink manufacture; miscellaneous (High Street) trades; drum and tank cleaning)

- Production, refining and bulk storage of industrial gases not otherwise covered (profile: fine chemicals)

Engineering and Manufacturing Processes

- Manufacture of metal goods, including mechanical engineering industrial plant or steelwork, motor vehicles, ships, railway or tramway vehicles, aircraft, aerospace equipment or similar equipment (profiles: heavy engineering works; engineering works; car manufacturing works; shipbuilding)

- Storage, manufacture or testing of explosives, propellants, ordnance, small arms or ammunition (profile: heavy engineering)

- Manufacture and repair of electrical and electronic components and equipment (profiles: electrical and electronic equipment manufacture; miscellaneous (High Street) trades)

Food Processing Industry

- Manufacture of pet foods or animal feedstuffs (profile: food preparation and processing)

- Processing of animal by-products (including rendering or maggot farming, but excluding slaughterhouses, butchering) (profile: animal processing works; miscellaneous (High Street) trades)

Paper, Pulp and Printing Industry

- Making of paper pulp, paper or board, or paper or board products, including printing or de-inking (profiles: pulp and paper manufacture; printing works; miscellaneous (High Street) trades)

Timber and Timber Products Industry

- Chemical treatment and coating of timber and timber products (profiles: wood preservative industry and timber treatment works; miscellaneous (High Street) trades)

Textile Industry

- Tanning, dressing or other process for preparing, treating or working leather (profiles: animal processing works; miscellaneous (High Street) trades)

- Fulling, bleaching, dyeing or finishing fabrics or fibres (profiles: textile and dye industry; miscellaneous (High Street) trades)

- Manufacture of carpets or other textile floor coverings (including linoleum works) (profile: textile and dye industry)

Rubber Industry

- Processing of natural or synthetic rubber (including tyre manufacture or retreading) (profiles: fine chemicals; tyre manufacture)

Infrastructure

- Marshalling, dismantling, repairing or maintenance of railway rolling stock (profile: heavy engineering; docks and railway land)

- Dismantling, repairing or maintenance of marine vessels, including hovercraft (profiles: shipbuilding and shipbreaking; docks and railway land)

- Dismantling, repairing or maintenance of road transport or road haulage vehicles (profiles: road transport and road haulage; garages and filling stations)

- Dismantling, repairing or maintenance of air or space transport systems (profiles: engineering works; airports)

Waste Disposal

- Treating of sewage or other effluent (profile: sewage works and farms)

- Storage, treatment or disposal of sludge including sludge from water treatment works (profile: to be determined)

- Treating, keeping, depositing or disposing of waste, including scrap (to include infilled canal basins, docks or river courses) (profiles: landfills and other waste treatment and disposal sites; scrapyards; drum and tank cleaning)

- Storage or disposal of radioactive materials (profile: radioactive materials)

Miscellaneous

- Premises housing dry cleaning operations (profile: miscellaneous (High Street) trades)

- Laboratories for educational or research purposes (profiles: research laboratories; miscellaneous (High Street) trades)

- Demolition of buildings, plant or equipment used for any of the activities in this schedule (profile: demolition)

Further Reading

Conveyancing Contaminated Land
Campbell G (1997, 1 85811 114 5) CLT Professional Publishing

Eco-management and Eco-auditing: Environmental Issues in Business
Spedding L S, Jones D and Dering C (2nd ed 1993, 0 471 93693 6) Chancery Law Publishing, a division of Wiley

The ENDS Report
Environmental Data Services Ltd

Environmental Law Monthly
Monitor Press

Environmental Liability
Campbell G (2nd ed 1998, 1 85811 137 4) CLT Professional Publishing

International Environmental Policy and Management
Spedding L S (1995, 0 7487 2132 0) Stanley Thornes

International Environmental Risk Management
Voorhees J and Woellner R A (1998, 1 56670 291 7) CRC Press Ltd

Official Journal of the European Communities

Risk Management Bulletin
Ark Publishing

Waste Management Law: A Practical Handbook
Garbutt J (2nd ed 1995, 0 471 95227 3) Wiley

Index

302